JOHN HEARNE

For Miriam

JOHN HEARNE

Architect of the 1937 Constitution of Ireland

EUGENE BRODERICK

IRISH ACADEMIC PRESS

First published in 2017 by
Irish Academic Press
10 George's Street
Newbridge
Co. Kildare
Ireland
www.iap.ie

978-1-911024-53-8 (cloth)
978-1-911024-54-5 (Kindle)
978-1-911024-55-2 (Epub)
978-1-911024-71-2 (PDF)

British Library Cataloguing in Publication Data
An entry can be found on request

Library of Congress Cataloging in Publication Data
An entry can be found on request

Interior design by www.jminfotechindia.com
Typeset in Garamond Premier Pro 10.5/14 pt
Cover design by edit+ www.stuartcoughlan.com

Jacket front: John Hearne on the occasion of his appointment as a senior counsel,
20 June 1939. Private collection, reproduced with permission.
Jacket back: Éamon de Valera's dedication of a copy of the draft constitution
given by him to John Hearne. Ms. 23, 508. Courtesy of the National
Museum of Ireland.

Printed by TJ International Ltd, Padstow, Cornwall.

CONTENTS

FOREWORD

There has been a significant lacuna in Irish legal history: unlike other jurisdictions, we have not appropriately honoured the draftsmen of our Constitution. For decades, little attention has been paid to the role played in its drafting by public servants, the most influential of whom was John J. Hearne. *John Hearne: Architect of the 1937 Constitution* redresses this with its in-depth description of Hearne's role in the creation of Bunreacht na hÉireann, 1937.

This publication is timely, in the eightieth year since the Constitution was enacted in 1937, and as we prepare to celebrate the life and work of John Hearne at a conference in his native city of Waterford. The author tells the story of Hearne, his family life, politics, education and religion, all of which enriched his work as a lawyer, public servant and diplomat, and provides us with a valuable historic account of Hearne's involvement in the making of the Constitution.

A fascinating insight is also provided into the relationship between Hearne and Éamon de Valera. The seeds of a strong professional relationship were sown following de Valera's election as President of the Executive Council of the Irish Free State, when Hearne was legal adviser to the Department of External Affairs. After de Valera made the decision to draft a new Constitution, and gave instructions to Hearne to commence the work, their relationship flourished during many hours spent discussing and preparing the basic law, which has shaped our State. De Valera later dedicated a copy to Hearne, whom he described as 'Architect in Chief and Draftsman' of the Constitution.

It was a prescient document. Drafted in the 1930s, it set out the framework of government, guaranteed fundamental rights, and gave the power of judicial review expressly to the Superior Courts. These provisions have generated a rich source of case law and a unique jurisprudence. We are fortunate to have such a written Constitution, which the People alone can change.

The author enlightens us about the significant role Hearne played in the inclusion of key provisions. Knowledgeable in constitutional law, he drew from the constitutions of other jurisdictions, in order to advise de Valera and draft the Constitution. His drafts included features of the new Constitution, which remained in subsequent drafts, and found their way into the Constitution as finally adopted.

Eugene Broderick describes how, when de Valera instructed Hearne to draw up the heads of a new Constitution, handwritten notes by de Valera indicate an exchange of views between the two men, during which Hearne advised de Valera on matters including the possibility of a Constitutional Court and the office of President. Both de Valera and Hearne believed that there should be entrenched in the Constitution the power of the Superior Courts to judicially review the compatibility of legislation. In October 1936, Hearne drafted a version of articles relating to judicial review. An independent judiciary, entrusted with the power of judicial review, enabling courts to uphold rights, has been an important aspect of our constitutional democracy ever since.

This book elegantly captures the commitment of John Hearne to the protection of the rights of Irish citizens, and his unwavering service throughout his life to the Irish State. I congratulate the author on a magnificent publication and I recommend this book to everyone interested in the history of our Constitution.

Susan Denham
Chief Justice
Four Courts
Dublin.
January 2017

PREFACE BY
THE MAYOR OF WATERFORD CITY
AND COUNTY

This year, 2017, marks the eightieth anniversary of the Constitution of Ireland, Bunreacht na hÉireann. Waterford-born civil servant, John J. Hearne (1893–1967) was described by Éamon de Valera as the 'architect in chief and draftsman' of the document, and his part as 'fundamental' in its production. De Valera's own words establish beyond doubt Hearne's importance and central role in the making of this state's fundamental law. It is only proper on this anniversary of the Constitution to recognise and acknowledge Hearne's contribution.

Dr Eugene Broderick's *John Hearne: Architect of the 1937 Constitution of Ireland* gives us an insight into John Hearne's part in Irish constitution-making. He highlights the fact that Hearne was involved at all stages in the document's evolution and that he insisted on an emphasis on human rights at a time when Europe was fast descending into fascist dictatorship.

John Hearne was a member of a family which contributed much to the political and economic life of Waterford. His father, Richard, was twice mayor of the city, 1901–3, and a partner in the manufacturing firm, Hearne and Cahill. John Hearne went on to serve this state with distinction not only by his part in the drafting of the Constitution, but as first Irish Ambassador to the United States, 1950–60. It was he who initiated the ceremony of presenting a bowl of shamrock to the American President on St Patrick's Day.

Waterford has much to be proud of in the achievements of John Hearne and this book will stand as a record to his illustrious career of public service.

Councillor Adam Wyse
Mayor of Waterford City and County

ACKNOWLEDGEMENTS

In writing this book I accumulated many debts and I am only too happy to acknowledge the kind help and assistance of many people. The archivists and library staff of a number of institutions were generous with their time and expertise: Irish Military Archives, National Archives of Ireland, National Library of Ireland, University College Cork, University College Dublin Archives, and Waterford City and County Archives. Dr Michael Kennedy, Editor, *Documents on Irish Foreign Policy*, generously facilitated access to the papers of John J. Hearne.

Fr Gerard Chestnutt, PP, Sacred Heart Parish, Waterford, obtained information relating to the Revd Maurice Hearne from the archives of the Roman Catholic Diocese of Waterford and Lismore. Mr Richard McNamara, former executive legal assistant to the Chief Justice of Ireland, made available to me documentation pertaining to the legal career of John J. Hearne. The late Mons. John shine shared his memories of Waterford in the 1930s and 1940s, shedding light on Hearne's family. Mr Seán Aylward, under-treasurer, Honourable Society of King's Inns, has taken an interest in my research and has been generous in his practical assistance.

Family and acquaintances of John Hearne were all too ready and willing to speak of a man they evidently admired and this enriched my understanding of the man behind the persona of lawyer, diplomat and civil servant. I thank Alice Bowen (niece), Fr Ignatius Fennessy, OFM (nephew), John R. Bowen (grand-nephew), Nuala Quirke (a member of the Cahill family, Hearne's father's business partner) and Phyliss Doolan (family friend).

Chief Justice Susan Denham has taken an interest in the publication from its beginning. Her support and ready willingness to write the foreword and launch the book are very much appreciated.

A very special thank you to Mr Justice Gerard Hogan for his guidance and help. He very kindly read a draft of the proposed book, offering insightful comments and criticisms, and took an interest in it at all stages. Dr Hogan's scholarship and very generous support were fundamental to the completion of the text. His wife, Karen Quirke, also gave help, shedding light on the Hearne and Cahill business partnership and by arranging contact between her mother, Nora, and me, where Mrs Quirke shed much light on the character of John Hearne.

John Hearne's daughter-in-law, Bernadette Kilduff, deserves special mention. She has been interested in my research and writing since I began work on this book and gave me access to papers which were of central importance to recounting Hearne's story. In particular, she gave me notes prepared by her late husband, Maurice, on his proposed biography of his father. She also gave copies of photographs which grace this publication. I cannot express too much my appreciation to Bernadette.

The professionalism and commitment of Irish Academic Press to the production of this book were exemplary. Conor Graham, managing director, Fiona Dunne, managing editor, and Myles McCionnaith, marketing and editorial executive, have embraced their task with enthusiasm and have been unstinting in their determination to ensure a publication of the highest quality.

I wish to acknowledge and thank Waterford City and County Council for financial assistance towards the publication of this book and the generous financial contribution of Toni Delaney towards the reproduction of many of the photographs.

Rosemary Ryan, Donnchadh Ó Ceallacháin and Peigi Devlin, Waterford Treasures, have been a source of much support and practical help. Their generous assistance reflects their on-going commitment and contribution to the preservation of the history and heritage of Waterford.

My mother-in-law, Mary Leamy, my brother-in-law, Paul Leamy, and my good friend, Ann McEneaney, undertook the difficult and demanding task of proofreading the text. I thank them most sincerely for undertaking this most necessary task and their patience, advice and observations made an invaluable contribution to this book. For this, I owe them much. Pat McEvoy also read some of the chapters and his helpful input is happily acknowledged.

Two people have been an integral part of this book since its inception: Miriam Broderick and Eamonn McEneaney. My friendship with Eamonn goes back a long way and he has offered much practical help and counsel in seeing the text to completion. More importantly, he has been a source of inspiration and encouragement and for this I owe him a great debt of gratitude.

My wife, Miriam, has been the constant support in the writing of this book and, indeed, in all my endeavours. Without her unfailing support and encouragement, it simply would never have seen the light of day. On a practical level, she proofread the various drafts and made many worthwhile suggestions. In readily and happily acknowledging her vital support, I dedicate this book to her, with all my love and gratitude.

Finally, any errors or deficiencies in this book are entirely my responsibility.

Eugene Broderick, Waterford, March 2017

INTRODUCTION

On 29 December 1937, Ireland celebrated Constitution Day, the day on which the country's new fundamental law, Bunreacht na hÉireann, came into operation. To mark the occasion the government organised a rare, if modest, display of ceremonial.[1] The national flag was flown on all public buildings throughout the country. In Dublin, at 9.30am, a twenty-one-gun salute was fired at the Royal Hospital, Kilmainham. In all military barracks, garrisons assembled at this time. Reveille was sounded and the tricolour raised. A *feu de joie* was fired, the national anthem played and soldiers attended mass. At 9.40am, in Dublin, Éamon de Valera, now styled 'Taoiseach' under the Constitution, and his ministers assembled at Government Buildings and were driven, with an escort of mounted cavalry, to the Pro-Cathedral for a solemn votive mass. Services were also held by other religious denominations – the Church of Ireland, Quakers and Jews. On his return to Government Buildings de Valera greeted the Chief Justice, Timothy O'Sullivan, who made and subscribed to the declaration as required of every judge under the Constitution. On his return to the Four Courts, the Chief Justice witnessed the declaration of the President of the High Court. At 12.40 pm, the Presidential Commission, one of the new constitutional organs of state, met at Dublin Castle. It discharged a number of functions, as required, pending the election of a President of Ireland in 1938. In honour of the day, the post office issued a special commemorative stamp. That evening de Valera made a radio address to the people of the state.

Among the congregation in the Pro-Cathedral on that day was a 44-year-old, slightly built civil servant, John Joseph Hearne, legal adviser at the Department of External Affairs. Unknown to most of those in attendance, he had played a very significant role in the making of Bunreacht na hÉireann. This fact was acknowledged by de Valera; in a copy of the document presented to Hearne, the Taoiseach wrote the following dedication in his own hand:

> To Mr John Hearne, Barrister at Law, Legal Adviser to the Department of External Affairs, Architect in Chief and Draftsman of this Constitution, as a souvenir of the successful issue of his work and in testimony of the fundamental part he took in framing this, the first free Constitution of the Irish People.
>
> Éamon de Valera
> Constitution Day 29 XII 1937[2]

Beyond a small number of politicians and senior civil servants, Hearne's role remained unacknowledged and unrecognised for decades by a wider public. This was in keeping with the practice of the civil service which was regarded by its members and politicians as an 'anonymous corps',[3] charged with meeting the needs and demands of ministers, behind a wall of secrecy and discretion. Civil servants were expected to work under cover of anonymity, preserving traditional boundaries that existed between them, the government and the public. The state's administrative system was founded on the belief that a transgression of this principle would undermine ministerial prerogative and responsibility.[4] Nearly thirty years after the introduction of Bunreacht na hÉireann, in December 1965, the Taoiseach, Seán Lemass, was asked by Deputy Patrick Harte to name those who in any way assisted in the drawing up of the Constitution. In his reply Lemass stated that 'it would be contrary to the civil service tradition of anonymity to disclose the names of civil servants who were engaged in the drafting work'.[5]

A consequence of the general ignorance of the role of Hearne and other civil servants in the making of Bunreacht na hÉireann was that its production was attributed to de Valera alone. There was a clichéd image of him drafting it in long hand.[6] A sense of this was conveyed by his son, Terry:

> I have recollections of him in his study as he worked on the draft, but his eyesight continued to cause him trouble. He would only write by using a pen with a very large nib, which meant that vast amounts of paper often overflowed from his desk onto the floor. One day I remember going into his study, where I was warned not to walk on the many sheets of paper which were scattered on the floor. In time I believe these drafts were destroyed, but I often think it would have been interesting to see those portions of the new Constitution which were rejected or otherwise as first drafted.[7]

In a book published in 1973, the distinguished historian F.S.L. Lyons wrote: 'The Constitution was a remarkable document – remarkable for what it contained and for what it omitted, remarkable still more because, as we now know, it was very largely the work of one man, Mr de Valera himself.'[8]

De Valera did not disabuse people of this notion. As head of the government which proposed the Constitution, he accepted and endorsed the view that the role of civil servants was an anonymous one. He was also happy to bask in the glory of his perceived constitution-making prowess. He informed the British Ambassador to Ireland, Sir Andrew Gilchrist, at a meeting on 27 February 1967: 'Of course, I wrote most of the Constitution myself.'[9] The acceptance of this fact among his more ardent followers contributed to his mystique and charisma. A charismatic leader is someone who is credited with having achieved seemingly impossible tasks and who, in the eyes of his followers, possesses qualities which mark him not just as rare or exceptional, but almost superhuman. 'The vital dimensions of real charisma are not, therefore, necessarily attributes of the leader but, rather, qualities he is believed to possess by his followers who place a blind trust in him.'[10] The complexities of constitution-making rank as a skill of the highest order and were probably akin to de Valera's supposed prowess in mathematics. This prowess was, according to admirers, awe-inspiring to the point of being disconcerting.[11]

In 1970, two official biographies of de Valera, in English and Irish, were published. Both of them contained what was probably his first public acknowledgement of Hearne's role in the process which led to the 1937 Constitution. Interestingly, there is a marked difference in the description of this role between the two publications. In the English version there is a reference to Hearne by name and this is in relation to his preparation of draft heads for a new constitution in 1935.[12] In a second reference he is unnamed. This reference concerned the appointment, in 1936, of two civil servants to a commission to consider the functions and composition of a Senate, if one were established under a new constitution. The two, Hearne and John (Seán) Moynihan (secretary to the Executive Council) were, according to the English biography, 'intimately associated with the drafting of the proposed constitution'.[13] In the Irish biography, Hearne's role is given a much more expansive treatment. He is named ten times and there are at least five references in which he is clearly identified, but not named. In the matter of the Senate commission, Hearne and Moynihan are named, with the added comment (as in the English version) that they were both very closely involved ('baint an-dlúth acusan araon') in the drafting of the Constitution.[14] It should be noted that the English biography was much more widely read and more readily available.

A year before the appearance of the biographies, John Hearne died, on 29 March 1969. His obituary in the *Irish Times* referred to the fact that he was 'prominent' in the drafting of the Constitution,[15] while the *Irish Independent* noted his 'big part' in its preparation.[16] It was not until the pioneering research of Professor Dermot Keogh that there was a greater knowledge and appreciation of this role. In a book published in 1986, writing about Bunreacht na hÉireann, he stated that 'the central figure in the process was unquestionably John Hearne, an able and knowledgeable civil servant'.[17] He published an article in the following year on the document, on the occasion of its fiftieth anniversary. Keogh described Hearne's contribution thus: 'Apart from de Valera himself, no individual was so centrally involved in the drafting and shaping of the new Constitution.'[18] In the same year, University College Dublin academic Brian Kennedy, in an article in the *Irish Times,* under the heading 'The special position of John Hearne', described him as 'a distinguished civil servant – the man behind the

1937 Constitution'.[19] On the seventy-fifth anniversary (2012), Hearne was described in a publication as 'the person who played the most consistent and central part in the drafting process'.[20] A year later, Seán Faughnan wrote that Hearne 'with de Valera, was to prove to be the principal architect of the 1937 Constitution'.[21] More recently, scholars have confirmed this assessment. Diarmaid Ferriter has commented: 'Nor was its creation possible without the contribution of civil servants like John Hearne and Maurice Moynihan' (secretary to the government, 1937–48).[22] Bill Kissane identified Hearne as the most important of the civil servants involved in its production[23] and, in the opinion of Judge Gerard Hogan, 'the supremely gifted John Hearne was the principal drafter'.[24]

While the role of John Hearne in the making of the 1937 Constitution has emerged from obscurity, it is important, however, never to forget that the document's prime mover and originator was Éamon de Valera. The Irish version of his biography conveyed this point with powerful directness: 'Bhí rian láimhe de Valera go trom ar an mBunreacht agus é á dhréchtadh. Chaith sé dua agus dícheall le gach alt agus gach focal ann.' (De Valera's handwork was very much on the Constitution as it was being drafted. He put labour and effort into every paragraph and word.)[25] Professor Ronan Fanning wrote in 1987:

> It is historically accurate to speak of the 1937 Constitution as de Valera's Constitution, not merely because he was the head of the government that enacted it but because the records recently released by the Department of the Taoiseach and by the Franciscan Institute in Killiney, where de Valera's own papers are housed, put his personal predominance beyond any shadow of doubt.[26]

Faughnan commented that 'ultimately it was de Valera's decision what should or should not be included. The drafting of the Irish Constitution of 1937 was a process which was controlled and, in all essentials, inspired by de Valera himself'.[27] Hearne's son, Maurice, acknowledged this fact in notes he prepared for a biography of his father: 'The Constitution of 1937 sprang from the nationalist ideals of Eamon de Valera, it was his political brainchild and it was he and he alone, among the Irish political figures at the time, who had the courage to shepherd it to its successful conclusion between 1935–7.' Of his father's role, he added: 'It is equally clear to me that it was my father whom Mr de Valera most trusted to bring his ideal to that successful conclusion.'[28]

Notwithstanding a greater knowledge and appreciation of John Hearne's part in the process which led to Bunreacht na hÉireann, Professor J.J. Lee was correct when he observed that 'much remains to be uncovered about the planning and drafting of the Constitution, including not least the role of John Hearne and Maurice Moynihan'.[29]

This book concentrates on Hearne and attempts to identify more precisely, describe more thoroughly and assess more critically his role. It is a task made difficult, however, by the absence of any personal papers belonging to him and of official sources at important times in the process of writing the document. Hearne confirmed this fact in a letter to Maurice Moynihan in 1963:

> As regards the English version [of the Constitution], I kept no records at all of my conversations with the President or others in the course of the drafting, and made none afterwards. On one occasion during the drafting, the President asked me whether I was making notes of our conversations and I said I was not doing so. As to whether there is any summary account of the discussions, their general nature, and so on, I should say there is no such account. There is none prepared by me and none of which I am aware.[30]

Nevertheless, it is important to try and understand Hearne's role more completely. It is also an opportunity to assess the document from the perspective and through the prism of Hearne's contribution – a document regarded by de Valera as one of his [de Valera's] two greatest achievements,[31] and of which it has been commented that 'little else in his career throws such a shadow over contemporary Ireland'.[32]

CHAPTER 1

Family, Education and Politics, 1893–1921

John Joseph Hearne was born on 4 December 1893 at 8 William Street in the city of Waterford. He was the fifth son and the seventh of eight children, five boys and three girls, born to Richard Hearne (1850–1929) and Alice Mary Hearne, née Power (1856–1934).[1] The William Street home in which he lived was not much more than 250 metres from the Viking Triangle, a small area of approximately two hectares, where the Vikings first settled in 914 and which came to define the historic centre of the city, the oldest in Ireland. As he grew up, Hearne came to appreciate the rich heritage of his birthplace and the significant role his family played in it. He always retained affection for the city of his birth and regarded it as 'home', often visiting it at Christmas while his parents were alive.[2] In December 1945, returning after the War from Canada, where he was Ireland's High Commissioner, he again came to Waterford for Christmas. On 18 December, he and his son, Maurice, then aged about ten, were both granted the freedom of the city on the basis of hereditary application, his father Richard having been a freeman.[3] The fact that he applied for this suggests Hearne's sense and appreciation of family history and municipal tradition, expressed in claiming a privilege, albeit strictly honorary, defined by familial right and in accordance with the old and established practice of the city's Corporation.

Waterford at the turn of the twentieth century

The city of Hearne's birth recorded a population of 20,852 in the 1891 census.[4] This was to increase to 27, 464 by 1911;[5] indeed, between 1901 and 1911, Waterford's population grew faster than that of any other southern Irish city, except Dublin. Prosperity depended on the provisions' trade. In the 1890s, bacon curing was one of the few significant industries, employing 850 people in four factories and supporting

150 pig buyers.[6] The number of jobs available in Waterford, however, failed to keep pace with the rising population. Unemployment continued to rise steadily though, by 1911, the number of males out of work had fallen. As a consequence of joblessness, poverty was pervasive. Appalling housing conditions, with attendant problems of poor drainage and lack of hygiene, meant that the city recorded the highest death rate of any town in Ireland in the 1880s. By the 1890s, the Corporation began tackling the housing problem but conditions were far from satisfactory and, in 1909, a particularly high number of deaths from tuberculosis was recorded.[7]

The most densely populated area in Waterford was the Centre Ward and it was here that some of its poorest inhabitants lived.[8] Although William Street was not far from this part of the city, the life experience of John Hearne was very different to that of many of the people in that ward. Society was structured according to a graduated class system[9] and the Hearne family was middle class. Their house was located in Tower Ward, where 70 per cent of residents were house owners; by contrast, the comparable figure for the Centre Ward was only 3 per cent.[10] The Hearnes had a live-in domestic servant.[11] In what has been described as 'the endemically stratified social life of the city',[12] John Hearne very likely had no significant contact with those less socially advantaged than he. This is apparent from an account of a conversation his son Maurice remembered having with him, in which his father recounted an event while serving in the Free State army during the Civil War:

> One experience when he was a junior officer remained with him and he related it to me as a small boy in Canada, probably, I think, to let me know how well off we were in comparison with so many others. He was passing by the NCOs' mess one dinner time and he heard a soldier, when asked what was on offer for dinner, reply almost in disbelief: 'Mate, again, begob'. It only dawned on him that the average Irish family could afford meat but once a week at the very outside.[13]

Richard Hearne: businessman

The Hearne family's middle-class status was due to the business success enjoyed by Richard Hearne, John's father. He was born in 1850, at Drumrusk, near Passage East, a village just over thirteen kilometres from Waterford.[14] As a young man he began working in the city as an apprentice at Messrs Walsh, a leather store situated in Broad Street. On the death of Edward Walsh, Richard Hearne and James Cahill took over the business. Under the new name of Hearne and Cahill, it soon became one of the city's best known industries, manufacturing boots. In a book published in 1894, Patrick Egan gave a detailed account of it:

Entering the cutting room we counted twelve hands cutting out ... Passing on to the machine room we counted in one room twenty-two girls employed working sixteen machines ... Those machines include all the newest designs which the art of invention has developed up to the present time, they having replaced within the present year older ones, now obsolete. We also witnessed the machine for sole sewing, 'Keats Fortuna', at work, which is the only one of its kind in Ireland, and the fifth made; and which is capable of sewing five hundred pairs daily. There are several finishing rooms, all filled by busy workmen, and the leather stores, in a factory where upwards of ninety hands are constantly going, with all the machines at their disposal, are of necessity well stocked by large quantities of the different leathers required.

Reflecting his admiration for the factory, Egan proclaimed: 'Waterford may feel justly proud of having one of the very few boot factories in Ireland.' Inspired by its example, he made a political point: 'If Waterford had many industrial resources such as this, it might look forward to the day when it would be able to recover all the native industries which have been filched from the country during ages of misdealing, through inimical laws and other grooves, by which the lifeblood of the Irish nation has well-nigh been exhausted.'[15]

On the death of Richard Hearne in 1929, the business was inherited by his son, also called Richard. In 1933, the factory was extended and new machines acquired with the potential to increase production by almost 50 per cent. By this time, the company was also producing light and more fashionable footwear, including ladies' shoes, in addition to boots.[16] Its importance as a source of employment in Waterford was highlighted in April 1948, when its closure, for a number of weeks, was raised at a meeting of the city's Corporation. It appears that this was due to overproduction but it did reopen.[17] However, manufacture ceased in 1951, dealing a major blow to the local economy.

Richard Hearne: public man

Like many successful businessmen in an era of a very restricted local franchise, Richard Hearne was elected a member of Waterford Corporation, representing the Custom House Ward.[18] He was a supporter of the Irish Parliamentary Party led by Charles Stewart Parnell, which was campaigning for Home Rule for Ireland. In 1889, members of the Corporation elected him High Sheriff of Waterford.[19] However, in 1890, when the Irish Parliamentary Party split over the issue of Parnell's affair with Catherine O'Shea, Hearne opposed Parnell. He was one of the founders of the National Commercial Club which met at Paul's Square in the city. It became the focus of anti-Parnellism[20] in a city that continued to be one of Parnell's strongest areas of support and which, in 1891, returned a Parnellite, John Redmond, to parliament in a by-election.

Notwithstanding this fact, Hearne continued to oppose the Parnellite majority locally – not a popular position to espouse in a decade of intense political bitterness and division. His obituarist commented: 'Into that movement [anti-Parnellism], despite fierce opposition and threats of harm, with all his moral consciousness, he threw the full weight of his great energy and enthusiasm.' The obituary continued: 'Then, when the blessed reconciliation came, and the leaders joined hands again as united Irishmen, Ald. Hearne became as devoted to Parnell's successor, the late Mr John Redmond, as he had been strenuously opposed to the policy Mr Redmond championed during the split.'[21] On Sunday, 22 April 1900, when John Redmond returned to Waterford as leader of the Irish Parliamentary Party, Hearne was among those present at a public meeting to welcome and congratulate him.[22]

In 1901, Hearne was elected Mayor of Waterford.[23] The *Waterford News* welcomed his election, despite the fact that it had 'disagreed very materially' with the position he held on the issue of Parnell's leadership. The newspaper described the Corporation's choice 'as wise and judicious from every point of view', the new mayor being 'a sound businessman and large employer, experienced in corporate affairs'.[24] Hearne recognised the significance of his election in the context of a reunited Irish Parliamentary Party, declaring at his installation: 'I am proud to be the first mayor after unity has been restored.'[25] He was re-elected the following year for a second term.[26] As the first citizen of the city, he proposed that the freedom of Waterford be conferred on John Redmond,[27] which happened on 12 September 1902.[28]

Arguably, the most important event, in political terms, during his tenure as mayor was the setting up of a branch of the United Ireland League in the city in December 1901. This was the constituency and fund-raising organisation of the Irish Parliamentary Party. The invitations to the public meeting to discuss the branch's establishment were issued by Hearne, in his capacity as mayor.[29] He was to play an active role in its affairs.

In addition to membership of the Corporation and two terms as mayor, Hearne also served in a number of other public and semi-public offices. He was a borough magistrate,[30] poor law guardian and Master of the Holy Ghost Hospital, a charity tracing its origins back to the reign of King Henry VIII.[31] In January 1920, when Sinn Féin secured control of the Corporation in the local elections, Hearne retained his seat,[32] suggesting that he was a figure who commanded a degree of regard. His funeral in May 1929 was, in the words of the *Munster Express*, 'one of the largest demonstrations of sympathy and respect seen in Waterford for years' with 'every section of the community in the city and county' represented.[33] A motion of sympathy passed by the Corporation noted the loss of a person 'who was close on half a century so honourably associated with [Waterford's] public and commercial life'.[34] Clearly, Richard Hearne was a man of some substance in the economic and political life of the city for many years.

Education

John Hearne attended Waterpark College, run by the Irish Christian Brothers, which was approximately 300 metres from his home. According to Christian Brother and historian, Barry Coldrey, this school and Christian Brothers' College Cork 'were intended for the type of middle-class clientèle who would be unlikely to send their children to an ordinary school' conducted by the order.[35] A description of the school, published in 1914, suggests that it would appeal to parents ambitious for their children's educational and professional prospects:

> Waterpark College ... was established in 1892. It is pleasantly situated on the river bank in the suburb of Newtown ... The Christian Brothers have built a large study hall and recreation rooms and have enlarged the recreation grounds. Pupils are prepared in this excellent educational establishment for commercial life or for the legal, medical or engineering professions. The highest distinctions possible in all departments of public life have been won by Waterpark students.[36]

For a prominent family such as the Hearnes, the character of the school was probably the deciding factor rather than simply its proximity.

Christian Brothers' schools were noted for their nationalist ethos and an extraordinary bond was forged between them and Irish nationalism.[37] In 1901, on the occasion of the order's centenary, the Gaelic League congratulated the Brothers on the work they were doing for the Gaelic cause.[38] John Hearne is recorded in the 1901 census as being able to speak Irish,[39] though in his career in the civil service there is no evidence of his having any great degree of proficiency in the language.[40] While Christian Brothers' schools were often credited with inculcating an ethos of robustly anti-British values and endorsing radical nationalism,[41] this was probably not as pronounced in a more middle-class school such as Waterpark, the parents of whose pupils were not always as sympathetic to such tendencies. This may explain why, when reminiscing to an American audience in 1957, Hearne commented that, as a boy, the only history he knew 'was a kind of birth-and-death register of defunct British monarchs'. He knew the dates on which all the kings of England died and the name of the diseases which killed some of them.[42] Though he was to express robust nationalist views when older, these were, very definitely, in the Home Rule and

Redmondite traditions. His education may have influenced his political views; time spent in a Christian Brothers' school should not be equated simply with the espousal of Sinn Féin nationalism.

Having completed his education at Waterpark College, Hearne entered St John's College, Waterford, in September 1910, to commence study for the Roman Catholic priesthood.[43] Opened in 1871, this establishment trained students for Waterford and other dioceses.[44] On 12 September 1911, he began studies at Maynooth College, the national seminary. The course of training for clerical students involved three years' study for a BA degree in philosophy and arts, followed by a four-year theology degree. For some reason, Hearne studied four years for a BA and was awarded one in 1915, his subjects being Latin, English literature, logic and psychology, and metaphysics and ethics. He commenced studies in the Faculty of Theology in the academic year 1915–16, but left the seminary sometime during the academic year 1916–17.[45]

The timetables at the seminaries Hearne attended show a heavy schedule of lectures and classes which demanded a great deal of intellectual vigour. The young Hearne studied philosophy, morality, Church law, ethics, logic and politics. He also studied languages such as Latin, Greek and Hebrew.[46] According to Chief Justice Susan Denham, 'this experience undoubtedly enriched his work as lawyer, public servant and diplomat … The formative years spent at the seminaries in Waterford and Maynooth clearly influenced John Hearne's understanding of the world and human nature, and graced the stylishly written drafts he wrote, which ultimately became part of our Constitution.'[47]

The decision to leave Maynooth cannot have been an easy one for Hearne. He was a very religious person throughout his life, as will be seen later. The fact that he spent a total of seven years preparing for the priesthood suggests a strong personal belief in his having a vocation. His son, Maurice, in his contents for a 'proposed biography' of his father, made a note which highlighted some of the difficulties Hearne faced: 'Left Maynooth a short time before due to be ordained. His family disappointed and [include] a short discussion on the trauma associated with such a decision at the time in provincial Ireland.'[48] When he wrote of 'trauma', what Maurice had in mind was that his father would have been regarded as a 'spoiled priest'.

> Having a priest, nun, or brother in the family was not merely socially acceptable, it conferred a unique respectability, as well as presumed advantages in the order of grace. The social attitude towards the priesthood carried the further assumption that any young man who commenced a clerical career was, *ipso facto*, 'called' to the priesthood; he had a 'vocation'. Therefore, a clerical student who failed, for whatever reason, to proceed all the way to ordination was called a 'spoiled priest'. The particular Irish Catholic usage carried a certain social stigma.[49]

This social stigma was explored in a play written in 1912 by Thomas C. Murray (1873–1959). Entitled *Maurice Harte*, the eponymous protagonist decides to quit his clerical studies at Maynooth, to the deep shock of his parents and brother.[50] His mother proclaims: 'If you don't return [to Maynooth] how can I ever face outside this door, or lift up my head again? ... How could I ever face again into the town of Macroom? ... I tell you, Maurice, I'd rather be lying dead a thousand times in the graveyard over at Kilnamartra.'[51]

While it is not being suggested that the Hearne family reacted with such melodramatic intensity, the play does give a valuable insight into contemporary attitudes. Maurice Hearne was aware of the Hearne family's 'disappointment' and the social attitudes then prevalent. His source of information for both was almost certainly John Hearne himself. This reinforces the sense that, for personal, family and social reasons, it was probably an anxious and difficult time in his life. The fact that he had an older brother, Maurice, who had been trained in St John's College and ordained on 17 June 1906,[52] could have either exacerbated or mitigated this anxiety. Whatever the case, significantly for John Hearne, he had the support of his father.[53] This made things somewhat easier for him, but the distress the decision might have caused him should not be underestimated in the Ireland and Waterford of 1916.

Hearne was a committed Catholic throughout his life. He was known to his contemporaries as a devout man,[54] a view confirmed by his niece, Alice Bowen, who knew him well and remembers him as being very religious.[55] A letter he sent her in acknowledgement of her expression of sympathy on the death of his son, Justin, aged twenty, as result of a shooting accident in September 1957,[56] suggests a person with a deep sense of personal faith.[57] The influence of his clerical training revealed itself in particular ways. While acknowledging a letter of sympathy from a nephew, Fr Ignatius Fennessy, again on the occasion of his son's death, he observed that a Catholic priest would be able to appreciate what he felt at that time.[58] This was a remark respectful of the Catholic priesthood and informed by his association with clerics, especially at the seminaries he attended. While serving as Irish Ambassador to the United States (1950–60), his younger son, David, was involved in a motor accident in which an elderly woman was killed. Hearne insisted on going to the woman's funeral in South Carolina and preaching the sermon at the funeral service.[59] During his tenure as ambassador, he was invited to speak at Catholic universities and his addresses were inspired by deeply-held religious beliefs. He delivered a speech on the occasion of the commencement exercises at the University of Notre Dame on 4 June 1950 and included the following:

It will depend on you [the graduates] whether or not this country can weather the maelstrom [of challenges facing it]. Be prepared for that. Be prepared by being practical, day to day, men of faith; not believers merely, but doers also. Let the excellence of your lives shine for all to see in the community in which you live, in your professional relations and your social surroundings. Be intellectually honest and intellectually humble. Teach your friends and neighbours, aye, and your enemies, how to distinguish money from wealth, interference from influence, notoriety from fame, pride from self-respect, speed from progress, luxury from elegance, glamour from distinction, fashion from taste, respectability from worthiness – I mean the spurious from the genuine and the temporal from the eternal.

He continued with an exhortation founded on Christian principles:

Never before has mankind been so much in need of the true pattern as well as the true tradition of human life formed in the mind of the Designer and spun from the hand of its Author. The world needs teachers much, but it needs models more. And if we be not the models there will be none. On us and our example will depend the issue of whether or not the image of God is written upon the character of this and the next generation.[60]

Throughout his life he retained a deep interest in philosophy and theology, interests which served him well during the drafting of the Constitution.

In 1916, Hearne entered University College Dublin, graduating with a LLB degree in 1919.[61] He was also admitted to the King's Inns as a student in the Michaelmas term, 1916, and was called to the Bar in 1919.[62] His career at the King's Inns was an illustrious one. He received three gold medals for his achievements in the year 1917–18: for oratory, legal debate and the Lord Chancellor's Prize for oratory and legal debate combined.[63] For 1919–20, he served as auditor of the Law Students' Debating Society of Ireland.[64] In that capacity he delivered the inaugural lecture, entitled 'University Culture and the Rule of Law', at the opening meeting of the society's nineteenth session. Some of the sentiments he expressed, as reported in the *Freeman's Journal*, are of interest in light of the future part he was to play in the making of the state's new basic law in 1937 and as a diplomat at the League of Nations:

[the] ... upshot from all their [the audience's] knowledge of the world war was that international law as a governing force in the world had signally failed. He believed that the power and permanence of their legislative and executive establishments in the state, and of progressive international polity in the world, would depend increasingly in the future upon the degree of advancement obtained by the

common people of the nations in moral culture and self-discipline, in public virtue, in knowledge to appreciate their liberties, and prudence to use them wisely, in light to understand those of others, and to recognise them generally, in the consciousness of their power as the makers and administrators of the law, and a corresponding sense of their responsibility as citizens of the state and the custodians of its destinies ... Self-discipline and social betterment would carry us a long way further at this moment than the world had yet advanced, and make the new citizenship the chief and primal sanction of a reformed international system and of the capital institutions of every free land.

The same newspaper reported that the vote of thanks was proposed by the Lord Chief Justice, who complimented Hearne on his address and 'predicted for him a great career at the Bar'. Seconding the motion, Timothy Healy, KC, a future Governor-General of the Irish Free State, joined the Lord Chief Justice in prophesying for the auditor 'a high place' in the profession.[65]

Hearne was to practise law on the Leinster Circuit, which included Waterford, until 1922. However, before he began his legal career, his oratorical skills were to be employed in the political bear-pit of local and national politics.

Politics

On 6 March 1918, John Redmond, MP for Waterford City, died and a by-election was called for 22 March. His son, Captain William Archer Redmond, was selected to contest the seat by the local United Ireland League; his opponent was Dr Vincent White, representing Sinn Féin. This political contest, an important one locally and nationally, was bitterly fought. Prominent in their support of Captain Redmond were the Hearnes, John and his father, Richard. For the younger Hearne, it was to be his first public engagement in electoral politics and, by his involvement, he revealed the extent of his commitment to the Home Rule cause and the Redmondite tradition.

For the two parties the election had a practical and symbolic significance. Sinn Féin had won four by-elections in 1917, though it had suffered a defeat in Armagh South in February 1918.[66] In practical terms, a victory in Waterford would represent a continuation of successful progress in its determination to supplant the Irish Parliamentary Party as the dominant force in Irish politics. There was also a deep symbolic significance attached to a win. The election was for John Redmond's old seat and the opposing candidate was his son. His nomination was regarded by Sinn Féin as 'the last kick of the dying "home rule upon the statute book" Irish Parliamentary Party'.[67] Defeat for Redmond would deliver a political coup de grace, sending his party into a spiral of irreversible decline. Therefore, there was no doubt that Sinn

Féin understood the importance, even the necessity, of victory. Its local director of elections, Nicholas Whittle, recorded the fact that:

> all members of the executive ... participated in the election in Waterford City and canvassed the city daily ... The republican movement in Ireland threw everything it had in to the by-election. Sean Milroy, general director of elections, wrote daily letters to prominent republicans throughout the whole country to come to Waterford and lend a hand.[68]

For the Irish Parliamentary Party the stakes were even higher. It appeared to be in decline following a series of election defeats. On a practical level, a victory would halt the progress of Sinn Féin; it might even reverse it and herald a restoration of the Party's fortunes. The contest was also charged with a deep emotional symbolism – the memory of John Redmond cast a shadow over his supporters in Waterford. He was viewed by them as a martyr for the Home Rule cause just as Patrick Pearse had come to represent martyrdom for the republican one. They were seeking to vindicate and protect Redmond's political legacy and to use his memory as an inspiration for party renewal and revival against the Sinn Féin onslaught.

For supporters of Home Rule, even more fundamental than these practical and symbolic considerations was their revulsion at the direction politics was taking. The restoration of constitutionalism was of paramount urgency in the face of what was regarded as the dangerous revolutionism of Sinn Féin. The mayor, David McDonald, asserted that the country could get what it required 'by constitutional means ... Was it worth spilling untold quantities of Irish blood? ... For eighteen months these marauders have gambled with the destinies of Ireland ... Waterford can finish the humbug that has been going on for the past eighteen months'.[69]

Given the importance of the election for both parties, it was a very hard-fought contest. Arthur Griffith was to comment to Whittle: 'Do you know this has been the roughest election in Irish history, not excepting the famous Galway election?'[70] Notwithstanding Sinn Féin's election successes in 1917, the Waterford contest presented a real and serious challenge, as it had to contend with the formidable Redmondite political machine in the city. John Redmond had first been elected in a by-election in 1891, defeating Michael Davitt, of Land League fame.[71] He retained his seat in all six subsequent general elections, in four of which he was returned unopposed.[72]

Central to his victories was the support he enjoyed from the Pig Buyers' Association, located in Ballybricken, in the heart of the city. Of this body Egan observed that 'in every movement, social, political and commercial, the men of Ballybricken, owing to their high position and influence as traders in the city, play an important part'.[73] On the basis of their support, Redmond built a powerful constituency organisation[74] which 'permeated and suffocated local politics'.[75] The Irish Parliamentary Party became the near monopoly leader of local nationalism and had the 'copyright' of the national movement and its machine.[76] William Redmond could count on this organisation and machine in March 1918.

A spectre of violence, actual and threatened, hung over the election campaign. When Griffith's newspaper, *Nationality*, complained that 'constitutionalism was upheld by "constitutional" stones and bludgeons', it was telling the essential truth.[77] Much of the violence and disorder which characterised the contest was instigated by Redmond's supporters, who outnumbered and were more organised than Sinn Féin's.[78] The former could rely on the pig buyers, former soldiers and wives of serving soldiers. The women interrupted Sinn Féin meetings with singing and heckling. De Valera was attacked and his party's candidate spent a week in hospital after an assault.[79] Sinn Féin responded by bringing in Volunteer units from outside Waterford to protect its election workers.[80]

Clearly, the March by-election was one fought with intensity and ferocity and all participants appreciated this fact. The Hearnes, father and son, played a central role in it. On 8 March, Richard Hearne, in his capacity as president of the city branch of the United Ireland League, was on the platform at a meeting in the City Hall to express sympathy to the Redmond family on its bereavement.[81] He attended the opening meeting of Captain William Redmond's campaign on 12 March.[82] Three days later he presided at a meeting in Ferrybank, regarded as a Sinn Féin stronghold, introducing Redmond to the crowd.[83] On St Patrick's Day he played a prominent part in Redmond's last election rally at Ballybricken, again introducing him to the gathering.[84]

On 12 March, at the opening meeting of Redmond's campaign, John Hearne delivered what was probably his first speech in his native city; it might, in fact, have been his first ever speech delivered at an election meeting. In this address, he articulated the views and concerns informing the attitudes and aspirations of Home Rule supporters. He began by acknowledging the emotions and symbolism of the occasion, declaring that it was fitting that it was in Redmond's adopted city that 'the first staggering blow should be struck for Redmondism and reason, when John Redmond himself, the living embodiment of political sound sense, is no more'. He announced the intention of his supporters not to cede political ground to any other party: 'We are to be here this time, next time and all the time.' In fact, they were resolved to 'smash Sinn Féin' and he asserted that 'Waterford was safe for political sanity.'

He then sought to motivate his audience by appealing to their sense of history: 'Daniel O'Connell told Isaac Butt that it was not the Clare election that won [Catholic] emancipation; he said that it was the Waterford election [1826] that turned the tide finally for religious freedom. It was the Waterford election of 1891 which gave us John Redmond for our member, and gave him to Ireland as the "Chief".' Hearne was very clear in his assertion that the election was essentially about the political legacy of Redmond: 'Let it be the Waterford election of 1918 that will vindicate the greatness of his chieftaincy.' In a rhetorical flourish, he summarised the significance of the occasion and what was at stake: 'We are going to lift up the old flag and unfurl it upon our City Hall, upon our Cathedral and upon the castles and towers of our dear ancient city, and we are going to proclaim Waterford the greatest, the most powerful and the most impregnable stronghold of the principles of John Redmond and constitutional home rule.'[85]William Redmond won the by-election, by 1,242 votes to White's 745.[86]

In the early hours of Sunday 24 March, John Hearne delivered another political speech, this one at a meeting celebrating victory. It was a trenchant and uncompromising address, motivated and shaped by the bitterness of the campaign. He began with an emotional proclamation that the city had been true to John Redmond and his son. He quickly launched into a vitriolic attack on Sinn Féin: 'The life blood of the late Mr John E. Redmond and the late Major William Redmond [his brother][87] went forth for the same imperishable ideals of nationality. One was shot dead by the enemies of civilisation abroad, the other's heart broken by the enemies of civilisation at home.' He referred to Sinn Féin supporters, who had been drafted in for the election, leaving the city after their defeat: 'Was it any wonder that they [Redmond's supporters] opened their windows and let in the pure splendour of God's sunlight, because they knew that the pestilence had gone from the city.'

He continued in a menacing tone: 'They knew that if they did not go in time, the people of Waterford would see that they would go in eternity.' Jeeringly, he announced that 'Mr Darrell Figgis[88] had fled from Waterford as he fled from British soldiers in Easter Week and Mr A. Griffith had gone to Clontarf to meditate on Brian Boru.' He reserved particular bile for those who had voted for White, especially former Redmond supporters: 'There were men in the city who should hang their heads in shame. There were men even in Ballybricken who might hang their heads in shame – men who stood by John Redmond in sunshine and deserted him in the dark days.' Hearne then turned his attention to the British government, denouncing its treatment of Redmond, accusing it of doing all it could to ensure that his position was made 'unbearable' in the country: 'They knew that he was the only man powerful enough and with brain enough to restore to Ireland what they had filched from it, their national self-government.' He linked the behaviour of the government and Sinn Féin together to discredit both: 'Sinn Féin was the strongest ally the government had in keeping their country in subjection. The government gloried in Sinn Féin, because they knew that as long as the country was in a state of insufferable anarchy, they could say that Ireland was unfit for home rule.'

However, Waterford, he declared, had transformed the situation by showing the world that the country was fit to rule itself. In an assertion inspired by the moment of victory, he proclaimed: 'It was quite impossible to exaggerate the importance of that tremendous moment in the history of their country. For the past two years there had been an avalanche of abuse launched at the head of John Redmond ... Waterford had, once and for all, turned the tide in the teeth of Sinn Féiners and the government.' Coming to the end of his speech, he urged preparation for the general election, appealing to Home Rule supporters to remain united: 'They must try to bring their forces together, for the Sinn Féiners did their traitorous work well.' He finished on a note of menace: 'Those men should never have been allowed to poll 700 votes in the City of Waterford, and that must not occur again.'[89]

The importance of the Hearne family in the Home Rule movement in Waterford was confirmed in the aftermath of the March election, when Richard Hearne was re-elected president of the city branch of the United Ireland League.[90] In October, a Young Ireland branch of the league was inaugurated. This was inspired by, and modelled on, the branch founded in Dublin in December 1904, which had as its aim the encouragement of a younger membership in the party,[91] so that it could 'infuse new lifeblood into the increasingly sclerotic arteries of the home rulers'.[92] John Hearne was the principal speaker at its inaugural meeting. His association with the branch was consistent with his call on supporters during his March victory speech to organise themselves. According to a newspaper report, he was invited to speak because 'his speeches made such an impression during the election campaign'.[93] Canon Furlong, who presided, said in his short address that 'the eloquence of Meagher,[94] Sexton[95] and Leamy[96] was not dead while they had John Hearne among them'. He was to deliver a significant speech in terms of outlining his political ideas.

Hearne began by delivering a panegyric to John Redmond, who was described as the 'embodiment' of nationalism and whose 'illustrious' name would be 'the bright symbol in hopeful future years'. Once again, it was evident that the emotional attachment of Redmond's followers to their dead leader was akin to that of Sinn Féiners for the 1916 leaders. Both groups of followers operated in the shadow of dead men and, in their public utterances, these followers were in thrall to their political legacies. Hearne stated that it was 'fitting to inaugurate a Young Ireland branch in Waterford to carry on the old fight, along the old lines ... with the master mind of Redmond still controlling the work and his extended hand pointing the steadfast way forward'. He outlined the purpose of the branch and his words echoed those of Redmond: '[it] proclaims the unabated, unbroken and unbreakable allegiance of the youth of our city to the age-old principle of parliamentary representation for Ireland, to work for and to win full and final self-government, absolute and unconditional, for our native land'.

Of course, this 'full and final government' was to be achieved in the context of Ireland's continuing membership of the British Empire. Hearne utterly rejected the charge that Home Rule was setting boundaries to the march of the Irish nation. He argued that the alternative to Home Rule was not an Irish republic: 'The controversy does not lie between these two alternatives, for the one is a practicable and attainable national policy, the other is a morbid and an amorphous and delusive national idea.' Elaborating briefly on what he meant as a 'practicable' policy, he explained that it was to work to win for Ireland 'a dignified and self-developing status among free peoples'. This policy he contrasted with Sinn Féin's 'political extravagances' and 'erroneous and maudlin patriotism'. The supporters of Home Rule were 'not prepared to continue this turmoil that exists in Ireland today on the steadily receding chance of setting up a national republic somewhere about the time the archangel will set one foot upon the water and the other upon the land'. Rather than pursuing a futile dream of a republic, there were urgent issues demanding attention:

> In the financial readjustment that will follow the war, the present ghastly and unreal prosperity of Ireland will be made the pretext for taxing our agricultural and industrial interests out of existence by our enemies in Great Britain and Ireland, unless our position be safeguarded and secured by the united, nation-supported efforts of our people in parliament. The status of the teaching profession, the great invaluable secular asset for the island of saints and scholars, must be uplifted from its present scandalous and disreputable condition. Turn where you will, the immediate needs of the nation call for vigorous and violent parliamentary agitation.

In focusing on taxation and education, Hearne was echoing opinions and concerns articulated by leaders of the Irish Parliamentary Party. John Redmond had spoken about over-taxation and education on a number of occasions, claiming that misguided British policies in these areas had 'annihilated' Ireland. Thomas Kettle[97] had identified these issues as among the two most pressing ones for a native government.[98] In the light of much work to be done, Hearne called on Home Rule supporters to be organised and disciplined. He concluded his speech with a rousing, rhetorical flourish:

> Let them concentrate their energies, let them define their aims, let them pursue them in every circumstance of derision and defeat with fearless and steadfast confidence, and let them persevere to the very end. Let them remember, above all, that when the long night is past, and Ireland stands forth again in the white

glory of her risen generation as the spiritual law-giver to the free nations of the earth, as the great commercial emporium between the continent of Europe and the cities of the western world, as the leader in the vanguard of the new freedom which is truth and justice and charity, the achievements will be attributable first, above all, to the men who fought with the emblem of peace and goodwill upon their banners, and the virtues of mutual trust and tolerance in their hearts.[99]

1918 general election

Within a few weeks of this speech, Waterford City was convulsed by the 1918 general election. Again, Richard and John Hearne played prominent roles in the campaign. William Archer Redmond's selection as its candidate by the local United Ireland League was seconded by the former[100] and he also seconded his formal nomination papers.[101] John Hearne addressed meetings in the city; he spoke at Grace Dieu on 10 December[102] and at a rally in Broad Street on 12 December.[103] An indication of his increasing stature in political circles was an invitation to speak at a meeting in the county in support of the candidacy of James John O'Shee, the Home Rule candidate. In its account, the *Freeman's Journal* listed the speakers, but made a particular reference to Hearne, commenting that 'he delivered a powerful speech'.[104] Unfortunately, no details were given of this or, indeed, of any of his speeches during the election.

Unsurprisingly, it was a bitter contest marked by incidents of disorder and violence on both sides. Volunteers were again drafted into Waterford to protect Sinn Féin canvassers who were outnumbered by their opponents. One volunteer recorded his impressions of the campaign thus: 'I was in Waterford city for the most exciting election contest in the 1918 general election ... I have never met anything since to equal the fanaticism of the Redmond supporters in that contest, who at times went berserk.'[105] On the eve of polling, there were street brawls[106] and disorder on polling day itself.[107]

Redmond retained his seat with 4,915 votes to White's 4,431. For the Irish Parliamentary Party the election was a disaster nationally: it won six seats as against Sinn Féin's seventy-three. Though Sinn Féin secured 48 per cent of the total votes cast and the Irish Parliamentary Party 23 per cent, the first-past-the-post system ensured the spoils to the victor. Constitutional nationalism was not dead but it had lost its voice for the moment. As Meleady has written: 'Thus died, within months of his own death, all of the projects that had absorbed Redmond's energies – home rule within the empire and the party fashioned to bring it into being.'[108] John Hearne and his father also saw their political dreams, beliefs and commitment pushed aside as the country embarked on a new course.

Nearly forty years later, while serving as Irish Ambassador to the United States, John Hearne summed up his experiences of 1918 in an address to American lawyers: 'I supported a political party which not only lost control of the country the year I joined its political hopefuls, but at the same time passed out of existence.' He also shared with his audience the assessment of T.M. Healy of his venture into politics: 'Young man, your political career was short, brilliant and disastrous.'[109] While brutal in their directness, Healy's words were accurate.

John Hearne's political views: a summary description

At this point it may be useful to review and attempt a summary description of Hearne's political ideas and views. This presents some real difficulties: 'The reconstruction of mentalities is notoriously difficult, particularly when few records of intimate thoughts and aspirations, as those which sometimes appear in diaries and personal letters, are available.'[110] However, his two election speeches and his address to the Young Ireland branch give a reasonable, if necessarily limited, insight into Hearne's mentality. Clearly, he was an ardent and uncompromising supporter of Home Rule for Ireland. He spoke of it as giving the country a 'self-developing status among free peoples'. Perhaps here he was subscribing to an idea, albeit inchoately, that it would not be in itself a final settlement – Ireland in time would achieve all the attributes of freedom associated with a sovereign state. Whatever about reading too much into that comment, he was, undoubtedly, committed to constitutionalism and parliamentarianism as the means of winning self-government. Given this view, his admiration for John Redmond and his achievements was real and understandable, an admiration reinforced by the fact that he had been the MP for Waterford City.

A corollary of this dedication to Home Rule was Hearne's rejection of Sinn Féin and its policies. He regarded them as impractical and unattainable – the advocacy of a republic, in particular, a delusion – when considered against the practicality and attainability of Home Rule which was on the statute book. Believing Sinn Féin's revolutionary proposals and methods to be damaging to Irish national interests, he promoted the primacy of the constitutional agenda. However, he had no illusions about, and was very critical of, English policy towards Ireland and condemned the attitude of the government. He articulated the language that was already fully developed within the Home Rule movement and used during the crises of 1914 and 1916–18 against what was regarded as a succession of English betrayals. Like many advocates of Home Rule, he was steeped in the bellicosity of language, sense of victimhood, glorification of struggle, identification of the movement's enemies and antipathy to England which suffused provincial nationalist orthodoxy.[111] John Hearne thus revealed himself as a typically robust nationalist in the constitutional, Redmondite tradition.

His engagement in politics affords us also some insight into his personality. He showed himself to be more than able to involve himself in the rough and tumble of a very tempestuous election campaign. The particularly embittered nature of the electioneering did not seem to bother him. Indeed, he himself contributed to the heat engendered by the contest by excoriating, even eviscerating, the Sinn Féin opposition. What emerges from a consideration of his political involvement is a man of determined views, convinced of their integrity, trenchant in their expression and lucid in their enunciation.

It is interesting to remember that Hearne was campaigning for Home Rule and Captain William Redmond while Éamon de Valera was on the opposite side, supporting Sinn Féin and an Irish republic. Hearne attacked with deliberate vitriol the party led by the man with whom he was to work so closely in the 1930s. To one of his antagonists in the crucial election in Waterford in 1918, de Valera later entrusted one of his most important concerns – a new constitution. This is a fascinating and dramatic illustration of how political circumstances change with the passage of time.

John Hearne and the revolutionary generation

Scholars have studied the revolutionary generation, the men and women who participated in the 1916 Easter Rising and those inspired by it, who rejected Home Rule and constitutional politics. Roy Foster surveyed the lives and beliefs of some of this generation, born roughly between the 1870s and the 1890s.[112] In an earlier study, Tom Garvin considered the revolutionary elite who constructed the independent Irish state and their political formation in the years 1890–1914.[113] There is an overlap in both studies in terms of personnel and time frame. What emerges from both is a fascinating political portrait of some of Hearne's contemporaries. 'The fact remains that during this era enough people – especially young people – changed their minds about political possibilities to bring about a revolution against the old order, which included not only government by Britain but the constitutionalism of the previous generation.'[114] In considering these studies and the generation they examine, light can be shed on the political formation of Hearne and why he, in contrast with others, continued to espouse the cause of Home Rule.

A central tenet of this generation of revolution was their alienation from British rule and rejection of Home Rule. Constitutional nationalism was spurned and self-government, as promoted by John Redmond, regarded as 'a corrupt and exhausted compromise'[115] which would impose on Ireland 'a grubby, materialist, collaborationist, Anglicised identity'.[116] As the person most associated with it, Redmond was utterly scorned, as was his party. Patrick Maume has commented that 'it is a shock to rediscover the ferocity and extent of contemporary separatist invective denouncing

Redmond as a conscious traitor who was deliberately selling Ireland and sending her to destruction'.[117] When Seán T. O'Kelly spoke of the need to rid the country of the Irish Parliamentary Party 'incubus',[118] he was articulating a common view of those disposed to revolutionary means.

The previous generation was often perceived as the enemy, every bit as much as the British government and the Irish Parliamentary Party were. Patrick Pearse declared that 'there has been nothing more terrible in Irish history than the failure of the last generation',[119] and there were those who agreed with him. 'For radical nationalists ... the previous generation had sold the pass to craven constitutionalism, by deciding that the Fenian agenda of achieving separation from Britain through physical force was outmoded and opting for parliamentary agitation instead.'[120] What was emerging was a new generation alienated 'not only from British rule but from the values and ambitions of their parents, and finally from the alternative offered by the constitutional Irish Parliamentary Party'.[121]

Members of the new generation felt like this because they were frustrated, their education often leaving them to face limited opportunities.[122] Feeling also excluded from political power, they began to critically assess the status quo and became intent on self-transformation.[123] After the 1916 rebellion, the police were convinced that many of the local leaders were people who turned to revolutionary politics in a society that offered them little opportunity.[124] Garvin has observed: 'In Yeats' classic phrase many of them indeed possessed great hatred and suffered from little room; little room was accorded them by Irish society or by the Anglo-Irish establishment and great hatred was commonly the consequence.'[125] In their assessment and rejection of the status quo there was also impatience with the power of the Catholic Church.[126]

On Hearne's part, there was no rejection of Home Rule or of the previous generation. As we have seen, he and his father figured prominently in the Home Rule movement in Waterford. He promoted the same politics as his father. He was not impatient with the Catholic Church; on the contrary, he had been a seminarian for many years. It would seem that he did not feel or share in the frustration of the revolutionary generation. He did not experience 'great hatred' because he did not experience 'little room'; his personal circumstances, because of the status and position enjoyed by his family, offered him the opportunity of a meaningful role in society. Crucially, there was also the influence of his father. Foster has noted that, in the life stories of many revolutionaries in this era, as confided to the Bureau of Military History in the 1940s and 1950s, the influence of a family member who provided a powerful nationalist conditioning was emphasised.[127] Richard Hearne provided a different but no less powerful conditioning for his son. John Hearne grew up in a home where Home Rule politics were a central part of family life; and just as some learned revolution in and from their families, he learned constitutionalism.

He also shared things in common with the revolutionary generation. He was educated by the Christian Brothers, who may have influenced his nationalism. He could be robustly critical of the British government. He wanted freedom for his country and saw Home Rule as giving this. He was a nationalist, a representative of the 23 per cent who voted for the Irish Parliamentary Party in the 1918 election. John Hearne serves as a reminder that not all voters subscribed to the Sinn Féin version of nationalism; there were significant numbers who were recusants. This minority was to be silenced and marginalised in the years 1919–21, but their silence must not be allowed to obscure the fact of their existence.

John Hearne and the 'lost generation'

Among those silenced and marginalised were many of the Catholic university elite who had expected to be leaders in a Home Rule Ireland. Their circumstances have been studied by Senia Pašeta.[128] These young men and women were self-consciously preparing themselves for important roles in a self-governing country[129] and expressed, confidently and regularly, their expectation that one day they would compose Ireland's ruling class.[130] Economist George O'Brien (1892–1973) commented:

> We all took it for granted that if Home Rule was achieved, we would be among the politicians of the new Ireland. A Home Rule parliament in College Green in those days would, no doubt, have been dominated by the Irish [Parliamentary] Party, which would have earned the credit for its establishment. We, in the college [University College Dublin] had many connections with the Irish Party ... We all confidently expected that in a short time we would be exercising our oratory, not in the dingy precincts of the old physics theatre in 86 [Earlsfort Terrace], but in the 'old house in College Green'... I remember Arthur Cox saying to me that there were only three positions for which we were being fitted by our education – prime minister, leader of the opposition and speaker of the House of Commons.[131]

Pašeta has made the important point that 'the years between Parnell and Pearse ... was a period of preparation, not for independence but for Home Rule and a central place in the empire'.[132] This world, however, disappeared with the 1916 Rising and the advent of Sinn Féin's revolutionary politics. Thus the demise of constitutional nationalism dealt a death blow not only to Redmond's party but to those members of the Catholic university elite preparing to be leaders in the new political era of self-government. The triumph of Sinn Féin doomed many talented men and women to become a lost generation of leaders.[133] Some could not find a place in the Ireland of the Irish Free State.

Hearne was a member of this Catholic university educated elite. He might have expected to play an important role in an Irish Home Rule parliament. This would not have been an unreasonable expectation, considering his family's status in one of the party's strongholds, his political activism, his education and undoubted abilities, particularly in law, a profession with strong links to politics. Such speculation, such engagement in counterfactual history, while diverting, is of no value here. What did happen was that he had no role in a Home Rule Ireland because there was no such thing. Rather he came to play a significant role in the new political dispensation after the Anglo-Irish Treaty settlement of 1921. Instead of being one of the 'lost generation' of Home Rulers, he was to become a member of the ruling elite in a newly independent state.

CHAPTER 2

In the Service of the Free State, 1922–1932

John Hearne accepted the Anglo-Irish Treaty of 1921 and this influenced him to support the Cumann na nGaedheal party led by William T. Cosgrave.[1] This party was to have a strong neo-Redmondite presence,[2] the old parliamentary nationalist tradition being seen as its natural constituency.[3] For example, in March 1923, at a Cumann na nGaedheal meeting in Waterford City, an extremely conciliatory mood was evinced towards the old Irish Parliamentary Party, with many in attendance advocating the adoption of William Redmond as the Cumann na nGaedheal candidate in an election.[4] Four years later, in 1927, at a meeting in Mayo to select candidates to represent the interests of Cosgrave's government, twenty-two of the thirty-one members of the election committee of the old Irish Party were in attendance and one of the candidates considered for nomination had contested a seat for the same party.[5] Cosgrave took satisfaction in bringing together the different nationalist traditions, a fact illustrated when both the sons of John Redmond and his successor, John Dillon, joined Cumann na nGaedheal.[6] In fact, as Patrick Maume has observed, 'the involvement in the Cosgrave government of middle-class Catholic professionals who might loosely be described as Redmondites ... meant that Redmondites could claim some degree of credit for the creation of the new state.'[7]

The Irish Parliamentary Party tradition was mediated in the highest levels of government by ministers such as Kevin O'Higgins, Vice-President of the Executive Council and Minister for Justice, and James Hogan, Minister for Agriculture.[8] The former, who was particularly influential in the development of Cumann na nGaedheal,[9] had strong family connections with Home Rule politics.[10] Writing about the two ministers, John Regan observed:

> O'Higgins and Hogan were in power, it might be argued, in spite of it [the Irish revolutionary period, 1918–21]. O'Higgins, in particular, acted and behaved,

even in his days with Collins in the provisional government, as if he should or one day would lead. School, university, the practice of the law, family, status, politics, their nationalism had all been framed within a history, perhaps a story of Ireland, the terminal point of which was to be the achievement of home rule. As part of a small, educated, and connected Catholic nationalist elite rapidly on the way up, they would be part of that achievement and benefit from it.[11]

These observations have strong resonances with Hearne's circumstances, as described in the previous chapter. He too was university educated, a lawyer and the scion of a family of status which was steeped in Home Rule politics. Therefore, he could entertain reasonable expectations of benefiting from the establishment of a Home Rule parliament. This explains why he had more in common with the Cumann na nGaedheal regime than a putative Sinn Féin one; the former was more consonant with his political beliefs and formation.

Moreover, O'Higgins, in his politics and approach to government, wanted to integrate into the new political system being established in the Free State the Irish nationalist Catholic elite.[12] Some had once been 'members of the Roman Catholic establishment in waiting',[13] pending the advent of Home Rule. Their rightful place was now in leadership roles in the Free State, according to O'Higgins. It is interesting to note, as will be seen in this chapter, that it was the same O'Higgins who first identified Hearne as a possible candidate for a position in the service of the new state.

For a strident opponent of Sinn Féin, such as Hearne, Cumann na nGaedheal in government won his support as it jettisoned much of the revolutionary Sinn Féin policy and its rhetorical republicanism after the 1923 general election.[14] In Cumann na nGaedheal's election manifesto, it was argued that 'the essence of a republic is the effective rule of the people, responsibility of governments to the people through their parliamentary representatives, the authority of the laws of the country derived from the people and exercised through a legislature elected by the people'. This had been established by the Constitution of the Free State; therefore, the republic had effectively been won.[15] Sentiments such as these would have struck a chord with Hearne, as he had denounced Sinn Féin's irresponsible policies in 1918, his views likely being reinforced by the country's apparent descent into anarchy in 1922–3, as a consequence of that party's pursuit of its illusive republic. Cumann na nGaedheal committed itself to an agenda of stable and efficient government and this represented a sensible and reasonable contrast and antidote to what Hearne would have regarded as the deplorable excesses of Sinn Féin.

The negation of extremism by Cosgrave and his ministers was more in keeping with the politics of an erstwhile follower of John Redmond than the more radical views of de Valera and his supporters. Interestingly, Kevin O'Higgins was criticised

for his failure to understand what the Irish revolution of 1918–21 was all about
– he was accused of having reduced it to the notion of the Irish people getting a
parliament.[16] Such an opinion is one with which Hearne might have identified and
sympathised, given his ardent support for a Home Rule parliament for Ireland, and
in the context of the perilous political situation in the country in 1922–3. Perhaps
applicable to him also, to some degree at least, was an observation made by de Valera
in the course of a press interview he gave on 15 January 1922. In it he argued that
the Treaty would undermine Ireland's position. He said that people did not realise
this and explained why.

> The national policy of the dominant political leaders of the last century, and
> of the present century up to the time of Mr Redmond's death, has so affected
> the mental background of all who are now above middle age that they slip back
> quite easily over the last decade as if it had not existed and regard this Treaty
> from the point merely of a Home Rule Act that cannot 'fix the boundary of the
> march of a nation'.[17]

While the reference to middle age is not relevant to Hearne, the Treaty viewed
in the context of the Home Rule Act may be. It is interesting to remember that, in
the course of his address to the Young Ireland branch in Waterford in 1918, discussed
in Chapter 1, he rejected the charge that the Home Rule movement was setting
boundaries to the march of the nation. He would have appreciated how much more
freedom the Free State enjoyed under the Treaty settlement than it would have
enjoyed under the Home Rule Act – the boundaries had been further extended.
This represented real progress and was not to be discarded in a quixotic pursuit of
republican constitutional dreams. Thus, by the mid-1920s the Free State's ruling elite,
in terms of composition and dominant political culture, appeared to share much
in common with the pre-revolutionary elite of the Irish Parliamentary Party.[18] For
Hearne, in the turbulent years of the new state's foundation, when citizens had to
decide their political loyalties, it meant transferring support from Redmond's party
to Cosgrave's. In truth, it was a decision which was neither surprising nor difficult.
    Hearne served the Free State in a number of capacities. He was an army officer
from 1922 to 1923. He then obtained employment in the Office of the Attorney
General as an assistant parliamentary draftsman, a position he retained until 1929,
when he became the legal adviser at the Department of External Affairs. He was
a member of one of the elites within the new state – 'civil servants, soldiers, legal
advisers, republican brothers [members of the Irish Republican Brotherhood] – all of
whom influenced policy and should be seen as forming extended and less recognisable
elites within what might be termed the Treatyite establishment'.[19] John Regan has

written that the non-political nature of many of the elites makes their more subtle contributions difficult or impossible to identify and that this remains 'especially true in the case of the senior civil servants in the early years of the new state'.[20] In relation to Hearne, he played a pivotal role in the state's Anglo-Irish and Commonwealth policies and, therefore, it is possible to identify and assess his contribution to some degree. He does not remain as anonymous as other civil service contemporaries.

Legal career

Before embarking on a career in the public service, Hearne was to practise as a barrister on the Leinster Circuit from 1919 to 1922. These years coincided with the struggle for independence waged by Sinn Féin and the Irish Republican Army. Sinn Féin set out in 1919 to create 'a polity within a polity' and nowhere was it more successful than in the creation of an alternative system for the administration of justice.[21] Courts owing their allegiance to Dáil Éireann were established and became quite formalised in their procedure, issuing injunctions and summoning juries.[22] Hearne appeared before them, acting as a counsel.[23]

Army officer

The Treaty was adopted by Dáil Éireann on 6 January 1922 but, for much of that year, the country was on the verge of anarchy. It was a very difficult time for those assuming the government of the newly independent state, a reality conveyed by one of its leaders, Kevin O'Higgins, in a memorable description:

> The provisional government was simply eight young men in the City Hall standing amidst the ruins of one administration, with the foundations of another not yet laid, and with wild men screaming through the keyhole. No police force was functioning through the country, no system of justice was operating, the wheels of administration hung idle, battered out of recognition by the clash of rival jurisdictions.[24]

With the Garda Síochána in the process of being formed and trained, the only instrument at the disposal of the government with which to enforce its authority was its fledgling army. The Dáil, therefore, approved the establishment of military courts in September 1922.[25]

In the autumn of 1922, Cahir Davitt was appointed Judge Advocate General to head up the army's legal section. He decided to attach to the headquarters of each command a legal staff officer, who would, if possible, be a qualified barrister or solicitor.[26] He began recruiting suitable staff and met with Kevin O'Higgins, Minister for Justice, who was in the process of appointing district justices. Davitt has left an interesting account of the meeting:

> I was told that Kevin O'Higgins, who had now become Minister for Justice, had received quite a number of applications from barristers and solicitors for positions as district justices to replace the old justices of the peace and that there were more applicants suitable in every way than there were vacancies to be filled. I called to see him and he gave me the names of those whom he would have liked to, but could not, accommodate. He made special mention of John Joseph Hearne, whom I had known in UCD and later as a counsel appearing before me in the Dáil courts. He was a Waterford man, whose family had always been staunch supporters of John Redmond and the Irish Parliamentary Party. He had himself in the 1918 general election ardently and eloquently supported John Redmond's son, William Archer Redmond ... O'Higgins told me that he would have appointed Hearne, of whose character and ability he had a high opinion but that there had been opposition within the government, which he had been unable to overcome.[27]

It is clear that Hearne's credentials as a Home Rule activist were militating against him; he had made an enemy or enemies in high places.[28] O'Higgins expressed the hope that Davitt would find a place for him on his staff and the latter readily agreed.[29] Thus Hearne became a command legal staff officer.

He was appointed to the army's Western Command. The circumstances of this have been described by Calton Younger in an account which captures the drama and hazardous nature of serving the young state:

> Seán Mac Eoin had recently been promoted to major-general and appointed G.O.C. of the Western Command, an appointment he accepted reluctantly. He was a man of action and didn't want to be tied down by administrative work. He would accept the command, he told Michael Collins, only if he were given a legal officer and a quartermaster. Collins quickly produced John Hearne, who afterwards reached ambassadorial rank. Hearne was rushed down to O'Callaghan's, the military outfitters, where he exchanged his natty lawyer's dress for an army uniform. He emerged with a Sam Browne belt that creaked its newness and a small holster. Having been issued with a large revolver, he took his place in McEoin's car to travel to Athlone. As they set off, Hearne suddenly realised that McEoin had no escort and asked rather anxiously where it was. McEoin laughed. 'Haven't I got you?' he said and, pointing to the revolver added, 'and that'.[30]

Hearne was commissioned at the rank of commandant, effective from 12 October 1922.[31]

The duties of a command legal staff officer were to advise the general officer commanding on all matters relating to military law and courts martial; to direct and generally supervise the administration of military law in the command area; and to provide for the attendance of a legal officer at every court martial held in that area.[32] The position was an important one in a country experiencing major civil disturbance, where military courts took the place of civilian ones. The courts had jurisdiction to try persons for offences such as attacks upon the national army; unauthorised possession of arms, ammunition or explosives; and the seizure and destruction of property.[33] These same courts had powers to inflict punishments which included fines, penal servitude, imprisonment, deportation, internment and death.[34] As legal officer of the Western Command, Hearne was responsible for the conduct of military courts in an area which included the western seaboard counties, as well as Longford, Roscommon, Sligo and Leitrim.[35]

His son, Maurice, has recorded that his father's military promotion and attendant duties 'placed Dad in somewhat of a dilemma'. He did not believe that capital punishment acted as a deterrent to criminality, especially in times of armed conflict, and that it left no margin for human error. The matter became a subject of discourse between them when they lived in Washington during Hearne's tenure as Ambassador to the United States. In 1951, both of them went to hear the unsuccessful appeal of Julius and Ethel Rosenberg against the death sentences imposed on them for espionage. According to Maurice, it was to his father's great relief that he was never appointed to conduct any case before a military court involving capital punishment.[36]

In considering Hearne's attitude to his role and to the prevailing disorder, recourse must be had to surmise in the absence of personal papers. Cahir Davitt offers us an insight. Referring to those to whom he offered positions as legal staff officers, he commented that 'once they had been given the opportunity of serving the state when it appeared to be in some danger, they felt it to be their duty, as citizens, not to refuse it [the position]'.[37] Furthermore, reflecting on the position in the country, he observed:

> Like the majority of the people, I regarded the provisional government as being the *de jure* as well as the *de facto* government of the state. I believed that it was not only its right but its plain and manifest duty to assert its authority and to protect the citizens in the exercise of their fundamental rights, to the undisturbed possession and enjoyment of their property and the lawful expression of their opinions. I believed that in order to do this it was essential to suppress the opposition of the Four Courts executive [anti-Treaty IRA leaders] and to prevent the use and abuse of the power they had unlawfully usurped. I believed that for

the purposes of doing so the government had every right to use military force as well as other legitimate means, including the taking of human life, if necessary ... Many attacks, in a sense all attacks, upon members of the government forces were made by men whom those attacked had every right and reason to regard as civilians. The Catholic hierarchy in a statement made from Maynooth in April [1922] had condemned the usurpation of power by the Four Courts executive; and in a joint pastoral letter of October 10 had stigmatised such attacks as being 'morally only a system of murder and assassination'.[38]

It is reasonable to suggest that Hearne would have shared many, if not most of the sentiments recorded by Davitt relating to the circumstances facing the government and the response of Cosgrave and his ministers to them. Like their author, Hearne was loyal to the Free State and would likely have agreed with the view of the Civil War articulated by O'Higgins at Oxford University in 1924: 'The right of the people to found a state on the basis of the Treaty which had been signed by their plenipotentiaries and endorsed by their parliament had to be vindicated beyond question.'[39]

As the Civil War petered out in 1923, the command legal staff officers became increasingly concerned about their future prospects. In May, they expressed these concerns in a letter sent to Cahir Davitt and signed by six officers, including Hearne.[40] In response, Davitt met with them but could not offer any reassurances.

As for Hearne, his career in the army ended when he tendered a letter of resignation, dated 19 November 1923, to Davitt, who recommended its acceptance, adding 'I do so with great regret, as this officer has been in every way satisfactory.'[41] His commission was terminated on 20 December.[42] He took up new employment in the Office of the Attorney General, as assistant parliamentary draftsman, in 1924.

Assistant parliamentary draftsman, 1924–9

In 1956, John Hearne reflected on his joining the civil service, recalling:

It happened that when I was of three years standing at the Bar an event took place which changed the course of the lives of many Irish lawyers and gave the legal profession a new place, and a new responsibility and a new influence in the country – I mean the establishment of the Irish Free State in the year 1922. For my own part, I was invited to work with the first Attorney General and spent five years in that department of the new government.[43]

The civil service John Hearne joined was a British type in miniature.[44] On the establishment of the Irish Free State, 21,000 of 28,000 civil servants transferred to the service of the new government.[45] The effect of this was administrative continuity both in terms of personnel and practice, a fact acknowledged in an official report in 1934:

> The passing of the state into the control of a native government, however revolutionary it may have been as a step in the political development of the nation, entailed, broadly speaking, no immediate disturbance of any fundamental kind in the daily work of the average civil servant. Under changed masters the same main tasks of administration continued to be performed by the same staffs on the same general lines of organisation and procedure.[46]

This was a formidable inheritance for the new state, given the tradition of the British civil service and the quality of professionalism it displayed.[47] The newly formed Irish civil service contributed to the establishment and consolidation of parliamentary democracy in the Free State.[48] That post-independence generation of civil servants was imbued with profound loyalty and commitment to public service,[49] being determined to ensure the survival and vitality of the new state.

As assistant parliamentary draftsman, John Hearne worked under Arthur Matheson, described by Maurice Hearne as 'legendary', and who was 'reputed to be the most skilful legal draftsman not only in Ireland but throughout these islands'.[50] According to the same source, Hearne formulated much of the legislation establishing the institutions of the state sector, notably the Electricity Supply Board (ESB).[51] The draft bill relating to the ESB was described by Matheson as 'highly technical, very detailed and very lengthy'.[52] In an accompanying memorandum to the Attorney General, he wrote that the draft 'far transcends in magnitude and difficulty anything which was contemplated by you, or in this office (or, I imagine, by the minister) when the work was undertaken two months ago'. He continued:

> I am glad to take this opportunity of letting you know that much the larger share of the credit for having produced this draft in the short time and on the meagre instructions available belongs to Mr Hearne; the draft bill as it now stands is not a draft prepared by me with Mr Hearne's assistance, but is a draft prepared by him under my supervision, a very different thing and one for which he should be given full credit.

Matheson explained, in some detail, the difficulties faced and included a timetable of meetings with various officials.[53] He was determined to leave the Attorney General in no doubt as to the problems associated with the drafting of the bill. The skills Hearne learned as a draftsman were to serve him well when working on constitutional matters later in his career.

John Hearne and the Imperial Conference, 1926

In his capacity as assistant parliamentary draftsman, Hearne attended the 1926 Imperial Conference. Between 1922 and 1932 the foreign policy of the Cosgrave government was dominated by the paramount objective of achieving full and unrestricted sovereignty for the Irish Free State.[54] This was to be realised by seeking to transform the British Commonwealth into a free partnership of sovereign independent states,[55] all equal in terms of constitutional and international status. In practical terms, this meant equality between the United Kingdom and the self-governing Dominions. For Cosgrave and his ministers the international recognition of Irish sovereignty would represent the true measure of independence. The Irish Free State, however, could not be regarded as a full international entity because of the limited sovereignty of the Dominions in foreign relations.[56] In fact, the degree of legal sovereignty they enjoyed in terms of international law was a matter of real controversy.

Notwithstanding these obstacles, there was a vital factor that was to work in favour of Irish policy. The Free State had acquired the status of a Dominion at a stage of development of the British Empire when the Dominions, 'which had long enjoyed unfettered control of their domestic affairs and, more recently, limited treaty-making powers, were moving, if unevenly, towards autonomy generally, including autonomy in their foreign relations'.[57] Such a development was viewed favourably and enthusiastically by a government ruling a country where Dominion status had never enjoyed popular support, having been imposed as part of the Treaty settlement.[58] In a very real way, therefore, the Free State was never a member of the Commonwealth, in the sense of accepting it freely and warmly;[59] and British beliefs that the country would become a Dominion psychologically as well as constitutionally were mistaken.[60]

The forum in which the Irish state pursued its policy and engaged in controversy with the government of Great Britain was the Imperial Conference, a gathering of the leaders of Dominion governments, held at periodic intervals. It was regarded as 'the chief buttress of imperial unity and the tangible expression of imperial co-operation';[61] it was to be the stage on which the Dominions advanced towards full equality and sovereignty. The Irish first attended in 1923, but it was the Conference of 1926 where the Irish delegation played a full role. At this and other Conferences, the Free State delegates, in co-operation with other Dominions, notably South Africa and Canada, expanded the meaning of Dominion status.

John Hearne was among five civil servants who attended the 1926 Conference. The others were Diarmuid O'Hegarty, secretary to the Executive Council, Joseph Walshe, acting secretary of the Department of External Affairs, and two typists.[62] Apart from the latter, Hearne was the most junior of the officials.[63] This did not mean, however, that he was an unimportant member of the group. A small team such as the Free State delegation had no room for a superfluous member; all would have been expected to make a real contribution and were chosen accordingly. His expertise as a draftsman, together with his legal knowledge, were the determining factors in his selection. His presence in London was probably on the recommendation of the Attorney General, John A. Costello, in whose office he worked and who was an adviser to the ministerial delegation comprising Cosgrave, O'Higgins, Desmond FitzGerald, Minister for External Affairs and Patrick McGilligan, Minister for Industry and Commerce. Joseph Walshe prepared the significant documents that formed the basis of the Irish position at the Conference,[64] though Hearne did contribute to a memorandum prepared by Costello on the complex area of merchant shipping.[65] In addition to his general advisory role, he acted as an adviser to Kevin O'Higgins, the Free State's representative on a committee dealing with the issue of nationality, and he was also nominated as the representative on a committee on overseas settlement.[66]

Before the Conference began, the Irish government proposed that the status of the Dominions be discussed and that anachronistic obstacles to the exercise of their sovereignty be removed.[67] The Irish contributed to the clarification of the meaning of Dominion status and, according to D.W. Harkness, their major contribution in this regard was contained in what he described as a 'remarkable memorandum' drawn up by ministers and officials, the latter almost certainly including Hearne. Dated 2 November 1926, it was written two weeks into the Conference, which had begun on 19 October. Thus it represented an analysis and restatement of Irish aims, informed by the discussions of constitutional and diplomatic issues at the Conference. Entitled 'Existing Anomalies in the British Commonwealth of Nations', Harkness has described it as a document

> of great breadth and it recognises that matters which affected one Dominion had repercussions upon all. Far from being a list of domestic grievances its aim was to create throughout the whole Commonwealth an atmosphere of co-operation based on the fellowship of equality ... It raised questions of a penetrating nature that went to the heart of the imperial structure: questions that required the closest scrutiny at the highest level.[68]

The memorandum[69] was predicated on a central contention of the Irish delegation that 'the principle of the absolute equality of status and the judicial and constitutional independence of the members of the British Commonwealth of Nations is now admitted beyond controversy'. Accordingly, attention was drawn to the outstanding anomalies and anachronisms which appeared most to detract from that principle. The Free State insisted on the fundamental right of the government of a Dominion to advise the King on all matters relating to its own affairs. In effect, what was being demanded was that a Dominion government should enjoy the kind of constitutional relationship which existed between the monarch and the government in Britain, when the former acted solely on the advice of the latter.

The memorandum identified what it regarded as an anomaly in the role of the Governor-General in each Dominion – he was both representative of the King and the British government. This dual role gave the Governor-General the constitutional right to interfere in the affairs of a Dominion. To remedy this, the memorandum argued he should represent the King alone and act solely on the advice of the Dominion government. Consistent with this view was the insistence that the powers of reservation and disallowance conferred on the Governor-General be abandoned. In keeping with the assertion of the constitutional independence of the Dominions, their legislative enactments should enjoy extra-territorial effect. Finally, the assumption in international treaties that the signature of plenipotentiaries, appointed solely by the British government, was binding on the governments of the Dominions was utterly unacceptable. Rather, the principle should be accepted that no Dominion could bind another; only the signatures of plenipotentiaries appointed by a Dominion government could have the effect of binding it by international agreement.

The 1926 Imperial Conference is famous for the so-called 'Balfour Declaration', which described the Commonwealth as founded on the root principle of the equality of status of the Dominions: 'They are autonomous communities within the British Empire, equal in status, in no way subordinate one to another in any aspect of their domestic or external affairs, though united by a common allegiance to the Crown, and freely associated as members of the British Commonwealth of Nations.'[70] Decisions made at the Conference reflected this declaration of equality. The Governor-General would cease to be the representative of the British government and was to represent solely the monarch, holding in all essential respects the same position in a Dominion as the King in Great Britain.[71]

It was recognised that it was the right of the government of a Dominion to advise the monarch in all matters relating to its affairs; the corollary was that the British government did not have the right to offer the monarch advice contrary to that of the Dominion government.[72] Equality had implications for matters such as reservation and disallowance of legislation and its extra-territorial effect; the Conference recognised that these were complex legal and constitutional matters which would require detailed consideration by a committee of experts to be established for that purpose.[73] This was the origin of the Conference on the Operation of Dominion Legislation, to be discussed later in this chapter. Finally, no Dominion was to be committed to obligations by another, and this included Great Britain.[74]

Hearne and Conference committees

The committee on nationality, on which O'Higgins was the Free State representative and Hearne his adviser, made little progress.[75] The Irish were anxious to establish their own nationality; the British were determined to allow only Irish citizenship within British nationality. For Britain, allegiance to the Crown was crucial. The Irish were determined to refute what they regarded as the British 'umbrella' theory – that all the Commonwealth members should embrace British nationality. Minor matters were settled; it was decided to refer the more complex ones to the Conference on Dominion Legislation.[76]

John Hearne was the Free State representative on the subcommittee on overseas settlement, a body concerned with the problems associated with this policy in the Commonwealth. The policy had been defined at the 1923 Imperial Conference as 'a redistribution of the white population of the Empire in the best interest of the Empire as a whole'.[77] This definition was accepted by the committee which proceeded to examine proposals for its successful implementation. Matters discussed included the selection and recruitment of migrants; their reception and welfare; family settlement; the settlement of juveniles; and the settlement of women and girls.[78]

The report of the subcommittee was very comprehensive[79] and adopted by the Imperial Conference on 19 November.[80] The fact was, however, that, in terms of Irish concerns, both the report and the activities of the group which produced it were unimportant, if not actually irrelevant. The parts of the Commonwealth interested in overseas settlement were Canada, Australia, New Zealand and Southern Rhodesia. It was not a matter of any concern to the Irish government and there was little evidence of active participation in discussions by Hearne. His one reported contribution served to underscore the tangential nature of the subject for the Free State: 'The representative of the governments of Newfoundland and the Irish Free State intimated that conditions in their territories precluded co-operation on their part.'[81]

This effective disengagement by the Irish delegation perhaps explained the acceptance of language in the report which otherwise might have elicited objections. It spoke of the need to stimulate the outward flow of population from the 'Mother Country' to the general advantage of the whole Commonwealth.[82] In other circumstances, the description of Britain as the 'Mother Country' might have been challenged and rejected by the Irish; here it was tolerated in the context of a policy which was the product of colonialism and the colonial legacy in terms of the other Dominions, and apparently accepted as such by them. These regarded Britain as the 'Mother Country'. Consequently, a country that was a reluctant Dominion was not going to raise objections to an issue that did not impact on it.

Nor should there be any surprise that the Free State, a country with an anti-imperial history and reputation, did not object to or even express a view on a policy that was a variation on the idea of plantation, a concept in Irish history redolent with notions of cultural, religious and racial superiority. After all, overseas settlement entailed the distribution of white people in the Dominions, who differed culturally, religiously and racially from the indigenous peoples. The Irish remained silent – this aspect of overseas settlement, as with the entire policy, simply did not have consequences for the Free State. Once again this aspect reflected the colonial legacy of the Dominions, lands essentially peopled by white settlers. Any comment might have caused offence among other Commonwealth governments and the Irish delegation would not have wished to cause such offence – it would have served no purpose in terms of Irish self-interest.

The official Irish response might also have been influenced by another consideration. Jason Knirck has written of the Irish tendency to write indigenous peoples out of their references to the other Dominions.[83] This raised the vexed question of the relations between Irish nationalism and non-white regions of the Commonwealth. The Irish, it would seem, did not want to be too thoroughly connected with peoples widely perceived as inferior.[84] In any case, this was not a major issue for the Irish Free State, as the matter of settlement was not one which preoccupied the attention of Irish policy makers. Nevertheless, the impact on indigenous races did not act as a spur to voice even the mildest concern. For the Free State, overseas settlement and its related matters were incidental and, therefore, principled observations and objections, if there were any, went unspoken.

Hearne's membership of this committee probably reflected the fact that he was the most junior of the officials in the Free State delegation. He was appointed to represent the state on a body regarded as unimportant. He was the diplomatic rookie who drew the proverbial short straw and his nomination was a kind of apprenticeship. He did what was required of him: he said little and discharged his duties unobtrusively. The resultant report meant nothing in the Free State. Tellingly, the Free State was not represented on the committee on overseas settlement at the 1930 Imperial Conference.

The 1926 Conference was a success for Irish ministers and officials. This is evident when the November memorandum identifying anomalies is compared with the final report – very many Irish concerns had been addressed. The Balfour Declaration certainly gave cause for much satisfaction. In the Dáil, Desmond FitzGerald asserted that the Conference would 'be regarded by historians as marking a definite step forward in the development of the individual states of the Commonwealth as distinct political entities in the general society of nations'.[85] Listing the various decisions taken by delegates, he stated that relations between Great Britain and the other Dominions were now based on the root principle of equality of status.[86]

The commitment, competence and hard-work of the civil service advisers were a very significant factor in the success of the Irish delegation. The daily routine of Hearne and his colleagues was demanding and exhausting. They were accommodated in the Hotel Cecil, located between the Thames Embankment and the Strand,[87] and here Hearne stayed for thirty-six days.[88] The civil servants were virtual prisoners, a fact described by Diarmuid O'Hegarty, secretary to the Executive Council:

> The points arising out of the conference and the memoranda which had to be prepared and submitted required careful consideration by the officials from the Department of External Affairs, the Draftsman's Office [Hearne] and the executive council, who were in constant attendance on the ministers ... Daily and even hourly conferences were necessary. Instructions, decisions, and memoranda were urgently required and given. Correspondence had to be attended to without delay. The volume of work was very heavy. During the days which I attended the conference not one of the officials engaged thereon on our staff had the opportunity of taking a walk. They were practically confined to two rooms – one used by the typists and the other employed as a conference room and dining room.[89]

For John Hearne, the 1926 Conference was an important occasion in his career. It was a significant conference in terms of the constitutional development of the Free State and he had been one of the advisers who had contributed to this development. He was to attend two other conferences – a clear indication that his contribution in 1926 was adjudged valuable by his ministerial and civil service superiors –where he was to play a more important role in terms of the Free State's continuing constitutional evolution. However, he attended in a different capacity – as legal adviser at the Department of External Affairs.

Appointment as legal adviser, 1929

In 1929, John Hearne was appointed legal adviser.[90] Together with two cadets recruited as a result of the first public competition for the Department of External Affairs, he joined an establishment which had endured many difficulties from its inception, not least the belief that its very existence was unnecessary.[91] This department was a completely new institution of government, necessitated by the Free State's constitutional status as a Dominion, and did not enjoy the advantage of the tradition of other offices in the former British administration, which were transferred into government departments, with comparatively little difficulty, on the setting up of the Irish state. During the Dáil debates in 1923 on the Ministers and

Secretaries Act, which gave government departments their formal and legal basis, deputies questioned the need for a foreign ministry.[92] The threat hanging over it was its possible absorption into the Department of the President. It was not until 1927 that its civil service head, Joseph Walshe, was given the rank of secretary and, by 1929, the threat to its independent existence had been dispelled with the recruitment of a legal adviser and cadets. These circumstances have prompted Dermot Keogh to write that 'it was possible to speak for the first time of a *Department of External Affairs*'.[93]

Conference on the Operation of Dominion Legislation, 1929: Hearne's memoranda

The Irish government was anxious to continue and expedite the process of transforming the character of the British Commonwealth. The 1926 Imperial Conference and, in particular, the Balfour Declaration had advanced this objective, but to the outside world it still had the appearance of an association dominated by Britain.[94] A momentous step in altering this perception was taken at the Conference on the Operation of Dominion Legislation, which had its origins in the 1926 Conference and which, after some delay, was organised for October 1929. Its terms of reference were comprehensive:

To enquire into, report upon and make recommendations concerning

(i) Existing statutory provisions requiring reservation of Dominion legislation for the assent of His Majesty or authorising the disallowance of such legislation.

(ii) (a) The present position as to the competence of Dominion parliaments to give their legislation extra-territorial operation.
(b) The practicability and most convenient method of giving effect to the principle that each Dominion parliament should have power to give extra-territorial operation to its legislation in all cases where such operation is ancillary to provision for the peace, order and good government of the Dominion.

(iii) The principles embodied in or underlying the Colonial Laws Validity Act 1865, and the extent to which any provisions of that act ought to be repealed, amended or modified in the light of the existing relations between the various members of the British Commonwealth of Nations.

In addition to the above, the whole area of merchant shipping was referred to the 1929 Conference in order to 'consider and report on the principles which should govern, in the general interest, the practice and legislation relating to merchant shipping in the various parts of the Empire, having regard to the change in the constitutional status and general relations which have occurred since existing laws were enacted'.[95] The report of the Conference on Dominion Legislation was to be submitted to an Imperial Conference for its consideration.

The purpose and importance of the Conference on Dominion Legislation was explained earlier in 1929 by Patrick McGilligan, Minister for External Affairs, in the course of a Dáil debate on the estimates for his department:

> The Commonwealth conception imports no limitation of the internal sovereignty of any of its members, and imposes no restrictions upon the exercise of its external sovereignty by any such member ... In the autumn of the present year a committee of experts from every state of the Commonwealth will meet to discuss the formal amendment or modification, or repeal of enactments still on the statute book of the United Kingdom, which are inconsistent with the existing legislative powers of the member states' parliaments. Our purpose is that whatever remnants there may be of the old order of imperial control will be removed and the last vestiges of the organisation now superseded swept away. The entire legal framework in which the old system of central rule was held together will be taken asunder and will never be put together again. A new legal structure will take its place ... The free co-operation which is the basis of the Commonwealth idea ... will be clothed in forms which reveal rather than conceal its reality.

McGilligan observed to deputies that 'the House will realise what an amount of watchful, painstaking and highly technical labour that work involves'.[96] John Hearne, as legal adviser at the department, did an immense amount of legal preparation, drawing on what D.W. Harkness has described as 'his voluminous knowledge of British constitutional history',[97] and his memoranda were to inform, support and summarise the arguments of the Irish delegation at the Conference.

In a preliminary memorandum, dated 15 July 1929,[98] Hearne gave an overview of some of the issues facing the Free State's representatives. He emphasised that the new character of the Commonwealth found expression in the formula 'freedom and constitutional equality', thus indicating the freedom of the members to co-operate or act separately and equally in the exercise of every function of government – legislative, judicial and executive.[99] The rapid development in the constitutional relations between the Dominions and the British parliament had resulted, however, in a situation in which the laws governing that relationship did not always reflect the new reality.[100] Hearne explained this in almost poetic terms:

The statute book of the British parliament is crowded with imposing but antiquated legal structures in the shadows of which the new group of buildings – as it were – erected in the course of world reconstruction are lost to view. The Commonwealth will not appear to the world in its true perspective for the group of constitutional edifices which it is – each unit in the group, although not symmetrical with each other, yet splendidly proportioned to the ends and aims of all – unless and until the shadows cast upon it out of a dead age are lifted. 'The state', 'the Commonwealth', 'status' are spoken words. The written text of the statute law either belies them or gives them legal sanction, life and permanence. Step by step the written law must form up with the advances of the new constitutional doctrines.[101]

He had the Balfour Declaration in mind when he wrote of 'momentous developments' resulting 'in a constitutional situation in which the United Kingdom as at present constituted is no more than one of the self-governing states of the Commonwealth'.[102]

Hearne addressed a fundamental issue in terms of the relationship between Commonwealth states and, in particular, their relationship with Britain – the extent of the legislative powers of Dominion parliaments. Regarding the Free State, the matter had to be viewed in the context of the situation resulting from the Treaty of 1921. Citing legal opinion, that of Justice Murnaghan in the High Court in 1925, the effect of Article 1 of that instrument was to create an independent state.[103] Therefore, Hearne asserted a fact which 'needed no emphasis', that the Treaty was an agreement between two independent nations[104] and, in theory, there could be no limitation to the legislative power of an independent state.[105] He declaimed the view that 'to speak of a disability to legislate arising out of the status of "an independent state" seems to do violence to the plain meaning of words'.[106] He accepted that British legal theory might not accept his arguments but this was not material to the purpose of his memorandum. Indeed, he realised that the student of British constitutional history was familiar with the long-drawn-out controversy as to the extent of the legislative power of Dominion parliaments.[107] He highlighted the two areas of particular contention where the British government insisted on the limitation of the power of these parliaments – the extra-territorial effect of legislation and the application of the Colonial Laws Validity Act 1865.

According to prevailing British legal theory, laws enacted by a Dominion legislature operated only within its territorial area, except where extra-territorial operation was given by the British parliament. In his memorandum, Hearne contended that nothing in the constitutions of the Dominions imposed any territorial limitation on the operation of any law made by a member of the Commonwealth. When necessary for 'the peace, order and good government' of a Dominion, its legislature was able to enact laws with extra-territorial effect. In his view, the words of the Dominion constitutions were wide enough to sanction such operation and, therefore, it followed that an act of the Oireachtas was not necessarily *ultra vires* if it had extra-territorial effect.[108]

Hearne's interpretation, however, was not the main reason why the Irish government asserted the extra-territorial effect of Free State legislation. Rather, it was founded on a deep-seated perception of sovereignty and the consequent rejection of a Dominion status which denied this.[109] Hearne articulated opinions informed by such beliefs in a subsequent memorandum, dated 26 August 1929, devoted entirely to the subject.[110] He restated the view given in the preliminary memorandum that the right of extra-territorial legislation 'must be regarded as inherent in the parliament of a Dominion' and any contrary opinion[111] had its origins, according to Hearne, 'in the arbitrary limit set to the powers of the Dominions by judicial minds steeped in the law-lore of the British colony'.[112] He asserted that 'whatever the parliament of the United Kingdom can do, the parliament of any other of the associated states can do'.[113] He advised, with certainty and conviction, on the necessary course of action to be pursued by the Irish delegates at the Conference: 'The law must become and be this: that a member state of the British Commonwealth is in precisely the same position as is the United Kingdom or any other state in the world.'[114]

The second limitation on the powers of a Dominion parliament insisted upon by the British government had its basis in the Colonial Laws Validity Act 1865.[115] Section two declared that any law made by the legislature of a colony, which was repugnant to any act of the imperial parliament extending to that colony, was, to the extent of the repugnancy, void and inoperative. Successive British governments insisted that the act applied to the Free State, an opinion rejected by the Irish government.[116] Nor were the provisions of this act regarded by the latter as an abstract threat. In 1926, the Judicial Committee of the Privy Council used the statute to invalidate a section of the Canadian Criminal Code 1888. This decision had a particular resonance in Ireland, linked as it was to the constitutional position of Canada by the terms of the 1921 Treaty. Many observers on both sides of the Atlantic believed that the Privy Council was sending a message to the Free State, in the parliament of which there had recently been debates on the matter of retaining the right of appeal to the Privy Council from Irish courts.[117] The Canadian case confirmed the Irish belief that the act was a direct threat to, and indeed a usurpation of, the attributes of sovereignty of the Free State, since its laws could be declared null and void if found to be repugnant to statutes passed by an external parliament.

In his preliminary memorandum, Hearne rejected the application of the Colonial Laws Validity Act to the Irish state, citing section three of the Irish Free State Constitution Act 1922,[118] enacted by the British parliament on 5 December 1922, to give legal effect to the Constitution of the Irish Free State. This section stated that, if the parliament of the Free State made provision to that effect, any act passed before the Constitution Act, which applied to the Dominions, would also apply to the Free State. Hearne submitted that this section was based on the assumption that imperial statutes passed before the act did not apply to the Irish state; they could only do so if adopted by the Oireachtas.[119] The Irish parliament had not adopted the Colonial Laws Validity Act.

In another memorandum, dated 3 September 1929, he developed his views on the Colonial Laws Validity Act.[120] He was trenchant in his condemnation of it:

> What is meant when it is said that the Colonial Laws Validity Act 1865 is repugnant to the legislative independence of the member states of the Commonwealth of Nations? Just this: that, as there is now in fact no supremacy of the British parliament over the parliament of, say, Australia or the Irish Free State, the retention on the British statute book of the Colonial Laws Validity Act is inconsistent with, in the sense of being irreconcilably opposed to, the *constitutional fact*.[121]

Its presence on the imperial statute book was contrary to the notion of an association of co-equal states and 'the whole theme and theory of status and statehood as it exists in the Commonwealth today'.[122] As in the case of extra-territorial legislation, Hearne was definite as to the approach the Free State must take at the forthcoming Conference: 'But we *must* at least go to the length of seeking a formal repeal of the offending sections of the act of 1865 with something in the nature of a renunciation declaration in the recital of the repealing statute.'[123] This suggestion was the least he could make in relation to a law he had forcefully described in figurative terms as 'the sword of contingent invalidity hanging over Dominion legislation'.[124]

The essential legal import of Hearne's submissions contained in the four memoranda regarding the extra-territorial operation of Dominion legislation and the Colonial Laws Validity Act was that 'there exists no limitation of the legislative power of the Irish Free State arising out of status'.[125] This was a powerful statement in the context of a state which was asserting its sovereignty and preparing for a conference which would be critical in relation to its international acceptance.

In terms of the development of the Commonwealth, one of the most complex areas was that of merchant shipping legislation.[126] This fact was acknowledged in the report of the 1926 Imperial Conference, when it was observed that 'it was difficult to reconcile the application, in its present form, of certain provisions of the principal statutes relating to merchant shipping, the Merchant Shipping Act, 1894 ... with the constitutional status of the several members of the British Commonwealth of

Nations'.[127] This fact certainly concerned the Irish delegation, whose main concern was that the Free State should be able to fly its own flag on its ships, and that these be recognised internationally as Irish not British ships, as under existing laws.[128] The Conference decided to refer the issue of merchant shipping to a special sub-conference which was to meet at the same time as the committee of experts reviewing Dominion legislation.[129]

Hearne produced a memorandum on merchant shipping, dated 24 July 1929,[130] while also referring to it in his preliminary memorandum. In the former he asserted the power of the Oireachtas to legislate in regard to merchant shipping[131] and that any bill so enacted would require all ships registered in the state to fly the national colours.[132] He was very aware, however, of the fact that there existed throughout the world an administrative machinery established by the existing Merchant Shipping Act, which was of enormous advantage in the commercial life of the Free State.[133] He was of the view, therefore, that Free State legislation would be determined by 'considerations of expediency and practical convenience'.[134] 'Theoretical exactitude' in the legal position of the Free State would have to take account of practical realities, Hearne summarising the situation thus: 'In the event, all our problems may merge into one: the problem of how far the British government will allow us to enjoy the benefits and advantage of their merchant shipping system, while permitting us to depart in important particulars from the theoretical basis around which the system swings.' In place of the existing system, Hearne envisaged the enactment by members of the Commonwealth of a series of reciprocal statutes to establish a system of merchant shipping laws based on mutual co-operation.[135]

This idea was developed in a memorandum entitled 'Proposals for Reciprocity'.[136] Merchant shipping laws should be enacted in a series of reciprocal agreements, the enforcement of which should be on the basis of mutual recognition and assistance. The authority of a statute of one member of the Commonwealth should, as far as practicable, bind all or at any rate be enforceable in the courts of all. According to Hearne, 'merchant shipping laws should be enacted as conventions of the Commonwealth association'.[137] The laws of all Commonwealth members should 'hold good' in the ports of the United Kingdom and in the ports of other member states.[138] It is evident why this suggestion appealed to Hearne – the principle of reciprocity recognised the co-equal status of all Dominions and the consequent right to regulate their own merchant shipping laws, while preserving a mutually beneficial system of administrative machinery.

Arguably, the most interesting of Hearne's memoranda was an undated one entitled 'Reservation and Disallowance of Acts'.[139] He was categorical in his view that reservation and disallowance 'must be deleted absolutely',[140] as their existence 'imperilled' the constitutional position of the whole Commonwealth.[141] He submitted that the Dominions were 'now so completely independent that each can validly amend its constitution by legislation'.[142] In an opinion strongly influenced by a spirit of nationalism and the autochthonous redoubt from which the Irish argued their view point, he continued:

> The colony status is at the root of the whole attempt to perpetuate the idea that the status of the member states of the Commonwealth is a thing conceded by the British parliament rather than a thing asserted, claimed and achieved by the states themselves ... Any compulsory limitation at all upon its [a Dominion's] self-rule deprives it of the right to be recognised as a member of international society. The states of the Commonwealth must shed all the disabilities which marked the separate stages of their development. The removal of these disabilities is fundamental to the continued existence of the Commonwealth. The member states of that organisation have grown out of the scheme in which they came into being; the scheme itself, in fact, no longer exists and the principles which held it together do not apply at all to the scheme or system which has superseded it. Once the idea is grasped that the sovereignty of the Irish Free State, the sovereignty of Canada, the sovereignty of South Africa etc. exist prior in the order of thought to the group called the Commonwealth of Nations, so much so that if the sovereignty of those states disappeared the Commonwealth of Nations could not continue to exist, it becomes clear with what vigilant care the sovereignty of those states must be safeguarded.[143]

He then turned his attention to the role of the Crown in the Commonwealth. He did this because he believed that opponents of recent constitutional developments in the Commonwealth, particularly in Britain, would focus on the King's position as a means of stymying progress towards Dominion equality. Hearne stated with absolute forthrightness that 'there falls on the Commonwealth states no shadow of a feudal king' but that, when some British statesmen spoke of the 'king bond', they were using language of 'absolute loyalty'[144] and this had no place in a modern association of equal states. If the King were to retain a role in the Commonwealth, he was firm about what it should be:

> If you must continue the kingship as so characteristic a note in the old system that it could not be abandoned, you must refashion it to fit the accepted facts of the new system. You tool it, first of all, as it has stood for some hundreds of years before in the United Kingdom, an entity without initiative, a constitutionally unconscious automaton, in practice controlled by the executive, or the legislature, or the judiciary.[145]

Hearne conveyed the essence of his view when he described the position of the King in the United Kingdom as 'a constitutional form'.[146]

In an important part of the memorandum, he turned his attention to a consideration of the matter of the sovereignty of the Irish Free State. His submission was again stated with certainty and conviction:

> I do not know of any definition of a sovereign state in the post-war organisation of the world but this: a sovereign state is an organised political community which is independently capable of undertaking international obligations and which is recognised as so capable by international society. Is there any doubt whatever that the Irish Free State is such a community? ... Is there any doubt whatever that there is no limitation upon the internal sovereignty of the Irish Free State and no limitation upon its external sovereignty save those which are freely self-imposed on every full international person by reason of their acceptance of the obligations of the Covenant of the League of Nations.[147]

Having defined the Free State as a sovereign entity, Hearne turned his attention to the contention that the Treaty of 1921 imposed 'disabilities' on the newly established state. It was essential to address this central matter, as the British preliminary memorandum, prepared for the Conference, argued that there was an 'express limitation' on the Free State that its legislation must conform to the Treaty.[148] He contended that 'if the Treaty of 1921 was a treaty at all, it presupposed the antecedent competency of this country – by whatever name it was called – to exercise the treaty-making power'. He continued: 'And if that be so, the "limitations" imposed by the Treaty are not in fact limitations at all, but obligations of exactly the same character as those accepted by other states when they became parties to an international treaty'.[149] In effect, as in the preliminary memorandum, he submitted that the Treaty of 1921 was an agreement between two independent states. Furthermore, regarding Article 50 of the Irish Free State Constitution, which stated that amendments to it had to be within the terms of that Treaty, he rejected this provision as a status-limitation upon the law-making competency of the Oireachtas; rather it amounted 'simply to a declaration by the provisional government of the Treaty obligations of the state'.[150] In amending the Constitution, the Irish state would have regard to the fact that there were obligations between it and another state but this did not mean that these obligations precluded the right of changing the Constitution.[151]

Hearne's memoranda: an overview

Having considered many of Hearne's memoranda, it may be useful, at this juncture, to give an overview of them by way of summary and assessment. He submitted that the Irish Free State was a sovereign, independent country and that the Treaty was an agreement between two such states. The corollary of this assertion of sovereignty was that there could be no limitation on the legislative competency of the Oireachtas. As a member of the Commonwealth, the Free State enjoyed complete equality with all other members, including the United Kingdom, as a consequence of the Balfour Declaration. However, the existing laws regulating Commonwealth relations did not reflect recent constitutional developments and obscured the sovereignty of Dominions, thus causing them to be denied their true international status. Such laws, accordingly, had to be changed to reflect the internal and external sovereign character of Commonwealth states. Hearne recognised that his views would be contested, if not actually rejected by Britain, and he had no illusions as to the resistance the Free State and the other Dominions would meet from British statesmen determined on preserving an old constitutional scheme which, heretofore, Britain had dominated.

Hearne's views were influenced and informed by a number of related factors. He possessed an extensive knowledge of British constitutional law and legal developments in the Commonwealth. For him, the Balfour Declaration was a fundamental statement of the character of its Constitution and he was ever mindful of the equality it conferred not just on the Free State but on all Dominions. As regards factors within the Irish state, he was deeply conscious of the policy of Cosgrave's governments to extend the meaning of Dominion status. Irish ministers conceived of the sovereignty of the Free State in absolute terms[152] and were deeply committed to protecting this sovereignty and to resisting British attempts to treat the Commonwealth as an indivisible whole.[153] Legal opinion, particularly the High Court ruling that the Free State was an independent country, supported both this policy and Hearne's opinions. Finally, his nationalism, and that of the ministers he served, was a very substantial influence. It is important to recall again that he was a nationalist and his memoranda are evidence and reminders of this.

The memoranda were characterised by a clarity of style which, according to Harkness, was invaluable to those delivering his briefs.[154] He was certain in his submissions and there was a forthrightness and trenchancy in their expression. The style had a dramatic and rhetorical quality, redolent of the gold medal winner in oratory who composed them. Figurative language also featured and gave legal briefs an occasional poetic flavour.

These memoranda were lengthy documents: the one on the Colonial Laws Validity Act numbered thirty-six A4 pages, while that which considered merchant shipping totalled fifty-one. They were organised in a clear and logical structure, often being divided into sub-headings for the ease of the reader. The memorandum on extra-territorial jurisdiction was structured as follows:

(i)   Extra-territorial jurisdiction in international law.

(ii) Territorial limitation of Dominion legislation:

    a.   The meaning of the limitation.

    b.   Recent interpretation of the doctrine.

    c.   Its removal at the forthcoming conference.

The length gave them a comprehensiveness and completeness. To refer again to the memorandum on extra-territorial jurisdiction, it is full of references to legal enactments and the case law of Dominions. The memorandum on merchant shipping contains a detailed summary of merchant shipping legislation in the Commonwealth.

Finally, in considering Hearne's legal submissions, there is an overriding and overarching fact which must not be forgotten. These legal opinions served a political purpose and were written to inform and reinforce the policies of the government. Therefore, they were, at times, as much political as legal documents.

Conference deliberations and report

The Conference on the Operation of Dominion Legislation eventually began on 8 October 1929 and continued until 4 December of the same year. The Irish Free State delegation included Hearne, Joseph Walshe, Diarmuid O'Hegarty, John A. Costello and Patrick McGilligan, all of whom had attended the 1926 Imperial Conference. There were seventeen plenary meetings[155] and Hearne attended most, if not all of them.[156] In addition, he was appointed to a committee to draft a declaration pertaining to extra-territorial legislation[157] and acted as an adviser on a committee considering the Colonial Laws Validity Act.[158]

The minutes of the plenary sessions suggest the extent to which Hearne's memoranda informed, supported and summarised the arguments and contributions of the Irish delegates. In his opening statement, McGilligan emphasised the coequality of all participating Commonwealth states and that the United Kingdom was no more than a coequal member of the association.[159] The second meeting considered the extra-territorial operation of dominion legislation, with the Irish minister asserting that the legislative power of dominion parliaments should be as wide and unfettered as that of the United Kingdom parliament.[160] As noted earlier, Hearne was a member of a committee selected to draft the relevant declaratory clause for inclusion in future legislation. This was composed of four civil servants and it considered a number of submissions, including one from McGilligan. The clause produced by the committee and approved by the Conference was entirely consistent with the views expressed by Hearne in his memorandum on the matter: 'It is hereby declared and enacted that the parliament of a Dominion has full power to make laws having extra-territorial operation.'[161]

The fourth meeting, held on 11 October, discussed reservation of legislation. McGilligan rejected the retention of this power in any Dominion constitution. Furthermore, he argued that the power of reservation contained in the Merchant Shipping Acts did not apply to the Free State as the Oireachtas had not adopted them.[162] On 15 October, the Irish minister attacked the Colonial Laws Validity Act. This enactment he described as 'anomalous and an anachronism', and he asserted that it could not be reconciled with the constitutional practices of the Commonwealth. He reiterated Hearne's characterisation of it as 'the threat of contingent invalidity' hanging over Dominion statutes.[163] At another meeting of the Conference on 31 October, the Free State's Attorney General, John A. Costello, asserted the right of Dominion parliaments to amend their constitutions. Regarding the provision in the Irish Free State's Constitution that legislation enacted by the Oireachtas could not be repugnant to the Treaty, he placed on record the contention of the Irish government that this was not so much a limitation of the state's legislative power as a recognition of its obligations under the Treaty.[164]

The committee on the Colonial Laws Validity Act, of which Hearne was a member, had a demanding workload. Its terms of reference were: 'To consider and report what action in relation to the provisions of the Colonial Laws Validity Act and matters ancillary thereto will be necessary to give effect to the principles laid down in the report of the inter-imperial relations committee, 1926.' The first meeting, held on 31 October 1929, proceeded to consider *seriatim* the act's provisions.[165] There were fourteen meetings and several revisions of its final report before its work was completed[166] and incorporated as 'Part V' of the Conference report.[167] McGilligan was to describe this part as 'the critical portion of the report',[168] a view reflecting the central part the act had played in the constitutional and legal architecture of the British Empire. The committee produced a declaration consistent with the recommendations and spirit of Hearne's memorandum on the subject: 'The Colonial Laws Validity Act of 1865 shall cease to apply to any law made by the parliament of a Dominion.'[169]

From the very start of the Conference, the Irish delegation was determined to make its point and 'to invest every corner of the Commonwealth framework with that autonomy and equality declared in 1926'.[170] It was demanding and strenuous work[171] and the Irish had to be constantly vigilant to resist what Diarmuid O'Hegarty described as 'the usual attempts to introduce into the documents words and phrases of a sapping nature'.[172] The report of the Conference, released in all the Dominion capitals on 3 February 1930, contained much to please the Free State. It acknowledged that the principles of freedom, equality and co-operation had slowly emerged from the experiences of the self-governing communities constituting the Commonwealth. The Conference considered that it was its task to apply those principles to areas where law and practice were inconsistent with them.[173] Therefore, it recommended the abolition of the powers of disallowance[174] and reservation.[175] Dominion legislation should have extra-territorial operation[176] and the Colonial Laws Validity Act should no longer apply to such legislation.[177] There were many recommendations relating to merchant shipping,[178] but arguably the most important was the one that there be no longer any doubts as to the full and complete power of Dominion parliaments to enact legislation in this area.[179]

John Hearne's participation in the 1929 Conference was yet another significant event in his professional career. His inclusion in the small and high-powered Irish delegation was again a testimony to his ability. He justified his place by the production of memoranda which were central to the presentation of the Free State's position on a number of highly contested and controversial issues. Moreover, he was an adviser at meetings in London and so contributed to the decision-making process. Thus he was a participant at a conference that was a significant milestone in the progress and development of the constitutional and international status of the Free State, not least in laying the foundations for the 1930 Imperial Conference and the 1931 Statute of Westminster.

John Hearne and the Imperial Conference, 1930

The Imperial Conference of 1930 met from 11 October to 14 November and Hearne was again in attendance. The Irish came with a clear purpose, as was explained by Patrick McGilligan in the course of a statement at the first plenary session: 'the recognition of our position as a free and sovereign state comes before all other considerations'.[180] In practical terms this meant the adoption of the report of the Conference on Dominion Legislation, which recorded the advances in the meaning of Dominion status achieved in the previous ten years. Early in the proceedings it was decided to set up a committee under the chairmanship of Lord Sankey, the Lord Chancellor, to consider the matter of inter-imperial relations. It was to be a body of major importance and became the battleground of the Conference.[181] Hearne was one of the main advisers to the Free State's delegation. In addition, he was appointed to two subcommittees, concerned with merchant shipping and nationality.[182]

The Sankey committee had thirteen meetings,[183] in addition to which there were some plenary sessions of the Conference.[184] In relation to the report on the operation of Dominion legislation, substantial agreement had been reached in the previous year and the Conference accepted the document without any major alterations. Thus, among other things, the Colonial Laws Validity Act no longer applied to Dominions, the parliaments of which were recognised as having the power to repeal or amend any imperial statute pertaining to them. The same Dominion parliaments were also recognised as having the power to enact legislation with extra-territorial operation. The powers of reservation and disallowance were abolished. The decisions of the Conference were given legal expression in agreed legislation – the Statute of Westminster.[185]

The Conference report also contained a draft agreement on merchant shipping.[186] It was the product of a subcommittee appointed to consider the matter and Hearne represented the Free State. It met for the first time on 20 October, with other meetings agreed upon for 21–3 October inclusive. The Sankey committee considered the deliberations of the subcommittee on 24 October. Hearne spoke at this meeting, informing the participants that the subcommittee was discussing the text of a long agreement and that there were several minor points which still needed discussion. He believed that at least three more subcommittee meetings would be necessary.[187]

The final agreement adopted by the Imperial Conference addressed many Irish concerns, as identified by Hearne in his 1929 memorandum on merchant shipping legislation. All ships were to be allowed to fly their national colours.[188] Article 9 referred to a merchant shipping system based on mutual co-operation and reciprocity.[189] It was agreed that all British Commonwealth ships were to enjoy a common status and were entitled to the recognition accorded to British ships.[190] This decision addressed a matter highlighted by Hearne: that the Free State would enjoy the benefits of the Commonwealth merchant shipping system, while at the same time being able to regulate its own ships. A merchant shipping agreement was signed in December of the following year, which was in accord with the agreement adopted at the Conference.[191]

The other subcommittee of which Hearne was a member concerned itself with the subject of nationality. This highly complex and controversial area had always been one of the Free State's long suits and had been considered at the 1926 Conference.[192] It may be remembered that Hearne had been an adviser to Kevin O'Higgins, the Free State's representative on the committee which considered the matter on that occasion. The Irish were then anxious to establish their own nationality and rejected the British view that the entire Commonwealth should shelter under the umbrella of British nationality. The matter was referred to the Conference on the Operation of Dominion Legislation, the report of which recognised a number of general principles pertaining to nationality. Members of the Commonwealth were united by a common allegiance to the Crown and this allegiance was the basis of the common status possessed by all subjects of the King.[193] The recognition of this common status, however, was in no way inconsistent with the recognition of the distinct nationality possessed by the citizens of the Commonwealth's individual member states.[194] The complexity of the subject was again evident when it was observed that the practical application of the principles was not an easy task and was beyond the scope of the report.[195]

The Free State delegation brought to the 1930 Conference a draft of its proposed nationality bill. In a letter to Desmond FitzGerald, Minister for Defence and one of the delegates, Hearne summarised the bill's intentions: 'The scheme of our bill is that we define our own nationals and give to the nationals of other parts of the Commonwealth (i.e., old British subjects), while in the Free State, all the privileges and advantages given to British subjects at the present time.'[196] He prepared a memorandum for the Irish delegates on the major sections of the proposed legislation, which were in accordance with the conclusions of the Conference on Dominion Legislation. Hearne advised the delegates that 'in future the citizens of each state will look to the law of that state for the ultimate legal basis of their status'.[197] In Harkness's words, 'this basis was infinitely preferable, the self-conscious Dominion felt, to the old, all-embracing category of "British subject"'.[198] With regard to the concept of common status, the memorandum explained the policy of the Irish government:

> Our law should provide that British subjects and Canadian subjects etc., living in Saorstát Éireann shall have the same status as citizens of Saorstát Éireann ... The Department of External Affairs hopes ... that by virtue of their citizenship of Saorstát Éireann our nationals will be entitled to the status of British subjects while in London, of Canadian subjects while in Ottawa and of South African citizens while in Pretoria.[199]

At the 1930 Conference, Free State representatives explained that they wanted their own citizenship first, as defined by their own laws, and would be happy to add the superstructure of a Commonwealth agreement on common status on top of this.[200] There was British opposition to any alterations in the concept of Commonwealth nationality, but the principles of the 1929 Conference report were confirmed.[201]

The Irish delegation and the Imperial Conferences

The Irish delegates found the 1930 Conference a difficult experience. Harkness has observed that an Imperial Conference was never a 'soft assignment' but this one was 'harder than most',[202] as it displayed 'an unusual degree of temper and engendered unprecedented bitterness'.[203] The British were less than happy with aspects of the report on Dominion legislation[204] and chose to argue with 'a medieval scholastic mentality'.[205] Frustrated, Desmond FitzGerald informed his wife that things were 'very trying'; and, writing to her on 6 November, he commented: 'Yesterday was appalling. Massed British guns directed on us – I never had such a day ... Faced with dishonesty, treachery and cowardice.'[206] Notwithstanding this somewhat dystopian atmosphere, the Irish had every reason to be pleased with the outcome of the Conference. Irish representatives played a prominent role in drafting the Statute of Westminster.[207] This helped remove all lingering doubts as to the status of the Irish Free State and the

Dominions as full subjects of international law.[208] It did not give the Free State all it wanted but did give the means to facilitate progress towards the eventual achievement of many of its objectives.[209] Therefore, it may be regarded as a watershed in Anglo-Irish relations.

The successes and achievements of the Free State at the Imperial Conferences were due to the calibre and expertise of its delegations. These attributes owed much to the fact that there was a striking continuity of personnel over the three Conferences, from 1926 to 1930. In terms of ministerial representation, Patrick McGilligan attended all three; and Desmond FitzGerald attended in 1926 and 1930. Attorney General, John A. Costello, was present on all three occasions, as were civil servants Diarmuid O'Hegarty, Joseph Walshe and John Hearne. By 1930, Irish ministers were the longest-serving members of any Dominion government and were advised by highly experienced civil servants. Moreover, the Irish delegates and their advisers were all around the same age[210] and from the same social class. They were not just colleagues but friends and this made real teamwork possible and natural.

This teamwork was inspired and strengthened by a sense of clear and common purpose: to achieve and secure recognition of Irish sovereignty. This objective was pursued, consistently and determinedly, from 1926 to 1930. The same arguments and counter-arguments ran through each Conference and each one represented a milestone in the pursuit of the Free State's goal. When McGilligan told the Dáil that he regarded the report of the 1930 Conference 'as being the end now achieved to the work which the then vice-president of this state, Mr Kevin O'Higgins, started in 1926',[211] he was expressing an essential truth and fact.

According to Harkness, McGilligan was the best-briefed delegate at the 1926 Conference[212] and, for the 1930 Conference, the Department of External Affairs prepared its usual thorough briefs.[213] As we have seen, Hearne did an immense amount of legal preparation for both events. This was his greatest contribution – he prepared the documentation central to the presentation of the Irish position; as it was stated earlier: he informed, supported and summarised the arguments of the Irish delegates. Commenting on John A. Costello's contribution to the delegation at the 1926 Conference, former Taoiseach, Garret FitzGerald, described him as 'the legal genius' of the team whose 'immense legal skill, his brilliance in any aspect of constitutional law, gave to our delegation of ministers and civil servants such a basis of knowledge, experience and skill, that they were able to outmanoeuvre not just the delegations of the other countries of the Commonwealth, but the British themselves'.[214]

While this may be an overstatement, it contains much that is true and it can be applied also with some justification and accuracy to Hearne's role at the Conferences of 1929 and 1930. While describing the achievements of the 1930 Conference, McGilligan stated that 'the system which it took centuries to build up has been brought to an end by four years of assiduous, concentrated collaboration between the lawyers and the statesmen of the states of the Commonwealth'.[215] It is interesting that he highlighted the role of the lawyers; as one himself, he appreciated their contribution. And Hearne was one of those lawyers.

Regarding the 1926 Conference, Kevin O'Higgins was of the opinion that the best team at it was the Irish one: 'The onus of the "status" push – anomalies and anachronisms – has fallen largely on ourselves.'[216] Certainly, Irish politicians and officials involved in Anglo-Irish relations shared this view. There was a real sense of pride in their successes, a fact articulated in very definite terms by Hearne in 1929: 'There is little doubt that whatever advances in constitutional practice and whatever contributions to the new constitutional doctrines are made by or as a result of the forthcoming sub-conferences will be made upon the showing of the Irish Free State representatives, that is to say, upon their advocacy of the New Policy forming in the Commonwealth generally ...' By the 'New Policy' Hearne meant the demand for coequality with Great Britain by many of the Dominions. According to him, this policy was 'forming in the Commonwealth generally as a result of the special constitutional position of the Irish Free State'. He continued: 'It is in the perspective of the Irish Free State Constitution, what it is and what it involves, that the contents of the entire Commonwealth conception are coming more and more into focus.'[217] This 'special constitutional position' Hearne attributed to the fact that the Irish state came into being as a consequence of the Treaty which was an international agreement between two independent states; this gave the Free State Constitution 'an international character not shared in their origins by the Constitutions of the other member-states of the Commonwealth'.[218]

In a memorandum to Éamon de Valera, dated March 1932, Hearne gave the newly elected President of the Executive Council an exposition of the Anglo-Irish and Commonwealth policies of Cosgrave's government:

> During the last nine years we have developed a very definite and wholly satisfactory technique abroad. We have posited certain facts on the basis of the Treaty of 1921 as an international treaty. We have done everything which an independent state can do ... We have forced upon Great Britain the acceptance of our position abroad much against her will. And we have split the Commonwealth into a number of separate legal, political, diplomatic and international entities, that is, a number of separate international persons. We have broken down the theory that the Commonwealth is a legal, a political or diplomatic or international unit by making each member of it a legal, political, diplomatic and international unit in the fullest known sense of these terms. And we have done all that on the basis of the contention that the Treaty of 1921 was an international treaty ... I

am sure it is recognised all over the British Commonwealth and throughout the entire world that the lever of international advancement for each member of the Commonwealth during the past nine years has been 'the Irish Treaty'. By reason of its international beginnings – namely, a treaty – the Irish Free State has made the international method the rule of the inter-state relationship in the Commonwealth itself, and has reformed that association in the light of the individual international responsibilities of its members towards each other and towards the other states of the world. Without the Irish Treaty the work could not have been done.[219]

Was Hearne overstating the role of the Free State in the development of the Commonwealth? Clearly, the Cumann na nGaedheal government was obsessed with the question of Irish sovereignty and was determined to thwart any attempts to limit that sovereignty.[220] Hearne, however, ignored the fact that the state became a member of the Commonwealth at a time when the Dominions themselves were in the process of constitutional development and Dominion nationalism was expressing itself. Moreover, he also ignored the contribution of other Dominions to the constitutional evolution of the Commonwealth in the 1920s and of the importance of Irish co-operation with them in pursuit of the Free State's objectives. While there are historians who are less inclined to accord the Irish state the credit Hearne gave it,[221] a balanced assessment of its achievement is to be found in the opinion that:

> at the Commonwealth Conferences of 1926 and 1930 and at the Conference on the Operation of Dominion Legislation of 1929 the Irish Free State diplomats and legal experts began to exert a considerable influence over the reform of Dominion status. Working closely with the Canadians and the South Africans, the Irish developed an agenda of radical change that resulted in the Balfour Declaration of 1926 and the Statute of Westminster of 1931 ... Irish Free State Commonwealth and Dominion policy was an incremental battle in which each small gain was of large significance because it set important precedents for the independence of the Dominions generally.[222]

There is another perspective from which to consider and assess Hearne's views, as expressed in his memorandum to de Valera and in earlier memoranda. They almost certainly made an important contribution to the creation and maintenance of an *esprit de corps* among Irish delegates at Imperial Conferences. These men approached their task with a growing sense of confidence and conviction in terms of what they were seeking to accomplish, and opinions and arguments articulated by Hearne contributed to and reinforced this sense. If he exaggerated on occasions, he did the Free State cause no harm; on the contrary, he did it some service. The

Irish delegates at these Conferences were the representatives of a country demoralised by, and recovering from, the Civil War. Its diplomatic service was at an embryonic stage, its very existence questioned by politicians who argued that the country did not need a foreign ministry. These same representatives were negotiating with a British government and diplomatic machine that was highly developed and sophisticated and which regarded its Irish opposites with condescension, even contempt. When Lionel Curtis, adviser on Irish affairs at the Colonial Office, commented that the Foreign Office wanted the Irish 'to be content to run like good dogs after the British coach',[223] he gave an insight into the challenge facing Irish negotiators – it was the Irish Davids against the British Goliaths. In such circumstances, a David needed inspiration, self-belief and self-confidence. Hearne's words helped address the needs of his colleagues in this respect and his memoranda may be regarded, among other things, as a valuable, even essential source of motivation and inspiration.

Abolition of the right of appeal to the Privy Council

In spite of the most determined efforts of the Cosgrave government, there was one aspect of the Irish Free State's membership of the Commonwealth which remained unchanged – the right of appeal to the Judicial Committee of the Privy Council.[224] An unavoidable consequence of attaining the constitutional status of Canada, as defined in Article 2 of the Anglo-Irish Treaty 1921, was the imposition of this right of appeal.[225] It was enshrined as Article 66 of the Constitution of the Irish Free State. The effect of this clause was to deny the state full judicial independence and the government itself felt that it was the 'chief slur' on its claims to sovereignty.[226] Its political opponents pointed to this appeal as proof of the subservient status of the Free State in the Commonwealth. Nor was it an abstract constitutional provision – by 1931 there were at least nine petitions for leave to appeal to the Privy Council from the Irish Supreme Court, though only two came to judgement.[227]

A contemporary observed that, in such a situation, there was 'inevitable conflict between the autonomy, legislative and judicial, of the Dominions and any attempt made by an extra-Dominion tribunal to which they did not consent and which they did not create, or control, to set aside or override their laws'.[228] The removal of this right of appeal to the Privy Council, described by Minister for Finance Ernest Blythe, in 1929, as 'a bad, unnecessary and useless court',[229] was one of the principal objectives of Cosgrave's governments and John Hearne was to play an important role in their endeavours. The Free State, however, was to encounter the obdurate resistance of British governments which believed that the issue had fundamental implications for the defining role of the Crown in the Constitution of the Free State and throughout the Commonwealth generally.[230]

The matter was raised at the 1926 Imperial Conference, when Kevin O'Higgins was persuaded by Lord Birkenhead, who was accepted as a friend of Ireland, to postpone the question until the next Conference, where he would support the Irish demands for abolition of the appeal.[231] However, by 1930 both men were dead and the Irish delegates at that year's Conference were resolute in renewing their demands. The previous year it had fallen to Hearne to prepare the relevant memorandum for the Conference on Dominion Legislation, outlining the Free State's case.[232]

Consistent with views expressed in other memoranda, he argued that no question whatever arose as to the power of the Oireachtas to amend Article 66 of the Free State Constitution. However, the matter was not that simple, as the right of appeal was preserved in Article 2 of the Treaty, which accorded the Free State the same status as Canada in the Commonwealth; the right of appeal applied in Canada and, consequently, Article 2 ensured its application in the Irish Dominion. An even further complication was Article 50 of the Constitution, which stipulated that amendments to it must be 'within the terms of the scheduled Treaty'.[233]

Hearne suggested that the Free State could seek deletion of the offending Article 66 by agreement with Britain but, according to Hearne, this course of action was unlikely to yield success. Article 2 of the Treaty, with its implicit recognition of the right of appeal, defined the fundamental British conception of the constitutional relationship between the Crown and the Dominions. The Irish, therefore, would be met by assertions that the prerogatives of the King were 'impregnable and immutable' and that only an act of the imperial parliament could divest him of them.[234]

The solution to the impasse proposed by Hearne was the assertion and vindication of a principle he regarded as central to the constitutional conception of the Commonwealth and iterated in other memoranda: the equality of all member states as defined by the Balfour Declaration. The acceptance of this principle meant that the King could exercise no prerogative in any Dominion except on the advice of its government;[235] and, by extension, the exercise of any prerogative preserved by Article 2 of the Treaty required the same advice. He contended that it was 'contrary to the whole Commonwealth notion and to the principle of coequal sovereignty and co-operation ... that His Majesty in his capacity of King of any one of the member states can be advised in matters affecting that member by a body external to it'.[236] With typical trenchancy, Hearne summarised his opinion and advice:

> It would appear, therefore, that an Irish Free State government has a complete case for removing the right of application for leave to appeal to the Privy Council based upon the separate constitutional existence of the member states of the Commonwealth and the inevitable implications of that constitutional fact. The judicial sovereignty of the Irish Free State is as inalienable as the legislative

sovereignty or the executive sovereignty. I am satisfied that the Oireachtas cannot legislate away its law-making competency, nor can it legislate away its judicial sovereignty without destroying its status and statehood.[237]

Two months or so before the 1930 Conference, Hearne informed Martin Eliasoff, second secretary in the Irish High Commissioner's Office, London, that the government did not consider the Privy Council as a court in the strict sense, as advice was given to the King by a number of privy counsellors and this advice was not the same as a judgement of a court of law. He described the continuance of the right of appeal as 'a menace to the judicial sovereignty of the Free State'.[238]

At the 1930 Imperial Conference, the Irish were looking for an amicable solution and were confident that the right of appeal would be abolished.[239] The importance of its removal for the Free State government was highlighted during the Conference in a radio address by Patrick McGilligan to the Irish diaspora in America, when he stated that there 'was no intention of allowing this infringement of our sovereignty to continue'.[240] However, on 25 October, McGilligan reported to Cosgrave on the resistance being experienced by the Irish delegation to their demands relating to the Privy Council.[241] Among the arguments advanced by the British side to reject Irish demands was the contention that the Treaty settlement 'had only given the Irish Free State the status of Canada as it had existed in 1921, without the benefits of subsequent constitutional advances achieved by the other Dominions'.[242] In effect, the Balfour Declaration and its consequences did not apply to Ireland. The Irish were to be unsuccessful once again, as the British proved unyielding.[243] The seriousness of this failure was underscored in a message from McGilligan to Cosgrave at the end of proceedings: 'Concluding this morning. No agreement reached on Privy Council which is not mentioned in the report. Avoid all publicity, if possible, concerning this.'[244]

The effect of the failure was to make the Irish angry and resentful.[245] These feelings can only have been exacerbated by the outcome of a meeting between Hearne and Seán Murphy, assistant secretary of the Department of External Affairs, and officials of the Dominion Office, held in London on Thursday 23 April 1931. Among the matters discussed was the controversial issue of the appeal. Having listened to the contributions of the British side, Hearne expressed the view to his opposites that the essential issue of its abolition was not being addressed. The two Irish civil servants wrote in their report to Dublin:

Mr Murphy and Mr Hearne consulted together on the whole situation on Monday night and Tuesday morning. Their joint impression was that there was no intention whatever in the Dominion Office to abolish the appeal by agreement and that in all the recent discussions the British government had one objective in view, namely to delay the introduction of bills in the Oireachtas to abolish the appeal or render it ineffectual.[246]

The reference to bills in the report relates to a decision by the Cosgrave government to pursue a unilateral policy of abolition of the right of appeal.[247] Hearne drafted a series of bills to give effect to this course of action.[248] The Constitution (Amendment No. 17) Bill proposed the abolition of the right of appeal contained in Article 66. Two other amendments were considered: the Constitution (Amendment No. 18) Bill defined more precisely the extent of the original jurisdiction of the High Court and the appellate jurisdiction of the Supreme Court; and the Constitution (Amendment No. 19) Bill proposed the deletion of the words 'within the terms of the scheduled Treaty' from Article 50, thus removing the Treaty as an obstacle to constitutional change. Two other bills were drawn up by Hearne in the event of the government not proceeding with the outright abolition of the appeal; the intent of these bills was to render the appeal de facto inoperative. The Supreme Court (Confirmation of Judgment) Bill permitted the executive council to immediately give statutory effect to any Supreme Court decision and thus give it immunity from interference by the Privy Council. The other proposed law, the Judicial Committee Bill, prohibited the enforcement of a decision of the Privy Council in any case concerning the Free State.[249]

None of the proposed bills was presented to the Oireachtas while Cosgrave was president. His government was awaiting the passage of the Statute of Westminster which would remove all doubts as to the power of the Free State parliament to enact such legislation.[250] A general election intervened in 1932, in which Cumann na nGaedheal lost power. It was to fall to Éamon de Valera to secure the prize of the abolition of the right of appeal.

In the election campaign Cumann na nGaedheal emphasised its record and relied on scare tactics to discredit the Fianna Fáil opposition party.[251] In effect, the electorate was offered a clear choice between a government defending the status quo and offering a conservative manifesto and a party proposing more radical constitutional, economic and social changes; and, in the words of Ciara Meehan, 'ultimately the people voted for the future, not the past'.[252] One thing is certain: the government which had ruled the Free State for a decade was not rewarded for its achievement in reshaping Ireland's relationship with the Commonwealth. In the course of the contest, Cosgrave declared that he did not know what more the Free State could ask than the decision of the Imperial Conference of 1926: all the Dominions were recognised as being coequal with Britain.[253] The problem, however, was that the government's foreign policy lacked public appeal; at best, the domestic political return was modest. In fact, Fianna

Fáil 'successfully turned the government's obvious enthusiasm for Commonwealth gatherings against it by caricaturing its delegates as top-hat-and-tailed imperialists cravenly aping their social superiors'.[254] The electoral outcome was determined not by achievements in the diplomatic sphere; more pressing social and economic issues concerned the voters.

In the interval before Éamon de Valera's election as President of the Executive Council, W.T. Cosgrave wrote to Hearne on 8 March 1932, thanking him for his 'official and personal services'. Hearne's reply on 6 April was respectful, warm and even affectionate. He expressed his 'sense of the great honour it has been to have worked for so long in close association with those more nearly placed to the head of government in the labour and achievement of the past ten years'. He continued: 'Nor can I express to our beloved President my gratitude for his graciousness and goodness on so many occasions during that time, for his patience with so many shortcomings, and the kindly appreciation and encouragement which lightened many a burden.'[255]

Whatever his personal feelings, Hearne had to accept that a new government was taking office; he had to accommodate himself to this reality. What he can never have anticipated was that he was to play a central and pivotal role in some of the most significant events in the early years of de Valera's rule.

CHAPTER 3

Serving de Valera, 1932–1936

On 9 March 1936, Éamon de Valera, with the support of the Labour Party, was elected President of the Executive Council of the Irish Free State and appointed his first Fianna Fáil government. Notwithstanding rumours of a planned coup by the outgoing administration, there was a smooth transfer of power. The change of government caused apprehension in the civil service as no one knew what to expect from the new ministers. In particular, there were fears that de Valera would introduce a spoils system and install his supporters in key positions.[1] John Hearne expected to face dismissal.[2] There were at least three reasons for him to be concerned. He had been an open supporter of John Redmond and a bitter opponent of Sinn Féin in the two elections in Waterford in 1918. During the March by-election, de Valera had been in the city and would likely have heard of Hearne and his speeches. Exacerbating his concerns was the fact that his Redmondite associations had already militated against his appointment as a district justice by the Cosgrave government. Secondly, he had served in the Free State army, regarded by republicans as the ruthless instrument of their defeat and oppression. Finally, he was legal adviser in the Department of External Affairs, to which de Valera had appointed himself minister. It was not unreasonable to speculate that Hearne was apprehensive that the new minister might appoint another in his place, one who shared de Valera's outlook and would be his preferred choice to help implement his controversial Anglo-Irish policy.

Fortunately for Hearne, there was no purge of civil servants. The new President was happy to exploit the talents of many former opponents.[3] What Fianna Fáil regarded as hostile in the shape of Cumann na nGaedheal, it embraced as neutral, disinterested, professional and expert in the shape of the civil service.[4] De Valera was to defend the service in the face of criticism by republican hardliners, arguing that it was loyal to the state. Deirdre McMahon has commented that his success in establishing a firm working relationship and continuity with the civil service was perhaps one of the most notable achievements of his early administrations.[5]

Arguably, nowhere was this relationship more apparent and more important than in the Department of External Affairs. De Valera assumed this portfolio because, according to his biographers, 'he always felt that this was a post which should, if possible, be held by the head of government, that there might be no doubt as to the authority with which the minister spoke'.[6] This consideration was to be all the more relevant as Fianna Fáil's Anglo-Irish policy was to prove contentious and 'the dark legacy of the Treaty split forged his determination to retain the control of the day-to-day detail of this policy in his own hands'.[7] The department de Valera headed was a small one; hence a good working relationship with its personnel was very desirable. In 1935, it employed fifteen to twenty people and was situated on the top floor of the Department of Agriculture in Government Buildings.[8] In 1930, the senior staff consisted of the secretary, assistant secretary, two junior administrative officers, a legal adviser and an assistant legal adviser.[9] The members of this small service had generally enjoyed a peculiarly personal and highly influential relationship with their minister[10] and de Valera was to be no exception. His first meeting with Joseph Walshe, the department's secretary, did much to assuage anxieties among the staff at the arrival of the new minister. According to former diplomat Con Cremin, 'all five or six diplomats at headquarters [Hearne was probably one of them] sat around a table awaiting Walshe's return. When he finally returned, he proclaimed de Valera as "charming, simply charming"'.[11]

Walshe came to realise that de Valera's election was an opportunity to increase the standing and influence of his department. The new President was also his minister and therefore the most influential member of the Executive Council. During the 1930s, External Affairs grew in respectability and stature within the civil service.[12] Walshe's biographer, Aengus Nolan, has observed that he and de Valera established 'a healthy relationship',[13] as he provided his minister with 'extensive and expert information' on the constitutional issues relating to the government's Anglo-Irish policy.[14] During the 1933 general election, he seemed to pledge his support to the Fianna Fáil leader.[15] According to Nolan, Walshe was ably assisted by John Hearne when it came to advising de Valera;[16] and, in her magisterial study of Anglo-Irish relations in the 1930s, Deirdre McMahon identified Hearne as an official who was to play an important role during this decade. She described him as de Valera's 'adviser during the period of his constitutional reforms'.[17] Ronan Fanning has confirmed Hearne as one of a 'troika of senior officials' on whom de Valera came to rely for counsel, the others being John Dulanty, Irish High Commissioner in London, and Walshe.[18] Unlike the latter, however, it appears that Hearne remained a supporter of the Cumann na nGaedheal–Fine Gael political tradition, his son, Maurice, commenting in his plan for a proposed biography of his father that 'Dad was ... not even a supporter of that party [Fianna Fáil].'[19]

Meetings between de Valera and Hearne

Hearne recorded details of one-to-one meetings he had with de Valera in 1933 and 1934.[20] Between 27 June and 18 August 1933 he had nine meetings, during which a wide range of topics with implications for the Free State's relations with foreign countries was discussed. On 27 June, Australia's candidacy for a seat on the Council of the League of Nations was considered, with de Valera deciding to support a fellow Dominion. The following day, both men addressed the possible appointment of a new American Minister to Dublin. On 24 July, Hearne read for de Valera a report from the Irish legation in Berlin concerning a recent newspaper article printed in Germany alleging de Valera's Jewish ancestry and his association with Jewish bankers. The minister directed the legation to make a strong protest.

The coverage of Blueshirt activities in the foreign press was the subject of a meeting on 18 August 1933. A draft statement, approved by de Valera, was to be sent to Irish legations describing such reports as 'sensational' and 'inspired by enemies of Ireland and of the present government'. It is very likely that the minister and his legal adviser had more meetings than the nine recorded by Hearne. According to Dermot Keogh, perhaps he 'was the person with whom de Valera had the closest contact during the early years of his coming to office.'[21] These meetings facilitated the establishment and development of a good professional relationship between the two men, the minister coming to appreciate and value the advice and abilities of his department's legal adviser. He came to realise that Hearne was a civil servant he both trusted and admired.

De Valera and the quest for sovereignty

A preoccupation with Irish sovereignty was the defining feature of Éamon de Valera's long political career, Gearóid Ó Tuathaigh writing:

> Throughout the whole of de Valera's public life ... this central question – the status of Ireland, the extent of her independence, the exact measure of sovereignty (in all its manifold forms, economic, social and cultural, no less than political) – this central question was to be the governing passion of his political life, the source from which were to spring the bulk of his ideas, aspirations, policies and, indeed, prejudices.[22]

De Valera declared that his fundamental opposition to the Anglo-Irish Treaty of 1921 was rooted in his conviction that it represented a denial of the basic principle of the sovereignty of the Irish people, having been imposed under the threat of immediate and terrible war.[23] In fact, he never wavered in his view that this settlement was morally worthless because it had been signed under duress.[24]

The Constitution of the Irish Free State, enacted in December 1922, made the Treaty an integral part of Irish municipal law. As a consequence, this Constitution contained numerous provisions abhorrent to republicans, including an oath of allegiance to the British monarch by members of the Oireachtas, a right of appeal to the Privy Council and the appointment of a representative of the King in the person of the Governor-General. Thus the organs of the state's authority were stained with the stigma of external domination in the eyes of the Treaty's opponents.[25]

While Cosgrave's government had advanced and affirmed the sovereignty of the Free State in international terms, it adopted an attitude of entrenched defence of the Constitution in the face of republican attacks. This is explained by the fact that, having fought the Civil War to defend the Treaty, the agreement became something of an article of faith[26] and its terms were considered sacrosanct by ministers.[27] In contrast, de Valera was determined to dismantle it, this being one of the core objectives of the Fianna Fáil party he founded in 1926. Dismantling the Treaty and purging the associated Constitution of its imperial impositions was a prerequisite for winning over the bulk of republicans who, with de Valera, had challenged the Free State in arms during the Civil War. This was an important group in terms of his party's support base. The legitimacy of the state had been rejected by them; the dismantling of the Treaty settlement was essential to restore this legitimacy. Reinforcing de Valera's determination was a strong conviction, shared by a long line of Irish nationalist leaders, in the creative possibility of political sovereignty for economic and social development; in fact, a satisfactory constitutional status was a prerequisite for such development.[28]

With his election as President of the Executive Council, de Valera began his assault on the Treaty. It was this recognition of the central role Anglo-Irish relations would play during the term of his government that prompted his decision to retain for himself the External Affairs portfolio. He was to exert total control over the conduct of this policy area. This approach reflected his determination never to let the debacle of the Treaty divisions happen again. Deirdre McMahon has written: 'In any assessment of de Valera's life and career it can be stated simply that the Treaty scarred him personally and politically for the rest of his life. It was his private avenging fury.'[29] Not only was he clear in his policy objectives, he was also clear as to the means of their achievement. Fianna Fáil would proceed gradually, as he explained as early as 1926 at the inaugural meeting of the party. Addressing the gathering, de Valera stated that 'a young man's appreciation' of the situation, as it then stood, would lead him to certain conclusions:

He would see that by isolating the oath for attack, the whole situation, and England's ultimate control, would be exposed. He could scarcely doubt that, the real feeling of the people being what it is, the oath would fall before a determined assault, and he would set out to attack it as being the most vital and, at the same time, the part most easily destroyed of the entire entrenchments of the foreign enemy. He could see, once the oath was destroyed, promising lines for a further advance, with the nation moving as a whole, cutting the bonds of foreign interference one by one until the full internal sovereignty of the twenty-six counties was established beyond question.[30]

As Ó Tuathaigh has observed, this 'was indeed to be the running order for constitutional change when Fianna Fáil eventually came to power in 1932'.[31]

Relations with Britain absorbed de Valera's thoughts from the time he assumed leadership of government. He was certain in the principles, policies and practices of his Anglo-Irish strategy; it had been a long time in gestation and this made him a formidable proponent of the reordering of the constitutional architecture between the Free State and Britain. It soon became clear that he was intent on a revolutionary departure from the Dominion settlement.[32] His ultimate aim was the recognition of Ireland as a republic, some form of association with the Commonwealth and the acceptance of the King as head of that association. This was his policy of 'external association', proposed during the Treaty negotiations and contained in 'Document No. 2' during the Treaty debates in the Dáil in 1921–2.[33] It was still uppermost in his mind as President.[34]

Removal of the oath of allegiance

In accordance with Fianna Fáil's 1932 election manifesto, the oath of allegiance in the Free State Constitution was to be abolished and the de Valera government moved with great speed to honour this pledge. On 12 March, the cabinet met to discuss the immediate introduction of the necessary bill to remove the offending Article 17. In the Department of External Affairs, Walshe and Hearne were uneasy. The former wrote to the minister counselling delay and urging him not to take any precipitate action which could jeopardise his ultimate objective.[35] He also submitted a memorandum prepared by Hearne.[36] Consistent with views expressed in memoranda prepared for the Conference on the Operation of Dominion Legislation and considered in Chapter 2, Hearne asserted the authority of the Oireachtas over the Constitution: 'It can repeal the entire Constitution from beginning to end.' He reiterated the opinion that Article 50, which required amendments to be within the terms of the Treaty, was simply a declaration of the fact that the state was bound by treaty obligations to another state; it did not impose limitations on the competency of the Oireachtas. In the copy of the memorandum retained in the National Archives, these opinions are marked in red ink on the margin, suggesting their importance to the reader, who may well have been de Valera.

There appears to have been a concern at government level that, notwithstanding the repeal of Article 17, Article 4 of the Anglo-Irish Treaty, which related to the oath, would still have the force of law in the Free State. Hearne addressed this matter by restating his view that the Treaty be regarded as an agreement between two sovereign states. Therefore, the essential issue was how the courts might interpret this article. He advised de Valera: 'It is a settled rule of law that the courts of a treaty-bound state are bound to recognise and enforce the statutes of that state, even when they are in conflict with clear and unequivocal treaty obligations.' Again, this sentence is marked in red ink on the margin of the memorandum.

On the question of what was the best approach to be adopted by the government, Hearne set out three possible courses of action: a review of the Treaty by both parties; submitting the oath to arbitration; and diplomatic discussions with the British government, the last of which was his preferred option.[37] Such discussions should seek an agreement to delete Article 4 of the Treaty: 'That is the only safe legal course to take and, in my view, the claims of the government to such an agreement would stand upon a solid and unassailable basis.' He was clear in his view that the Irish government must give careful consideration to its choice of response: 'But what matters most of all is the method adopted to secure the end.' According to McMahon, de Valera compromised and the following day sent the British Dominions Secretary a statement announcing his intention to abolish the oath; there would be no immediate introduction of legislation. She regarded this as significant:

> The views of Walshe and Hearne are important because they demonstrate that from the very beginning de Valera was prepared to listen to and act on their advice. It is also significant that the statement to the Dominions Secretary does not appear to have been discussed or even approved by the Irish cabinet.[38]

Walshe and Hearne clearly hoped that British ministers, having been given notice of Irish intentions, would seek to engage in discussions and offer concessions. In their advice, however, they underestimated the distrust of the new Fianna Fáil government in London.[39] There was a deeply hostile reaction to de Valera's stated intentions and this unleashed a 'veritable Pandora's box of fear and suspicion on the British side'.[40]

British ministers were adamant that the oath was an obligation under the terms of the Treaty and demanded full compliance on the part of the Free State. This intransigent attitude and their implacable opposition to de Valera were founded on the deeply held view that the Crown was the fundamental link of unity in the Commonwealth. There were genuine fears and concerns, moreover, that the Irish government was seeking to unravel the entire 1921 settlement and reopen the whole issue of the nature of the constitutional relationship between Ireland and Britain, which the British government believed had been settled.[41]

John Hearne got an insight into British attitudes at a meeting in London, in July 1932, with Sir Harry Batterbee, the assistant undersecretary at the Dominions Office. The official memorandum recorded that Sir Harry wanted a few minutes' private conversation with Hearne. The latter agreed and 'Sir Harry proceeded at once to express his views on the general political situation between the two countries.'

> He said that everybody connected with official life in the Dominions Office had been very much hurt by the treatment the British government had received at the hands of the new Irish Free State government. The attitude of 'declining to discuss' the oath of allegiance was quite unprovoked and uncalled for. But the real gravamen of the existing situation was not this particular difficulty or that particular difficulty, it was the background of the situation, the fundamental unsettling of things that had been regarded as settled, the tendency behind all the particular points at issue to put an end to the basis of the existing relations between the two countries ... One felt the hopelessness of dealing with this or that dispute as long as the main position was not definitely settled ... He personally felt that the Irish people themselves would have to decide in one way or the other the fundamental question of the continuance of the Irish Free State in the British Commonwealth. It would be for them to say *after experience* what their decision was to be. It all came to that in the end.[42]

The hostile reaction among British politicians to de Valera's policy raised concerns regarding possible implications for Irish people resident in Britain. A memorandum produced by Hearne examined this matter and probably calmed the fears of Irish ministers.[43] The legal adviser explained that the residency of most Irish people in Britain was regulated by the Nationality and Status of Aliens Act 1914, by the terms of which all persons born within His Majesty's Dominions were deemed to be natural-born British subjects. A change in this law would be necessary to deprive them of this status. Assuming that steps were taken to change this, Irish residents would then be classed as 'aliens'. This would impact on many of the benefits they enjoyed, such as the right to practise medicine on the same terms as English doctors. Moreover, aliens could be deported on various grounds. Hearne pointed out, however, that a person could not be deported simply because she or he was an alien; such a person had to be adjudged as 'undesirable' within the terms of the act, for example on account of a criminal record. Even if their status changed, he concluded that a considerable portion of Irish nationals in Britain might escape the more drastic forms of hardship.

It was against a backdrop of an increasingly toxic climate in Anglo-Irish relations that de Valera introduced the proposed legislation to abolish the oath on 20 April 1932. John Hearne was the civil servant in charge of the bill.[44] It contained three sections. The first deleted Article 17 of the Free State Constitution. The second repealed section 2 of the document of the Irish Free State (Saorstát Éireann) Act 1922, which required that the document be construed with reference to the Treaty. Under the last section, Article 50, which governed the amendment procedure, was itself amended by the deletion of the words which stipulated that all amendments had to be 'within the terms of the scheduled Treaty'. Clearly, the bill did much more than simply abolish the oath.[45] It also removed the repugnancy clause, a far more significant provision from a legal perspective because 'it unlocked the potential to unravel the Treaty settlement'.[46] This removal was, in fact, 'the preliminary step' to this unravelling and, 'ultimately, for the enactment of the current 1937 Irish Constitution'.[47]

It is possible, perhaps, to identify Hearne's influence on de Valera's speech to the Dáil during the bill's second stage on 27 April 1932. The President argued that the oath's removal was consistent with the Free State's position as a coequal member of the Commonwealth,[48] a theme iterated by Hearne on many occasions. He almost certainly influenced de Valera's statement that, in cases when the courts were required to interpret municipal law which contradicted treaties, the courts favoured municipal law,[49] an opinion consistent with the view expressed in Hearne's memorandum on the oath, which was noted earlier. The bill passed all stages in the Dáil on 19 May 1932 and was sent to the Seanad, where it was delayed; it finally became law on 3 May 1933.[50]

The annuities' controversy

The newly elected Fianna Fáil government also announced its intention to withhold payment to the British Treasury of the land annuities due under various land acts enacted by the imperial parliament. A cornerstone of Fianna Fáil's refusal to pay them was that the financial agreements between the Free State and Great Britain in 1923 and 1926,[51] under which the Irish government agreed to collect the annuities and pay them to the British government, were not binding because they had not been submitted to the Dáil for debate and ratification.[52] Hearne prepared two memoranda in response to information sought by de Valera on this aspect of his government's objection to their payment. The first, dated 11 April 1932, outlined the practice in other countries regarding parliamentary approval of agreements and treaties.[53]

The second, dated 12 April 1932, considered the authority of the Cosgrave government to bind the state to the payment of the annuities.[54] Hearne wrote that he could not give a final opinion until all the relevant facts and documents were before him. He did, however, explain the general principles relating to such an agreement. Having been signed by President Cosgrave, an external government would have no reason to believe that the head of government of the Irish Free State was not entitled to bind at least the government of the Free State by his signature. Furthermore, Cosgrave's signature had not been repudiated by the government. Lastly, the state had acted on the agreement by paying the annuities. Given the opinions expressed by Hearne, the overall import of this memorandum was not particularly helpful to the position of de Valera's government.

In retaliation for de Valera's refusal to pay the annuities the British government imposed special duties on Irish imports in July 1932. The Free State countered by putting duties on English imports. The 'Economic War' had begun. The two controversies in Anglo-Irish relations – the oath and annuities – became conflated in the responses and attitudes of British ministers, and the special duties came to be seen as a means of putting pressure on de Valera to capitulate. Thus there was the effective pursuit of a policy of economic sanctions for political ends in response to the abolition of the oath.

As a means of resolving their differences over the annuities, both governments gave consideration to arbitration.[55] However, there was a fundamental difference between them: British ministers insisted that the matter be submitted to a Commonwealth tribunal, as described in the report of the 1930 Imperial Conference. This tribunal was to be composed of representatives of member states and was to be resorted to as a means of settling intra-Commonwealth disputes.[56] Despite reservations about arbitration, de Valera indicated, in June 1932, that he would accept it in principle, but with the proviso that the arbitral tribunal should not be restricted to Commonwealth personnel.[57] The British government insisted on this restriction and so the prospect of arbitration foundered.[58]

During the July meeting between Hearne and Batterbee, referred to earlier, Hearne had given his views on the question of arbitration. In the memorandum recording the encounter, Hearne was reported as stating that 'he had no authority to go into the general position or to discuss the particular issues, e.g., the oath or the land annuities'; he was giving 'a purely personal opinion'.[59] This opinion he expressed with his usual trenchant forthrightness:

The government of the Irish Free State had accepted the principle of arbitration as a method of settlement. The two governments were definitely agreed on that; they had not agreed on the method of constituting the arbitral tribunal. But in that state of facts the British government brought in the Import Duties Bill against Irish Free State goods and produce. While discussion of ways and means of arbitration – the principle already accepted – was going on this bill was introduced. It would be difficult to find an instance of mishandling of a difficult situation so extraordinary as that.

In his contention that both governments had definitely accepted the principle of arbitration, Hearne was overstating the level of agreement and understanding. The fact was that, at best, 'arbitration was a half-hearted compromise about which both governments had serious reservations'.[60] Regarding Britain's insistence on a Commonwealth tribunal, Hearne declared that the Irish government refused to regard the report of the 1930 Imperial Conference pertaining to this putative tribunal as 'the edict of a super-parliament'. Hearne was correct in his view. The report, while agreeing to the composition and remit of the proposed body, recommended the adoption of a voluntary and not an obligatory system.[61] Speaking in parliament on 3 July 1932, Labour MP Clement Atlee attacked British demands for a Commonwealth tribunal; the conclusions of the 1930 Conference were, according to him, 'a pious view'.[62] McMahon was accurate in her comment that British ministers were 'clearly ignorant of the chequered history of the Commonwealth tribunal'.[63]

Hearne was definite in his opinion of the implications of the British refusal to consider a tribunal composed of non-Commonwealth representatives: it was a denial of the Free State's international sovereignty: 'If the Irish Free State had any international existence at all it was entitled to an international tribunal to arbitrate an international financial issue.' In his discussion with Batterbee he referred to an earlier statement made by the British civil servant:

You say that the people of the Irish Free State must decide the question of membership of the Commonwealth. What considerations will operate in their minds when taking that decision? You know that since the Treaty was signed they have been assured that membership of the Commonwealth in no way derogates from the substance of international statehood. If you steadily decline to accept that situation, if you insist that membership of the Commonwealth does derogate from statehood and does deprive members – other than great Britain – of certain elementary international rights, what decision do you think the Irish people will take?

Batterbee was unmoved, the memorandum recording his reaction: 'Sir Harry said that the Commonwealth tribunal will be insisted upon: it was fundamental.' Hearne utterly disparaged this notion: 'Was the half-worked-out idea of a Commonwealth tribunal going to be set up as a sort of judicial constitution of the British Commonwealth?' Showing an understanding and appreciation of the evolution of Dominion status over the previous ten years, he informed the British official that 'the existence of the Commonwealth in the future would depend upon the very fact of its having no judicial constitution or other constitution of any kind'.[64] Throughout this meeting John Hearne defended the position of the Irish Free State, employing arguments which displayed a consummate, even prescient knowledge of Commonwealth development, while Batterbee articulated the views of a dying imperialism.

Governor-General controversy

In 1932, de Valera found himself embroiled in a controversy involving the Governor-General, James McNeill. The manner in which he dealt with it contrasted sharply with his handling of the matters of the oath of allegiance and the annuities. He was certain and considered in dealing with them; the situation with McNeill took what McMahon has described as 'a maverick course'.[65] This was due to the fact that the matter arose unexpectedly.

Fianna Fáil regarded the position of Governor-General with unrelenting hostility. Representing the King, it was a tangible symbol and reminder of the hated Treaty settlement. It was also attacked as being too costly and as an absolutely useless office, filled by a 'rubber stamp'.[66] De Valera did not initially intend to act against the representative of the monarch in 1932; that was for the future. Events, however, conspired otherwise.

Confrontation arose between McNeill and the government because of his disrespectful treatment by ministers. Shortly after their appointment in March, Sean T. O'Kelly, Vice-President of the Executive Council, and Frank Aiken, Minister for Defence, made a pointed departure from a reception at the French legation on the arrival of the Governor-General. McNeill complained to de Valera and demanded an apology but without satisfaction. Tensions came to a head in July after a series of petty snubs during the Eucharistic congress. McNeill published his correspondence with de Valera, in spite of warnings to the contrary from the Executive Council. The Fianna Fáil government decided to force his resignation,[67] which took effect in November.

De Valera decided to use the opportunity to diminish the status of the office by appointing an acting Governor-General. His subsequent handling of events was confused, even haphazard. Ill-prepared because of the unexpectedness of this controversy, he was also distracted by more pressing matters, such as the oath and annuities. Chief Justice Hugh Kennedy was considered for the position but was unwilling to serve.[68] De Valera proposed that he himself assume the role in an acting capacity. However, the King's secretary replied that the Treaty and Constitution appeared to make it impossible for the offices of President and Governor-General to be held by the same person.[69] De Valera then made the proposal that the powers be vested in a commission, composed of himself, the Ceann Comhairle and the Chairman of the Senate. The King refused to consider this.[70]

Hearne became involved in the controversy surrounding the Governor-General. He prepared a memorandum on the letters patent constituting the office for the assistant secretary at the Department of External Affairs Seán Murphy.[71] In another memorandum, he advised abolition of the office and that the government deal directly with the King. He was very clearly of the mind that the government should take a firm stand on that basis in any possible future negotiations.[72] De Valera was not ready for such a course of action at this stage – it simply was not on his agenda of constitutional change for the year 1932. The most significant part played by Hearne in this affair was his accompanying the Attorney General, Conor Maguire, to a meeting with Chief Justice Kennedy. A memorandum, prepared on 20 November for the Executive Council, recorded that both men called on the judge 'with a view to discussing with him the question of his assumption of the duties of office of acting Governor-General pending the appointment of a successor to McNeill'.

De Valera's emissaries were singularly unsuccessful, the memorandum noting that 'the Chief Justice stated that in his opinion it would be obligatory to take the oath of office and the oath of allegiance and that he did not desire to take these oaths'.[73] This unequivocal refusal thwarted de Valera's plans to use the opportunity of McNeill's resignation to nullify the office he was vacating. The President was effectively forced to appoint Domhnall O'Buachalla.[74] Even though O'Buachalla was to discharge the office in an anonymous fashion,[75] thus marginalising its public significance, de Valera nevertheless was forced to make this appointment in 1932, having gone to great trouble to avoid making a permanent appointment in that year.[76]

De Valera's decision that Hearne accompany the Attorney General suggests that the President increasingly appreciated his knowledge, competence and abilities. He was probably the obvious choice, given his position in the Department of External Affairs, but, considering the urgency of the situation, indeed its near crisis proportions, de Valera would not have entrusted this sensitive and important task to a civil servant in whom he did not repose confidence, simply because of that civil servant's position. That he did was an indication of the growing professional closeness between the two men.

Privy Council appeal

On 9 September 1932, John Hearne wrote a secret memorandum listing outstanding issues between the Irish and British governments. The second item on the list was the Privy Council appeal.[77] Its inclusion was unsurprising given that it was an ongoing source of discord. During his July meeting with Batterbee, Hearne had expressed his frustrations on this matter, as recorded in the official memorandum:

> But as a purely personal opinion he would like to say to Sir Harry Batterbee that he had always regarded the Privy Council issue as a test issue, a test of the reality of Commonwealth Conference decisions. He had expressed a certain view to Sir Edward Harding [permanent under-secretary, Dominions Office] previously when Sir Edward was in Dublin with Mr Thomas [Dominions Secretary]. He would repeat it now. It was this. If those whose duty it was to carry out the directions of successive governments had been able to say to President de Valera when he took office that the Privy Council had been regarded by the British government as a Treaty issue, just as the oath was now so regarded by the British government, but that the Privy Council issue had been settled by agreement without any difficulty whatever because of the wishes of the Irish people in the matter, what a difference that might have made. But what had been the position? The President had to be told – if indeed he had not known it already – that negotiations lasting over years had been a failure, and that an absurd interpretation of the Treaty was solemnly advanced over and over by successive British law officers to defeat the Privy Council policy of the government and people of the Irish Free State.[78]

In January 1933, Éamon de Valera called a snap general election. Fianna Fáil won an overall majority in a campaign dominated by Anglo-Irish relations. With a renewed and stronger mandate, de Valera continued what British ministers, implacably wedded to the status quo, regarded as his 'constitutional rake's progress'.[79] On 9 August 1933, he introduced three bills to amend the Constitution, thus demonstrating his steely determination to dismantle the Treaty settlement. All of them were enacted by November. The Constitution (Amendment No. 20) Act transferred from the Governor-General to the Executive Council powers relating to the appropriation of money under Article 37. The Constitution (Amendment No. 21) Act removed from Article 41 provisions about the withholding, by the Governor-General, of the royal assent to bills and the reservation of bills for the signification of the King's pleasure. The third measure (Amendment no. 22) abolished the right of appeal to the Privy Council contained in Article 66. Hearne prepared a memorandum on the matter of the appeal,[80] which he was directed to send to the Attorney General, in whose department the bill was being drafted. He also sent copies of the bills he had prepared for the Cosgrave government, which are noted in Chapter 2. On 15 November 1933, this amendment completed its passage through the Houses of the Oireachtas.[81]

That same evening, the Erne Fisheries Company announced its intention to appeal a judgement of the Supreme Court to the Privy Council in defiance both of the amendment and the wishes of the Irish government.[82] As part of the appeal, the company requested that the Privy Council determine the legitimacy of the abolition of the right of appeal.[83] This was a crucial case for the Free State: at issue was the right of its parliament to amend the Constitution and the validity of this and other constitutional amendments. Should the Privy Council reject the legitimacy of the constitutional amendment abolishing the right of appeal, this would have the effect of subverting the state's claims to full judicial sovereignty and, by extension, its claim of being an independent sovereign state.

De Valera received conflicting advice from the Attorney General and Hearne as to what the government's response should be to the decision of the Privy Council to hear the appeal. Maguire favoured making a diplomatic protest, while the legal adviser advocated tendering advice to the King to accept the terms and significance of the amendment.[84] The monarch, according to Hearne, had no constitutional option but to accept the advice of his government in the Irish Free State. Hearne's advice was informed by his conviction of the state of the constitutional development of the Commonwealth, which was founded on the fundamental principle of the coequality of all members:

> Their [the government's] action must be based on the supreme authority of the Oireachtas to regulate and control the prerogatives of the King. The whole issue is a constitutional issue between the parliament and government of Saorstát Éireann, and the King. The correct course for the government to take will be to advise the King in terms of the Constitution (Amendment No. 22) Act ... The government should firmly decline to be drawn into any discussion with the British government on the question of the propriety or otherwise of advice tendered to the King ... The King will not refuse to accept the advice of the government of Saorstát Éireann. This advice would be correct on every conceivable ground. It would be correct on the legal ground of the statute of the Oireachtas barring the prerogative of appeal in express terms; correct on the constitutional ground of the relations which exist between the King and the government of Saorstát Éireann in an opinion so obviously internal as the organisation of the judicial system; correct on the political ground of a unanimous Dáil and practically undivided public opinion; correct on the international ground of the judicial sovereignty of the Irish Free State and its responsibility in international law for the acts of its judicial tribunals.[85]

De Valera did not accept the advice of either official; rather, he instructed that the Free State ignore the proceedings of the Privy Council.[86] The case was heard in April 1935.[87] Finally, on 6 June of the same year, the Privy Council ruled that the

Irish Free State had the right to abolish the appeal. It summarised its judgement in one sentence: 'The simplest way of stating the situation is to say that the Statute of Westminster gave to the Irish Free State a power under which they could abrogate the Treaty, and that, as a matter of law, they have availed themselves of that power.'[88]

This judgement resulted in the collapse of British legal arguments concerning the maintenance of the Treaty settlement. While the British government would continue to oppose de Valera's constitutional reforms, it could never again seriously challenge the legality of the measures.[89] This decision must have given Hearne great satisfaction, even pleasure. It vindicated his view, expressed in many memoranda, regarding the sovereignty and coequality of all members of the Commonwealth. As a man of the law, he would likely have concurred with Thomas Mohr's assessment: 'As a result of this decision the date of June 6, 1935 can be considered the day in which Ireland finally won undisputed judicial sovereignty and therefore can be considered a great victory for Irish sovereignty as a whole.'[90]

The 'nationality code'

One of the most complex issues which faced the Commonwealth was that of nationality, a fact noted earlier in accounts of Imperial Conferences. De Valera believed that each member state had a distinct and separate nationality[91] and decided to give a legal basis to Irish nationality in the Free State. On 15 November 1934, the Dáil began debating the Nationality and Citizenship Bill. This was an area which usually came within the remit of the Department of Justice, but de Valera, as Minister for External Affairs, promoted the legislation[92] because it had implications for Anglo-Irish and Commonwealth relations. Speaking in the Dáil, the President explained that the bill contained proposals for the regulation throughout the world of Irish citizenship and sought to govern the conditions for its determination and acquisition.[93] De Valera's involvement meant that Hearne became involved in the legislative process, by virtue of his position as legal adviser. On 2 January 1935, in reply to queries from Stephen Roche, secretary of the Department of Justice, regarding the effects of the bill on the validity of certain wills, Hearne explained some of the consequences if it were to be enacted. He stated categorically that 'No person shall be a citizen of Saorstát Éireann and a British subject thereunder.'[94] The bill heralded the end of the notion of common status among Commonwealth citizens as far as the Free State was concerned.

On 14 February 1935, the Dáil began consideration of the Constitution (Amendment No. 26) Bill, pertaining to Article 3,[95] which was concerned with citizenship. Hearne had explained the bill's purpose in a memorandum in November 1934: it was to remove the territorial restriction on citizenship created by this article. Under it, a citizen of the Free State was only such 'within the limits and jurisdiction of Saorstát Éireann'. The amendment proposed 'to delete the quoted words so that in future the citizenship created in Article 3 will have extra-territorial effect and will follow those who possess it throughout the world'.[96] On the same day, the Dáil also debated the Aliens Bill. De Valera stated that it contained proposals 'to deal with those who are not regarded as citizens'.[97] Hearne had also explained its purpose in an earlier memorandum: 'The proposed bill is necessary having regard to the fact that we require a new definition of "alien" in the light of the new Citizenship Bill and a new code to regulate the position of aliens in Saorstát Éireann.'[98] On 3 December 1934, he issued another memorandum on the Aliens Bill, which repeated much of the information and details contained in the earlier one.[99] De Valera told the Dáil that the three bills together could be regarded 'as comprising our whole nationality code',[100] and Hearne wrote that it was intended that the Constitution Amendment and Aliens Bills would become law at the same time as the Nationality and Citizenship Bill.[101] This is what happened effectively, with the amendment being enacted on 5 April 1935 and the two other bills on 10 April.

Absence of provisions for common status presented a major difficulty for British ministers, as it was believed that this would lead to a breach in the unity of the Commonwealth. The Nationality Bill made no reference to such status and de Valera was uncompromising in his position: 'the British view of common status was not one in which representatives of this state at any time concurred'.[102] In fact, the bill was very much along the lines of the proposals put forward by Irish delegates at the 1930 Imperial Conference. The Aliens Bill further antagonised British opinion by including British subjects in the definition of aliens as anyone who was not a citizen of the Free State.[103] However, the Irish government had power to exempt certain classes of people from this definition and when the bill became law it made an order exempting citizens from the other Commonwealth countries from the status of aliens. Notwithstanding this fact, the language used in the acts of Ireland's 'nationality code' pointed not towards membership of the Commonwealth but towards de Valera's concept of external association as he had sketched it years before in 'Document No. 2'.[104]

Abolition of the Seanad: the 'Hearne affair'

On 22 March 1934, de Valera introduced the Constitution (Amendment No. 24) Bill, to amend Article 12 and abolish Seanad Éireann as a constituent House of the Oireachtas.[105] The bill was enacted on 29 May 1936, the Seanad sitting for the last time on 19 May, when it adjourned *sine die*.[106] Fianna Fáil's attitude to the Free State Seanad will be considered in the next chapter; here we are concerned with an incident involving John Hearne in the course of the abolition debate in that house on 15 January 1936.

During the discussion, there was criticism of the fact that de Valera was not present in the chamber. Senator William Quirke, the Fianna Fáil group leader, offered an explanation. According to him, an official from the President's Department, unnamed by Quirke, was sent to take notes on the debate. He was approached by an official on the Seanad staff and informed that he could not sit where he was, unless accompanied by a minister, but that a seat would be provided in the public gallery. De Valera's official left. Quirke described this as 'an unprecedented incident' and he alleged that it was 'premeditated' and 'indicative of the vindictive policy of the majority of this house against the President personally'.[107]

The Cathaoirleach, Senator T.W. Westropp Bennett, intervened at this juncture to clarify the situation. It transpired that Hearne was the official in question, and that

[he] came in at three o'clock and sat in one of the seats reserved for those in attendance on ministers. He was asked who was coming, or if the President were coming, and he said he did not know: that he was not aware that he was coming. Mr Coffey [an official of the Seanad] was then asked to tell him that he could not remain there if a minister were not in attendance – those seats were reserved for ministers and their attendants – but that a seat would be provided for him in the front row of the [public] gallery. He replied 'Tell him [the Cathaoirleach] to communicate that to me in the proper way', and he subsequently left. That was communicated to me by the Clerk of the House. I then prepared this letter, which I signed, and which would have been handed to him if he came back. It was not handed to him, as he did not come to the House later. The letter reads as follows: –

'Legal adviser to the Minister for External Affairs.

I am afraid I cannot allow you to sit behind the chairs reserved for ministers if no minister is in attendance. A seat in the gallery will be found for you. This procedure is in accordance with precedent'.

–Cathaoirleach[108]

The next day the event was reported in the three national newspapers. Under a heading, 'An unusual incident', the *Irish Times* carried a description based on the statements of Senators Quirke and Westropp Bennett.[109] The *Irish Press* used the heading 'A remarkable incident'.[110] The *Irish Independent* described the affair and continued: 'It is understood that the President regarded the action which caused his adviser to withdraw as a grave discourtesy to himself and that he would probably not attend the debate today'.[111]

Senator Westropp Bennett wrote to de Valera on 16 January to explain the matter from his point of view. In the detailed letter, he emphasised the protocol governing the attendance of ministerial officials in the Seanad chamber and assured the President that he never intended to offer any discourtesy to him or his officials.[112] De Valera's curt, two-sentence reply simply noted the explanation which had been offered.[113]

This incident, an essentially minor one, underscored the tensions between de Valera and the Seanad. 'The Hearne affair', if it may be so styled, was the product of turbulent political times, an overly sensitive upper house and a head of government determined in his antipathy towards it. It was unfortunate that Hearne was caught in the crossfire, and this may be explained by the fact that, according to the *Irish Independent*, 'he usually accompanied the President in the Senate when the abolition bill and certain other bills were discussed'.[114] He happened to be there when a defensive Seanad decided to stand on its dignity by invoking precedent. Throughout his career, Hearne was quintessentially the self-effacing and unobtrusive civil servant and it is reasonable to assume that he would have found the publicity unwelcome – though he was no shrinking violet, as was evidenced in his attitude and reply to Mr Coffey. While de Valera exploited the incident for political advantage, it is likely that he did take umbrage at the treatment of his legal adviser. What he regarded as the insulting treatment of Hearne was, in fact, directed at him; Hearne was simply a vicarious target. It is also possible that the President was unhappy that a civil servant was drawn into a political spat. This unhappiness may have been exacerbated by the fact that the official in question was Hearne, for whom he had a high regard.

The close professional relationship that developed between John Hearne and Éamon de Valera in the years 1932–6 was founded on the latter's appreciation of Hearne's judgement, competence and expertise. The President came to realise that the Waterford-born lawyer and civil servant possessed attributes which facilitated the realisation of his policy objectives. Hearne responded by serving his minister with consummate professionalism. This relationship was to be the foundation of the trust reposed in Hearne by de Valera when it came to the advancement of his radical programme of constitutional change.

CHAPTER 4

Towards a New Constitution, 1932–1936

In June 1936, Éamon de Valera informed King Edward VIII of the Irish Free State's decision to draft a new constitution. It was a decision which was to herald a momentous change in the constitutional relationship between the two countries and represented the culmination of the process of dismantling the Treaty settlement of 1921. This decision was not taken hastily; rather it was in gestation for a period of over four years, from 1932 to 1936. There were significant milestones along the way. In fact, it is possible to identify four stages in the evolution of Bunreacht na hÉireann. First, there was the removal from the Free State Constitution of those articles which were particularly offensive to republicans. These were articles implanting the Crown in the constitutional framework of the state and were removed by amendments in 1932 and 1933, as was outlined in the previous chapter. The second stage was the establishment, in 1934, by de Valera, of a civil service committee to review the 1922 Constitution. The next stage, in 1935, was the formulation of draft heads of a new fundamental law. Finally, a year later, de Valera decided to draft an entirely new constitution and this represented the final stage in the progress towards Bunreacht na hÉireann.

John Hearne was to be involved in all these stages. His role in amending the 1922 Constitution has already been noted in Chapter 3. He served on the civil service committee which reviewed this document. It was to his legal adviser that de Valera turned to draw up draft heads in 1935 and, most significantly, Hearne was selected by the President to draft a new constitution. His various roles in relation to the development of the state's basic law are a tribute to his legal and drafting skills. These same skills were recognised by de Valera and there developed between the two men a professional relationship of the highest order, a relationship which helped shape modern Ireland.

Constitution Review Committee, 1934

In 1934, de Valera set up a committee to review the 1922 Free State Constitution. This decision had its origins in opposition concerns regarding the Fianna Fáil government's decision to abolish the Seanad in 1933.[1] One consequence of this was that the state's basic law could be amended by the Dáil alone, in accordance with Article 50. As originally conceived, this provided for amendments by the Oireachtas for a period of eight years from the date of its coming into operation, i.e. 6 December 1922. After the expiration of this transitional period, due in December 1930, future changes were to be subjected to a referendum. However, in May 1929, the Executive Council secured the passage of the Constitution (Amendment No. 16) Act which extended this period by a further eight years. Consequently, the 1922 Constitution would continue to be amended by ordinary legislation enacted by the Oireachtas. This change had radical implications, as constitutional provisions guaranteeing the fundamental personal and democratic rights of citizens could potentially be restricted or removed altogether at the discretion of parliament. Realisation of this fact prompted some Fine Gael deputies to table an amendment on 17 May 1934, in the course of a debate on the government's proposals to abolish the Seanad. Motivated by fears that de Valera was intent on establishing himself as a dictator by means of a unicameral legislature, this amendment sought to ensure that, in the event of the abolition of the Seanad, certain provisions of the Constitution could no longer be changed by ordinary legislation, unless a general election had intervened in the meantime. Proposing this amendment, John A. Costello, a former Attorney General, identified twenty-one articles which were safeguards of citizens' rights,[2] describing them as 'fundamental articles of the Constitution'.[3]

While rejecting the proposed amendment, de Valera explained his attitude to fundamental constitutional rights: 'There are in the Constitution two types of articles. There are those which might be inserted in the constitution of any democratic state and there are those which everybody knows were inserted in the Constitution here because of a threat of war and outside pressure.'[4] Continuing, he stated that he proposed to have the 'fundamental articles dealing with the democratic foundations of the state' carefully examined. He also indicated his preferred method of safeguarding them: 'I do not mind if these are fixed so that they cannot be changed by ordinary legislation without some such provision as a referendum of the people. I hold that the method by which the will of the people should be tested in regard to the articles of the Constitution should be by way of referendum.'[5]

He made one other significant comment: 'When we talk about constitutions we are dealing with very fundamental things.'[6] In keeping with his intention to have the fundamental articles examined, de Valera established a committee on 24 May

1934. Under its terms of reference the committee was charged with examining the Free State Constitution 'with a view to ascertaining what articles should be regarded as fundamental, on the ground that they safeguard democratic rights, and to make recommendations as to steps which should be taken to ensure that such articles should not be capable of being altered by the ordinary process of legislation'.

The persons appointed to serve were: Stephen Roche, secretary of the Department of Justice; Michael McDunphy, assistant secretary in the Department of the President; Phillip O'Donoghue, an assistant in the Office of the Attorney General; and John Hearne.[7] All of them had legal training and expertise.[8] The committee met on ten occasions, from 28 May to 3 July 1934, when it produced its report. Hearne attended all but two meetings.[9] At the second meeting on 29 May, the members examined the Constitution, article by article, and agreed that the report should take the form of an entirely new constitution.[10] De Valera, however, made it clear to the committee that what he really wanted was 'not a new constitution, but a selection within the framework of the present Constitution of those articles which should be regarded as fundamental'. Furthermore, he required 'a recommendation as to how these should be rendered immune from alteration by ordinary legislation'.[11]

These instructions were very significant, as they indicated that de Valera had not yet decided to introduce a new fundamental law. At its third meeting, the committee noted de Valera's clarification of its role, the minutes recording that Hearne's concurrence was secured by telephone. The members present continued their examination of various articles of the Constitution.[12] A first draft of a report, compiled by McDunphy, was circulated to members on 9 June.[13] At a meeting held on 18 June, McDunphy's draft was used as the basis of a discussion of nineteen articles.[14] The next day five more articles were discussed.[15] On 20 June, it was resolved that another draft be prepared by McDunphy[16] and this was circulated on 25 June,[17] for consideration on 27 June.[18] There were three more meetings and the text of the final report was approved on 3 July.[19]

The Review Committee produced a report consisting of an introduction and eight appendices.[20] Twenty-two articles or parts thereof were regarded as fundamental and recommended to be rendered immune from easy alteration. These were identified in Appendix A:[21]

Article 6: Liberty of the person.
Article 7: Inviolability of citizens' dwellings.
Article 8: Freedom of conscience and free practice of religion.
Article 9: Right of free expression and peaceable assembly.
Article 18: Immunity of members of the Oireachtas.
Article 19: Privilege of official reports etc. of the Oireachtas.

Article 24: Oireachtas to hold at least one session a year.

Article 28: General election and reassembly of Dáil.

Article 41: Presentation of bills for royal assent.

Article 43: Prohibition on retrospective legislation.

Article 46: Oireachtas to have sole right to raise and regulate army.

Article 49: Participation in war.

Article 50: Amendments of the Constitution.

Article 61: Central funds.

Article 62: Appointment of comptroller and auditor general.

Article 63: Removal of comptroller and auditor general.

Article 64: Organisation of courts.

Article 65: Powers of High Court in the matter of validity of laws.

Article 66: Jurisdiction of Supreme Court.

Article 68: Appointment and removal of judges.

Article 69: Judicial independence.

Article 70: Military tribunals.

In identifying the articles, Appendix A contained a note on the committee's views respecting each of them.[22] In the case of eleven of the articles, it was observed that 'we do not suggest that any alteration should be made in the text'.[23] In relation to ten others, the committee's notes varied both in degree of detail and the extent of suggested alterations for the purpose of improving the sense of the article.[24] The note pertaining to Article 24 may serve as an example of this aspect of the committee's work.[25] The article read: 'The Oireachtas shall hold at least one session each year. The Oireachtas shall be summoned and dissolved by the representative of the Crown in the name of the King and subject as aforesaid Dáil Éireann shall fix the date of re-assembly of the Oireachtas.' The committee observed that the article provided for three distinct matters:

(a) The holding of at least one session of the Oireachtas each year.
(b) The summoning and dissolving of the Oireachtas by the representative of the Crown in the name of the King.
(c) The right of Dáil Éireann subject to (b) to fill the date of re-assembly.

The principles embodied in (a) and (c) were deemed to be fundamental. It was recommended that they be separated from (b) and made the subject of a distinct article or articles. Regarding (a), it was observed that the obvious intention of this provision was to ensure that democratic control through parliament was not defeated by unduly prolonged non-assembly of that body. However, the article did not prescribe any specific mechanism or charge any individual or institution with the responsibility of putting it into effect. The committee was not unduly concerned at this juncture as the Oireachtas was required to assemble annually for the purpose of voting monies to the executive (under the terms of Article 36). What did concern the four civil servants was a situation 'in which the Oireachtas might be induced to forgo this practice and to empower an executive to obtain the necessary monies without having to resort annually to parliament'. The relevant provisions of other constitutions were considered to address this issue. Those of seven countries – Czechoslovakia, Denmark, Estonia, Germany, Yugoslavia, Mexico and Poland – were examined and their relevant provisions reproduced in Appendix E of the report.[26] On the basis of this examination, the committee concluded that the possibility of prolonged non-assembly could be addressed by requiring

(i)   That parliament shall meet on a specified date in each year, if not previously convoked, and/or

(ii) That if a certain proportion of the total number of its members so requires, parliament must be convened within a prescribed time.

The observations on Article 65 were perhaps some of the most interesting and significant. This article stated: 'The judicial power of the High Court shall extend to the question of the validity of any law having regard to the provisions of the Constitution.' The committee's members accepted as a fundamental principle that some court should have the power to determine the constitutional validity of laws. They could not, however, agree on the judicial mechanism to achieve this:

In the course of our consideration of this article, the following points were discussed, *viz*:
    Whether the power of deciding the validity of laws, having regard to the provisions of the Constitution, should be vested
(a) In the Supreme Court alone, or
(b) In a special 'Constitution' Court appointed or designated for that purpose, e.g. a combination of the Supreme and High Courts, or
(c) In the High Court with a right of appeal to the Supreme Court as at present.[27]

The idea of a constitutional court was a radical one and the fact that it was discussed by the committee highlighted that its members were willing to consider suggestions which were not constrained by the conservative legal system prevailing in Ireland at the time. Moreover, this discussion demonstrated that they 'must have had a very sophisticated understanding of the dynamics of constitutional law'.[28]

In relation to the same article, there was a discussion as to 'whether a time limit, commencing from the date of enactment in each case should be fixed within which the question of validity of any law could be submitted to or decided on by the courts'.[29] This was considered because constitutional lawyers recognised that a procedure which allowed for a swift and certain determination as to the constitutionality of a particular law might prove of great value. However, again the committee could not reach unanimity on this matter, but it could be that this proposal contained the germ of Article 26 of the 1937 Constitution, by which the President may refer a bill passed by the Houses of the Oireachtas to the Supreme Court to decide on its constitutionality.[30]

Finally, the committee's observations on Article 50 deserve some attention. This determined the procedures for amending the Constitution. The members stated that they would address this constitutional provision in a separate report, as the subject matter of the article had a direct bearing on the second part of the committee's terms of reference: 'a recommendation as to how the articles regarded as fundamental should be rendered immune from alteration by ordinary legislation'.[31] This second report was never produced. In the memorandum recording the signing of the first part, the following sentence was added, apparently sometime later: 'No action was taken on part 2 of the committee's terms of reference. The matter gradually became one of government policy and was dealt with on that basis.'[32] Article 50 was considered, however, in the first draft of the report. Significantly, all the members, except Stephen Roche, favoured 'requiring that there must be a popular vote in a referendum in favour of any change in any of the fundamental articles before such changes can become law ...'[33]

Emergency provisions

For much of the first decade of its existence, the Free State was forced to counter the threat presented by a republican minority that rejected the Treaty settlement and sought to subvert the constitutional dispensation established by it. The government had recourse to emergency legislation which conferred on the authorities exceptional powers to address a difficult security situation.[34] One of the most draconian measures was enacted by the Constitution (Amendment No. 17) Act 1931, which inserted Article 2A into the document. This, in fact, was an elaborate anti-terrorism law, containing thirty-four sections.[35] This highly controversial measure was suspended by de Valera's government; significantly, it did not repeal it. The new President appreciated the threat presented by political extremism and, in due course, he faced the Charybdis of republican militants and the Scylla of Blueshirt activists.[36] In a comment informed by this appreciation, de Valera told the Dáil in April 1934 that 'it is necessary to ensure, in cases of real urgency and real public emergency, that an executive would not be prevented from taking the action that might be considered necessary to safeguard public interests'.[37]

The Constitution Review Committee gave detailed consideration to the issue of emergency legislation because of the presence of Article 2A. A memorandum prepared by Stephen Roche described its inclusion in the Constitution as 'grotesque'[38] and, in his opinion, 'It must go'.[39] He presented alternative proposals to deal with periods of emergency and this and another memorandum[40] formed the basis of the Committee's deliberations.[41] Its observations and recommendations were contained in the report's introduction and in Appendix B attached thereto.

In the introduction, the members of the Committee stated that they had given special consideration to Article 2A and it was their view that, in its present form, it was 'not a proper one for retention in the Constitution'. They realised the 'great importance' of providing safeguards to prevent special powers being resorted to except in a state of public emergency. At the same time, however, it was necessary to ensure that a government which had a real need to invoke such measures was not hampered or defeated by appeals to the courts based on the exercise of normal constitutional rights.[42]

In Appendix B,[43] the opinion was expressed that the first serious phase in the development of a grave state of disorder was the failure of the ordinary courts to secure the conviction of offenders. The proposed solution was that the Constitution should contain a permanent provision to supplement the operation of these ordinary courts by the establishment of special ones. This proposal, for convenient reference, was called 'Scheme A' and was regarded as a 'preventive measure', aimed at stopping the development of a state of public emergency. Should such an emergency occur, the state would have to respond and the proposed response was termed 'Scheme B'. This would entail the substitution of a new article for 2A, authorising the Oireachtas to provide by ordinary legislation such powers as were considered necessary to counter this threat, including the right to temporarily suspend any articles of the Constitution. This proposed article should state that nothing in the Constitution or in any act of the Oireachtas could be invoked to invalidate anything in the article or any legislation enacted under it.[44]

Constitution Review Committee: an assessment

In discharging their responsibilities, the members of the Constitution Review Committee were methodical and meticulous, displaying a very high level of professionalism and competence. Their exacting approach has been illustrated by the earlier account of their discussions on Article 24. In his history of the Special

Criminal Court, Fergal Davis described their work in relation to emergency provisions as 'thorough': 'This group was to spend some time developing a suitable compromise between the need for constitutional legitimacy and the need to properly equip the government in dealing with extremism.'[45] The accuracy of this assessment is apparent in the discussion of Appendix B in the previous section.

The consideration of other articles resulted in the production of relevant appendices. Regarding Article 9, which protected the free expression of opinion and peaceable assembly, the provision in seven other constitutions was examined (Appendix D),[46] while provisions for the declaration of war were reviewed in eleven constitutions (Appendix F).[47] In all, during deliberations on these and other issues, various provisions of thirteen constitutions were considered.[48]

The most significant and important aspect of the work of the Committee's members was their identification of those articles which were fundamental in terms of protecting the personal and democratic rights of citizens. They sought to devise a mechanism to safeguard those same rights against abrogation by ordinary acts of the Oireachtas and, as was noted earlier, considered the option of a referendum to achieve this. The drafters of the report were determined to reinforce fundamental constitutional rights and regarded judicial review as a central element of the Constitution's capacity to protect them. The majority valued judicial review of legislation[49] and were so committed to it as an essential feature of the constitutional life of the state that they considered the establishment of a separate constitutional court.

The work and report of the Committee were to contribute to some of the more notable features of the 1937 Constitution. A few have been mentioned briefly already: Article 26 (providing for presidential reference of bills to the Supreme Court for a determination of their constitutionality) and the referendum. The proposals on emergency powers were also to be influential. Therefore, the report had an impact on the drafting of a number of provisions contained in Bunreacht na hÉireann and was a significant, even critical step in the process that led to the 1937 Constitution. Much groundwork was done by the 1934 Committee and this facilitated the transition between the two documents.[50] Crucially, it did this by identifying the articles of the 1922 document necessary for the maintenance and preservation of democracy and basic rights, and these were to be incorporated in the later version. The determination to preserve judicial review was also carried through and informed the work of its drafters.[51] Therefore, to quote Gerard Hogan: 'It may thus be stated that the success of the 1937 Constitution is due in no small measure to the foresight and legal acumen of the members of the 1934 Constitution [Review] Committee, whose report paved the way for its enactment.'[52]

Hogan's praise for the members of the Committee highlights that the report heralded the key role to be played by civil servants in constitution-making. Three of the four who served on this Committee were to be involved in the drafting of the 1937 Constitution (Roche was excepted) and the central figure, John Hearne, was to be heavily influenced by his membership of it.[53] While it is not possible to identify his personal contributions to the work of the Committee, he was, nevertheless, an active contributor to its deliberations and recommendations. Through this he achieved a thorough understanding of the Free State Constitution and an appreciation of the significance of fundamental rights and judicial review. He was willing to consider innovations such as a constitutional court, radical in terms of the prevailing conservatism of the legal profession. Hearne's membership of the 1934 Constitution Review Committee may be considered a kind of intense preparation for his later and more significant endeavours and he was to emerge from this Committee a mage in matters constitutional as they pertained to the Irish Free State.

Draft heads of a constitution: the 'squared paper draft', 1935

No action was taken on the 1934 report. De Valera and his government were preoccupied with the Economic War and the threat presented by the Blueshirts.[54] Another significant political consideration in determining his response was the fact that the desirability of identifying and protecting fundamental articles of the Constitution had been suggested by deputies from the opposition Fine Gael party. De Valera was not going to give his opponents any credibility by appearing to respond to their concerns. In any case, he had other plans when he again turned his attention to constitutional matters in April 1935.

On 30 April and 2 May, de Valera had meetings with John Hearne. A record of these conversations has been preserved in a document which has come to be known as 'the squared paper draft'.[55] This was written in de Valera's own handwriting on thirteen pages of a mathematics copy. It was his contemporaneous personal record of the conversations between the two men. It was not a draft of a constitution; rather it was a record of discussions regarding a proposed draft, an unofficial memorandum of dialogue and instructions. While, unsurprisingly, de Valera dominated the deliberations, Hearne made a significant contribution, as is apparent from an examination of the document.

In the first three pages, de Valera noted what were, in effect, six fundamental principles of any proposed new constitution. It was to herald a new constitutional dispensation, fundamentally different from that based on the Treaty settlement. Thus the state was to be called Éire, a name change in which the President intended to consign the Irish Free State and all its repellent associations for republicans to history. Secondly, Éire was to be sovereign, independent and democratic in character. Mindful of the practical implications of partition, the third principle stated that 'the territory of Éire shall be such as from time to time may come within the jurisdiction of Éire'. The fourth envisaged that the ultimate 'sovereign power'[56] was to rest with the people, 'who shall be the ultimate court for deciding all national and practical problems'. The fifth principle was a development of the previous one: 'all governmental authority – legislative,[57] executive[58] and judicial' – was to be derived from the people, 'under God'. All power was to be exercised by organs of government established by the Constitution. Finally, consistent with the ideal of the sovereignty of the people, the state's fundamental law could only be changed by referendum.

The rest of the draft concerned itself with the more practical implications of a revised constitution. The fourth page recorded that the legislature would be composed of Dáil Éireann, elected by proportional representation, and Seanad Éireann. There was a question mark, however, placed after the word Seanad; clearly, de Valera was undecided about the restoration of a second parliamentary chamber which he was then in the process of abolishing.

A reading of page five indicates that eight very diverse topics were addressed: 'flag', 'language', 'religion', 'coat of arms', 'constitutional court', 'council of state', 'regional and subordinate parl[iament]s' and the proposal to establish an office of President of Éire. In the case of the first seven items, no details of substance were given; words naming them were simply recorded. It is possible to identify, with a measure of certainty, specific subjects on which Hearne made a contribution. The concept of a constitutional court was one with which he was more familiar than his minister. He certainly advised de Valera in relation to the new office of President. The words 'German President' were written – he was discussed as a possible constitutional model for the new Irish President. This was confirmed by a note: 'page 187'; this referred to a page in a book entitled *Select Constitutions of the World*, which contained the articles in the Weimar Constitution pertaining to the President of Germany. It is likely that Hearne, a constitutional expert, gave de Valera this reference and information on the German presidency.

The notes on page six were not completed but their substance is clear. The Constitution was to permit association with 'any league or group of states'. The league in question was the League of Nations and the group of states the British Commonwealth of Nations. Regarding the latter, de Valera's concept of external association was to be given constitutional expression. The importance of this issue was highlighted by the fact that it was discussed again by the two men. On page ten, it was recorded that 'Éire may associate itself with any other state or group of states or become a member of any league of states or nations.'

Page seven listed areas to be covered by 'organic laws', i.e. laws which the Oireachtas would be empowered to enact to give effect to basic constitutional principles. The concept of an organic law was one with which Hearne was very familiar[59] and he probably made a significant contribution to this part of the discussion. Nine areas which could possibly be covered by such laws were listed, including: election of the Dáil and its constituencies; election and composition of the Seanad; the setting-up of the judiciary; and treason. Emergency powers were also identified, as evidenced by a reference to 'Constitution, 2A Law'. On this matter, Hearne was certain to have made some observations as it had been discussed in detail by the Constitution Review Committee of which he was a member.

In the 'squared paper draft', de Valera noted an incomplete and very rough outline of a preamble: 'The Irish[60] people acknowledges[61] their dependence on Almighty God, thanks him for the preservation of their nation, dedicates themselves to his service, accepts the ten commandments[62] as fundamental[63] law, give themselves this Constitution so as to' (this was the extent of the text). At the end of the page was a note to 'see' the Proclamation of 1916;[64] the Declaration of Independence 1919;[65] and the Democratic Programme.[66] The preamble envisaged by de Valera was to be Christian (though it was not specifically Roman Catholic in this draft) and nationalist, thus giving expression to the two great influences which he believed shaped the Irish state.

The next matters considered by de Valera and Hearne were the transitional arrangements to apply in the event of a new constitution. This was a technical aspect of the whole process of constitution-making and, in the 'squared paper draft', it was recorded that 'the next parliament shall be at liberty to pass organic laws with immediate effect, but [these] must be ratified by referendum at [the] time of the next general election'. Apparently, what was being envisaged was a means whereby unforeseen issues or defects in the document could be addressed immediately and ratified later by referendum. The laws which would have to be carried over were identified and some of them recorded: 'electoral boundaries', 'judiciary' and the 'Ministers and Secretaries Act'.[67] Given the technical nature of the subject under consideration, Hearne would almost certainly have had a significant input to the discussion.

On page eleven, there is evidence that there was a discussion of the fundamental rights to be enjoyed by all citizens. No details were noted, apart from two incomplete sentences: 'The state guarantees to all its citizens'; and 'To the family it guarantees etc.' Most of this page recorded a conversation concerning the relationship between Ireland and Britain – the heading on the top of the page was 'Br', meaning Britain. The first point referred to the fact that 'S.W.F note ... shows no real apprec[iation] of the fundamentals in the problem'. S.W.F. was an abbreviation for Sir Warren Fisher, the permanent under-secretary of the British Treasury. It would appear that the discussion centred on the implications of a particular note. De Valera recorded: 'many times pointed[68] out that the I[rish] people have no imperial[69] interests or aspirations. They want to keep out of war. The only right they concede is that I[reland] should[70] not be used as basis of attack on Britain'. The discussion was a recognition that constitutional changes would impact on the fundamental relationship between the two countries. The conversation also serves as a reminder of the tensions in Anglo-Irish and international relations which formed the backdrop to de Valera's decisions regarding constitutional change.

The last two pages of de Valera's notes refer to a wide range of topics which he and Hearne considered. No significant details were given, just headings and incomplete sentences. The headings included: 'secret voting', 'laws', 'recall' and 'tribunal'. The incomplete sentences allow for reasonable conjecture about what was being discussed. On page twelve, under a heading 'laws of treason', a note suggested that the constitutional court would determine those matters which would not come under the category of treason. On this same page, de Valera recorded: 'powers and duties in addition to those prescribed in constn [constitution] by law' – this could refer to additional powers being conferred on the President by law. On page thirteen, there was a note which may refer to the circumstances in which a referendum was envisaged. The first referred to amendments of the Constitution.[71] The second reads: 'organ[ic] laws at discretion of P' – a possible reference to a discussion between the two men on the power of the President to refer a proposed law to the people for their decision in a referendum. The third point, as noted by de Valera, referred to 'major legislation at request of majority of 2nd H[ouse]', possibly a reference to an idea that the second House of the Oireachtas could be empowered to request that a bill deemed to address a matter of importance be submitted to the people in a referendum.

In the course of their meetings on 30 April and 2 May, de Valera and Hearne had wide-ranging discussions on constitutional changes. This was the President's personal political project; he was very certain of the essential elements to be contained in the draft to be drawn up by Hearne. The legal adviser, however, made significant contributions to the deliberations, not least ideas relating to a constitutional court, the proposed new office of President of Éire, the issue of organic laws, emergency provisions and transitional arrangements. The handwriting in the 'squared paper draft' was often untidy, even illegible; words were abbreviated and sentences not completed, evidence of de Valera writing in great haste during what appears to have been, at times, a prolific exchange of ideas. The principal purpose of the meetings was for de Valera to issue instructions. However, on the evidence of the notes, it is clear that Hearne made a significant contribution to what turned out to be a real dialogue between the President and the legal adviser.

Draft heads of a constitution

Arising out of their conversations, Hearne prepared draft heads of a constitution. The instructions given to him by de Valera were recorded in an explanatory memorandum, dated 17 May 1935, which accompanied the document. It stated: 'In general, the instructions of the President were to prepare a draft of the heads of a new constitution for Saorstát Éireann.' In particular, the draft was to contain certain basic articles guaranteeing fundamental human rights:

(a) To place the said articles in a specially protected position, i.e., to render them unalterable save by the people themselves or by an elaborate constitutional process;

(b) To provide for the suspension of the said articles during a state of public emergency only;

(c) To contain machinery for effectively preserving public order during such emergency;

(d) To provide for the establishment of the office of President of Saorstát Éireann, the holder of which would fulfil all the functions now exercised by the King and Governor-General in internal affairs; and

(e) To contain provisions for the retention of the King as a constitutional officer of Saorstát Éireann in the domain of international relations.[72]

Hearne completed the draft heads by 17 May and submitted them to de Valera. The document was composed of a preamble and fifty-three articles, arranged as follows:

Article 1: Nature of the state.
Article 2: Citizenship.
Article 3: Language.
Articles 4–14: President.
Articles 15–30: Oireachtas.
Articles 31–3: Council of Ministers [government].
Articles 34–5: Judicial power.
Articles 36–7: Comptroller and auditor general.
Articles 38–42: Fundamental rights.
Articles 43–5: Trial of criminal offences.
Article 46: Emergency powers.
Articles 47: War and defence.
Articles 48–9: Treaty-making power.
Article 50: Amendment of the Constitution.
Articles 51–3: Technical sections.[73]

Hearne's draft contained a number of notable features. Article 1 defined the Free Sate as 'an independent sovereign state'. It continued: 'All powers of government and all authority, legislative, executive and judicial, derived from God through the people, shall be exercised in Saorstát Éireann through the organisations continued or established by, or established under, and in accord with this constitution.' Eleven articles related to the newly created office of President. He was to be elected by the people and a citizen had to have completed his thirty-fifth year to be eligible for election.[74] The presidential term of office was to be seven years and a President was eligible for re-election. Should a President die in office, an election for a successor was to be held not later than two months from the date of the President's death. In the event of a President becoming ill or incapacitated for more than six months, the Council of Ministers was empowered to call on Dáil Éireann to appoint a Deputy President to act until the President could resume the functions of office. Article 5 prescribed an oath to be taken by the President when entering upon office.

Seven articles related to the powers and functions of the President. The supreme command of the defence forces was vested in him. Article 7 declared that 'The President shall ... represent Saorstát Éireann in international relations.' The duties in this respect were to include: the appointment of diplomatic representatives in other states; the negotiation and conclusion of treaties; the signing of the full powers of plenipotentiaries empowered to conclude international treaties and the signing of the instruments of ratification of such treaties. The President was to have power to remit or commute sentences imposed by courts. Under the terms of Article 9, he was to appoint the Prime Minister on the nomination of Dáil Éireann and ministers on the nomination of the Prime Minister. He was also to appoint the judges of the Supreme and High Courts. Bills passed by the Dáil were to be presented to him for his assent and all the powers and duties of the Governor-General were to be performed by him. Article 14, however, stated that all the powers and duties conferred on the President by the Constitution were exercisable only upon the advice of the government.

Hearne's draft provided for a unicameral legislature, Dáil Éireann, and, by the terms of Article 34, the power to determine the validity of any law having regard to the Constitution was vested in the High Court, with a right of appeal to the Supreme Court. Thus judicial review was enshrined in the draft heads. The fundamental rights of citizens were recognised in Articles 38 to 42 inclusive. These rights included recognition of freedom of conscience and free expression of religion; the right of free expression of opinion and peaceable assembly; personal liberty; and the inviolability of citizens' dwellings. Article 46 addressed the matter of emergency powers. In essence, Dáil Éireann, or the government should the Dáil not be in session, was to be empowered to declare a state of emergency, if satisfied that a grave state of public disorder existed. Such a declaration would suspend temporarily the operation of specified articles of the Constitution for the duration of the emergency period.

Nothing in the same document could be invoked to nullify any provision of this article or legislation enacted under it. Article 50 was concerned with amending the basic law. It stated that the Oireachtas could amend any articles with the exception of those pertaining to fundamental rights. Such articles could only be altered by referendum. Critically, Article 50 itself was also protected from amendment by the Oireachtas, it too requiring change by referendum.

The last three articles of the draft heads dealt with technical aspects of any proposed constitutional changes. Articles 51 and 52 were concerned with the state seals and the continuance of laws should the Constitution of 1922 be repealed. The last article, under the heading 'Transitory Provisions', addressed the situation of the Free State's continuing association with the British Commonwealth and the practical implications regarding foreign relations. It was stated that specified documents 'shall before being issued be countersigned by the Minister for Foreign Affairs'. What was not mentioned was that they would also be signed by the King.

Draft heads and the 1922 Constitution: the differences

The draft heads differed in many and important respects from the 1922 Constitution. Hearne's document fundamentally redefined the Free State's relationship with Britain. There was no reference to the Treaty; the British Commonwealth was mentioned only in terms of the state being associated with it for the exercise of functions in the area of foreign policy. The King was removed from the internal affairs of the state, this break with the Crown being highlighted by the establishment of the office of President. The composition of the Oireachtas was altered and it became a unicameral legislature. A procedure regarding amendment of the Constitution was included to protect fundamental rights and the amendment article itself. Hearne's draft also addressed the issue of emergency powers in time of grave public disorder. These differences from the 1922 document were reflected in twenty-two new articles in the draft[75] and were in accord with the instructions de Valera gave Hearne.

Influences on the draft heads

The most significant influences on the draft heads were the instructions of de Valera, as detailed in the explanatory memorandum, and Hearne's meetings with him, into which the 'squared paper draft' gives an insight. The memorandum referred to guarantees of fundamental rights; provisions to address a state of emergency; and the establishment of an office of President. The 'squared paper draft' recorded these and other concerns. The latter included: an expression of the sovereign and independent character of the state and provisions for a referendum. The draft heads contained articles relating to all these matters, a fact which is hardly surprising given the President's views on them.

The Constitution of 1922 also had an influence on Hearne's draft heads. Twenty-eight articles in the draft were identical or essentially identical to articles in that document. Fourteen articles were transposed from the 1922 Constitution.[76] Many of these related to the institutions of state: six to the Dáil or Oireachtas;[77] and one to the comptroller and auditor general.[78] Four of the articles guaranteeing fundamental human rights were inserted unchanged.[79] Fourteen of the articles in the draft heads were essentially identical; by this is meant that the principles and sense underlying them were unchanged from the 1922 Constitution, as was much, if not most of the language in many instances.[80] Some of the changes simply reflected the removal of the Crown from the state's internal affairs. Article 37 of the Free State Constitution may serve as an illustration; it read: 'Money shall not be appropriated by vote, resolution or law, unless the purpose of the appropriation has in the same session [of the Dáil] been recommended by a message from the representative of the Crown acting on the advice of the Executive Council.' In Hearne's draft Article 30, the President (newly created) replaced the representative of the Crown and the Executive Council was renamed the Council of Ministers. Hearne wrote two articles in the draft pertaining to the courts[81] and these were an amalgam of six articles in the 1922 document.[82]

Clearly, the 1922 Constitution had a very significant influence on Hearne's draft. This inclusion of many articles taken from the former was greatly facilitated by the report of the Constitution Review Committee. As was noted earlier, this report had identified twenty-two articles in the Constitution which were deemed fundamental. Hearne effectively included twenty of them.[83] His membership of that Committee ensured that its report was to be another influence on his draft heads.

One of the more innovative features of the draft was the establishment of the office of President. In this regard, Hearne was greatly influenced by the articles in the Weimar Constitution relating to the German presidency, a fact noted earlier in the discussion of the 'squared paper draft'. There are striking similarities between the provisions in both documents, as is evident below:

Articles in draft heads relating to the President	**Articles in Weimar relating to the President**
Article 4	
To be elected by the people.	Article 41
To be at least 35 years old.	Article 41
To serve seven-year term.	Article 43
To be eligible for re-election.	Article 43
May not be member of Dáil.	Article 44

Article 5

Oath to be taken by President.   Article 42

Article 6

To be supreme commander of armed forces.   Article 47

Article 7

To represent state in international relations.   Article 45

Article 8

Right to pardon and remit sentences   Article 49

Article 9

Appoint ministers on nomination of Prime Minister.   Article 53

Equality provision, Article 38 and other aspects

In accordance with de Valera's instructions, fundamental human rights were identified and guaranteed in the draft heads in Articles 39–42. However, this emphasis on human rights reflected Hearne's concerns more than those of de Valera. As a constitutional lawyer, he had a more developed sense of such rights and of the means to protect them. This fact becomes more apparent in a consideration in Chapter 6 of Hearne's advocacy of a constitutional court and judicial review, and of addresses he gave while on diplomatic service in Canada and the United States. An additional stand-alone article was included by Hearne in the draft heads, which had no counterpart in the 1922 document. This Article 38 read as follows: 'All citizens of Saorstát Éireann are equal before the law.' An identical provision was to be found in the Weimar Constitution: 'All Germans are equal before the law.'[84] Other constitutions also had such an article, using similar language. The Polish Constitution declared: 'All citizens are equal before the law,'[85] while that of Austria stated: 'All citizens of the federation are equal before the law.'[86] Hearne's draft article was clearly based on equality articles in various European constitutions and it was also influenced by the fourteenth amendment of the United States' Constitution guaranteeing the equal protection of laws for all citizens.[87] Article 38 was a 'conscious innovation' and intended by him to be 'progressive and egalitarian'.[88] It was a testimony to Hearne's determination that the fundamental law of the Irish state protect the rights of all its citizens.

Two other aspects of Hearne's draft deserve attention. One was his preamble, written in an elegant and direct style:

In the name of Almighty God, We, the sovereign Irish People through our elected representatives assembled in this Dáil Éireann sitting as a constituent assembly, in order to declare and confirm our constitutional rights and liberties, consolidate our national life, establish and maintain domestic peace on a basis of freedom, equality and justice, ensure harmonious relations with neighbouring peoples, and promote the ultimate unity of Ireland do hereby, as of undoubted right, ordain and enact this Constitution.

What is striking is that it bore little relationship to de Valera's rough version in the 'squared paper draft'. His was pronouncedly religious; Hearne's was not. Nor was Hearne's overly nationalistic. Perhaps this draft gave expression more to the ideas of its drafter than its instigator; it owed more to Hearne's ideas than de Valera's and may be one of the occasions in the process of constitution-making when John Hearne revealed some of the idealism which informed his vision of the state's basic law.

The second aspect deserving comment is that Hearne's draft was conspicuously secular in tone when compared to the 1937 Constitution. A former Chief Justice Ronan Keane, commenting on the document, observed:

The special position of the Catholic Church was not mentioned, there was no prohibition on divorce legislation and his draft preamble was in stark contrast to the overtly religious preamble in the Constitution as enacted. Nor was there any equivalent to the articles ultimately included guaranteeing private property and family rights and heavily influenced by Catholic social teaching.[89]

Gerard Hogan has commented: 'It was perhaps asking too much of the Ireland of the 1930s to adopt a draft as noble, as fair-minded and secular as this.'[90] It is important, however, not to read too much significance into the secular tone. This draft was heavily influenced by the Constitution of 1922, reflecting the essentially secular tone of that document. Crucially, as will be seen later in this chapter, Hearne's draft heads were intentionally framed within the structures of that fundamental law. The draft preserved much of it and this included its secular tone. This secular tone owed more to the influence of the 1922 Constitution than to any personal disposition of the author of the draft heads.

An essentially democratic and liberal document, Hearne's draft of 1935 is an important landmark in the history of the making of the 1937 Constitution. It is also a document of considerable merit in its own right. Ronan Keane has paid it the following tribute: 'If radical new constitution-framing becomes unavoidable, we could do worse than adopt as our template the spare and elegant draft produced all those years ago by an unknown civil servant, John Hearne.'[91] The fact that Hearne produced such a document single-handedly in such a short time is a tribute to his skill and imagination in the complex area of constitution-making.

The completion of the draft heads did not mean that all issues relating to constitutional change had been addressed in that document. In his explanatory

memorandum of 17 May 1935, Hearne referred to the 'specially difficult problem of
fitting the King as a constitutional officer for the purposes of international relations
only into the framework of a state internally organised on a presidential basis'.[92] As
described earlier, two articles, 7 and 53, concerned themselves with the President's
role in international relations and with diplomatic arrangements regarding the
state's relationship with the Commonwealth respectively. The whole matter of the
role of the King required further consideration. In a memorandum from Hearne
to de Valera in October 1935 the legal adviser wrote of the 'particular problem to
which you referred in our recent conversations, namely, that of excluding the King
from the internal constitution of the state, while at the same time continuing (with
some modifications) the existing practice in the sphere of international relations'. He
presented the President with four other possible drafts of Articles 7 and 53, these
being variations on the ones contained in the draft heads.[93] The retention of the King
in the international and diplomatic sphere was necessitated by the fact that de Valera
did not envisage formally severing all ties with the British Commonwealth. In terms
of the state's foreign and diplomatic relations, the monarch remained the country's
head of state and was regarded as such by foreign states.

De Valera was also concerned with the constitutional mechanism to determine
the validity of laws. In December 1935, Hearne prepared a memorandum for Seán
Murphy, assistant secretary of the Department of External Affairs, which explained
the practice in other countries. This document was given to de Valera, annotated
by Murphy: 'President, herewith memorandum on constitutional courts in other
countries which you asked for this morning.' In it Hearne referred to the relevant
provisions from the constitutions of six countries – Czechoslovakia, Austria, Spain,
Poland, United States and France – with the observation that only three of them
had a constitutional court so called, namely Czechoslovakia, Austria and Spain.[94]
Obviously, judicial review and the best means to achieve this were being examined by
de Valera and the option of a constitutional court was under consideration.

De Valera decides on a new constitution

At what stage the idea of a completely new constitution crystallised in de Valera's
mind is not clear.[95] Initially, he pursued a policy of constitution-cleansing, purging
the 1922 document of those articles reviled by republicans. He began with the oath
of allegiance and, with a renewed mandate in 1933, he accelerated the pace. Speaking
in the Dáil in May 1933, he stated that 'it was quite clear to the Irish people that
we had in mind the removal of every mark or badge of inferiority, everything in
the Constitution which is not consistent with the rights of the Irish people'. He
announced, in somewhat inelegant terms, that he proposed in a very short time to

introduce 'quite a batch of articles of that sort that will go', a reference to the various amendments he introduced later that year, and described in Chapter 3.[96] A month later he recognised and acknowledged that the proposed amendments would have a significant impact on the character of the 1922 Constitution and that it 'is not at the present time in anything like the form it will finally be in', and with classic understatement observed: 'I think it is bound to change.'[97]

A year later, he spoke of being in a 'transitional period' with regard to the Free State Constitution.[98] But whither was it in transit? While he was engaged in a vigorous policy of amendment, it would appear that he did not intend proceeding at this point to its complete repeal. This sense is confirmed by his instructions to the Constitution Review Committee in May 1934. As noted earlier, Hearne and his civil service colleagues decided that their report would take the form of a new constitution, to be told that the President did not want this. They were to conduct the review within the framework of the existing Free State Constitution. What is clear is that de Valera had not yet decided to introduce a new fundamental law.

Nor is there any evidence of a significant change in attitude when the draft heads are considered. In his instructions to Hearne in 1935, de Valera had dramatic alterations in mind but the proposed draft heads were not presented in the form of a new constitution. In his explanatory memorandum, Hearne wrote that they were 'an attempt to write down the President's instructions and insert them into the text of the existing Constitution rather than an effort to construct, at this stage, a completely new constitution'. This approach Hearne described as 'a preliminary method' which had been adopted for the following reasons:

> The task to be undertaken appears to be to effect a far-reaching constitutional reform within the framework, as far as possible, of the existing state rather than to establish a new state within a constitutional system fundamentally different from that now obtaining. The method adopted has, it is thought, the advantage of showing the precise extent to which the changes contemplated will modify the Constitution of 1922.[99]

In a memorandum to the secretary of the Executive Council Seán Moynihan, dated 18 May 1935, he explained that the draft 'would form a suitable basis for a general discussion with the President at this stage on the scope of the project as a whole'.[100] These memoranda suggest that de Valera had not definitely decided on what course of action to adopt in respect of constitutional change. It would appear that he had not as yet concluded, with certainty, that there was a need for a completely new constitution. While de Valera had radical changes to the existing basic law in mind, these did not necessarily entail, at this juncture, repeal of the existing Free State Constitution of 1922.

There is another matter which may be significant. In the 'squared paper draft', de Valera recorded the name of the state as 'Éire'; this name featured seven times in his notes and the houses of parliament were styled 'Dáil Éireann' and 'Seanad Éireann'.[101] In the draft heads, however, the name 'Saorstát Éireann' was used. This usage was certainly a deliberate decision. In his explanatory memorandum, Hearne wrote of the 'existing state' and a 'new state'. The draft was produced within the framework of the existing Constitution; hence the use of 'Saorstát Éireann'. 'Éire', as understood in the discussions recorded in the 'squared paper draft', suggested a more radical constitution and the draft heads did not justify this description. The draft heads were presented as having been constructed according to 'a preliminary method': they were to be a basis for a discussion of the constitutional project; they were part of a work in progress. The draft did not represent the full consummation of the aspirations suggested by the name 'Éire'. This whole approach to the name of the state was probably adopted subsequent to further instructions from de Valera, of which there is no record. The 'squared paper draft' may not be giving the full picture.

However, nearly two weeks after receiving the draft heads, de Valera declared in the Dáil, on 29 May 1935: 'It is true that we are operating a constitution which has not been wholly ours. I hope before our term expires that we will be able to bring in a constitution which, so far as internal affairs at any rate are concerned, will be absolutely ours.'[102] A month or so later, speaking at Ennis, he told his listeners that 'before the present government left office they would have an Irish constitution from top to bottom'.[103] These sentiments would appear to suggest that he had resolved on a completely new document. However, it is not possible to be absolutely certain of this. De Valera could still have been considering accommodating significant constitutional change within the framework of the existing 1922 Constitution, though the reference to 'a constitution from top to bottom' would indicate an inclination towards a new one.

From the summer of 1935 to the early summer of 1936, de Valera did not significantly advance his constitutional programme. Ongoing economic difficulties and concern over the activities of the Irish Republican Army and the Blueshirts demanded the attention of the President and his government. On a personal level, he was devastated by the death in a riding accident of his son, Brian, in February 1936. It was during a Dáil debate on 28 May 1936 that he stated that the Executive Council hoped to introduce a new constitution in the autumn. This announcement was made in an undramatic manner, as part of his contribution to a debate on the abolition of the Seanad.[104] When the decision to write a new constitution was actually taken is not known; there is no archival record of it.[105] On 8 June, the government gave formal notice to King Edward VIII of its intention in that regard:

The government of Saorstát Éireann, in pursuance of their policy of establishing conditions for permanent peace and harmony amongst the Irish people and providing a more secure basis for friendship and co-operation with the people of Great Britain, intend, at the beginning of the autumn session of parliament, to introduce a bill for the purpose of setting up a new constitution. This constitution will deal with the internal affairs of Saorstát Éireann, leaving unaffected the constitutional usages relating to external affairs. Amongst the provisions of the new constitution will be the creation of the office of President of Ireland and the abolition of the office of Governor-General.[106]

There were many factors which convinced de Valera that such a course of action was essential. According to his official biographers, he believed that he had almost reached the limit of reasonable amendment of the existing Constitution.[107] It had been amended twenty-four times by Cumann na nGaedheal and Fianna Fáil by June 1936 and more than half of its original articles had been altered. A policy of continuous amendments was regarded by de Valera as no longer realistic and had to be abandoned in favour of a new basic law, as he explained to the Dáil in December 1936:

We had intended at one time to continue constitutional amendments, just like those we have put through in the old Constitution, to bring the law in the Constitution into accord with the practice and the real position. But when we had reached a certain position ... I said the time had come when we ought now, with full freedom of action in regard to it, to consider what should be, in our circumstances, our own constitution.[108]

The result of all these changes had been to reduce the Free State Constitution to tatters[109] and to diminish its status as the fundamental law of the state, a fact on which de Valera commented in June 1936, not more than three weeks after the announcement of the government's intention to introduce a new one:

Has anybody, I wonder, looked at a copy of the Constitution and tried to bring it up to date or tried to know exactly what is the Constitution at the moment. I shall be rather interested to know how clear they are in their minds as to the Constitution at the moment. There is no place to which you can refer anybody. I have here a copy of the Constitution which I got specially marked for myself and there are far more lines erased in it than lines left whole.[110]

In a speech prepared for him by Hearne for delivery in late 1937, de Valera observed that the Free State Constitution had

Seventy-two articles (not including certain transitory provisions), of which, as a result of these amendments, only thirty-one remained intact, and of which seventeen had been repealed altogether. When one recalls that the Constitution of the United States had been amended only nineteen times in a period of one hundred and fifty years and the Constitution of the French Republic has been amended on only five or six occasions in the period of half a century, one begins to see the extent of the havoc wrought in so short an interval on the Irish Constitution of 1922.[111]

A second factor, identified in de Valera's Irish biography, was that legal doubts had arisen regarding the amendments to the Constitution introduced by him,[112] a circumstance which had serious implications for the state of constitutional law and his policy of dismantling the Treaty settlement. These doubts arose due to a ruling by the Supreme Court in the matter of *The State (Ryan) v. Lennon* in 1934. The particulars of the case need not concern us here; it was the decision of the judges which was relevant. In it, they accepted that the 1922 Constitution derived its authority from an act of the Dáil, sitting as a constituent assembly but that the Oireachtas did not have the power to amend this same act, the Constitution of the Irish Free State (Saorstát Éireann) Act 1922.[113] This was due to the fact that the constituent assembly which had established the Oireachtas had not conferred on the Oireachtas the power to amend the Constitution of the Irish Free State Act. The significance of this was that the act removing the oath of allegiance also deleted section two of the Constitution Act, by which it was required to construe the Constitution with reference to the Treaty. This was the foundation of this and subsequent amendments but the Supreme Court denied that the Oireachtas had such authority. This placed a large question mark over the validity of all the amendments enacted at de Valera's behest because they all related to the Treaty settlement.[114]

Then in 1935, as was described in Chapter 3, the Privy Council ruled on the validity of the amendment deleting the right of appeal to that body, adding a complication to an already unsatisfactory constitutional situation. The ruling was based on the fact that the Statute of Westminster gave Dominion parliaments the authority to amend statutes passed by the imperial parliament and the Privy Council held that, since the Constitution of the Free State had its legal basis in an act of the British parliament, the Free State Constitution Act 1922, the Dáil could amend it. As a result of both rulings, de Valera found himself, in Gerard Casey's words, 'in a kind of legal limbo'.

He must of necessity have accepted the Supreme Court view of the Constitution's root of title; anything else would have been a denial of his previous career. Yet that view led to unacceptable results. On the other hand, the Privy Council's conclusion was eminently acceptable – but unfortunately it was based on an inadmissible premise.[115]

That de Valera considered himself in this 'legal limbo' was confirmed in a speech prepared for him by Hearne, dated 12 June 1937, and intended for delivery during the final stage debate in the Dáil on the proposed constitution. Though undelivered, it conveyed the legal dilemma in which the Irish government found itself:

> On the dicta of the judges of our own courts – based on the theory that the provisional parliament [the second Dáil] was a constituent assembly – the Treaty of 1921 must remain the legal criterion of the validity of the enactments of our parliament and of the decisions of the people themselves on constitutional questions so long as the system survives. On the view of the position as expressed by the British courts ... the Treaty may be abrogated as a statute of the British parliament ... But here in our own country the Treaty of 1921 is still apparently the law which our courts regard as paramount, basing their judgment on the theory that the provisional parliament of 1922 was a constituent assembly. I hope I have not laboured the point. If I have dwelt upon it for a moment it is because I want to say once and for all that the government were unwilling to allow the national position to be bedevilled any longer by a confused legal situation of that kind.[116]

Neither Irish nor British courts provided acceptable avenues of constitutional development from the President's perspective.[117] Therefore, a new constitution was necessary to resolve the dilemma.

A third factor in his decision was precisely one which the Supreme Court and Privy Council had highlighted – the root of constitutional authority in Ireland. This was fundamental for de Valera and, in the words of his biographers: 'No matter how republican the Free State Constitution was made by amendment, it could never escape its basis in British law. What was needed was a new beginning which drew its strength from Irish roots.'[118] A new constitution would be approved by the people to dispel, finally and convincingly, any doubts as to its legitimacy. 'Given that there was no provision in the existing legal order for an entirely new constitutional dispensation to be enacted, a plebiscite allowed the authority of the new Constitution to be grounded ... [in] the consent and affirmation of the voting "people".'[119]

It is certain that de Valera sought the advice of Hearne on the matter of making a new constitution. While the evidence is incomplete, it is reasonable to assume that the legal adviser favoured such a course of action. He was acutely aware of the ravages wrought on the text of the Free State Constitution by the policy of multiple amendments.[120] He had played a central part in the abolition of the oath and the amendment pertaining to nationality and citizenship.[121] According to Maurice Moynihan, 'when Hearne provided drafts of these bills, he included his conclusions regarding the constitutional implications of their introduction. He was pointing to the need for a new constitution if these bills were introduced'.[122] The Supreme Court's ruling casting doubts on the legal basis of amendments to the Constitution would have offended Hearne's sense of legal order, not least because he had advised that the Oireachtas had the power of amendment. He was a man of very strong and definite views, as was revealed in his memoranda: he would have been trenchant in the expression of his opinion as to the necessity for a new constitution.

In his approach to constitutional change from 1932 to 1935, de Valera sought and was willing to take advice. His principal advisers were civil servants. Foremost among these was John Hearne. The thoroughness and professionalism which de Valera's legal adviser displayed helped advance the process of constitutional development by 1936 in a coherent and considered fashion. Unsurprisingly, it was to his highly accomplished legal adviser that de Valera turned to draft his new constitution. But before he could begin work in earnest, de Valera had yet one more task for him – membership of a commission pertaining to the second House of the Oireachtas.

Second House of the Oireachtas Commission

During the final Dáil debate on abolition of the Seanad in May 1936, de Valera made an interesting, if not surprising comment:

> There is general agreement, perhaps more general agreement on this than on any other political issue in the country, that the Seanad as at present constituted should go, and I am asking the Dáil here to pass the final sentence and to send it off. I say to those who are not convinced that the country would be better served by a single legislative chamber than by two, that the door is not definitely closed.[123]

His apparent willingness to consider the restoration of a second parliamentary chamber in the context of a new constitution (which had been referred to in the debate) reflected 'the considerable support bicameralism had in ecclesiastical, academic, commercial and opposition circles'.[124] De Valera's appreciation of this fact resulted in the establishment, by the Executive Council, on 9 June 1936, of a commission to consider and make recommendations as to what should be the function and powers of the second chamber of the legislature in the event of its being decided to make provision in the constitution for such second chamber and, further, to consider and make recommendations as to how in that event such chamber should be constituted as regards number of members, their qualifications, method of selection ...[125]

There were twenty-three persons nominated to serve on it, including John Hearne. It was a body of some substance: the Chief Justice, Hugh Kennedy, served as chairman and the Attorney General, Conor Maguire, was the vice-chairman.[126] Other notable members included Joseph Connolly,[127] a former Fianna Fáil minister and senator, and distinguished academics and public figures, Michael Tierney[128] and Alfred O'Rahilly.[129]

The commission met on twenty-seven occasions, completing its report on 30 September 1936. Hearne attended twenty-one of the meetings and appeared diligent in the performance of his duties.[130] Sixteen preliminary memoranda were submitted, including one from him.[131] In this document, he detailed his ideas for a second chamber under a number of headings. Regarding the functions of such a body, he argued that experience had shown that, in the examination and criticism of bills, the recently abolished Seanad 'did excellent work of the kind appropriate to a reading of bills in committee'. He was very critical, however, of its attitude to a measure, unspecified by him, relating to an amendment of the Constitution. He had, almost certainly, the abolition of the oath in mind and, although the Seanad was within its constitutional right to act as it did, it did not appear to him 'to be an action appropriate to a second house': 'It is submitted that a second chamber in this country shall not have the constitutional right to pronounce upon questions of domestic or external policy, no matter how clearly such questions arise in the course of the examination of measures in that house.' Hearne was adamant that, as a second chamber could do useful committee work, 'its function should be confined to work of that kind'. This was all the more necessary because 'a bill emerging from the Dáil is frequently an unworkmanlike document, sorely in need of skilful second aid'. Hence, the Seanad's 'sole function should be to discuss and make recommendations upon matters of detail'. It should have 'no power to challenge the principle or policy of bills'.

Concerning the constitution of a second chamber, it should be an integral part of the legislature and a representative assembly. By representative, Hearne meant that 'its members, as regards a portion of their number, might represent particular interests, and as regards the remainder, should be men of practical knowledge and experience of public affairs'. The entire membership of this house would, in his scheme, be nominated by or on the advice of the head of government. Half would be nominated at his discretion, half on the recommendation of certain vocational or other organisations to be defined. It should not have more than forty members, a number Hearne believed to be in keeping with the character and functions of a committee. He 'strongly urged on the commission' that it should not be an elected body, as 'two elected chambers in our parliament will inevitably tend to become competitors, i.e. rival competitors for popularity, no matter what the technical distribution of constitutional functions'.

The issue of the Seanad's role in two particular matters was considered: constitutional amendments and a referendum. Hearne was very definite that it should have none whatsoever in either. He explained that his proposals on the functions of the second chamber related only to 'ordinary legislation' in which constitutional amendments were not included. As for giving it the right to determine the matters or the occasions in which a referendum should take place, he submitted that this would give to the Seanad 'the status of a plebiscitary organ in our Constitution', something he believed to be unacceptable.

In the course of the commission's deliberations, he was to change his mind about the entire Seanad being nominated. At a meeting on 30 June, he proposed that 'a portion' of the membership be appointed on the nomination of the President of the Executive Council. This proposal was not voted on, but on 8 September he presented a modified one. He now favoured one third of the chamber being nominated by the President.[132] It is not possible to identify Hearne's other personal contributions to the commission's work, as the records of its meetings only identify the proposers of motions. He did, however, suggest changes to the text of the report on 11 and 12 September.[133]

Three reports were submitted by the commission for the consideration of the Executive Council, a majority and two minority ones. The majority report, an amalgam agreed on by close and by no means unanimous votes,[134] was signed by nine members, including Hearne. This report recommended that the number of members of the second house should be forty-five,[135] and these to be chosen on account of their 'ability, character, experience and knowledge of public affairs'.[136] Regarding the powers of the chamber, among the recommendations was the provision that no bill could be enacted into law until it had been sent to the second chamber for its consideration.[137] A bill could be initiated in the second house of parliament, with the exception of a money bill.[138] Ministers should have the right to attend and be heard in the second house.[139] It was recommended that the removal of judges and the comptroller and auditor general require a resolution of both Houses of the Oireachtas.[140] In the matter of the method of selecting members to serve in the second chamber, the majority report recommended that one third be nominated by the President of the Executive Council.[141] It was proposed that the remaining members be elected from panels representing the national language and culture, the arts, agriculture and fisheries, industry and commerce, finance, health and social welfare, foreign affairs, education, law, labour and public administration.[142] The electorate would consist of every person who had been a candidate at the immediately preceding general election for the Dáil. This proposal envisaged a scheme of election whereby each elector would be entitled to cast one vote for every 1,000 first preferences received at the general election. A fraction of 1,000 exceeding 500 would be reckoned as 1,000.[143]

One of the minority reports recommended that the Seanad be constituted on a vocational or functional basis.[144] This issue of vocational organisation represented a significant point of difference between this report and the majority one, signed by Hearne. The minority report, recognising that important branches of the country's social and economic life were either unorganised or insufficiently organised along vocational lines, recommended that elected members of the second house 'should be elected by Dáil Éireann from four panels formed before each general election to the second chamber, and constituted largely, but not entirely, by vocational organisations of a substantially representative character'. The panels suggested were: farming and fisheries; labour; industry and commerce; and education and the learned professions.[145] The purpose of the panels was to secure the representation of unorganised or insufficiently organised vocational groups by a system of controlled nomination. This was intended as an interim measure: with the development of vocational organisation provision would ultimately be made for direct election to the Seanad by councils representing vocational interests.[146]

The panels proposed in the majority report served a different purpose. They were to be constituted as a means of selecting persons of responsibility and distinction in their own particular vocation or occupation, thus affording a wide choice of persons 'certainly qualified by their ability, character, knowledge and experience for membership of the house'. The panels were not 'contemplated for the purpose of making the second house a body to represent such vocations or occupations in the discharge of the functions and powers of the second house'.[147] In the majority report, therefore, the panels were a means of identifying eligible and suitable candidates; in the minority report they were a means toward the eventual vocationalisation of the Seanad.

John Hearne entered two reservations in respect of recommendations in the majority report. He dissented from a proposal that members of the second chamber be elected by an electoral college consisting of every person who had been a candidate at the immediately preceding general election for Dáil Éireann. In his opinion, the only 'practicable method' of election was by the Dáil on the system of proportional representation.[148] His second reservation related to a recommendation in the report that persons nominated to the Seanad and those nominated for election should have a competent knowledge of Irish.[149] Hearne, together with eight other members, expressed that they were 'strongly of the opinion that it is due to the dignity of the national language that effective provisions should be made at the outset to ensure and maintain the gradual predominance of Irish as the language of the second house'.[150] Such sentiments were consistent with the Gaelic ideals of the Irish Free State. Language revival existed in the realm of *Idealpolitik* and few were brave enough to set a boundary to the linguistic march of the nation.[151] This reservation, however sincerely expressed, was another example of the rhetoric and gesture which, it was hoped, would presage advance to a universally, if not exclusively, Irish-speaking state.[152]

When the majority report, signed by Hearne, and his preliminary memorandum are compared, it is apparent that he had much to be happy about, while having had to accept the inevitability of compromise on a commission composed of members with divergent views. He favoured a second house nominated by the President; he compromised by proposing one third be nominated and this was accepted. He proposed in his memorandum a membership of not more than forty; forty-five was proposed in the report. He had suggested that a portion of them might represent particular interests and the remainder be men of practical knowledge and experience of public affairs. Given that the selection process was the one where, in the words of the report, 'the greatest diversity of opinion prevailed',[153] the proposal of a panel system represented a reasonable compromise. Hearne was adamant that the second house not be an elected body and it was here that he had to make his greatest compromise. He had to accept that a proportion of the members be elected. He was pleased, however, that a proposal that these be selected by direct vote of the people was rejected.[154]

He, in his turn, rejected the recommended compromise of an electoral system based on general election candidates. This rejection was probably motivated by his concern that the proposal contained the potential for competition between the Dáil and the second chamber because of an element, however attenuated, of popular election in the system. This was the reason he wanted election by the Dáil, to limit this possible effect. Finally, Hearne's contention that the sole function of the second house should be to make recommendations on the details of bills was unrealistic. It reflected the very personal and particular opinion of a punctilious draftsman and represented an unduly narrow view of the role of the second house. The majority report favoured a wider range of functions.

John Hearne's membership of the Second House of the Oireachtas Commission was significant for a number of reasons. First, it confirmed the regard de Valera had for his professional competence and expertise, and the extent to which he reposed confidence in his department's legal adviser when it came to constitutional matters. Second, such membership allowed Hearne personally to make a substantial contribution to an important constitutional issue. Third, and most significantly, his membership meant that Hearne had been centrally involved in all of de Valera's initiatives as they related to the Constitution of the Irish state which pre-dated the one of 1937. He was involved in the drafting of constitutional amendments; he was a member of the 1934 Constitution Review Committee and the 1936 Second House of the Oireachtas Commission; and he drafted heads of a constitution in 1935. All these experiences gave him an unrivalled knowledge of Irish constitutional affairs and served as an unparalleled preparation for the task of drafting a new fundamental law.

CHAPTER 5

Drafting the New Constitution, August 1936–July 1937

É amon de Valera selected John Hearne to draft the new Constitution of the Irish state because he was a civil servant he trusted and admired. Hearne began work on the document in late August 1936 and produced a first official draft by 16 March 1937. For him it was an extremely demanding process and period in his life and, in his proposed biography of his father, his son Maurice wrote:

> Moreover, much of my father's constitutional work was done at night (after his day's work as legal adviser in Iveagh House) in the privacy of his study at no.3 Temple Villas, Palmerston Road, Dublin. On numerous occasions my mother told me – and not without some barely disguised asperity – that she was obliged to stay up late into the night making countless pots of tea and plates of sandwiches for the two men [de Valera and Hearne] as they laboured on. The notion of overtime and expenses was not in the lexicon of senior public servants and senior public representatives in the early days of the state ...[1]

According to an official memorandum dated 30 December 1938, 'the preparation of the original draft was done mainly by Mr John Hearne ... in consultation with the parliamentary draftsman, Mr Matheson, under the personal direction of the President.'[3] The working relationship between de Valera and Hearne was very close and personal, with few people penetrating the effective wall of exclusion decided upon and erected by the former.

One consequence of this is the absence of documentation when it comes to examining the making of the 1937 Constitution. While there are numerous drafts available, many are undated and memoranda explaining the many decisions made are simply not there. Hearne, in particular, kept no papers from this period, a fact noted in the introduction. Even when the Constitution was being prepared for printing, the controller of the stationery office was informed by a senior civil servant that the process was 'carried out under abnormal conditions; the draft was subjected to considerable alteration necessitating many successive amendments, of which it was not possible to keep a record'.[3] Memoranda, minutes of meetings and records of decisions were unnecessary because only two people were involved during most of the drafting. De Valera gave instructions verbally, and Hearne his opinions and advice in the same way, at what were probably regular meetings. While frustrating for historians, it proved to be a very effective modus operandi which perfectly suited the excellent professional relationship between the two men.

What follows in this chapter is an attempt to give a comprehensive narrative overview of the drafting of the Constitution. In relation to the production of the various drafts between August 1936 and March 1937, the focus will be on documents for which it is possible to determine, with reasonable accuracy, a date of composition. The next chapter will consider the factors which informed and shaped the document, and will consider particular articles in greater detail.

Planning the new Constitution, August–October 1936

John Hearne began the work of drafting the Constitution by drawing up a 'Plan of Fundamental Constitutional Law', dated 20 August 1936.[4] It gave an overview of the structure of the proposed document, including the headings of each section and the number of related articles:

A: The preamble.
B: The state: Articles 1 and 2.
C: The sovereignty of the people: Articles 3–5.
D: The national language: Article 6.
E: The national flag: Article 7.
F: The body of citizens: Article 8.
G: Fundamental rights of citizens: Articles 9–13.
H: The parliament: Article 14.
I: The President: Articles 15–26.
J: The Council of Ministers: Articles 27–30.
K: The judicial power: Articles 31–3.
L: The comptroller and auditor general: Article 34.[5]

A brief summary of the contents of each article was also given; for example:

C. The sovereignty of the people
Articles 3, 4 and 5

Article 3: All powers of government vested in the people. Form of state determinable by them. Their absolute right to decide the manner in which the powers of the government are to be exercised.

Article 4: Organic laws to provide and regulate the manner in which certain powers of government are to be exercised.

Article 5: Power to alter Constitution vested in the people.[6]

Most importantly, having outlined the structure and summarised the articles, Hearne wrote a preliminary form of wording for each, up to and including Article 30. Article 3 read as follows:

All powers of government, legislative, executive and judicial in É[ire][7] belong under God to the people of É[ire] and are exercisable only through the organs established by the people of É[ire]. The right of the people of É[ire] to determine the form of the state and to decide the manner in which the said forms of government (or any of them) shall from time to time be exercised or exercisable is hereby declared to be absolute and indefeasible.[8]

By 14 October 1936, Hearne had produced 'Draft Heads of a Constitution'.[9] These gave a more complete and detailed overview of the document, and an insight into the extent to which the drafting process had progressed after two months.

Preliminary: fundamental declarations:

1. The Irish nation.
2. The national territory.
3. The national language.
4. The sovereignty of the people.

Part I: The state: Exercise of sovereign powers: Articles 1–3.

Part II: The President of É[ire]:

A: Creation and tenure of office: Articles 4–13.

B: Powers and functions of the President: Articles 14–26.

Part III: The national parliament:

A: The constitution of parliament: Articles 27–8.

B: Legislative powers of parliament: Articles 29–33.

C: Dáil Éireann: Article 34.

D: Powers and functions of second House of the Oireachtas: Articles 35–44.

Part IV: The government of É[ire]: Articles 45–52.

Part V: The courts: Articles 53–6.

Part VI: The comptroller and auditor general: Article 57.

Part VII: The Council of State: Articles 58–9.

Part VIII: Constitutional guarantees:

Fundamental rights of citizen: Articles 60–5.

Part IX: Education: Articles 66–9.

Part X: Prosecution and trial of offences: Articles 70–2.

Part XI: General: Articles 73–8.

As with the August 'Plan of Fundamental Constitutional Law', a summary of the contents of each article was included. Those relating to the creation of the office of President suggest that steady and significant progress was being made:

Part II: The President of É[ire].

Creation and tenure of office.

Article 4: The office of President of É[ire] is hereby created.

Article 5: Save in the case of the first President, the President to be elected by direct vote of the people.

Article 6: The first President to be elected by Dáil Éireann for a limited period (say, one year).

Article 7: Election to the office of President to be regulated by organic law.

Article 8: Every person possessing Irish nationality who has completed his thirty-fifth year, who has resided for a specified period in É[ire] and who is nominated by a specified number of members of Dáil Éireann to be eligible for election.

Article 9: The President to take an oath of fidelity to the Constitution.

Article 10: Tenure of office seven years.

Article 11: Provision to place the functions of the office in commission during temporary absence (with permission) or incapacity of the President.

Article 12: Provision for Acting President in the event of the death, resignation, removal or permanent incapacity of the President.

Article 13: Removal from office for treason, corruption etc.

The 'Plan of Fundamental Constitutional Law' of August 1936 and the draft heads of October 1936 reveal that the drafting of a new constitution was following a clear and coherent sense of purpose and direction, a fact confirmed by another document dated 5 November 1936, entitled 'Summary of Main Provisions of the Constitution'.[10] What is noteworthy is that, from the earliest stage, the plan and draft heads established central elements of the state's new basic law, which were to feature in successive drafts and the final version. These included: the principle of popular sovereignty; a President; a Council of State to act as a consultative body to the President; amendment of the Constitution by referendum; a statement of fundamental constitutional guarantees; and the enshrinement of judicial review. The drafting process of several months was to refine these and other elements, which were to be given expression in increasingly elegant and precise legal language.

Draft considered by Executive Council, 20–2 October 1936

As well as planning, Hearne was also drafting the state's new basic law. By late October 1936, he had completed a version of a number of articles and these were discussed at a meeting of the Executive Council on 20–2 October.[11] The document was divided into four parts, each one containing a number of articles, most of which were divided into sections:

> Part I: The state:
> Articles 1–6.
> Part II: The President of É[ire]:
> Article 7: Creation and tenure of office.
> Article 8: Powers and functions of the President.
> Part III: The national parliament:
> Article 9: The Oireachtas.
> Article 10: Dáil Éireann.
> Article 11: The second house ('S').
> Part IV: The government:
> Article 12.

According to Article 1, the name of the state was to be Éire, while the second article described the state as 'sovereign, independent and democratic'. Article 3 stated that 'all powers of government legislative, executive and judicial' were vested in the people. Irish was to be recognised as the state's 'official' language, with English afforded recognition as a second official language (Article 5). The final article in Part I defined those persons entitled to Irish nationality and citizenship of Éire.

In relation to the President, Article 7 provided for election by direct vote of the people. The presidential term was to be seven years. In order to be eligible for election, a candidate had to have completed his thirty-fifth year and secured nomination by not less than twenty members of the Oireachtas. The form of declaration to be taken by him before entering upon office was given. In the event of his temporary incapacity or absence from the country, the functions of the President were to be discharged by two or more members of the Council of State appointed for that purpose by him. The President could be removed from office on impeachment by Dáil Éireann for 'treason, bribery or other high crimes and misdemeanours', and on conviction by two-thirds of the total membership of both Houses of the Oireachtas at a joint session. Should a President be removed from office, die, resign or become permanently incapacitated, an election for a successor was to be held within two months. In the interim, an Acting President was to be elected by the Dáil.

By the terms of Article 8, the President's functions included the right to summon and dissolve the Oireachtas on the advice of the Prime Minister, though it was not to be dissolved if the latter ceased to retain the support of a majority of Dáil Éireann. The President was to sign and promulgate laws. He was to exercise functions in relation to referendum provisions and the suspension of sections of the Constitution pertaining to fundamental rights during a period of declared emergency.[12] Supreme command of the defence forces was vested in him, the exercise of which function was to be regulated by law. He was to appoint the Prime Minister on the nomination of Dáil Éireann and other ministers on the nomination of the Prime Minister. All senior judges were to receive their appointments from him, and he could remove a judge from office for stated misbehaviour on passage of the appropriate resolution by both Houses of the Oireachtas. The draft articles gave to the President the right of pardon, as well as the power to commute or remit sentences imposed by the courts. After consultation with the Council of State, he could communicate with the Houses of the Oireachtas by message or address on such matters which he deemed to be of public or national importance. Additional powers could be conferred on the President by organic laws and all such powers and functions were to be exercised in accordance with those laws.

Article 9 addressed the powers of the Oireachtas – composed of the President and two houses of parliament – which was to be the 'supreme legislative authority of Éire'. Only the Oireachtas could raise and maintain armed forces. The reports, publications and utterances of either house were privileged, as were the members going to, returning from or while within the precincts of either house. Article 10 was concerned with the 'primary house' of parliament, Dáil Éireann. This was to be elected by a system of proportional representation. The Dáil was to have exclusive legislative authority in relation to money bills. Article 11 contained provisions pertaining to the second house, designated 'S' in the draft. It was to have a membership of forty-five and, to qualify for election, an Irish citizen had to have reached forty-five years of age. The second house was to have the power to consider any bill initiated in the Dáil while having the power to initiate a bill itself. This house was to have the power to delay a bill for 180 days. However, the central and critical issue of the method of selection of members was not described; according to the draft the 'decision was to be taken'.

The final part of the document prepared by Hearne, Article 12, described the government. It was to consist of a Council of Ministers of not fewer than nine and not more than fifteen members. The Prime Minister, the Deputy Prime Minister and the Minister for Finance had to be members of the Dáil, though provision was made for not more than two members of the council to be members of the second house. The council was to act as a collective authority and to prepare estimates of receipts and expenditure for each financial year. A minister could resign by placing his resignation in the hands of the Prime Minister. The latter could request the resignation of a minister at any time 'for reasons which to him seem sufficient'. Should a minister fail to comply with such a request, his appointment could be terminated by the President on the advice of the Prime Minister. In the event of a Prime Minister ceasing to retain the support of a majority of Dáil Éireann, the Prime Minister and the other members of the government were required to resign.

The Executive Council, at its discussion from October 20–2, suggested a number of changes to the draft. A copy belonging to de Valera is deposited in the archives of University College Dublin and these suggestions are recorded on it in the President's own hand.[13] Article 4, relating to the national flag, was deleted, as was section 4 of Article 6, dealing with nationality: 'Irish nationality shall not be conferred by naturalisation upon any person who disbelieves in or is opposed to organised government, or is a member of, or affiliated with any society or organisation entertaining or teaching disbelief in, or opposition to organised government.' Perhaps an even more interesting deletion concerned the President, *viz.* Article 8, 10: 'The President may, at the request of the Council of Ministers, with the concurrence of Dáil Éireann, become chairman of a national government during a period of national crisis or emergency, whether internal or external.' Other alterations to the articles on the President included that his election was to be by proportional representation and his declaration of office was to be made in the presence of members of the Oireachtas. All these changes were incorporated in a revised draft.[14]

Drafting progresses: November and early December, 1936

The drafting of a new constitution made considerable progress in November and early December. For example, among Éamon de Valera's papers is a typescript headed 'Articles 8–20', and dated '8/11'.[15] This contains detailed drafts pertaining to the President and the second House of the Oireachtas. Under the terms of draft Article 12, its membership was fifty, an increase of five from the October draft, eight of whom were to be nominated by the Prime Minister on behalf of the Council of Ministers and forty-two elected: three each by the two universities, the National University of Ireland and the University of Dublin, and thirty-six from five panels. Under the terms of Article 13, these five panels were to be composed of:

A.   Persons having practical experience of public administration in Éire;

B.   Persons engaged in the agricultural industry in Éire as farmers of land;

C.   Persons engaged in industry or commerce in Éire or the business of banking or finance or engaged in the profession of engineering or architecture or accountancy;

D.   Persons who earn their livelihood as workers in industrial or agricultural employment or by any form of manual labour in Éire;

E.   Persons engaged in the profession of teaching in any primary or secondary or technical school or engaged in the practice of law or medicine (including dentistry, veterinary surgery or pharmaceutical chemistry) in Éire.

For the purpose of electing the members of the second house, a college of electors was to be established, consisting of every person who had been a candidate for membership of Dáil Éireann at the previous general election and who had received no less than 1,000 first preference votes.[16]

These drafts were based on at least two earlier, undated versions.[17] The first, while proposing a second parliamentary chamber of fifty members, stipulated that nine be nominated and forty-one elected. There were articles which detailed the maximum number of persons on the various panels. The second draft was essentially identical to that dated '8/11', with the articles referring to the maximum number on panels removed. In both these versions the second house was described as 'S'; it was only in the '8/11' draft that it was named Seanad Éireann.

By early December, Hearne had completed a draft which contained fully worked out versions of articles numbered 1 to 20. This was labelled by de Valera in his own hand '2nd Draft. Latest from Hearne. Original English'. It is further annotated: 'checked to date 1/12/1936'.[18] Gerard Hogan has commented that 'the articles which had been so drafted were more fully formed and complex, with tighter language and more defined legal and political concepts'.[19] This second draft was organised as follows:

Part I: The state.
Article 1: Name of state.
Article 2: Political character.
Article 3: Sovereignty of the people.
Article 4: National flag.
Article 5: Irish language.
Article 6: Citizenship.
Part II: The President:
Article 7: Creation of office.

Article 8: Powers and functions of the President.

Part III: The national parliament:

Article 9: The Oireachtas.

Article 10: Dáil Éireann.

Article 11: Money bills.

Articles 12–16: Seanad Éireann.

Article 17: Initiation of bills.

Article 18: Consideration of bills by Seanad Éireann.

Article 19: Passage of bills.

Article 20: Promulgation of laws by the President.

There is an undated version of articles, numbered 21–7,[20] which was probably completed either late in December or early January, before de Valera left for Zurich on 11 January 1937 (see below). We may call this the 'Christmas draft' and Article 21 was an early version of what was to eventually become Article 26, one of the most significant provisions in the 1937 Constitution, *viz.* the power conferred on the President, having consulted the Council of State, to refer a bill, or any provision thereof, to the Supreme Court for an opinion as to its constitutionality. This was to be done by the President within four days of the bill's passage through the Houses of the Oireachtas. The court was required to pronounce its opinion not later than seven days after the bill's referral. The opinion of the court was to be that of the majority of the judges; dissentient opinions were not to be pronounced. Draft Article 22 contained provisions for the reference of a bill to the people by the President; while other articles referred to the government (Article 23) and the Council of State (Articles 24–7).

Drafting interrupted: the abdication of King Edward VIII

Progress on the proposed constitution was interrupted by the abdication of King Edward VIII on 10 December 1936. Aware of events in England,[21] de Valera summoned the Dáil to meet the next day to give consideration to two items of proposed legislation. The first was the Constitution Amendment (No. 27) Bill to remove all references to the King and Governor-General from the Free State Constitution. The second proposed piece of legislation was the Executive Authority (External Relations) Bill. Drafted by Hearne,[22] the principles contained in it had been under discussion by him and de Valera since 1935, in the aftermath of the draft heads of a constitution produced by the legal adviser in that year. The terms of the External Relations Bill had already been proposed by Hearne in September 1936, when he had drafted a Foreign Relations Bill. Section 4 provided that so long as Éire is associated with the association of states commonly called the British Commonwealth of Nations ... international instruments ... may be made and issued respectively in such a form or forms as now or may hereafter be recognised from time to time by the governments of the several states of the said association for the purpose of the exercise by each of those states of its treaty-making power or of its right of legation.[23]

In effect, this bill proposed that the British monarch act on behalf of the Irish state in foreign relations, on the advice of the Executive Council, and this was the substance of the External Relations Bill a few months later.

The abdication crisis forced de Valera to rearrange his preferred constitutional and diplomatic timetable. He had intended to address the issue of future relations with Britain and the Commonwealth after, and not before, the enactment of a new basic law. This resolution of the President had been explained in November in the 'Summary of the Main Provisions of the Constitution':

Side by side with the new Constitution, and subject to it, a law will be enacted that so long as the State is associated with the states of the British Commonwealth of Nations certain functions heretofore exercised in the domain of external affairs by the constitutional monarchy recognised by those states will continue to be exercised on behalf of the state, but only on the advice of the government.[24]

The adoption of a new constitution and then the adjustment in the relationship with Britain – this was, in de Valera's view, the best policy – but in the words of Nicholas Mansergh, 'convenience and logic had been minor casualties of royal impetuosity'.[25] He had to revise his plans, but his approach to the abdication crisis was decided upon within the context of his intention to draft a new constitution for the Irish state and to clarify its relationship with the Commonwealth.[26]

Drafting resumed: the 'Zurich draft', January 1937

With the abdication crisis out of the way, John Hearne turned his attention once again to the drafting of a new basic law. A near complete draft was ready in late December 1936/early January 1937 and was taken by de Valera with him on a visit to Zurich on 11 January.[27] The proposed articles were arranged as follows:

Part I: The state: Articles 1–6.
Part II: The President: Articles 7–8.
Part III: The national parliament: Articles 9–11.

Part IV: The government: Article 12.

Part V: The Council of State: Articles 13–16.

Part VI: The courts: Articles 17–23.

Part VII: The comptroller and auditor general: Article 24.

Part VIII: Amendment of the Constitution – the referendum: Articles 25–31.

Part IX: Constitutional guarantees: Articles 32–8.

Part X: Economic life: Articles 39–43.

Part XI: Power to suspend certain constitutional provisions: Article 44.

Part XII: General: Articles 45–9.

Part XIII: Transitory provisions: [blank].

There are a number of curious aspects to what we may term the 'Zurich draft', which may be explained as inadvertent administrative glitches. Articles 1–12 were identical to those discussed by the Executive Council on 20–2 October 1936 and they did not contain the changes suggested at that meeting. Nor did the Zurich draft include the articles of the second draft of early December 1936. Accordingly, there were no details, for example regarding the Seanad, such as the panels or the system of election. The copy of the Zurich draft in the de Valera papers shows a line just above the heading, 'The Second House' and the word 'changed' is written in the margin,[28] suggesting that the President realised that the articles he was reading had been superseded by other, revised ones. This meant that this draft did not record all aspects of the drafting process to that point and, therefore, fails to give a complete picture of the progress which had been made by early January.

Notwithstanding these defects, the Zurich draft included a number of very important features and confirmed ongoing progress by Hearne. Among these features were declarations, clearly at an early stage of drafting. One related to 'the national territory' which consisted of the whole island of Ireland; and the right of the nation to this territory was described as 'absolute and indefeasible'. This declaration was an early version of what became Article 2 of the 1937 Constitution. There was also a solemn declaration of the sovereign right of the people of Ireland to determine the form of the state and its constitutional organs, to the exclusion of every other power. The final declaration was concerned with 'relations with other states' and proclaimed that such relations and the extent of co-operation with any other state or group of states were matters 'within the exclusive competence of the sovereign Irish people to decide as they think right in the national interest'.[29] The Zurich draft also included proposed articles on the Council of State;[30] the courts;[31] the referendum;[32] and power to suspend certain constitutional guarantees during 'a grave state of public disorder'.[33]

The draft was especially significant because it included a complete version of constitutional guarantees to be enjoyed by every citizen. Article 32, dealing with fundamental rights, guaranteed equality before the law; freedom of conscience; right of peaceable assembly and free expression of opinions; liberty of the person; and the inviolability of a citizen's dwelling. Freedom of religion was guaranteed under the terms of Article 33. A feature of the draft was the presence of articles relating to the family and private property, numbered 34 and 35 respectively. The former guaranteed the state's protection of the family as 'the sure foundation of ordered society'. Divorce was prohibited, as was contraception. There was a commitment to encourage early marriage and to foster the production of large families. Article 35 dealt with the right of private property, affirming it as 'a natural human right and a basic principle of ordered society'.

Two articles were concerned with the rights of parents and the prevention of the corruption of public morals. The former, Article 36, recognised the right of parents to the custody of their minor children and that they were only to be deprived of this custody in accordance with law. Article 37 identified areas in which the state would seek to protect public morality. Article 38 on education contained much more than a statement that 'all citizens have the right to free elementary education'. Section 2 declared that the aim of primary instruction was 'the formation of character, the cult of moral and civic virtue, as well as the development of the physical and intellectual faculties'. By the terms of section 6, the teaching of religion to all pupils under the age of eighteen years was to be compulsory.

Part IX of the Zurich draft related to 'economic life' and included Articles 39–43. Under the provisions of Article 39, 3 the state's natural resources were dedicated to the maintenance of its people and were under the special control and supervision of the state. Their exploitation by private owners was to be with a view 'to the conservation and development of the said resources for the benefit of the community'. Article 40, 1 provided for 'the ownership, distribution and use of land under the special control and supervision of the state', in order 'to promote the creation and development of the maximum number of economic holdings privately owned'. Two other provisions, Articles 41 and 42, referred to the development of the sea fishing industry for the benefit of the community and the supervision of transport services with a view to facilitating agricultural development and commercial progress, respectively.

'3rd Draft', 11 January 1937

In early January, another draft was completed by John Hearne; in the de Valera papers it is annotated as '3rd Draft (11 January '37) (English)'.[34] This is a more useful and accurate measure of the headway being made in the process of making a new constitution, as it reflected the developments and progress in previous drafts, especially the second draft of December 1936 and the Zurich draft of January 1937.

The articles of this third draft were arranged as follows:

Part I: The state: Articles 1–6.

Part II: The President: Articles 7–8.

Part III: The national parliament: Articles 9–22.

Part IV: The government: Article 23.

Part V: The Council of State: Articles 24–7.

Part VI: The courts: Articles 28–30.

Part VII: Comptroller and auditor general: Articles 31–2.

Part VIII: The referendum: Article 33.

Part IX: Constitutional guarantees: Articles 34–8.

Part X: Power to suspend certain constitutional guarantees: Article 39.

Part XI: Amendment of the Constitution: Article 40.

Part XII: General: Articles 41–6.

Part XIII: Transitory provisions: [blank].

The declarations which were a feature of the Zurich draft were absent and replaced with a heading, 'Fundamental Declarations', and a general outline of the proposed contents:

1. The Irish nation.
2. The national territory.
3. National sovereignty.
4. The form of the state and its constitutional organs.
5. Relations with other states.

There were a number of changes to articles relating to the President. Gone was the idea of an Acting President during a vacancy in the office pending the election of a new one. The impeachment procedure for a President was more detailed and elaborate. Charges were now to be preferred before the Supreme Court, which would investigate them and report its conclusions to the two Houses of the Oireachtas. These would meet in joint session to consider the matter. A resolution supported by two-thirds of the total membership of the two houses was required to remove the President from office.[35]

The third draft was the first near complete one to give details of the proposed Seanad and the relevant articles were similar to those in the second draft. There were to be fifty members, eight nominated by the Prime Minister and forty-two elected, six by the two universities and thirty-six from five panels,[36] as originally described in the November 1936 draft articles. The electoral college was to be composed of Dáil candidates[37] in accordance with the same draft articles.

Article 21 of the third draft concerned the referral of bills to the Supreme Court by the President in order to determine their constitutionality and it was identical to the version in the Christmas draft. Article 22 also conferred a power on the President in relation to his function in the signing and promulgation of laws. If petitioned by a majority of the members of the Seanad and four-ninths of the Dáil to decline to sign a bill on the grounds that it contained a proposal of fundamental national importance on which the will of the people ought to be ascertained, the President was to consider the matter. Having consulted the Council of State, he could decide to sign the bill or else refer it to the people by way of a referendum.

The exercise of the functions by the President, described in Articles 21 and 22, required him to consult the Council of State before he arrived at a decision. Four articles, 24 to 27, in the third draft dealt with the composition and functions of that body. Article 24 listed the ex-officio members of the council and these included the Prime Minister, Deputy Prime Minister, Chief Justice, President of the High Court, Chairman of Dáil Éireann, Chairman of Seanad Éireann, Attorney General and former Presidents, Prime Ministers and Chief Justices. The President was to be empowered to appoint, at his absolute discretion, not more than five persons to be members. By the terms of Article 26, during the temporary absence of the President, his powers and functions were to be performed by a commission consisting of three members of the council, appointed by him for that purpose. In the event of the President's death or resignation, a commission of three members of the council, appointed by that body, were to exercise his functions. Article 27 stipulated that, pending the election and entry upon office of the first President, his powers and functions were to be carried out by a commission consisting of the Prime Minister, Chief Justice and Chairman of Dáil Éireann.

Versions of Articles 22–7 in the third draft had appeared in the Zurich draft[38] but those in the former were more elegant and refined. In fact, those in the third draft were identical to ones in the earlier Christmas draft and were similarly numbered. There was little difference in most articles pertaining to the courts between the Zurich and the third drafts. However, there was a significant and important one: in the earlier draft, the High Court was to have 'original jurisdiction to determine the question of the validity of any law having regard to the provisions of the constitution',[39] with a right of appeal to the Supreme Court.[40] Under Article 28, 4 in the third draft this jurisdiction was conferred on the Supreme Court.

The third draft contained five articles dealing with constitutional guarantees, two fewer than the Zurich draft. The articles pertaining to a citizen's fundamental rights and religion were identical, except for the inclusion of a prohibition on propaganda 'calculated to be subversive of the dogmas of the Christian faith'. The articles on private property and education were essentially identical in the two documents.[41] The article on marriage in the third draft (Article 36) guaranteed the state's protection of the family as the sure foundation of ordered society and not to enact legislation to dissolve a marriage, thus confirming similar provisions in the Zurich draft. However, what might be regarded as extraneous matters were removed from the later draft: there was no reference to contraception and the encouragement of early marriage. The provisions of Article 36 of the Zurich draft, recognising the custodial rights of parents, were also removed. The third draft contained no equivalent to Part X of the Zurich draft, 'Economic Life', except for a significantly briefer provision on natural resources, Article 41, which was included in Part XII under the heading 'General'.

Under the terms of Article 39, in Part X of the third draft, certain constitutional provisions could be suspended. Dáil Éireann, or if it was not sitting, the Council of Ministers, could proclaim a state of public emergency. Whenever the council made such a proclamation, the President was to summon the Dáil and the proclamation had to be confirmed within seven days or else it would cease to have effect. Upon confirmation of the proclamation by the Dáil, the President was to issue an order directing that certain sections of the Constitution were to be suspended. These sections were those relating to the right of free expression of opinions and peaceable assembly; liberty of the person; and the inviolability of dwellings. Article 39 empowered the Oireachtas to establish extraordinary courts. Critically, nothing in the Constitution could be invoked to invalidate any act done in pursuance of this article and any decision of a court established under it could not be appealed or reviewed by another court. These provisions were identical to those in Article 44 of the Zurich draft.

Part XI was concerned with the amendment of the Constitution. It was required that every proposal for an amendment be introduced in Dáil Éireann and, having been passed by both Houses of the Oireachtas, be submitted by referendum for a decision of the people.

'Fourth Draft', 13 February 1937

Drafting and redrafting continued and, by 13 February 1937, Hearne had prepared what was annotated as the 'Fourth Draft'[42] and the articles therein broadly confirmed those of the third draft. Regarding the President, however, there were some changes in the nomination procedure: the number of members of the Oireachtas required to support a nomination increased from not less than twenty to not less than thirty. A new feature was the power conferred in the county councils of not less than five counties to subscribe to the nomination of a candidate.[43] The criterion determining the entitlement to vote in Seanad elections was changed: rather than the requirement that Dáil candidates constituting the electoral college had to have secured not fewer than 1,000 first preference votes at the general election preceding the Seanad election, candidates had now to secure not fewer than 500 such votes.[44]

The Supreme Court no longer had a role in the impeachment of a President: he was to be impeached at the instance of the Seanad and the charge was to be preferred before Dáil Éireann and investigated by it. A resolution supported by three-fourths of the membership was to be required to remove the President from office.[45]

The most significant aspect of this draft was the inclusion of a new article, headed 'International Relations'.[46] Two sections affirmed the state's adherence to the principle of the peaceful settlement of disputes by international arbitration[47] and the acceptance of agreed principles of international law as the determinant of relations between Éire and other states.[48] Section 4 of the article was informed by de Valera's concept of external association, by permitting the government 'to promote friendly co-operation between Éire and any group or league of nations with which Éire is or becomes associated for the purpose of international co-operation in matters of common concern'. Another part of this same section gave constitutional expression to the principles of the External Relations Act 1936 and authorised the government 'to avail, for the purpose of the exercise of any executive function of Éire in or in connection with its external relations, of any organ, instrumentality, or method of procedure used or adopted for like purpose by the members of any such group or league of nations as aforesaid'.

This draft also contained a version of the transitory provisions, which related to the period during which the state went from the operation of the constitutional dispensation associated with the Free State Constitution to a new one heralded by the introduction of a new constitution.

Drafting process, October 1936–February 1937: a summary

It may be useful at this point to summarise the drafting process from October 1936 to February 1937. There were five drafts described in this account: the one considered by the Executive Council, 20–2 October 1936; the second draft, 1 December 1936; the Zurich draft, early January 1937; the third draft, 11 January 1937; and the fourth draft, 13 February 1937. At each stage, articles established key elements of the emerging Constitution, these being retained in subsequent drafts, though often in amended form. Gradually, this process gave the document its structure. The table hereunder identifies when key aspects of what became the 1937 Constitution were introduced:

Name and date of draft	Key element of the Constitution introduced
Draft considered 20–2 October 1936	Sovereignty of the Irish state. Sovereignty of the Irish people. The President. Bicameral legislature. The government.
Second draft, 1 December 1936	Composition/election of Seanad.
Zurich draft, early January 1937	Council of State. Courts. Judicial review of constitutionality of laws. Referendum. Constitutional guarantees. Suspension of constitutional guarantees.
Third draft, 11 January 1937	Reference of bills to Supreme Court.
Fourth draft, 13 February 1937	International relations. Transitory provisions.

While the making of a new constitution was a process by which new elements were introduced and earlier ones amended, deleted or retained, as drafting progressed, this same process saw the removal of other features which were often interesting, even radical. For example, it may be remembered that, in the October 1936 draft, there were provisions for an Acting President and for the President's appointment as chairman of a national government at the request of the Council of Ministers and with the concurrence of Dáil Éireann, during a period of national crisis, internal or international. Such provisions were removed from the third draft. The Zurich draft contained an article relating to the protection of public morals and a section prohibiting contraception; these did not appear in the third draft produced a month later.

Involvement of Arthur Matheson

Since August 1937, the making of the new Constitution had been the preserve of de Valera and Hearne. In early March 1937, however, the President invited Hearne's former superior, parliamentary draftsman Arthur Matheson to examine draft articles 'with a view to seeing whether any provision could be shortened by leaving the subject matter thereof to be dealt with by ordinary law'.[49] In this regard, Matheson made a number of suggestions: for example, the detail of the flag to be prescribed by ordinary law rather than by an article of the Constitution.[50] While this proposal was rejected, others he made had an influence on the drafting process. These included: a draft form of words for the provision relating to the automatic election of the Ceann Comhairle at a general election[51] and that the word 'decision' be used in place of 'advisory opinion' in the article dealing with the referral of bills to the Supreme Court by the President.[52] He presented a suggested version of the article dealing with natural resources, which became the basis of Article 10 in Bunreacht na hÉireann.[53]

'Preliminary Draft', 10 March 1937

By 10 March 1937, Hearne had progressed the drafting process to the stage that a version of the new basic law, entitled the 'Preliminary Draft', was ready. According to the relevant file in the Department of the President, it 'was circulated privately by the President'.[54] Twelve galley proofs of the draft had been pulled the previous day but it is not known who, besides members of the Executive Council, received a copy, as a list is not on file. Circulation was limited to de Valera's most trusted advisers. For example, Joseph Walshe was a recipient: his copy is retained on file in the National Archives.[55] It is likely that Michael McDunphy, assistant secretary in the President's Department, Arthur Matheson, parliamentary draftsman, and Patrick Lynch, the Attorney General, also received copies.[56]

The sixty articles of the preliminary draft were structured by Hearne thus:

The nation: Articles 1–3.
The state: Articles 4–10.
The President: Articles 11–12.
The national parliament: Articles 13–19.
Legislation: Articles 20–3.
The government: Article 24.
International relations: Article 25.
Attorney General: Article 26.
The Council of State: Articles 27–9.
Comptroller and auditor general: Articles 30–1.
Courts: Articles 32–5.
Trial of offences: Articles 36–7.
Personal rights and social policy: Articles 38–42.

Power to suspend certain provisions of the Constitution: Articles 43–4.

Amendment of the Constitution: Article 45.

The referendum: Article 46.

Repeal of the Constitution of Saorstát Éireann: Articles 47–9.

Transitory provisions: Articles 50–60.

The preliminary draft differed from the fourth draft in a number of ways: it included oaths to which members of the Council of State[57] and newly appointed judges had to subscribe.[58] There was an additional article in the section dealing with courts, which recognised the authority of quasi-judicial bodies,[59] and a new section, composed of Articles 36 and 37, headed 'Trial of Offences'.[60] The first of the articles of this new section declared that 'no person shall be tried save in due course of law'. Extraordinary courts were only to be established in time of war, armed rebellion or during a state of public emergency declared by the government. Article 37 was concerned with a definition of treason.

Perhaps the most significant difference between the preliminary and fourth drafts, and indeed all earlier drafts, pertained to the suspension of certain provisions of the Constitution guaranteeing the rights of citizens. Under the terms of Article 43 of the preliminary draft, a state of public emergency could be declared by the government if it was satisfied that a grave state of public disorder existed. Upon the issuance of the proclamation, the President was to make an order suspending specified provisions of the Constitution. The proclamation and order were to be confirmed by Dáil Éireann within fourteen days. The critical difference between these provisions and those of earlier drafts was that, under the latter, the Dáil had to proclaim a state of emergency or the proclamation of the government had to be confirmed by it before the President could make any order suspending constitutional guarantees. The new provisions had the effect of increasing the power of the government to act independently of the Dáil and so diminish the role of parliament in the matter of the declaration of a state of emergency. In the preliminary draft, there was a new article in the section dealing with suspension of constitutional provisions. This Article 44, concerned with the establishment of extraordinary courts, was composed of three sections which had previously been part of the article on the declaration of an emergency in earlier drafts; and the wording of the separate article was identical to that used in those three sections.

The draft contained two especially significant features. The first was a section entitled, 'The Nation'. This had its origins in the declarations which first appeared in the Zurich draft of early January 1937 and which were summarised in the third draft under the heading, 'Fundamental Declarations'. The preliminary draft presented a refinement of the declarations into three articles:

Article 1
The Irish nation hereby affirms its inalienable, indefeasible and sovereign right to choose its own form of government, to determine its relations with other states and within the national territory to develop its own life – economic, social and political – free from external interference.

Article 2
The national territory consists of the whole of Ireland, its islands and territorial seas.

Article 3
Pending the re-integration of the national territory, and without prejudice to the right of the parliament and government set up under this Constitution to exercise jurisdiction over the whole of the national territory, the laws enacted by that parliament shall have the like area and extent of application as the laws of Saorstát Éireann and the like extra-territorial effect.

The second significant feature was Article 42, concerned with religion and consisting of ten sections, the first four asserting:

1. The state acknowledges the right of Almighty God to public worship in that way which He has shown to be His will.
2. Accordingly, the state shall hold in honour the name of God and shall consider it a duty to favour and protect religion and shall not enact any measure that may impair its credit.
3. The state acknowledges that the true religion is that established by our divine Lord, Jesus Christ Himself, which He committed to His church to protect and propagate, as the guardian and interpreter of true morality. It acknowledges, moreover, that the church of Christ is the Catholic Church.
4. The state recognises the church of Christ as a perfect society, having within itself full competence and sovereign authority, in respect of the spiritual good of men.

Finally, an interesting aspect of the preliminary draft was the introduction of a new and distinctive nomenclature, having its basis in the Irish language, in respect of ministerial titles. The Prime Minister was henceforth to be styled 'Taoiseach'[61] and the Deputy Prime Minister 'Tánaiste'.[62]

On 12 March, the Executive Council approved the procedure regarding the enactment of the new Constitution. The draft was to be presented to the Dáil for approval and to be considered in the same manner as any bill. If approved by the Dáil, the draft was to be submitted to a plebiscite of the people, to be held on the same day as the forthcoming general election, scheduled for 1 July. If a majority of voters expressed support for it, the Constitution was to be brought into operation by a resolution of Dáil Éireann passed for that purpose.[63] Crucially, the Dáil's function was to approve, not adopt, the proposed constitution; its adoption was to be by a vote of the people. For de Valera, it was essential that the new basic law 'should not be cast as an amendment of the 1922 Constitution, but rather should involve a complete break with it'. Thus the process for its enactment 'was carefully designed to avoid contamination by the 1922 Constitution or its creation, the Dáil'.[64] This agreed procedure was regarded by de Valera and his ministers as a means of ensuring that the adoption of the state's new fundamental law would be an expression of the sovereign will of its people.

'First Official Draft', 16 March 1937

On 16 March 1937 copies of the printed text of what was described as the 'First Official Draft' of the proposed fundamental law were, according to an official memorandum, 'distributed confidentially to members of the Executive Council and to other selected persons, including Mr Conor Maguire, President of the High Court, Mr George Gavan Duffy, judge of the High Court and Mr James Geoghegan, judge of the Supreme Court'.[65] Its sixty articles confirmed the progressive evolution and development of the document since August 1936.[66]

Article 1: Sovereignty of the Irish nation.

Article 2: National territory whole of the island of Ireland.

Article 3: Laws to apply to the area of the state pending the re-integration of the national territory.

Article 4: Name of state – Éire.

Article 5: Éire is a sovereign, independent, democratic state.

Article 6: The sovereignty of the Irish people.

Article 7: The national flag.

Article 8: The Irish language.

Article 9: Irish citizenship and nationality.

Article 10: Natural resources of Éire belong to the state.

Article 11: The President – election, nomination and impeachment procedures.

Article 12: Powers and functions of the President.

Article 13: The Oireachtas.

Article 14: Dáil Éireann.

Article 15: Money bills.

Article 16: Seanad Éireann – composition and method of election.

Article 17: Tenure of office of senators.

Article 18: Elections to Seanad Éireann to be regulated by law.

Article 19: Election of senators by vocational councils.

Article 20: Legislation.

Article 21: Promulgation of laws by the President.

Article 22: Reference of bills to the Supreme Court by the President.

Article 23: Reference of bills to the people in a referendum.

Article 24: The government.

Article 25: International relations.

Article 26: The Attorney General.

Article 27: The Council of State – composition and functions.

Article 28: The President obliged to consult the Council of State.

Article 29: Members of Council of State to exercise the powers of the President in the event of his absence or death.

Article 30: All the state's revenues are to form one fund.

Article 31: The comptroller and auditor general.

Article 32: Powers and jurisdiction of courts.

Article 33: Independence of the judiciary.

Article 34: Matters pertaining to the courts to be regulated by law.

Article 35: Authority of quasi-judicial bodies.

Article 36: All persons to be tried in due course of law.

Article 37: Definition of treason.

Article 38: Personal rights.

Article 39: The family.

Article 40: Education.

Article 41: Private property.

Article 42: [Blank].

Article 43: Declaration of a state of emergency.

Article 44: Establishment of special courts to deal with emergency situations.

Article 45: Amendment of the Constitution.

Article 46: The referendum.

Article 47: Repeal of the Constitution of Saorstát Éireann.

Article 48: Government of Éire successor to government of Saorstát Éireann.

Article 49: Continuance of laws.

Articles 50–60: Transitory provisions.

A noteworthy feature of the first official draft was the omission of Article 42 on religion. It had provoked a negative reaction among some of those who had received a copy of the preliminary draft, a controversy to be discussed later. There were other differences between the first official and preliminary drafts, though none of these were as significant as the omission of Article 42. Excluding the eleven articles composing the transitory provisions and Article 42, of the remaining forty-eight articles, forty-three were effectively unchanged,[67] while five others contained changes of varying degrees of detail and importance.[68] Of the latter five articles, Article 46, dealing with the referendum in both drafts, displayed the most significant differences. The first official draft simply stated that every proposal for an amendment of the Constitution which is submitted by referendum to the decision of the people shall be approved if a majority of votes are cast in its favour. In the preliminary draft, however, the provisions were stated in the negative and the contents were more complex. Every proposed constitutional amendment 'shall ... be approved by the people unless ... a majority of the voters ... shall have signalled their disapproval ... by casting their votes against its enactment into law and the votes so cast shall have amounted to not less than thirty-five per cent of the voters on the register'.

Besides the provision on religion, the first official draft contained four other articles under the heading, 'Personal Rights and Social Policy'. These related to personal rights, family, education and private property, and were numbered 38, 39, 40 and 41 respectively. They were identical and similarly numbered in the preliminary draft. The provisions in these two drafts had appeared in earlier versions of the document: the Zurich, third and fourth drafts. In the preliminary and first official drafts, however, the language was more complex and legalistic; furthermore, it was theological and philosophical, the result of influences to be discussed in the next chapter. At this juncture, the concern is with the contents of the relevant articles.

Article 38, 1 declared that 'the state acknowledges that all citizens are as human persons equal before the law', a far more elaborate provision than the simpler declaration which had appeared in earlier drafts: 'All citizens are equal before the law.'[69] The article continued: 'The state shall, in particular, in its laws have due regard to individual differences of capacity, physical and moral, and of social function', words which had no counterpart in the earlier Zurich and third drafts; nor had there been an earlier equivalent of section 2:

1. The state guarantees to respect, defend and vindicate the personal rights of each citizen.
2. The state shall, however, protect, as best it may, from unjust attack, and, in case of injustice done, vindicate the person, life, good name and property rights of every citizen.

As in previous drafts, the article contained provisions regarding the liberty of the person and the security of dwellings. There were also sections guaranteeing the rights of free expression and assembly. The language used in the first official and other drafts was essentially similar. Furthermore, as with these other drafts, the exercise of rights was subject to public order and morality, though in the first official draft the conditions were expressed in more detailed and elaborate terms in relation to the free expression of opinion:

> The education of public opinion being, however, a matter of such grave import to the common good, the state shall see to it that the organs of public opinion, such as radio, press and cinema, shall not be used to undermine social order or public morality or, especially at times of war, the authority of the state.

The article on the family contained an elaboration, precision and complexity of language unlike previous versions in earlier drafts: 'The state recognises the family as the natural primary and fundamental unit of society, and as a moral and juridical institution possessing inalienable and imprescriptible rights, antecedent and superior to all positive law'.[70] The family, accordingly, was to be protected 'as the necessary basis of social order and as indispensable to the welfare of the nation'.[71] Particular recognition was given to the life of a woman within the home, 'without which the common good cannot be achieved'. Moreover, the state was to endeavour 'to secure that women, especially mothers and young girls, shall not be obliged to enter avocations unsuited to their sex and strength'.[72] However, as in all drafts since the Zurich one, divorce was prohibited.[73]

The pronounced emphasis of Article 40, concerned with education, was on the rights of parents and the family in the matter of the education of their children, the state guaranteeing 'to respect the inalienable right and duty of parents to provide, according to their means, for the religious and moral, intellectual, physical and social education of their children'.[74] Sections 2 and 3 recognised the right of parents to provide education in their homes or in private schools or in state established schools and not to oblige parents, 'in violation of their conscience and lawful preference', to send their children to state schools. This focus on parental rights had not featured in earlier versions of these provisions.

Article 41, dealing with private property, was surprising in its content and import, its title belying the expansive scope of many of its sections. The first two acknowledged the right to ownership of private property and guaranteed that the state would protect this same right. Such provisions had found expression in earlier drafts, though these lacked the complexity and forcefulness of language of this first official draft, which spoke of 'the natural right, antecedent to positive law, to the private ownership of external goods', a right that is 'not only allowable but is, for social needs, absolutely necessary'. Section 3 declared that 'since the use by individuals of private property ought, in civil society, be regulated by the principles of social justice', the state may lawfully delimit this use in the interest of the common good. This concept of the common good also inspired section 5: 'The state shall strive to promote the economic welfare of the whole people, by securing, protecting and defending, as effectively as it may, an economic order in which social justice and social charity shall imbue all the institutions of public life.'

Aspects of social policy were identified as a means of promoting the economic welfare of all the people of the state. These aspects included endeavouring to ensure that 'the adult working man, especially the father of families, shall receive a wage sufficient to meet adequately their domestic needs, present and future'. Section 6, 2 contained a radical proposal: 'In particular, the state shall see to it that the economic domination of the few, in what pertains to the control of credit, shall not endanger the common good of the community as a whole.' A pledge was given in section 7, 1 'to safeguard with special care the economic rights of the less favoured classes, to contribute to the support of the infirm, the widow, the orphan and the aged poor who are past their labour'.

Observations on the first official draft, March 1937

When the first official draft was circulated on 16 March, recipients were invited to respond, such responses to be returned by the 23rd of the same month. In a letter to P.J. Ruttledge, Minister for Justice, dated 16 March 1937, Maurice Moynihan, secretary to the Executive Council, made reference to Articles 38–42, which related to personal rights and social policy. He informed the minister that 'these are not as yet in their final form', a clear admission that they contained some of the more controversial elements in the proposed constitution.[75]

There were at least fifteen responses to the draft, ranging in length from four to over eighty pages.[76] Some departments confined their observations primarily to articles relating to their own activities and concerns, for example the Departments of Education[77] and Defence,[78] and the Revenue Commissioners.[79] Others commented in more general terms: responding on behalf of the Department of the President, Michael McDunphy made observations on most articles.[80] J.J. McElligott, secretary of the Department of Finance, also produced a detailed response of thirty-nine pages. It is deserving of some attention, not least because of his concerns regarding Articles 38–42, and, in particular, Article 41 (private property).[81]

In his opening remarks, McElligott observed that, 'in examining the draft of the Constitution, the Department of Finance has taken the line that it is not called upon to praise but rather to point out possible defects and difficulties, so what follows is conceived in that spirit'.[82] With this grant of self-permission, he proceeded to launch an attack on the articles relating to personal rights and social policy. 'These articles are not of a kind usually enshrined in a constitution,' he wrote, 'and they will not be helpful to ministers in the future but will provide a breeding ground for discontent and so create instability and insecurity.' They were, 'consequently, objectionable and even dangerous'.

He was especially animated by the references in Article 41, 6, 2 to the 'economic domination of the few in what pertains to the control of credit'. The fulminations of the orthodox economist denounced a phrase which 'could easily be worked up by agitators as a weapon of attack on the banks, the Agriculture Credit Corporation, the Industrial Credit Co., or against any large joint-stock concern'. The various declaratory phrases which characterised Article 41 were 'of an idealistic tendency which, while individually unobjectionable as a statement of social policy, may, launched out into the void in the draft Constitution, recoil like a boomerang on the government of some future day in circumstances not anticipated by the originators'. According to McElligott, the provisions of this article were putting 'in the hands of enthusiasts for any particular cause an unnecessarily powerful instrument of agitation which, it is feared, might be freely used in support of all sorts of unreasonable and impracticable proposals for further social legislation.'[83]

Appointment of an editorial committee, April 1937

John Hearne had carried the burden of drafting a new constitution up to the circulation of the first official draft on 16 March 1937. On receipt of ministerial and departmental observation, de Valera decided to appoint a committee, in late March/early April, to assist in the process, composed of Maurice Moynihan, Michael McDunphy, Philip O'Donoghue, legal assistant in the Attorney General's office, and John Hearne. Their function was, in the words of an official memorandum, 'to examine and revise the draft in the light of observations and generally to advise him [de Valera] on both the scheme and text of the Constitution.'[84] Clearly, this was intended to be more than an editorial committee: it had the responsibility to integrate all relevant observations, comments and suggestions into future drafts and to address queries and criticisms.[85]

When it came to the making of the new basic law one thing remained unchanged – de Valera retained personal and political control of the entire project. In a comment on the first official draft, Stephen Roche, secretary of the Department of Justice, suggested that 'a round-the-table discussion between a cabinet committee and officials is essential' to examine the document.[86] De Valera was never going to agree to this: admission to the exclusive world of Irish constitution-making was regulated and limited, authoritatively and vigilantly, by its prime mover. The President personally selected the members of the editorial committee: they were individuals he knew and trusted. Three of them were civil servants in his own departments; only O'Donoghue was not under his direct ministerial control. The memorandum recording the committee's establishment stated that it was 'to examine the draft constitution in detail in constant consultation with him [de Valera].'[87] April was to be a demanding month for Hearne and his colleagues; they would work long hours under the supervision of de Valera. An official memorandum gave an excellent summary of that intense period during which four revises of the proposed constitution were produced: 'The examination by the committee, who were in constant touch with the President, proceeded continuously, without a break, up to the end of April, some of the sittings lasting until midnight or later.'[88]

It was a process characterised by the imposition of rigorous secrecy by de Valera. Copies of the revises were circulated only to a small group, mainly ministers and senior officials. For example, it would appear that not more than twenty-two people received the third revise, issued on 24 April 1937. The copies were numbered and were required to be returned to the President's Department; they were then destroyed.[89] Printing arrangements were strictly confidential and were personally managed by de Valera, who met with the works' manager and chief compositor of Cahill Printers on 2 March 1937. No record of the meeting was kept, just the fact of its happening.[90] The original text was given personally by him or his secretary to the works' manager.[91] Thus the President of the Executive Council constructed a closed and secretive environment to revise the draft constitution and Hearne and his fellow committee members played a central and pivotal role in it.

First revise of the Constitution, 1 April 1937

The first revise of the proposed constitution was issued on 1 April 1937.[92] The most striking feature of the document was the omission of all five articles relating to personal rights and social policy. Two had attracted particularly adverse criticism, those concerned with religion and private property. In the preparation of the first revise, it was decided to subject all five articles to re-examination. Seventeen articles of the first official draft were changed in the revise.[93] Some changes were minor: Article 30, concerned with the state's revenues, was simply renumbered as Article 12 and repositioned in the section headed 'The State'. Many changes were as a consequence of departmental observations made on the draft,[94] these observations having been, in Moynihan's words, 'exhaustively examined'.[95] Article 13, 4, 5 of the revise stated that it was not necessary to proceed to a ballot if there was only one candidate for the office of President. James Ryan, Minister for Agriculture, had commented that he would like to see, in this article, that an unopposed candidate would be validly elected.[96]

He also expressed the view that the obligation on the Taoiseach to report to the

President on matters of domestic and international policy 'as and when desired by the President to do so', as required under Article 24, 2, 2 of the first official draft, could prove 'a heavy burden', especially 'if we had a conscientious and pernickety President'.[97] In the revise, this was changed to keeping the President 'generally informed'.[98] In the observations of the Department of the President, McDunphy had argued that the Attorney General should be heard by the judges of the Supreme Court when a bill was referred to it by the President for a decision on its constitutionality.[99] The revise included this proposal.[100] Regarding the comptroller and auditor general's membership of the Council of State, as specified in Article 27, 2 of the first official draft, McDunphy questioned in what respect his experience or function entitled him to this position.[101] He was removed as a member in the revise.[102]

The observations of Stephen Roche, secretary of the Department of Justice, had a major influence on the revision of the emergency provisions contained in the first official draft. In his memorandum, he described Articles 43 and 44 as 'quite satisfactory', adding, however, that he doubted if power to suspend articles of the Constitution was necessary, having regard to the effect in practice of laws under Article 44, which allowed for the establishment of extraordinary courts.[103] On 30 March, he, together with Philip O'Donoghue, composed a draft article to replace Articles 43 and 44.

This draft formed the basis of a revision of the emergency section of the document. It was they who suggested the heading for what became Article 45 of the revise: 'Special Provisions for the Preservation of Public Order'. In it there was no reference to the suspension of certain parts of the Constitution, which had been a feature of all previous drafts. Rather, under section 1, the Oireachtas was now empowered to enact legislation to maintain public order and establish extraordinary courts. This legislation would come into operation on the issue of a proclamation by the President, on the advice of the government.[104] Two elements of the provisions remained unchanged – the proclamation had to be laid before the Dáil[105] and nothing in the Constitution could be invoked to invalidate any legislation passed under the article.[106]

De Valera made a number of observations and, unsurprisingly, these were reflected in the revise. In response to a suggestion by McDunphy that the President be required to consult the Council of State before refusing to dissolve the Dáil when requested by a Taoiseach who had ceased to enjoy the support of a majority of deputies, de Valera replied in the negative and stated that the matter was, in de Valera's words, at the President's 'absolute discretion'.[107] These same words were incorporated in the relevant article of the revise.[108] De Valera wanted it made clear that members of Dáil Éireann 'shall act as public representatives of the country and not as delegates of particular constituencies or interests'.[109] These sentiments found expression in Article 15, 11: there was no equivalent in the first official or earlier drafts. The President also desired that the provisions relating to the Dáil and Seanad should 'as far as possible be arranged in the same logical sequence and grouped in the same number of articles corresponding generally in scope'. What he had in mind was that in the draft under consideration there was one article on the Dáil (Article 15) and three on the Seanad (Articles 16–18). He decided that 'Hearne was to do this.'[110]

Consequently, in the revise, there was one article on the Seanad, this being an amalgamation of the three in the previous draft. The wording of the composite article was identical to that of the three separate articles. Perhaps influenced by de Valera's instructions, Hearne organised other articles in a more logical sequence. Article 20 of the first official draft, a relatively long article of many disparate elements, was separated into three articles in the revise, 20, 22 and 23. These were concerned with the Seanad's consideration of money bills; the time period for its consideration of bills other than money bills; and the abridgement of this period for the consideration of bills respectively. The wording of the single article of the first official draft was that used in the three separate articles of the revise. Article 17 of the revise was formed by the removal of two sections from Article 15 of the earlier draft. These related to the obligation by the Dáil to consider the estimates of receipts and expenditure for a financial year.

Second revise of the Constitution, 10 April 1937

Having produced the first revise, that document was now considered again by Hearne and his three civil service colleagues, this work being completed on the night of 8 April and given to the printers.[111] The second revise was distributed on 10 April.[112]

The most significant difference between the two revises was the inclusion of articles omitted in the first, on personal rights, family and education, and now numbered Articles 41, 42 and 43 respectively. The provisions relating to property and religion, however, were still not included. Section 3 of Article 41, displaying a real elegance of expression, now read:

1. The State guarantees in its laws to respect, and, as far as practicable, by its laws to defend and vindicate the personal rights of the citizen.
2. The State shall, in particular, by its laws protect as best it may from unjust attack and, in the case of injustice done, vindicate the life, person, good name and property rights of every citizen.

The changes in the articles relating to family and education were relatively undramatic. In fact, the article on education in the second revise contained no significant changes, apart from tighter and more elegant language. Likewise, the provisions on the family were essentially similar, though the prohibition on divorce was expressed in more direct and simple language: 'No law shall be enacted providing for the grant by courts in Éire of a dissolution of marriage.'[113]

Comparing the remaining forty-five articles of the second revise with those in the first, and excluding the five articles on personal rights and social policy which had not been included in the first revise, and the eleven transitory articles, thirty-eight were unchanged.[114] Five articles were changed and sections of two deleted in the second revise, accounting for nine differences in all between the two documents. In the case of three articles in the second revise, the changes were editorial in character. Article 40, dealing with emergency provisions, was numbered 45 in the first. Article 13, 9 of the first revise, referring to the commission to discharge the functions of the President in his absence, was deleted, because its contents were effectively repeated in Article 32, 1, 1 which featured in both revises. Article 32, 5, referring to the requirements on this commission to act on the advice of the government or consult the Council of State, as required of the President under the Constitution, was a composite of Articles 32, 5, 1 and 35, 5, 2 in the first revise.

Three changes reflected observations made on the first official draft but not included in the first revise. These related to Article 25, the referral of bills to the Supreme Court by the President. A court of not less than five judges was specified in the second revise.[115] Commenting on this article in the first official draft, McDunphy had stated that the court considering a bill should be composed of all the judges of the court.[116] Hearne and his colleagues, according to McDunphy, examined the matter and decided on a court composed of five judges.[117]

A very rare insight was given into the deliberations of the committee in a letter written in 1941 by Hearne (who was then Irish High Commissioner to Canada) to his successor as legal adviser, Michael Rynne. According to Hearne, at the time of framing the Constitution, 'we had many discussions as to whether a provision should not be inserted prohibiting a challenge in the courts to the validity of a statute the bill for which had been signed by the President after a reference thereof to the Supreme Court and a decision by that court under Article 26 [as Article 25 was renumbered in the final version of the Constitution] pronouncing the bill valid'. The committee of civil servants decided not to insert this provision. Hearne informed Rynne of the basis for the decision:

> There is little likelihood, it was said, of a Supreme Court which had decided, on a reference to them under Article 26, that a bill is valid, holding that the same bill when enacted into law is invalid. In order to insure that it would be so, it was agreed to put in the provision contained in 26, 2, 1 that the Supreme Court should consist of not less than five judges for the purposes of the article.[118]

In the same article, the prohibition on the expression of dissentient opinions by members of the court was removed in the second revise.[119] George Gavan Duffy had criticised the inclusion of this stipulation in his observations on the first official draft, terming it 'undemocratic', and asserting that 'the people are entitled to know what their judges think'.[120] The third change in the article required that the Supreme Court give its decision on a presidential referral not later than fourteen days, as against seven in the first revise.[121] As a result of the changes relating to the referral of bills by the President, section 34, 4, 3, which stated that 'the Supreme Court shall not entertain any question as to the validity of a law the bill for which shall have been referred to the Supreme Court by the President', was deleted. The remaining three changes were relatively minor and included a requirement that the government be composed of not less than seven and not more than fifteen members.[122] McDunphy and McElligott had expressed the opinion that a maximum number was desirable.[123]

With the circulation of the second revise, departments were invited to submit observations to the President.[124] McElligott's were, characteristically, the most forthright.[125] He noted, with pleasure, that the article on private property was not included, and expressed the hope that it had 'been dropped for good as being too controversial, contradictory and dangerous'.[126] Even before the receipt of these observations and McElligott's original philippic on the same article, de Valera, together with Hearne and the other civil service advisers, had begun to conceive of a distinction between fundamental rights that would be justiciable in the courts and certain economic and social rights that would not be justiciable.[127] In fact, there is clear evidence that the President, doubtless under the guidance of his legal adviser, was thinking in such terms before the establishment of the editorial committee.

As early as 16 March, the day on which the first official draft was circulated, Moynihan wrote that the article (on private property) 'is still under examination with a view to having it placed in a special category in the Constitution. It is intended as an indication of the principles which should inform the policy of social and economic laws of the state'.[128] In a memorandum dated 23 March 1937, containing McDunphy's observations, he noted, in relation to the article, that 'the President's intention is that a number of these sections are merely statements of moral principles and should not be created positive rights'.[129] Judge Gavan Duffy suggested that these provisions might be entitled 'Guiding Principles of Social Policy'.[130] John Hearne corresponded in early April with Charles Bewley, Irish Minister in Berlin, regarding the implications of similar sections in the Weimar Constitution. Bewley replied on 5 April, stating that these provisions were not 'juridically enforceable' but were expressions of hope that the legislature would act in certain ways.[131]

Moreover, Hearne and his colleagues on the drafting committee were aware that such rights were not recognised in many liberal democracies, especially in the

Commonwealth. Nor indeed were they a feature in constitutional documents such as the United States' Bill of Rights or the French Declaration of the Rights of Man.[132] Accordingly, de Valera and his drafting team assigned some of the sections and provisions contained in the draft article on property to a new, non-justiciable one, entitled 'Directive Principles of Social Policy'.[133] This, together with a revised version of articles on private property and part of an article on religion, was circulated on 23 April for the observations of ministers and senior officials.[134]

Third revise of the Constitution, 24 April 1937

When the third revise was distributed on 24 April 1937,[135] it contained articles on private property, religion and one entitled 'Directive Principles of Social Policy'. The latter, Article 44, was introduced by a preamble: 'The principles of social policy set down in this article are for the guidance of the legislature. The application of these principles in the making of laws shall be the exclusive care of the Oireachtas and shall not be cognisable by any court under any of the provisions of this Constitution.' Sections 2–5 of the article had their genesis in sections 5–9 of Article 41 of the first official draft. For example, Article 44, 3, 4 of the revise read: 'In particular, the state shall take care that in what pertains to the control of credit the welfare of the people as a whole shall be the central aim', a more moderate version of Article 41, 6, 2 of the earlier document. The extent to which the original article had been changed was evident in the approving words of J.J. McElligott: 'The preamble which now introduces this article deprives it of the character of a declaration of rights enforceable in the courts, and to that extent meets the objections urged by the Department of Finance.'[136] Article 42 on private property in the third revise was also influenced by the first official draft, being based on sections 1–3 of Article 41 of the latter.

Article 43 on religion consisted of two sections, the first one of which was blank. Section two contained five subsections and these, among other things, guaranteed freedom of conscience and free expression and practice of religion. The state was not to endow any religion or discriminate on the ground of religious profession, belief or status. The provisions in this section were based on sections 6–10 of Article 42 of the preliminary draft.

Apart from the inclusion of these three new articles, the third revise did not differ significantly from the second. This fact reflected the rigorous process of redrafting and revising which had characterised the previous two revises. Not counting the transitory provisions, there were forty-nine articles in the third revise and fifty in the second. Comparing both, and omitting the articles on private property, religion and the Directive Principles which did not feature in the second revise, thirty-nine articles were the same in the two revises.[137] Three articles from the second revise, 2, 32 and 40, were deleted as a consequence of changes in the third revise. Article 20 in the second revise (concerned with the consideration of bills and money bills by the Oireachtas) was divided into two Articles, 19 and 20, in the third revise.[138]

There were changes in five other articles in the third revise. Article 12, concerned with the election and entry into office of the President, was more detailed than the corresponding Article 13 of the second revise. Article 13, 11 contained provisions referring to a commission to assume the functions and powers of the President during his absence or a vacancy in the office. This was to be composed of the Chief Justice, the Chairman of Dáil Éireann and the Chairman of Seanad Éireann. This commission had been prefigured in Article 38 of the third draft of 11 January 1937, which stated that, pending the election of the first President, his powers and functions were to be exercised by a commission consisting of the Prime Minister, the Chief Justice and the Chairman of Dáil Éireann. The third revise removed any role to be played by the Council of State during a presidential absence or vacancy; accordingly, as noted earlier, Article 32 of the second revise, which was concerned with this, was deleted.

The third change, which pertained to Article 25, gave the Supreme Court a longer period to consider its decision in the matter of the referral of bills by the President: it was increased from not later than fourteen days to not later than thirty. In relation to emergency powers, there was no separate article in the third revise; hence Article 40 of the second revise was deleted. However, new provisions were inserted in Article 37 of the third revise, which dealt with 'the Trial of Offences', for the establishment of special courts by law, 'when, in accordance with such legislation, it may be determined that the ordinary courts are inadequate to secure the effective administration of justice and the preservation of public peace and order'.[139] Military tribunals or courts could be set up to deal with a state of war or armed rebellion.[140] In addition, Article 37 stated that the provisions of Article 33, concerned with the normal operation of courts, were not to apply to a special court or military tribunal.[141] The final article to be changed was Article 27, 3 of the third revise. This contained a provision whereby nothing in the Constitution could be invoked to invalidate any law enacted by the Oireachtas for the purpose of securing public safety and the preservation of the state in the time of war or armed rebellion, a principle incorporated in earlier drafts of the document.

Fourth revise of the Constitution, 26 April 1937

The fourth and final revise of the new basic law was circulated on 26 April 1937.[142] It was identical to the third except in two significant respects: it contained a full version of the article on religion and a preamble. If the article on property presented difficulties, the one relating to religion was even more problematical. De Valera's official biographers have written that he was to admit that the religious provisions gave him more anxiety than anything else in the Constitution.[143] He informed the Church of Ireland Archbishop of Dublin, Dr John Gregg, that he had neglected to pay much attention to it because he felt it was relatively easy to compose.[144] It may be remembered that a limited number of complete drafts was privately circulated on 10 March. These contained an article on religion.[145]

It was very confessional in tone, and informed by a strident expression of ultramontane Catholicism's doctrine that the Church of Rome was the true church founded by Jesus Christ and that it alone taught all that was necessary for salvation. The article provoked a negative reaction among some of those who received a copy. It appears that de Valera was told that it was offensive to the Protestant community of the state and would constitute a barrier to the unification of the country as its sentiments would inflame Protestant opinion in Northern Ireland.[146] It became apparent to de Valera that the article would have to be replaced. It had not been included in the draft issued on 16 March or in the two subsequent revises. An incomplete version appeared in the third revise and it was not until the fourth revise was issued on 26 April that a complete article was made available.

Much of the month of April was spent in seeking an article acceptable to Catholic and Protestant opinion. Only a brief summary of events is required here.[147] Secret and intense negotiations ensued involving the leaders of the various churches. The most difficult meetings were those between de Valera and Catholic churchmen, who were seeking the retention of the 'one true church' formula. The President was very concerned that the controversy had the potential to seriously damage, if not irremediably subvert, his constitutional ambitions. He wished to avoid becoming embroiled in a public conflict with Catholic Church leaders during the plebiscite, into which the leadership of the Protestant Churches could be drawn. Having arrived at a compromise wording, he sent the secretary of the Department of External Affairs, Joseph Walshe, to the Vatican to secure papal approval. Pope Pius XI was unhappy with the wording, as it was not in full accord with the Catholic Church's teachings on the true church, but he agreed to preserve a public silence on the issue. This satisfied de Valera and the relevant sections were included in the article on religion:

The State recognises the special position of the Holy Catholic Apostolic and Roman Church as the guardian of the faith professed by the great majority of the citizens.[148]

The State also recognises the Church of Ireland, the Presbyterian Church in Ireland, the Methodist Church in Ireland, the Religious Society of Friends in Ireland, as well as the Jewish Congregations and the other religious denominations existing in Ireland at the date of the coming into operation of this Constitution.[149]

De Valera conducted this exercise for an acceptable constitutional formula on religion independent of the drafting committee as a body.[150] At a meeting between the Papal Nuncio and one of de Valera's ministers, Seán T. O'Kelly, to discuss a possible version of the article, the prelate was informed that 'the lawyers have not yet seen the draft, and may want some changes in the phrasing ... but the substance will be unchanged'.[151] However, it was likely that de Valera consulted with individual members of the committee. The opinions of John Hearne, a former clerical student, with an interest in theology and philosophy nurtured during his years at Maynooth, and a trusted confidant, would have been prescient and authoritative. When Joseph Walshe was sent to the Vatican, he was furnished with a document by de Valera in preparation for his meeting with Catholic Church officials. This document gave Walshe guidelines for his talks,[152] perhaps the most crucial in relation to the Constitution, as failure had the potential to open a Pandora's box of recrimination between the government and the churches, Catholic and Protestant. Dermot Keogh believes that it is probable that the guidelines were drafted by either Hearne or Maurice Moynihan, or both.[153]

In Hearne's 'Plan of Fundamental Constitutional Law' of 20 August 1936, there was reference to a preamble,[154] as there was in his 'Summary of the Main Provisions of the Constitution', dated 5 November 1936.[155] While the third, fourth, preliminary and first official drafts had a heading 'Preamble', the section was blank in the various documents. A version of the preamble is to be found in de Valera's papers, dated 28 February 1937[156] and it bears a striking similarity to the one which eventually appeared in the fourth revise. In the 'Summary of the Main Provisions of the Constitution' the preamble was described as 'acknowledging that all lawful authority comes from God and setting forth the ideals of the nation and the purposes of the people in establishing this new Constitution'.[157]

The preamble in the final revise certainly reflected these concerns. It began: 'In the name of the Most Holy Trinity, from Whom is all authority and to Whom, as our final end, all actions both of men and states must be referred ...' The purposes of the Constitution were declared: 'And seeking to promote the common good, with due observance of prudence, justice and charity, so that the dignity and freedom of the individual may be assured, true social order attained, the unity of our country restored, and concord established with other nations ...'

An interesting omission in this revise was the section pertaining to members of the Oireachtas being representatives of the country and not delegates of constituencies and interests. It may be remembered that it appeared in the first revise, at de Valera's suggestion, and it featured in the next two revises. In fact, the sentiments informing it were underscored with the introduction of the word 'merely' in the third revise, which resulted in the article reading: '... shall act as public representatives of the country and not merely as delegates of particular constituencies or interests'. McElligott lauded the proposal and, in his opinion, if it could be carried out, 'the effect on public life will be very beneficial'.[158] However, an annotation was made to these observations: 'This may be omitted. It obviously cannot be enforced.'[159] This section was removed and the parochial, local and clientelistic nature of Irish politics prevailed.[160]

Transitory provisions

As part of drafting a new fundamental law, John Hearne had to prepare articles entitled 'Transitory Provisions', which facilitated and regulated the transition between the Constitution of the Free State and the proposed new constitutional order. These provisions represented the technical dimension of the making of a new constitution for the state and, though now omitted by terms of the same Constitution from copies of the document,[161] they are a significant testimony to the legal, drafting and organisational skills of their author.

The Zurich and third drafts of the Constitution, both of which appeared in January 1937, contained a heading 'Transitory Provisions' but the relevant sections were blank. It was not until the 'Fourth Draft', dated 13 February 1937, that a complete version of them was included by Hearne.[162] The preliminary draft, circulated on 10 March, had eleven articles relating to the transitory provisions and these are summarised hereunder:

> Article 50: A general election was to be held for Seanad Éireann on the coming into operation of the Constitution.
> Article 51: Until the assembly of Seanad Éireann the Oireachtas was to consist of one house. Until the first President assumed office the Oireachtas was complete and capable of functioning and until he assumed office, bills were to be signed by the commission described in Article 54.
> Article 52: Members of Dáil Éireann under the previous Constitution would continue to be members under the new Constitution.
> Article 53: Members of the government under the previous Constitution would continue in office under the new Constitution.
> Article 54: The first President was to assume office and the first Seanad was to assemble not later than six months after the coming into operation of the Constitution. Pending his entry into office, the powers and functions of the President were to be exercised by a commission composed of the Chief Justice, the President of the High Court and the Chairman of Dáil Éireann.

Article 55: All judges were to continue to exercise jurisdiction upon making the declaration required in the new Constitution.

Article 56: The auditor and comptroller general was to continue in office under the new Constitution.

Article 57: All existing officers of the Free State were to continue in office under the new Constitution.

Article 58: The government of Éire was to be the successor of the government of the Irish Free State as regards property, assets, rights and liabilities.

Article 59: Any provision of the new Constitution, except the article pertaining to amendment of the Constitution, could be amended by the Oireachtas within a period of three years after the date on which the first President assumed office.

Article 60: Date of coming into operation of the Constitution.

Arguably, Article 59 was the most important of the transitory provisions. By limiting the period during which the Oireachtas could amend the Constitution and by expressly precluding this article from amendment itself, Hearne was determined to protect the new fundamental law of the state from the legal ravages which had reduced the Free State Constitution to a mere statute of parliament, devoid of any popular legitimacy. After the expiration of the three-year period, the Constitution could only be changed by referendum. Thus it would become subject to the sovereign will of the people.

In the course of the observations on the first official draft and the subsequent revises, comments and proposals were made on the transitory provisions.[163] By the time the fourth revise was finalised in late April, there were thirteen articles in this section of the Constitution. Nine of them were substantially the same as Hearne's original versions and frequently used similar language.[164] This fact is a tribute to an extraordinarily skilful draftsman and constitution-maker, John Hearne.

Overview of the revision process, March–April 1937

The work of the editorial committee, shrouded as it was in secrecy, was dominated by discussions on the articles relating to personal and social rights. The article on private property was especially problematical. The provisions on religion were the most controversial and, while de Valera dealt with the matter personally, he very likely consulted with Hearne, his most trusted adviser regarding a new constitution. Changes were made to other articles in the course of the revises, most notably the establishment of a commission to discharge the powers and functions of the President in certain circumstances, with the consequent removal of a role for the Council of State in this respect. Another noteworthy change was the removal of a dedicated article dealing with the suspension of constitutional guarantees and the declaration of a state of emergency. Emergency provisions were stream-lined, with the President ceasing, for example, to have a role in issuing proclamations. The relevant provisions were incorporated in a number of articles rather than in one dedicated one.

The pressure on Hearne, Moynihan, McDunphy and O'Donoghue to produce revises was intensified by the fact that they were working to a tight time schedule. The proposed constitution had to be ready for a plebiscite on 1 July. This was taking place on the same day as a general election; therefore, the draft of the document had to be prepared for discussion by the Dáil which was to be dissolved sometime in the middle of June. In practical terms, this meant having copies available to deputies early in May.

On completion of the fourth revise, final printing instructions were given at 4.40pm on 28 April to Cahill Brothers, printers. Copies were to be delivered on the next day[165] and, on the evening of 30 April, the proposed new fundamental law was posted to members of the Dáil. Copies were also given, at the same time, to the press and the text was published in the morning papers of 1 May 1937.[166] After a long and exhaustive process, the work of Éamon de Valera and John Hearne was finally in the public domain and was now to be the subject of debate in Dáil Éireann and in the country.

However, before the Dáil debates are considered, the influences and factors which shaped the Constitution will be examined in the next chapter.

CHAPTER 6

The Shaping of the Constitution

Addressing the annual meeting of the Harvard Law School Association of New Jersey in 1957, John Hearne, Irish Ambassador to the United States, reflected on his experience of constitution-making in Ireland:

> The task before the Irish lawyers, in their particular time and circumstances, was to frame a constitution that would not only be a framework of government, but would at the same time make for the restoration of an uninterrupted national tradition. In order, therefore, to understand the tardy and sometimes torturous constitutional development in Ireland during the time of which I am speaking it is necessary to interpret the collective mind of the lawyers and political leaders who directed it.[1]

The 'tardy and torturous path' which led to the 1937 Constitution has been described in earlier chapters. This chapter is concerned with attempting to describe and interpret the 'collective mind' involved in the making of the Irish state's fundamental law, especially the 'mind' of de Valera and Hearne. In effect, the concerns and influences which informed their endeavour are the focus of attention, as these shaped the contents of the document, in general, and those of its articles, in particular.

Éamon de Valera's concerns were paramount – after all it was his constitutional project – and they shaped the document to a pre-eminent degree. The destruction of the Treaty settlement, the principle of popular sovereignty and partition were uppermost in his mind. The need to provide for emergency conditions in the state and the status of the Catholic Church demanded attention. Hearne advised and guided the President and also gave expression to some of his own concerns, most notably, the incorporation of judicial review as an effective protection of citizens' rights. Ireland's new basic law was to be influenced by, among other things, the 1919 Weimar Constitution, the 1922 Free State Constitution and by the 1935 draft heads. Hearne's in-depth knowledge of these and other documents proved indispensable and invaluable as the making of the Constitution progressed. A close and dynamic professional relationship developed between the President and the legal adviser. An understanding of their 'collective mind' affords a unique insight into the factors and considerations which shaped the 1937 Constitution.

Sovereignty and partition

A central preoccupation with Irish sovereignty as the controlling idea of de Valera's career has already been noted[2] and, in its more immediate context, his proposed constitution was all about sovereignty.[3] The principle of popular sovereignty featured prominently in the text and it effectively overlapped and blended into the partner idea of national sovereignty.[4] Bunreacht na hÉireann represented the culmination of his unrelenting determination in the pursuit of a sovereign Irish state. Documents which laid the foundation of the new constitutional dispensation confirm this fact. Sovereignty informed the 'squared paper draft' and the draft heads of 1935. In the 'Draft Heads of a Constitution', dated 14 October 1936, John Hearne included a series of fundamental declarations, under the heading 'The Sovereignty of the People':

> Declarations as follows:
>
> Of the principle that sovereignty resides in the people.
>
> Of the right of the people, to the exclusion of every other power or authority, to determine the form of the state and the political institutions under which they desire to live.
>
> Of the right of the people to determine the extent of the co-operation of the state with any other state or any league or group of states.
>
> That all disputed issues of national or public policy, or expediency be decided by the people in the ultimate resort ...[5]

In his speech to the Dáil proposing approval of the draft constitution, de Valera asserted that 'the people are the masters';[6] and, in a radio address on the eve of its publication, he stated that 'sovereignty resides in [the people] as their inalienable and indefeasible right'.[7] This central conviction was given practical and concrete expression in a number of ways. Most importantly, the proposed constitution was submitted to the people in a plebiscite on 1 July 1937. In the President's opinion, a new fundamental law designed to legitimise the state, as an expression of the nation and the national will, required popular endorsement. In an undelivered speech prepared by Hearne for de Valera on 12 June 1937, entitled 'The Constitution and National Life', a contrast was drawn between the proposed constitution and that of the Irish Free State. According to Hearne, the latter was not based on the principle of popular sovereignty and, in the constitutional system established under it, the Treaty was made paramount and was, therefore, destructive of popular sovereign rights.[8] The circumstances of the proposed new basic law were different:

> We are asking the people to say definitely and clearly that their power to make what laws they please in the national interest is untrammelled by any commitment in the domain of our foreign policy or any theory of our relationship with any other state or group of states. We want to correct the cardinal political error into which the framers of the 1922 Constitution were led when, at the instigation of the British government, they agreed to the fantastic proposition that our laws were to be valid or void and were to stand or fall by the test of their conformity or otherwise with a formula of association with other states.[9]

The popular endorsement of the 1937 Constitution represented an end as well as a beginning for de Valera: its enactment completed the destruction of the Treaty settlement and heralded a new constitutional framework, validated by the people and purged of the stains of British imperial dictation and oppression.

The Constitution included articles which gave direct expression to the sovereign principle on which the state was to be based. Article 1, described by John A. Murphy, as 'a ringing declaration of popular sovereignty',[10] was an assertion of the right of the Irish nation to choose its own form of government, while Article 6 affirmed that all powers of government derive from the people. Finally, the fact that the document could only be amended by referendum was an enshrinement of the fundamental principle of popular sovereignty as the very basis of the new constitutional order.

Notwithstanding the restrictive nomination procedure, the fact that the President was elected by the people of the state reinforced the central principle of popular sovereignty. Direct election of a president was novel – only two countries in Europe employed this method in 1936, while eleven others had indirectly elected presidents.[11] The presidency highlighted the break with the Treaty settlement of 1921 and the Free State Constitution by this very visible removal, even expulsion, of the British monarch from the internal affairs of the state. The President was intended 'to symbolise the constitutional autochthony of Bunreacht na hÉireann'.[12] The Canadian High Commissioner to Ireland was correct when he observed in 1947 that 'his [the President's] most important functions are, probably, the satisfaction of a popular demand for the symbols of independence'.[13]

Another of de Valera's concerns when he came to power in 1932 was the creation of circumstances in which all the people of the state, with the most miniscule exceptions, could give their loyalty to its basic law.[14] His version of this law, therefore, was aimed at the republican core,[15] with the purpose of reconciling erstwhile diehards and dissidents to the state. He sought to satisfy what he regarded as their just and reasonable aspirations. To finally and definitively eclipse the Treaty settlement, he would have to secure the support of republicans for his new constitutional order.

De Valera was also under pressure from a vocal section of his own Fianna Fáil party to end partition. One of the most recalcitrant critics was Eamon Donnelly, an Ulster-born member of the Dáil, who represented the constituency of Laois-Offaly from 1933 to 1937.[16] He heckled de Valera at the party's 1933 ard fheis (party convention) over the division of the country.[17] By 1936, after four years in power, Fianna Fáil had little to show on the issue of ending partition. The prospect of a new constitution galvanised some of the more strident republicans in the party. A motion at the 1936 ard fheis called for the insertion in the proposed document of a clause enabling elected representatives from Northern Ireland to sit in Dáil Éireann. De Valera succeeded in having the motion withdrawn: 'As he did not feel the need to have a discussion among his government colleagues on the details [of the proposed constitution], it was not out of character for him to be reluctant to promote a discussion among mere party delegates at an ard-fheis.'[18] On 21 December 1936, Donnelly put a motion before Fianna Fáil's national executive calling for a special ard fheis in early February to discuss the planned new constitution, 'with special reference to partition'. De Valera ensured no such gathering was called.[19] These events highlighted that he 'was vulnerable to pressure from within his party to adopt a strong, if ill-defined, line on partition'.[20]

To counter republican pressures within and without his own party and to vindicate his own republican credentials and orthodoxy, the Constitution would have to be suffused with the spirit of republicanism and include an expression of territorial nationalism in some form or other to address the matter of partition. This was the genesis of Articles 2 and 3. The former claimed that 'the national territory consists of the whole island of Ireland', while the latter qualified this claim, declaring that the jurisdiction of the state was confined to the area of the former Irish Free State, 'pending the reintegration of the national territory'.

Maurice Hearne, informed by conversations with John Hearne, has claimed that his father designed this formula and wrote the articles. His father, moreover, 'was firmly of the view (which he often insisted upon) that the formula was deliberately included in the Constitution to copper-fasten the support for it from the more militantly republican supporters of Mr de Valera's Fianna Fáil party'.[21] Articles 2 and

3 were prefigured in the 'Draft Heads of a Constitution' drawn up by Hearne in a document dated 14 October 1936:

Article II

The National Territory
The national territory is the whole of Ireland and the territorial seas of Ireland. The right of the Irish nation to the whole and every part of the national territory is absolute and indefeasible. No part of the national territory can be surrendered. Without prejudice to the right hereinbefore declared provision may be made by the parliament of Éire for the application of the laws of Éire to such part of the national territory as is for the time being within the jurisdiction of the parliament and government of Éire.[22]

Thus the substance of these articles was established very early in the drafting process.

Maurice Hearne, very likely reflecting his father's views, commented that 'the phraseology was deliberately vague and ambiguous, and the articles were intentionally included in the section [of the Constitution] on "The Nation" rather than the section "The State", highlighting the distinction between the two constitutional concepts'.[23] The state clearly referred to the twenty-six-county entity of Éire, while the nation encompassed the entire population resident on the whole island. This distinction between nation and state was maintained throughout the text of the Constitution.

Commenting on the two articles, Maurice Hearne, himself a barrister, has observed that two court judgements 'came closest, I think, to my father's views of the meaning he and Mr de Valera intended these controversial articles to have'. The first was that of Chief Justice Thomas F. O'Higgins. In the course of his judgement in the matter of the President's referral to the Supreme Court of the Criminal Law Jurisdiction Bill 1977, he stated:

The Constitution contains more than legal rules: it reflects, in part, aspirations and aims and expresses political theories which the people acted on when they enacted the Constitution ... One of the theories held in 1937 by a substantial number of citizens was that a nation as distinct from a state had rights; the Irish people living in what is now the Republic of Ireland and in Northern Ireland together formed the Irish nation: that a nation has a right to unity of territory in some form, be it a unitary or a federal state and that the Government of Ireland Act 1920, though legally binding, was a violation of that right to national unity which was superior to positive law. This national claim to unity exists not in the legal, but in the political order ...

The second judgement was that of Mr Justice Barrington of the High Court in 1988:

> The national claim to unity made in Article 2 exists in the political and not in the legal order. If, therefore, it is expressly saved by Article 3, by the use of the words 'and without prejudice to the right of the parliament and government established by this Constitution to exercise jurisdiction over the whole of that territory', it is saved as a political claim and not as a legal right. At best, the right of a national parliament to legislate for the whole of the national territory is an inchoate right which Article 3 does not permit it to exercise in the legal order until the national territory has been reintegrated.[24]

In effect, the national claim made in Article 2 was for all purposes of domestic and international law withdrawn in Article 3 until such time as the unification of the country was achieved. The formula contained in the two articles was a subtle one in which de Valera and Hearne combined national ideals, common sense, political and legal caution and pragmatism. The reason for this approach was dictated by the consideration that, on the issue of partition, de Valera was politically vulnerable: he had to satisfy his supporters and appease his critics. This presented the President with a pressing and complex problem. An expression of unqualified irredentism would have inflamed tensions between Ireland and Britain; while a feeble expression of national aspirations would have inflamed domestic political opposition. Hearne understood de Valera's dilemma and devised a legal and constitutional formula and form of words which addressed the President's concerns, domestically and internationally. In this regard, he did de Valera great service.

De Valera's Constitution won the support of most republicans because it was regarded by them as a republican document; on that basis Hearne was able to declare, in 1950 that 'The state is republican in form.'[25] However, the word 'republic' was not used in the document. The reasons why de Valera did not use it have been well rehearsed by historians.[26] Such use could not be justified until the state had jurisdiction over the whole island; preserving vestigial links with the Commonwealth might make easier the ending of partition; and there was a strong desire to avoid a direct and overt challenge to Britain, which could have resulted in retaliatory actions against Irish immigrants in that country.

Another consideration, of which Hearne as legal adviser was very much aware, was that the King still had a role in Irish diplomatic affairs by virtue of the External Relations Act 1936. The *Irish Times* reminded its readers of this fact in an editorial on Constitution Day, 29 December 1937:

The King will continue to act as the head of the new state in all matters pertaining to representation abroad. If, and when, Éire appoints new ministers to some foreign country, their letters of credence will be signed by, or on behalf of, George VI, and every diplomat who comes to Dublin will be accredited not to the uachtarán, but to the King.

The editor's summary of this situation was thus: 'It simply means that His Majesty will be recognised when he is needed, and ignored when he is not required.' Therefore, between 1937 and 1949, when a republic was declared, 'the King and the President co-existed in an uncomfortable pairing under the Constitution',[27] their functions partitioned by de Valera: the former attending to external matters, the latter to internal.

The continuing role of the King in foreign relations was illustrated in 1939 when a difficulty arose in the appointment of an Irish Minister to Berlin. The King would not issue letters of credence to a country with which, as King, he was at war. Another diplomat had to act as chargé d'affaires for the duration of the conflict.[28] In the eyes of the rest of the world, Ireland was still a Dominion, like Australia and Canada. The use of the word 'republic' in the Constitution might have caused international and diplomatic complications and confusion, something de Valera and Hearne wished to avoid. Their solution, therefore, was a constitution that was republican in form, for a state whose international status remained that of a Dominion of the British Commonwealth.[29] The *Irish Times* observed, somewhat caustically, that the people of Ireland 'will be republicans at home and dominionists abroad. They will be in the Commonwealth, but not of it'.[30] Such acerbity aside, the decision not to use the word 'republic' meant that Britain chose to act as if nothing had changed in terms of Ireland's Commonwealth membership.[31] Conflict had been avoided.

De Valera believed that his old scheme of external association had been realised and the Constitution and the External Relations Act were the means whereby this had been achieved. This was important to the President. The Constitution was not just a political and legal document: it was much more – for him it was personal. It justified his actions and words in the 1920s, when he rejected the Treaty and presented 'Document no. 2' as his alternative. According to John Bowman, throughout his political career de Valera was preoccupied by the verdict of history: 'This was part of his own psyche but was reinforced by two considerations: self-doubt about his behaviour during the Treaty and the need to reply to the criticism of what he must have seen as his detractors and calumniators in the 1920s.'[32] From early on in his public life he showed what Roy Foster has described as 'an almost neurotic obsession with controlling the official version of events in which he played a part'.[33]

He repeatedly called for a historical commission to consider the Treaty and Civil War periods, before which he was prepared to give evidence, and Cosgrave could be one of his accusers. This did not happen; no such commission was established.[34] He did, however, recruit Frank Pakenham to write his version of Treaty history, every draft of which book was scrutinised by de Valera. It appeared in 1935 under the title *Peace by Ordeal*.[35] Moreover, he channelled his version of events through his strict control of an 'elephantine official biography' reverently written by Lord Longford (as Frank Pakenham was later styled) and Thomas P. O'Neill.[36] He also produced Bunreacht na hÉireann, which was shaped by his concept of external association first proposed in 'Document no.2'.

In a very real sense, this same Constitution may be seen, among other things, as his apologia for his words and actions in the 1920s. The importance he attached to this document was evident when he asked Maurice Moynihan, secretary of the Department of the Taoiseach (1937–60) to prepare a historical account of it, with particular reference to the Irish version. Moynihan produced two drafts in January 1949.[37] De Valera turned his attention to the matter again in 1961, when he approached Moynihan to resume work on the account.[38] In 1963, the latter was in receipt of government files pertaining to the Constitution.[39] In October of the same year, he wrote to John Hearne seeking any information he might have.[40] Three years later, in a letter to Hearne, Moynihan told him that work on the account was 'progressing slowly'.[41] It appears never to have been finished.

Protection of fundamental rights

De Valera and Hearne wanted the new fundamental law to guarantee and protect the rights of the citizens of the state. As was noted in Chapter 4, the legal adviser, as a constitutional lawyer, had a more developed sense of such rights than the President. Among the directions given in 1935 by de Valera to Hearne in relation to the draft heads of a constitution was a requirement that, 'in particular', certain basic articles guaranteeing 'fundamental human rights' be included.[42] These instructions, influenced by Hearne's conviction that the Constitution should guarantee human rights, were also relevant to the new basic law de Valera ordered to be drafted in June 1936. In the 'Plan of Fundamental Constitutional Law' drawn up by the legal adviser in August 1936, there was a heading 'Fundamental Rights of Citizens' and these were identified as:

> Article 9: Equality of citizens before the law.
> Article 10: Freedom of conscience.
> Article 11: Right of assembly and association. Right of free expression of opinion.
> Article 12: Liberty of the person.
> Article 13: Inviolability of the dwelling.[43]

The 'Draft Heads of a Constitution' he prepared in October 1936 also provided for citizens' fundamental rights.[44] The 'Preliminary Draft of the Constitution', dating from this time, included what were among the earliest versions of these articles by Hearne:

> Section 1: All citizens are equal before the law.
> Section 2: Freedom of conscience and the free expression and practice of religion are, subject to public order and morality, guaranteed to every citizen.
> [...]
> Section 3: The following rights are guaranteed to all citizens, subject to public order and morality:
> (1) The right of free expression of opinion,
> (2) The right to assemble peaceably and without arms, and
> (3) The right to form associations and unions. Laws may be passed to prevent or control open air meetings which are calculated to interfere with normal traffic or otherwise to become a nuisance or danger to the general public.
> Section 4: The liberty of the person is inviolable and no person shall be deprived of his liberty except in accordance with law.
> Section 5: The dwelling of each citizen is inviolable and shall not be forcibly entered except in accordance with law.[45]

The Zurich draft of early January 1937 and the third draft later in the same month included the fundamental rights in Articles 32 and 34 respectively, and these did not differ dramatically from the versions in the preliminary draft of 1937.[46] The section relating to the liberty of the person did contain an additional provision relating to *habeas corpus*.

Drafting continued and, in February 1937, a significant new dimension was introduced into the article dealing with fundamental rights. Part of it now read:

> 2, 1: The state now guarantees to respect, defend and vindicate the personal rights of each citizen. The state shall, accordingly, take all necessary measures to prevent any violation of these rights, enforce respect for social order and punish offenders.
> 2, 2: The state shall, in particular, protect as best it may, from unjust attack, and, in case of injustice done, vindicate the person, life, good name and protect the property rights of every citizen.[47]

Clearly, it was envisaged that the state play an active role in the matters of the fundamental rights of citizens. In addition to guaranteeing them, it was going to vindicate them. There is evidence that these proposed provisions produced much discussion between Hearne and de Valera. Among the papers of the latter is a typed script of the definition of the word 'vindicate' taken from the *Oxford English Dictionary*.[48] The President, it would appear, wanted clarification of the implications of the wording. In the course of the discussions, de Valera deleted the second sentence of the first subsection (beginning with 'The state shall accordingly').

The provision relating to the equality of all citizens before the law also included significant changes:

> 1, 1: The state acknowledges that all citizens are as human persons equal before the law.
> 1, 2: The state shall, however, in its enactments have due regard to individual difference of capacity, physical and moral, and social function.[49]

There was a prohibition on conferring titles of nobility, though orders of merit could be created. This latter provision had been included in the Zurich and subsequent drafts. The equality guarantee featured in Hearne's draft heads of 1935, Article 38 of which stated: 'All citizens of Saorstát Éireann are equal before the law.' As the drafting process progressed, the influence of Catholic social teaching became apparent, a fact which will be discussed later in this chapter.

The phrase 'as human persons' had its origin in this teaching.[50] The article came to be based on the principle of strict equality, by virtue of the common humanity shared by all citizens, and on the general understanding that for the state to pass laws which treat people unequally would be fundamentally unjust. The article also recognised that perfect equality of treatment cannot be always achieved. Accordingly, it was recognised that applying the same treatment to all persons could lead to indirect inequality because of the different circumstances in which citizens of the state could find themselves.[51] The concept of equality before the law had not been an aspect of the 1922 Constitution. On the basis of its presence in the 1937 document, one is entitled to assume that de Valera and Hearne were, albeit to an unascertainable extent, motivated by an egalitarian ideal.[52]

As the drafting of the article on fundamental rights continued, Hearne endeavoured to reflect and give legal expression to ideas and suggestions advanced by others, such as Fr John Charles McQuaid (see below), as well as his own. The article was presented to the Dáil for approval and was to become Article 40 of the Constitution, which reads:

> 40, 1. All citizens shall, as human persons, be held equal before the law.
> This shall not be held to mean that the state shall not in its enactments have due regard to differences of capacity, physical and moral, and of social function.

2, 1: Titles of nobility shall not be conferred by the state. Orders of merit, however, may be created.

[...]

3, 1: The state guarantees in its laws to respect, and, as far as is practicable, by its laws to defend and vindicate the personal rights of the citizen.

3, 2: The state shall, in particular, by its laws protect as best it may from unjust attack and, in the case of injustice done, vindicate the life, person, good name, and property rights of every citizen.

4, 1: No citizen shall be deprived of his personal liberty save in accordance with law ...

5: The dwelling of every citizen is inviolable and shall not be forcibly entered save in accordance with law.

6: The state guarantees liberty for the exercise of the following rights, subject to public order and morality:

The right of the citizens to express freely their convictions and opinions ...

The right of the citizens to assemble peaceably and without arms ...

The right of the citizens to form associations and unions ...[53]

This article was a more elaborate recital of fundamental rights than had been included in the Free State Constitution. This was a testimony to the commitment of de Valera and Hearne to recognise and protect these rights. They represented the freedoms essential for an acceptable life as a citizen in a constitutional polity.

Article 40, 3 is the most important provision in the Constitution and has given rise to an enormous volume of litigation.[54] It has become the basis for the determination of a range of 'unenumerated rights', i.e. rights not expressly declared in the text of the document (see Chapter 8). But what were the article's origins? There is very strong evidence that Article 6 of the 1933 Portuguese Constitution provided Hearne with his model: 'The state shall take all necessary measures to safeguard the common good in regard to the life, liberty, property, morals and all the natural or justly acquired rights of all of the citizens and to promote so far as possible their material, intellectual and moral interests.'[55] Significantly, in 1935, barrister George Gavan Duffy offered de Valera a copy of the new Portuguese Constitution,[56] an offer which he was happy to accept.[57]

Interestingly, Duffy's biographer, G.M. Golding, has suggested that he aided John Hearne in the drafting of the Constitution.[58] In fact, his son, Colum Gavan Duffy, claimed that his father was responsible for drafting Article 40, 3.[59] He was certainly well regarded by the President, being appointed to serve on the Commission on the Second House of the Oireachtas in 1936[60] and, more importantly, was one of those who received a copy of the first official draft on 16 March 1937.[61] Hearne, in a letter to Gavan Duffy's son on the occasion of his father's death, said that 'he would always be remembered as one of the architects of the Constitution'.[62] However, there is no evidence that Duffy drafted Article 40, 3; indeed, his biographer has written that 'nothing definite can be said of Gavan Duffy's contribution [to the Constitution]'.[63] While Colum Gavan Duffy was overstating his father's role, this is not to say that he did not have one as an adviser to Hearne and in his astute and valuable submissions to the editorial committee.[64] In that respect, he was one of the document's architects. However, Article 40, 3 was principally the work of Hearne,[65] the rights of the citizen being a matter which concerned him deeply.

While serving as Irish High Commissioner to Canada (1939–49) and Ambassador to the United States (1950–60), Hearne gave speeches from which it is evident that the position of the individual citizen in the state was an issue which preoccupied him. Speaking in America in 1950, he referred to the fact that the Irish Constitution addressed 'the crucial issue of the relation of the citizen, as a human person, to the state'.[66] A few years earlier he had spoken to a Canadian audience of the document's concern for 'the personal and political life of the individual citizen'.[67]

Hearne had a particular appreciation of the rights of citizens because the new Irish Constitution was being drafted at a time when democracy was under threat in many European states and fascist and communist totalitarianism was on the rise. He highlighted this fact in the undelivered speech he prepared for de Valera, referred to earlier:

> This Constitution is presented for the approval of the Dáil and country at a juncture in human affairs which has no parallel in the annals of mankind. The world is in the throes of a conflict of political philosophies which has divided it into two academies and bids fair to divide it into two camps. And the issues that hang on the outcome of that incredible conflict touch down to the deepest questions that concern the human mind. The questions of the relation of the individual to the state, the rights of one and the rights of the other, the duties of each to each ...[68]

Speaking in Pennsylvania in 1950, he told his audience that 'the Bolshevik revolution of twenty years previously, the fascist dictatorship in Italy and the National Socialist dictatorship in Germany had raised once again the old constitutional issue of the relation of the citizen to the political sovereign'.[69] In another address, Hearne observed that, when the Irish people surveyed the world scene in the 1930s, 'they found systems and schools whose doctrine is the denial of personal morality or state responsibility, whose method is force and whose object and effect is the establishment of a social order destructive of human dignity'.[70]

For Hearne, this dignity was a fundamental attribute of the human person. He told graduates at a ceremony in Notre Dame University in 1950 that

> man is the chief and ultimate subject of all literature and art. All the sciences are his handmaid. All the systems of law and of government which the world has known are of his making. The state is his minister and not his master. The whole course of history has been determined and is to-day being determined by his actions, his genius, his virtues and his crimes.[71]

Hearne's sense of human dignity was deeply rooted in his religious convictions; his beliefs were shaped within a Catholic moral and philosophical framework: '... the theme of man, the central figure in all history, his nature wonderfully instituted and still more wonderfully reformed, man the masterwork of God, made in his image, heir by divine redemption to an everlasting kingdom in a world to come'.[72] In an address in Pennsylvania in 1950, he gave a powerful exposition of his conviction regarding the inherent dignity of the human person:

> I want to refer ... to the part of our political system which relates to the life of the individual in the community, as a factor in the life of the nation and in the relations of the Republic of Ireland to the other states of the world. It is here that the philosophy of life of our people has most clearly determined the substance of our fundamental law. The members of the community are regarded not only as citizens, but, what is far more important in the development of civil society, as human persons. Their equality before the law is equality not as members of the community but as human persons. An individual is not antecedently a citizen of the state; he is first of all a human person, whose relation to the state is determined by his relation to God. We did not theorise about that when the Constitution was being framed. We began with the basic historic fact that man is a creature of God, made in God's image ... The state was made for time, the human soul for time and eternity. That was the standpoint from which we began. It is, I think, subject to correction, the standpoint of Jeffersonian Democracy ... We set out to enthrone in our law the historic human person arrayed in all the faculties of his created nature, robed in the full light of his supernatural destiny, the masterwork of God, who became the temple of the very spirit of God. We made provision for the protection of his life, his liberty, his right to work, and to a living wage, his property, the sanctity of his home, and so on.[73]

It is apparent that John Hearne was affected and impressed by Catholic teaching, which informed his deep conviction in the rights of the citizen. Consequently, 'a central part of Catholic social thought which it [the Constitution] embodied was concerned with human dignity through the protection of fundamental human rights'.[74]

Interestingly and significantly, Samuel Moyn, Professor of Law and History at Harvard University, has argued that dignity as a concept in a constitution entered constitutional history in Ireland in 1937,[75] while Bunreacht na hÉireann was being drafted. A version of the preamble, probably authored by McQuaid and which appears to date from late February 1937, included a reference to it:

> And seeking to promote the common good by due observance of the Christian principles of prudence, justice and charity, whereby the dignity and freedom of the citizens may be rightfully secured and true social order adequately established and maintained ...[76]

On 19 March of that year, Pope Pius XI issued the encyclical *Divini Redemptoris*[77] which condemned atheistic communism.[78] Its failure to respect the dignity of the human person was repeatedly identified and stated.[79] The encyclical concerned itself, among other matters, with the individual in the dignity of his human personality and the reconciliation of individual dignity with that of the state.[80] Pope Pius turned emphatically to personalism, with its concern for the uniqueness of the human person, as the Christian alternative to totalitarianism.[81] Crucial revisions of the new Irish Constitution were occurring in the immediate aftermath of the encyclical and it is hardly a coincidence that the reference to dignity was retained.

In his speech at Pennsylvania, Hearne also reflected on the fundamental freedoms of the human person, expressing views which may appear deeply conservative to many modern readers:

> The greatest danger to free nations today is not external aggression: it is the internal retrogression in one free country after another from the standards of life and behaviour on which western society was founded and western civilization sustained ... Freedoms were mistaken for rights conferred by the state. Freedom of speech, for example, was misinterpreted as a man's freedom to think and say what he liked. Whereas the only reason for freedom of speech was that a man must be free in order to fulfil his duty of speaking the truth... I want to say simply that we cannot defend a doctrine of personal liberty which comprises the independence of man's intellect of truth and reality. It is the truth which makes us free. And we cannot defend a doctrine of personal liberty which comprises the independence of a man's will, that is, his personal judgment, of any external rule whatever. As you cannot divorce freedom of thought from truth, neither can you

divorce freedom of action from morality; and you cannot divorce morality from the eternal law of God.[82]

These opinions must be regarded, once again, in the context of Hearne's deeply held religious views. It must also be remembered that his audience was made up of graduates of a Catholic university. He was expressing his idealised conviction relating to the responsibilities attached to the freedoms which he saw as the right of all human persons and this conviction was profoundly influenced by his Catholic Christian beliefs. According to Moyn, 'Jesus's truth had been intended to set men free, but not for the sake of their creative autonomy or the satisfaction of their preferences.'[83] Rights were seen as a necessity of free moral action but also understood in the overall context of the common good.[84] Hearne presented a vision of moral restraint. It was his opinion that all human persons must be conscious of the law of God – in his view, the source of all truth and morality – in exercising the freedoms they enjoyed by virtue of their humanity. Men and women should conform to God's will and the moral order.

In another of his speeches, Hearne declared that 'society is the safeguard of the citizen and not his total master. That is why, to use the language of the lawyers, government should be actually representative and constitutionally responsible.'[85] By 'constitutionally responsible' he meant that the actions of government had to be in accord with the Constitution which enshrined the fundamental rights of the citizen. Government did not have unfettered power – it was obliged to act with due regard to the state's fundamental law.

The Constitution, as envisaged by de Valera and Hearne, guaranteed and protected the fundamental rights of citizens in a number of ways. Firstly, and most obviously, the state guaranteed, by the terms of Article 40, 3, 1, to respect and vindicate the personal rights of citizens, which were enumerated in Article 43, 3, 2: life, person, good name and property rights. Secondly, the laws enacted by the Oireachtas could not be in any respect repugnant to the Constitution.[86] Thirdly, the Constitution could only be changed by referendum. This was a significant security. Under the Free State Constitution, any article could be abrogated by act of the Oireachtas. Thus fundamental rights were tentative and could be set aside, as happened with the enactment of the Constitution (Amendment No. 17) Act 1931, which inserted Article 2A into the Constitution.

As was noted in Chapter 4, the 1934 Constitution Review Committee favoured protection of the fundamental rights provisions of the Free State Constitution by proposing that they could only be changed by referendum. Hearne's 1935 'Draft Heads of a Constitution' included a provision influenced by this recommendation.[87] However, as the drafting of a new constitution progressed, the protection of a referendum was extended to include all articles. In his 'Plan of Fundamental Constitutional Law', drawn up in August 1936, Article 5 declared: 'Every proposal for the amendment of this Constitution or any provision thereof ... shall, in accordance with regulations to be made by the Oireachtas, be submitted by referendum to the decision of the people.'[88] This idea was confirmed in draft heads of October 1936, Article 73 reading: 'Constitution to be amended by referendum only.'[89] This principle was given expression in the Zurich draft in January 1937[90] and in subsequent drafts.

The resolve of de Valera and Hearne to secure the referendum as a real and effective safeguard of citizens' rights was highlighted in their determination to protect the document against amendment during the transitional period from the Free State Constitution to the full operation of the new one. Their concerns in this regard were informed by the fate of the former. As was explained in Chapter 4, Article 50 provided for amendment of the Free State Constitution by the Oireachtas for a period of eight years, but this was extended by a further eight years. This ensured that the referendum provisions of the article never came into effect. Thus Article 50 became a legal Trojan horse and was used to deconstruct the Free State Constitution.[91]

Their intention to avoid a repetition of such a circumstance became apparent during the discussions between de Valera and Hearne in 1935 and which were recorded in the 'squared paper draft'. Under the heading 'Transitional', the President wrote the following: 'The next parl[iament] shall be at liberty to pass organ[ic] laws to have immed[iate] effect – but must be ratified by referendum at time of next general election.'[92] It is apparent that the two men were anxious to ensure that limits were imposed on the power of parliament during the transition period of the Constitution. As the constitutional expert, Hearne was especially aware of this necessity to impose limitations and would have advised the President accordingly. Therefore, in Article 51, 1 of the transitory provisions of Bunreacht na hÉireann he included the following:

> any of the provisions of this Constitution, except the provisions of the said Article 46 [which regulated amendment of the Constitution] and this article, may ... be amended by the Oireachtas ... within a period of three years after the date on which the first President shall have entered upon office.

Hearne inserted an additional safeguard in section 2:

> A proposal for the amendment of this Constitution under this article shall not be enacted into law if, prior to such enactment, the President ... shall have signified in a message ... addressed to the chairman of each House of the Oireachtas that the proposal is in his opinion a proposal to effect an amendment

of such character and importance that the will of the people thereon ought to be ascertained by referendum before its enactment into law.

De Valera explained to the Dáil that the purpose of these elaborate provisions was 'to see that even within the three years [of the transition period], the foundations of the Constitution are not upset'.[93] Moreover, he rejected a suggestion from Deputy Frank McDermott that the three years be extended to eight.[94] Clearly, de Valera and Hearne were intent that there was to be no repetition of the baleful results of Article 50 of the Free State's Constitution in the new version of Ireland's basic law. Accordingly, the amending article itself was protected by Hearne against amendment, as was Article 51 of the transition provisions. In addition, in Article 46, he required that every bill proposing any future amendments after the Constitution came into operation 'shall be expressed to be "An act to amend the Constitution"'; and such a bill 'shall not contain any other proposal'. By requiring that the exact provision of the Constitution that was being amended be specified and its scope identified, Hearne was determined to secure against the lack of stability which characterised its predecessor.

The final protection of the human and democratic rights of citizens was Article 26, the power of referral of bills by the President to the Supreme Court to ascertain their constitutionality.

Fundamental to the protection of the rights of citizens was judicial review, whereby the courts could invalidate any actions of government or laws enacted by the Oireachtas if these conflicted with any provision of the Constitution. Article 65 of the 1922 Constitution provided for judicial review but it was never a significant or important feature of the constitutional life of the Free State. There were two main reasons for this. First, the concept was entirely new to Irish judges, trained as they were under the British system where parliament was sovereign. Therefore, they were not conditioned by their tradition or experience to adapt to a system which provided for judges reviewing laws.[95] Second, for the whole of the lifetime of the Free State Constitution the Oireachtas could amend it by ordinary legislation.[96] In fact, during the initial eight-year period when it came into operation, it was upheld by the courts that any legislation enacted by the Oireachtas which was found in conflict with the Constitution had the effect, *ipso facto*, of amending the Constitution, whether on a permanent or temporary basis.[97]

Moreover, this basic law was of so little weight that it was not thought necessary that an amending act should specify the exact extent of any amendment. Such circumstances robbed the Constitution of its potential as a check on the actions of the government and legislature and as a protection for the state's citizens.[98] This reality was confirmed in the ruling of the Supreme Court in 1934 in the case of *The*

State (Ryan) v Lennon, as it was established that, the terms of the scheduled Treaty aside, 'there were no legal barriers to amendments of the Constitution'.[99] Thus judges had no real power of judicial review. Laura Cahillane has observed: 'How could the judiciary act as guardians of the Constitution if the executive had a limitless power of amendment? The judiciary needed the security of an entrenched Constitution before more use could be made of the judicial review provisions.'[100]

De Valera and Hearne were determined to give the principles of judicial review based on constitutional criteria a new security. The best means to achieve this was the subject of serious discussions between them. The establishment of a constitutional court was given consideration. It was first mentioned in late April 1935, a fact recorded in the 'squared paper draft'.[101] The idea came from Hearne. As a comparative constitutional lawyer, he was aware of developments in other countries and that the establishment of such a court was very much in vogue in newly emerging European states.[102] In December 1935, the President was furnished with a memorandum by Hearne on the 'machinery established to determine the validity of laws' in various countries and this included references to constitutional courts.[103] His 'Plan of Fundamental Constitutional Law', prepared in August 1936, included a section which read:

> The judicial power
> Articles 31 to 33
> Article 31: Establishment of the constitutional court.[104]

In October 1936, Hearne drafted a version of articles pertaining to judicial review. The High Court was to have original jurisdiction to determine the question of the validity of any law having regard to the provisions of the Constitution, with appellate jurisdiction conferred on the Supreme Court.[105] Around the same time, he drafted another version of the article and, under the terms of this, a constitutional court was to be established:

> Section 4
> The Constitutional Court shall have exclusive jurisdiction to determine the question of the validity of any law having regard to the provisions of this Constitution. The decision of the Constitutional Court on every such question shall be final and conclusive.
> The Constitutional Court shall consist of seven members who shall be appointed as follows:
> The chairman and two others shall be appointed by the President.
> Two members shall be appointed by the judges of the Supreme Court.
> Two members shall be appointed by the judges of the High Court.

Section 5

The judges of the High Court, the Supreme Court and the Constitutional Court shall not be removed except for stated misbehaviour or incapacity and then only by a resolution passed by Dáil Éireann, or, in the event of a second house of the Oireachtas being established, by resolutions passed by both houses.[106]

The similarity between Hearne's proposal and that of the constitutional court of the Czechoslovak Republic is striking and certainly influenced his ideas.[107] There are two annotations, in de Valera's hand, on the margins of the draft, which suggest that the President was giving the matter of the constitutional court serious consideration. The composition of the court was the subject matter of the first annotated comment.[108] The second annotation also considered the court's composition and whether the court should be constituted each year or on a case by case basis.[109] Though the annotations are difficult to understand at times, clearly consideration was being given to the composition of the court's personnel.

The establishment of a constitutional court was a radical proposal for a country with a common law jurisdiction such as Ireland[110] and would have represented a seismic departure from the legal system inherited from Britain. Hearne was the constitutional expert and was the person advising de Valera. His readiness to propose the option of such a court to the President is evidence of the legal adviser's commitment to establish judicial review as an integral part of the new Constitution. That he was willing to advise an approach which was at variance with the traditional legal system and that de Valera was willing to consider this advice was clear evidence that both men were determined to incorporate a meaningful and robust system of judicial review into the new constitutional architecture.

Judicial review was to be incorporated into the Constitution. However, the option of a constitutional court was discountenanced; perhaps it was regarded as too radical. The last reference to it in a draft article was in early January 1937. At this stage, it was decided that the Supreme Court would perform the work of a constitutional court.[111] Notwithstanding this decision, the constitutional court was a subject which had seriously exercised de Valera and Hearne. The fact that it did meant that they foresaw a greater role for judicial review and were determined to accommodate it in the planned constitution. If that were not the case, in Gerard Hogan's words, 'then the suggestion that there should be a constitutional court would surely not have been seriously entertained'.[112]

While Hearne's plans for a constitutional court failed to come to fruition, traces of it may be found in the Article 26 reference procedure.[113] This was an innovative feature of Bunreacht na hÉireann, having no corresponding provision in the 1922 Constitution, and was included due to Hearne's expertise as a constitutional lawyer.

Its origins were to be found in deliberations of the 1934 Constitution Review Committee, of which he was a member. As was noted in Chapter 4, constitutional lawyers favoured a procedure which allowed for a swift determination of the constitutionality of a particular law. In giving legal expression to this idea during the drafting process, Hearne was influenced by pre-1922 legislative models.[114] Section 4 of the Judicial Committee Act 1833 provided for reference of disputed legal matters to the Privy Council.[115] In the opinion of Justice Ronan Keane, section 51 of the Government of Ireland Act 1920 bears a 'remarkably close resemblance to the Article 26 power':

> If it appears to the Lord Lieutenant ... expedient in the public interest that steps shall be taken for the speedy determination of the question whether ... any bill introduced in either of (the) parliaments [those of Southern and Northern Ireland] or any provision thereof ... is beyond the powers of such parliament ... the Lord Lieutenant ... may present the same to His Majesty in council, and thereupon, if His Majesty so directs, the said question shall be forthwith referred to and heard and determined by the Judicial Committee of the Privy Council.[116]

This decision to provide for judicial review was made despite opposition from powerful figures in the civil service. J.J. McElligott, secretary of the Department of Finance, expressed unease about the implications of such review: 'If Articles 38 to 41 [of the first official draft and Articles 40–4 in the 1937 Constitution] dealing with personal rights and social policy are retained, it is conceivable that many efforts will be made to upset bills properly passed and this would be undesirable.' He continued: 'In this [Article 38] and the three succeeding Articles 39, 40 and 41, there are a number of mandatory provisions making it compulsory on the state to do a number of vague and undefined things, e.g. "to have due regard to individual differences of capacity, physical moral and of social justice and social charity etc."'[117] The possible consequences of the inclusion of these articles caused him to be concerned.

McElligott's colleague, Stephen Roche, secretary of the Department of Justice, was also worried: 'The guarantees given in section 2 [of Article 38] are widely worded and may have unexpected results.'[118] A month later, in April 1937, he was blunt in the expression of his unease to Michael McDunphy: 'As you know, I dislike the whole idea of tying up the Dáil and the government with all sorts of restrictions and putting the Supreme Court like a watch-dog over them for fear they may run wild and do all sorts of indefensible things ...'[119] He was reiterating views he had expressed even more forcefully while serving as a member of the 1934 Constitution Review Committee:

I believe that what this country wants at present and probably will continue to want for years is a strong executive, not liable, so long as it has the support of the people, to be delayed, hampered and humiliated at every step by long arguments in the courts ... A government should not allow itself to be insulted. Further, I believe that the doctrine of 'judicial independence' and 'the separation of functions' are being overdone and the courts have been given or have assumed a position in our civic life to which they are not entitled. There was a time in England when the judges' job was to save the people from an irresponsible executive: it may be necessary, in turn, for a responsible executive to save the people *from irresponsible judges.*[120]

In spite of the opposition of McElligott and Roche and the alarm bells they sounded in relation to judicial review and the potential for judicial activism which the new basic law could afford, de Valera, supported by Hearne and his colleagues on the editorial committee, chose to retain this important principle and the attendant provisions in the Constitution. In his observations on the second revise, dated 13 April 1937, Stephen Roche realised that the committee was determined in its decision and that further protest was futile:

Generally, the Department [of Justice] felt that the draft constitution went too much into detail, whereas the department's feeling is that the shorter and more general the Constitution is, the less likely it is that the maintenance of law and order will be impeded by limitations on the power of the Dáil and by conflicts between the judiciary and the executive. The departmental view on these particular matters and on the general principle remains unchanged, but presumably a decision has been taken in favour of the opposite point of view and there is nothing to be gained by re-opening the matter.[121]

Judge Brian Walsh, formerly of the Supreme Court, observed that it was often claimed that de Valera did not relish the provision of judicial review but, according to Walsh, 'that claim can only be evaluated in the light of the fact that he expressly provided for it in the Constitution itself'.[122] And he did this in the face of the reservations voiced by key government departments. He made his decision to give the courts a role in relation to the review of legislation despite having been forewarned about the possible implications. Thus, in the words of James Casey, 'de Valera clearly and unequivocally provided for judicial review'[123] and was influenced and supported in his view by John Hearne and his colleagues. The President had the intellectual self-confidence to see beyond the standard civil service attitude and worked with civil servants who shared his opinions.[124] The convictions and determination of those involved in the making of the 1937 Constitution ensured that judicial review was enshrined as fundamental to the protection of the human rights of the citizens of the state.

Significantly, two years after Bunreacht na hÉireann came into operation, a court judgement severely tested de Valera's attitude to judicial review, but his subsequent response confirmed his favourable disposition towards its inclusion in the Constitution. The facts of the case need only be given in outline. In 1939, the Offences against the State Act was enacted.[125] On 22 August of the same year, with the prospect of war looming, Part IV of the act, which provided for internment, was activated. A month later, the Minister for Justice issued a warrant directing the arrest and internment of James Burke. An application for *habeas corpus* was heard on 28 and 29 November before Judge George Gavan Duffy, who ruled that the legislation governing Burke's detention was unconstitutional.[126] As a result of this decision, Burke and fifty-three other prisoners were released. On 23 December 1939, the Phoenix Park Magazine was raided by the IRA and over a million rounds of ammunition were seized. Some of the participants were believed by the security forces to have been among those released in the aftermath of the *Burke* case. In response, the government decided to amend the Offences against the State Act to take account of Judge Duffy's ruling.

In the course of the Dáil debate on 3 January 1940 on the proposed amendment, de Valera uttered sentiments which conveyed a pronounced disenchantment and frustration with the High Court's decision. In fact, he seemed to threaten that the system of judicial review might have to be re-examined if the judiciary were to continue to act in this fashion:

> I say if the Constitution which was brought in here, which used common-sense language and which had to be submitted to the people for enactment is not to have the meaning which the legislature and which the people think it has, and if we cannot get some common ground on which there is an understanding of words, then we certainly cannot get on. If the legislature and the judiciary are going to be at loggerheads in that way [interpretation of statutes] we shall have to change the situation ... because it means bringing everything here into confusion ... The judiciary, the executive and the legislature have all their proper functions. To a certain extent they are a check on abuses, one on the other, but if they cannot carry on in harmony, which is the premise upon which I am talking, if words like these have not the meaning which ordinary people attach to them, I say there is an end to working in that particular way.[127]

It would appear that these were intemperate words, perhaps spoken in the heat of the moment because, when addressing the Seanad on the following day, he made remarks which were more moderate:

This legislation, as I am sure the Minister [for Justice] has pointed out to you in his introduction, is brought in because of a certain High Court decision. It did not matter what view we took of the decision, whether we thought it right or wrong; we did what it was our duty to do, we acted upon it. That, to my mind, is the highest expression of acceptance of the rule of law. Judgments will be given; you will find lawyers, having stated cases to judges, holding – even after the judgment was delivered – that the judge was wrong, but accepting the finding. That must be the way; there must be somebody to determine a certain issue and somebody to determine it finally. We accepted the court decision as finally determining the issue of the liberation of the men concerned. If it should happen that the interpretation taken by the courts is different to that intended by the legislature, the legislature has, in general, the power of changing the law so that its own intention – taking into view the decision of the judges – will be expressed.[128]

In the course of the same debate, de Valera associated himself, clearly and unequivocally, with the making of the Constitution: 'There is no use in minimising my connection with the Constitution; no doubt I had a principal part in determining what the Constitution should contain.'[129] In the context of this public association, he made a very significant statement regarding the role of judicial review and the interpretation of Bunreacht na hÉireann:

This was intended to be a simple, straightforward, common-sense document and our hope was that, as it would be interpreted from time to time in accordance with developments – if it were to last without change and if circumstances were to change, the document might be, so to speak, frozen in its existing words – there would be a living body which would be able to take account of the changing circumstance and interpret the Constitution in accordance with those circumstances.[130]

He was acknowledging that the Constitution would evolve 'in accordance with developments' and that 'a living body' – by implication, the High and Supreme Courts – would be instrumental in that process. Continuing his speech, de Valera highlighted the importance of judicial review by referring to the consideration he gave as to the most appropriate judicial mechanism by which to interpret the Constitution. His remarks, not least those relating to a constitutional court, confirm what has been noted in this study – that the matter of effective judicial review had been a subject of serious discussion between him and Hearne during the making of Bunreacht na hÉireann:

This whole difficulty was so much present to my mind that I think you will find in the Dáil debates on the Constitution that I spoke of the devices used in other countries with regard to written constitutions by which a special constitutional court is set up, not being the highest court in the land in ordinary legal matters, but a court composed of some judges and other people experienced in public affairs – for example, the Council of State, as we have it here, or something of that sort – and that body is the body to interpret the Constitution, the reason again being the difficulty I have been speaking about of taking an instrument of that kind and interpreting it in regard to legislation from time to time. I still have the hope, and it was with this hope that the Supreme Court in the Constitution was intended to be the final authoritative body, that the Supreme Court in dealing with these things will deal with them in a way which will make it possible to have the Constitution a workable instrument.[131]

This was by no means the end of de Valera's engagement with the issue of judicial review. The Offences against the State (Amendment) Bill was referred to the Supreme Court by President Douglas Hyde under the provisions of Article 26.[132] The five judges, by a majority decision, upheld its constitutionality. It was noteworthy that at least one member of the court was prepared to find the measure unconstitutional. The fact that this was the situation at a time of grave national emergency 'ought to have sent its own signal that the Constitution had indeed endowed the judiciary with potent powers which might well be used to rebuff the other organs of government in more settled times.'[133]

In spite of the fact that the judiciary's interpretation of the Constitution presented the government with challenges at a time of national and international crisis, nevertheless de Valera did not dilute this aspect of his new constitutional dispensation. He could have done so, as an opportunity presented itself, but he chose not to. A few weeks after the Supreme Court's judgement, he established a committee to review Bunreacht na hÉireann and to propose amendments in accordance with the transitory provisions enshrined in Article 51, whereby the document could be altered by the Oireachtas for a period of three years after the date on which the first President entered upon office. (President Hyde assumed his position on 25 June 1938.) As a consequence of the Review Committee's report, there were no qualifications or restrictions introduced in respect of judicial review, except in the case of bills referred under Article 26. Once reviewed these could not be reviewed again. De Valera was in a position to modify the general application of judicial review in the Constitution. He decided not to do so, and this decision was made notwithstanding his government's experiences of its operation and his understanding of the power with which the judiciary was being invested.[134] Thus he confirmed by this decision his support for the inclusion of judicial review in the Constitution.

It can be convincingly argued that de Valera's commitment to judicial review was significantly influenced and informed by the ideas and concerns of John Hearne – as a constitutional expert he understood its central importance in the architecture of a basic law committed to the vindication of citizens' rights. Hearne was determined to enshrine such review in Ireland's new Constitution. Hence, he proposed, albeit unsuccessfully, a constitutional court. The principle of effective judicial review, however, was accepted by de Valera and the right of such review was conferred on the superior courts. The function of such review was to determine the validity of any law having regard to the provisions of the Constitution; in other words, to protect the constitutional rights and liberties of citizens.

Hearne drafted Articles 40, 3, 1 and 40, 3, 2, which are the key provisions regarding citizens' rights, and he was responsible for the inclusion of the original article guaranteeing the equality of all citizens. He had a profound sense of the rights and dignity of the human person. Therefore, the Constitution, as the document enshrining these rights, had itself to be protected. He devised the legal mechanisms which embedded the referendum and rigid transition provisions in the constitutional framework to guarantee such protection. A consummate lawyer, Hearne, inspired by deeply held religious beliefs, sought the vindication of human rights at a time in history when much of Europe was descending into the darkness of dictatorship and the consequent systematic denial of personal liberty and dignity.

Emergency powers

While the recognition and protection of fundamental rights was a central element of the Constitution, the same document provided for the suspension of such rights in times of emergency, when the preservation of public order was under threat. Such a threat existed in the early years of de Valera's government, in the form of the IRA and the Blueshirts.[135] Though the Fianna Fáil government had suspended the operation of Article 2A on assuming office, it did not repeal it. This emergency legislation was used first of all against the Blueshirts and later the IRA.[136] Speaking in the Dáil in May 1935, de Valera expressed regret about having to use it but asserted that such a response was necessary. Furthermore, he declared that he would include provisions to deal with emergency situations in any new constitution:

> If I were introducing a new constitution tomorrow ... I would have, as a result of my experience, to suggest ... that there should be a special provision to deal with emergency occasions in which there was a possibility of arms being used

against unarmed citizens, and the courts, the ordinary courts, being set at defiance ... The ordinary laws will operate under settled conditions. But the ordinary laws cannot operate if conditions are not as those for which these laws were designed. If we were introducing a constitution here – unless there is a big change, seeing the state of the world as a whole – we would have to introduce in that constitution certain emergency measures which would give powers to the executive, in case the ordinary courts were set at defiance, to bring those who were acting in an unlawful and illegal manner before courts which could not possibly be intimidated. We would have to do it.[137]

The inclusion of emergency provisions was an important consideration during the process which led to a new constitution. The 1934 Constitution Review Committee produced detailed recommendations.[138] In the 'squared paper draft', May 1935, de Valera made a note which read: 'const. 2A law', a reference to emergency legislation in the Free State Constitution, indicating that he and Hearne discussed this issue in relation to the draft heads.[139] One of the instructions given to the law adviser regarding the latter stated that they were 'to provide for the suspension of the said [human rights] articles during a state of public emergency only' and 'to contain machinery for effectively preserving public order during any such emergency'.[140] Article 46 of the draft heads, May 1935, was concerned with 'emergency powers'. The inclusion of emergency provisions was a feature of all drafts of the Constitution from the Zurich draft of early January 1937. For whatever reason, the final form of the provisions in the Constitution, presented to Dáil Éireann for its approval, were formulated very late in the drafting process, the wording of the majority of the articles having already been decided.[141]

The Constitution as a manifesto

De Valera was committed to a constitution that would inspire loyalty. The Free State Constitution was a factual and turgid document, rooted in substantial articles concerned with the building blocks of the new state. The 1937 fundamental law contained, for the most part, articles of a similar nature, but it also, according to a Supreme Court judgement of 1975 referred to earlier, reflected, in part, 'the people's aspirations and aims'. De Valera, therefore, conceived the Constitution, in part, 'as a manifesto rather than as a bare law'.[142] A remark made by him at the Fianna Fáil ard fheis of 1937 confirmed this, when he told his audience that 'down in this part of Ireland the Constitution is a declaration of freedom',[143] and like any such declaration it contained rhetorical elements and flourishes.

In relation to Articles 1 and 2, Hearne identified the rhetoric informing them:

You may wonder why it should be necessary to enact a self-evident principle of that kind in a national constitution. My answer is that as the freedom of which I have been speaking is the freedom of the whole Irish nation, this declaration is made for the whole nation and not for a portion of it merely, not for any geographical fragment of the national territory. You will observe that the national territory itself is defined as the whole of Ireland, its islands and its territorial seas, and that yet another declaration is inserted assuming the right of the majority of the people to the control of the whole of the national territory.[144]

Article 5 contained rhetorical and substantive elements in describing Ireland as 'a sovereign, independent democratic state'. Article 8, referring to the Irish language as 'the first official language', represented an aspiration presaging advance to a universally, if not exclusively, Irish-speaking nation.[145] As the Irish nation was being constructed in opposition to Englishness, the Irish language was a useful component,[146] de Valera declaring at his party's 1937 ard fheis: 'The only way to hold our nation is by securing our language as the language of the Irish people.'[147] Article 9, 2 was also more rhetoric than substance: 'Fidelity to the nation and loyalty to the state are fundamental political duties of all citizens.' The guarantees of fundamental rights, in particular those which respected the rights of the family, showed that 'law and manifesto could be intertwined'.[148] Article 45, 'Directive Principles of Social Policy', was the essence of a manifesto by virtue of its non-justiciability.

The preamble was, quintessentially, a rhetorical statement:

In the Name of the Most Holy Trinity, from Whom is all authority and to Whom, as our final end, all actions both of men and states must be referred,
We, the people of Éire,
Humbly acknowledging all our obligations to our Divine Lord Jesus Christ, Who sustained our fathers through centuries of trial,
Gratefully remembering their heroic and unremitting struggle to regain the rightful independence of our nation,
And seeking to promote the common good, with due observance of prudence, justice and charity, so that the dignity and freedom of the individual may be assured, true social order attained, the unity of our country restored, and concord established with other nations, do hereby adopt, enact, and give to ourselves this Constitution.

The language used reflected and embodied the victory of the national independence movement, after centuries of struggle, as an essential element in the identity of the state.[149] The Constitution represented the consummation of this same struggle, at least for the twenty-six counties of southern Ireland. The preamble included commitments to human rights, liberty, democracy and popular sovereignty as fundamental and over-arching principles of the entire Constitution. A pronounced religious tone and quality permeated this whole section of the document, identifying the state with the Roman Catholic tradition. The fact that the people adopted and enacted the Constitution signified, in a potent manner, that popular sovereignty was the foundation of Ireland's new fundamental law.

The manifesto quality of the document, with its accompanying rhetoric, was influenced by the three seminal documents of the revolutionary struggle of 1916–22: the Proclamation of 1916, the Declaration of Independence and the Democratic Programme, both dating from 1919. De Valera's hand-written notes on the preamble in the 'squared paper draft' made reference to the three documents;[150] while on the preliminary draft of the Constitution, October 1936, were also to be found references to the same documents, again in the President's own hand.[151] The mention in the preamble of 'centuries of trial' and 'the unremitting struggle to regain the rightful independence of our nation' echoed the opening section of the Declaration of Independence: 'And whereas for seven hundred years the Irish people has never ceased to repudiate and has repeatedly protested in arms against foreign usurpation.' The reference to 'justice' and 'concord established with other nations' were likely influenced by the phrases in the declaration which spoke of the Irish people being resolved 'to re-establish justice' and 'insure ... goodwill with all nations'.[152]

In Article 5, the description of the state as 'sovereign, independent and democratic' reflected the words of the Proclamation, declaring the Irish republic as 'a sovereign independent state'.[153] The inclusion of the Directive Principles of Social Policy may be regarded as a faint homage to the Democratic Programme. The three seminal documents heralded the establishment of a state based on the sovereignty of the people, so their impact on the Constitution was not surprising. If Bunreacht na hÉireann was, among other things, de Valera's apologia for past actions and decisions, it was also his version of the Proclamation of 1916, the Declaration of Independence and the Democratic Programme.

The manifesto element and its rhetoric owed its place in the Constitution because de Valera understood that, to his supporters, he was, in the words of Seán O'Faolain, the 'Irish nationalist oracle'[154] and, as such, he spoke through this document. 'He presented himself, as did his Fianna Fáil party, as the embodiment of the 1916 Rising, and his dismantling of the Treaty settlement in the 1930s ... as the fulfilment of the traditional genealogy of Irish nationality summed up by [Patrick] Pearse in *The Spiritual Nation*.'[155] His basic appeal was that he might recover for his people 'the vision splendid of Irish nationalism'.[156] He was regarded as a leader who achieved a sense of national self-respect for his people. To quote John A. Murphy:

Bread-and-butter issues aside, when a small nation has been placed by the facts of geography and history in uncomfortable proximity to a great power, the people of that small nation, scarred by such a history, crave not only material progress, not only political sovereignty but a psychological independence as well, so that their dignity and self-respect can be asserted against the superiority, contempt and disdain of the great power. In his time, particularly in the 1930s and 1940s – and pre-eminently in the celebrated reply to Churchill, de Valera made his unmistakable assertion of independence and dignity on behalf of his people.[157]

He hoped to inspire in his people this sense of dignity and self-respect by speaking for them, and to them, in the manifesto element of the Constitution.

The influence of the European constitutional heritage

De Valera's Irish language biographers recorded that, during his early years in office, he examined a number of constitutions of other countries. Particular reference was made to a publication produced by the provisional government in 1922, *Select Constitutions of the World*, which contained many of the basic laws written under the influence of democratic ideas in the aftermath of the First World War and which the President, according to his biography, found useful ('áisiúil').[158] In fact, those involved in the process of constitution-making studied an array of constitutions.[159] It was observed in Chapter 4 that the 1934 Constitution Review Committee, of which Hearne was a member, considered the basic laws of other states.

In 1935, he prepared a memorandum for de Valera regarding the operation of constitutional courts in various jurisdictions. Hearne was a constitutional scholar and, therefore, it was not surprising that such careful international comparative research was undertaken by him.[160] Speaking in Canada sometime in the 1940s, he acknowledged that the Irish state's new Constitution 'took account of the constitutional system in other countries and had regard to them';[161] Chief Justice Susan Denham has observed that 'it is significant that our Constitution's development was influenced by such a diversity of comparative constitutional law materials'.[162] Thus the Irish Constitution, like practically all others, was based on free borrowing from a wide range of other fundamental laws,[163] as Hearne sought out a broad European constitutional and legal heritage. Like any lawyer he looked for precedents – in this circumstance in the constitutional documents of other countries.

Principal among the Constitutions which influenced the drafting of Ireland's new basic law was that of the German or Weimar Republic 1919. It was reproduced in *Select Constitutions of the World*.[164] De Valera recorded a reference to it in the 'squared paper draft'.[165] Such was the extent of the way in which the Weimar Constitution shaped Bunreacht na hÉireann that Gerard Hogan has commented that its chief architect and drafter, Hugo Preuss, 'quite probably had as much influence on the drafting of our Constitution as anyone outside the drafting team and Mr de Valera himself'.[166] Certainly, the 1937 document has a distinctly 'Weimarian' feel to it,[167] as is evident in this brief overview of the two fundamental laws.

Article 6 of Bunreacht na hÉireann provides that 'all powers of government ... derive, under God, from the people', while Article 1 of the Weimar Constitution [hereafter WC] stated that 'all authority emanates from the people'. Article 7 prescribes the tricolour as the national flag; Article 3 WC defined the German flag. Under the terms of Article 15, sittings of each House of the Oireachtas are to be in public but provision is made for closed sessions in certain cases; Article 29 WC stipulated that proceedings of the Reichstag were to be conducted in open sessions but there was a provision for excluding the public. Article 15, 13 confers privilege on utterances made in either House of the Oireachtas; Article 30 WC contained a similar provision. The same article in Bunreacht na hÉireann confers privilege from arrest on members of the Oireachtas going to and returning from meetings of parliament; Article 37 WC was essentially the same. Article 16 confers voting rights on all citizens who have reached twenty-one years; Article 17 WC established the same principle. Article 16, 4, 2 requires that the Dáil meet within thirty days of a general election; Article 32 WC had a similar provision.[168]

The provisions in the Weimar Constitution pertaining to the German presidency informed the articles relating to the newly created office of President of Ireland. The German President had to be at least thirty-five years old (Article 41) and his term of office was seven years (Article 43). He was precluded from membership of parliament (Article 44) and was obliged to subscribe to a prescribed oath before entering on office (Article 42). The supreme command of the defence forces was conferred upon him (Article 17) and he appointed ministers on the nomination of the Chancellor (Article 53).[169]

More fundamentally, the influence of Weimar was not confined to what might be termed the 'organisational aspects of the Constitution'; it extended to key provisions concerned with equality, personal liberty, the family and the protection of a citizen's dwelling.[170] In a document dated 14 October 1936, Hearne drafted versions of articles relating to these matters and established, at an early stage in the making of Bunreacht na hÉireann, what was to be the essential substance of these articles in their final form. Under the heading 'Fundamental Rights of Citizens', he included the following: 'All citizens are equal before the law... No titles of nobility shall be conferred.'[171] This was, eventually, to become Article 40, 1 and 2 and was based on Article 109 of the Weimar Constitution:

All Germans are equal before the law ... Titles of nobility shall simply be part of the name, and may no longer be conferred ... Orders and badges of honour may not be conferred by the State. No German is permitted to accept a title or order from a foreign government.[172]

Hearne also drafted provisions which became part of Article 40 of the Irish Constitution. This guarantees liberty for the exercise of the following rights: the free expression of opinions and convictions, peaceable assembly and freedom of association. Sections of the Weimar Constitution clearly influenced the legal adviser:

Article 118: Every German has the right, within the limits of general laws, to express his opinion freely ...
Article 123: All Germans have the right without notification or special permission to assemble peaceably and unarmed.
Article 124: All Germans have the right to form unions and associations ...[173]

Article 114 of the German Constitution stated: 'Personal liberty is inviolable. No encroachment on or deprivation of personal liberty by any public authority is permissible except in virtue of law.'[174] This influenced a similar provision in Bunreacht na hÉireann (Article 40, 4, 1). The declaration in Article 40, 5 regarding the inviolability of a citizen's dwelling echoes that of Article 115 of Weimar, which stated: 'The residence of every German is an inviolable sanctuary for him; exceptions are only admissible in virtue of laws.'[175]

Hearne drafted an early version of an article, in October 1936, pertaining to family:

Section 1. The state guarantees the constitution and protection of the family as the source of the preservation and increase of the race, the basis of moral education and social discipline and harmony, and the sure foundation of ordered society.
Section 2 (1) The constitution of the family depends upon lawful marriage.
(2) Marriage, as the basis of family life, is under the special protection of the state; and all attacks on the purity, health and sacredness of family life shall be forbidden.[176]

This draft was to inform Article 41 of the 1937 Constitution, which recognises the family 'as the necessary basis of social order' and 'pledges to guard with special care the institution of marriage, on which the family is founded, and to protect it against attack'. The influence of Article 119 of the Weimar Constitution is evident:

Notes on Constitn.

Flag, Language, Religion
Coat of arms.

Regency; Constitutional Ct.

Council of State

✗ Regional & Subordinate Parlts

Page 187 - German — Pres of F.A.

By a 2/3 vote of Dáil the P. may
be invited to assume office
— a further men without Portfolio to
assist   [May have Extraordinary

If old. Presd die — new takes up
office immed — otherwise two months

Deputies' etc to abide by
Constitn Declaratn

'Squared paper draft'. Reproduced by kind permission of UCD-OFM Partnership.

To Mr. John Hearne, Barrister at Law
Legal adviser to the Department of
External affairs architect in chief
and Draftsman of this Constitution,
as a Souvenir of the successful
issue of his work and in testimony
of the fundamental part he took
in framing this the first Free
Constitution of the Irish People

Éamon de Valéra

Constitution Day. 29.xii.37.

Éamon de Valera's dedication of a copy of the draft constitution given by him to John Hearne. Ms.
23, 508. Courtesy of the National Museum of Ireland.

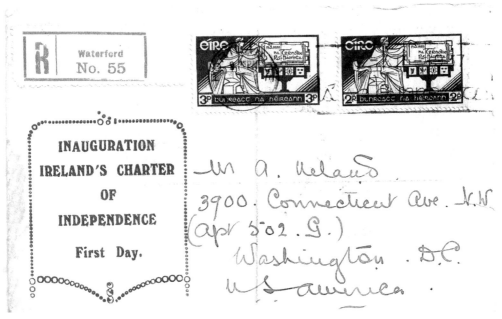

Commemorative stamp issued on Constitution Day, 29 December 1937. Reproduced by kind permission of An Post ©.

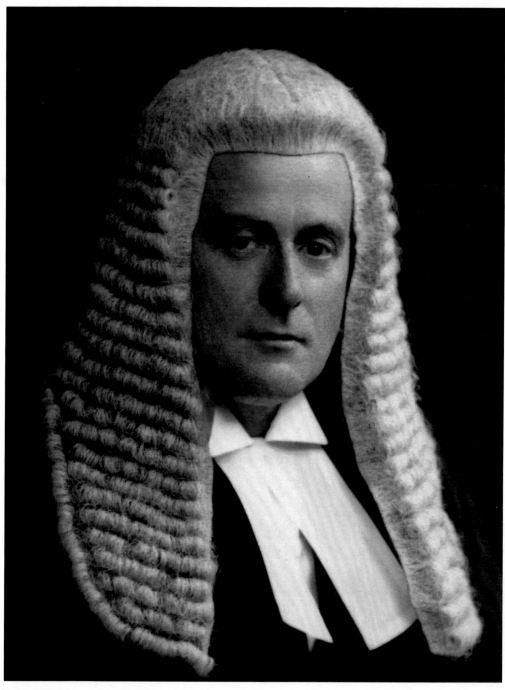

John Hearne on the occasion of his appointment as a senior counsel, 20 June 1939. Private collection, reproduced with permission.

Captain William Archer Redmond.
Courtesy of Waterford Treasures.

Éamon de Valera, Geneva, c.1932. Taken by C. Ed. Boesch,
Geneva. Reproduced by kind permission of UCD-OFM
Partnership.

'.T. Cosgrave. Reproduced by kind permission of
CD Archives.

Dr Vincent White. Poole Collection, courtesy of
the National Museum of Ireland.

Fr John Charles McQuaid, Papal Nuncio Pascal Robinson and Éamon de Valera in the grounds of Blackrock College, Dublin, 1932. Courtesy of *The Irish Times*.

Éamon de Valera with members of the Irish diplomatic service, 1930s. Back row, extreme left: John J. Hearne, High Commissioner to Canada (1939–49). G.P. Beegan, photographer, reproduced by kind permission of UCD-OFM Partnership.

John and Mona Hearne, with their son, Maurice, *c.*1940s. Private collection, reproduced with permission.

John Hearne (extreme left) with Taoiseach John A. Costello (fourth from right), Canada, 1948. Reproduced by kind permission of UCD Archives.

Cearbhall Ó Dálaigh, Chief Justice of Ireland (1961–72). Reproduced by kind permission of UCD Archives.

John Hearne and his family in the United States, *c.*1950. Reproduced by kind permission of UCD Archives.

Formal portrait of John Hearne, *c.*1950s. Reproduced by kind permission of UCD Archives.

legal heritage since the French Revolution, especially in the area of fundamental rights.[183] The draft heads, dated 14 October 1936, had a significant influence on the Zurich draft of early January 1937 and subsequent drafts.

The influence of the Free State Constitution, 1922

Another Weimar inspired basic law, the 1922 Irish Free State Constitution, as amended by 1936, had a central and pivotal influence on the shaping of the 1937 Constitution.[184] In fact, it was the proximate source of the influence of the German Constitution. In the words of Tom Garvin, 'behind Bunreacht na hÉireann lurks the unacknowledged ghost of the Free State Constitution,'[185] confirming Bill Kissane's observation that 'strong elements of continuity mark the constitutional record'.[186] Hearne transposed many sections of the 1922 Constitution into that of 1937:

> [a] very large part of our present Constitution is in fact the Constitution of 1922, with the language in many cases unchanged ... The extent to which this is true has, however, been partially obscured by the manner in which the content of the Constitution has been ordered as between the 1922 and 1937 versions. Nevertheless, this does not diminish in any way the political significance of the 1937 Constitution, nor the ingenuity with which it was drafted.[187]

An overview of both Constitutions conveys the extent of the continuity between them. Laura Cahillane has established that at least fifty-eight articles of the Free State Constitution influenced its successor.[188] What may be termed three technical articles in the 1922 version, Article 11 (pertaining to land, mines and minerals), Article 35 (definition of a money bill) and Article 61 (all revenues to form one fund) were transposed, becoming Articles 10, 22 and 11 respectively in 1937, the last two being absolutely identical in both documents. The provisions on personal rights in the Free State Constitution, Articles 5–9, influenced Article 40 in 1937. An examination of the articles relating to the institutions of state reveals a very significant degree of continuity. Articles 64–9 of the 1922 Constitution, dealing with the courts, were essentially transposed, becoming Articles 34–6 in 1937. A similar situation applied to other articles dealing with state institutions: Articles 62–3, concerning the comptroller and auditor general in the earlier Constitution became Article 33 in the later version; while Articles 12–15 and 18–27, dealing with the Oireachtas and the Dáil in 1922, are to be found as Articles 16–17 in 1937. In fact, a more detailed consideration of the articles concerning parliament highlights, very clearly, the relationship between the two versions of the state's basic law:

Free State Constitution	Provision	1937 Constitution
Article 12	Oireachtas sole power of making laws.	Article 15, 2, 1
Article 14	All citizens aged 21 years have right to vote.	Article 16, 1, 2
Article 18	Oireachtas members privileged from arrest.	Article 15, 13
Article 19	Utterances of Oireachtas members privileged.	Article 15, 12
Article 20	Houses of Oireachtas to make their own rules.	Article 15, 10
Article 21	Each house to elect its own chairman.	Article 15, 9, 1
Article 24	Oireachtas shall hold one session a year.	Article 15, 7
Article 25	Sittings of Oireachtas to be public.	Article 15, 8, 1
Article 28	General elections.	Article 16

It has been noted by Brian Walsh that, because of the care which these matters and others relating to the institutions of the state were dealt with in the 1937 Constitution, there has been very little litigation concerning them.[189]

De Valera's desire to avoid change for the sake of change helps to explain the continuity between the Constitutions of 1922 and 1937. That he and Hearne adopted this approach was reasonable. It did not make sense to discard any elements of the earlier Constitution which were regarded as satisfactory. As de Valera told the Dáil on 11 May 1937: 'I was anxious ... that the things that we were satisfied with should remain; that we should not change simply for change's sake.'[190] In this regard, it is also important to remember the work of the 1934 Constitution Review Committee, of which Hearne was a member. This group identified those articles of the 1922 Constitution which it considered fundamental and these served as a foundation for Hearne's work in drafting the new Constitution. The Committee's report bridged the two versions of the state's basic law and was a very significant factor in shaping the later one in 1937. Hearne's expert knowledge of the 1922 document proved invaluable and facilitated its influence on Bunreacht na hÉireann.

The earlier basic law established a framework for the state on which the 1937 Constitution could build[191] and that the 1937 document was a stabilising and reforming continuation of that of 1922 is fair comment.[192] However, there was much more than institutional continuity; more fundamentally, there was an ideological and philosophical continuity between the documents. Popular sovereignty was the central ideal of Irish separatist thought and it found expression in the two versions of the Irish state's basic law. It was noted earlier that Bunreacht na hÉireann was all about sovereignty and Laura Cahillane, in her study of the Free State Constitution, identified popular sovereignty as its foundation.[193] Commenting on the latter in a book published in 1932, Leo Kuhn wrote that 'the monarchical forms paled into insignificance in the light of the formal enunciation and the consistent application [of popular sovereignty] as the fundamental and exclusive source of all political authority'.[194] Those who drafted the 1922 Constitution

> wished to prove to the Irish people that the new state would not involve simply the painting of red post-boxes green. They hoped that by showing the people that they were the sovereign power, the people would have faith in the new system and would work together for its prosperity ... the dreams of Pearse and many other patriots would be realised in the form of an Irish Ireland with democratic institutions and popular sovereignty.[195]

De Valera and other republicans could not accept this constitutional dispensation. John Hearne, however, appreciated the achievements of the Treaty settlement and the Free State Constitution. He had spent the years of W.T. Cosgrave's rule seeking to give full expression to the ideal of a sovereign Ireland; his work on the 1937 Constitution was a continuation of this effort. The preambles of both the Irish Free State Constitution Act 1922 and Bunreacht na hÉireann enunciate 'with the metaphysical ethos of all revolutionary constitutions the divinely inspired sovereignty of the people as the transcendental basis'[196] of the two documents. Hearne understood and appreciated the significance of this fact and, by his involvement in the making of the 1937 Constitution, he was giving expression to a fundamental principle first declared in the Free State Constitution.

The influence of the Catholic faith and Catholic social teachings

It was noted earlier in this chapter that, as the drafting process progressed, the influence of Catholic social teachings became apparent in the text of the proposed constitution. In fact, as early as 14 October 1936, Hearne introduced a prohibition on divorce in an early version of the article on the family: 'The state shall recognise the inviolability of the marriage bond. Divorce *a vinculo* is prohibited.'[197] The inclusion of this outright ban may reveal the influence of Alfred O'Rahilly, one of the country's most distinguished Catholic social activists.[198] An academic at University College Cork,[199] he was a member of the committee which drafted the Free State Constitution, for which body he prepared a proposed version of the document that was rejected by the government.[200] There is clear evidence that he gave de Valera a copy of his proposed basic law.[201] O'Rahilly was also acquainted with Hearne and corresponded with the legal adviser seeking access to certain documents for a book he was writing.[202] Articles and provisions in O'Rahilly's version of a constitution for the Free State on marriage, parents and children influenced Hearne's draft heads.[203]

Another of Hearne's draft articles of 14 October 1936, entitled 'Preservation of Public Morals', represented a constitutional acknowledgement of, and a response to, concerns voiced by Catholic clerics and activists on issues of public morality.[204] It was comprehensive, nearly exhaustive, in the range of its provisions:

> Preservation of Public Morals.
> Section 1. The state will take measures to prevent the corruption of public morals.
> Section 2. The state undertakes to maintain and improve the laws for the protection of young girls, the suppression of brothels and prostitution, and the punishment of sexual crimes.
> Section 3. The state shall maintain a censorship of publications, cinematograph performances, stage plays and other public entertainments.
> Section 4. The licensing and supervision of clubs and public dance-halls shall be regulated by law.
> Section 5. The sale of noxious drugs and of intoxicating liquors shall continue to be subject to state control in accordance with the law.[205]

That the Constitution was influenced by Catholic concerns, values and social teachings was perhaps inevitable. Writing in the 1960s, American Jesuit Bruce Biever observed:

> No constitution of any culture area is drafted in a vacuum; rather it is an artifact of that cultural system, representing in its declarations an attempt to place in juridicial language some of the most deeply felt of that society's values and beliefs. This is as true of the Irish Constitution as any other.[206]

The Ireland of the 1930s was a country where the Roman Catholic faith played a central part in the life of the community and the Constitution of 1937 reflected this reality. In fact, the role of the Catholic Church in the drafting process has long dominated discussion and assessment of the document by historians and commentators.[207] This section is concerned with considering and assessing the role of religion and the Catholic Church in the shaping of Bunreacht na hÉireann.

The 1922 Constitution made no reference to the Catholic Church and afforded no recognition of distinctively Catholic values or concerns;[208] the 1937 Constitution was to declare the 'special position' of the Catholic Church, prohibit the introduction of divorce and include provisions based on the social principles of papal encyclicals.

This change reflected two factors: the growing importance of religion in the sense of Irish national identity[209] and the influence of the Catholic social movement in the 1930s.[210]

The post-revolutionary decades were ones of bitter disillusion for many of the participants in the struggle for independence.[211] The achievements of the Irish Free State counted for little or nothing with those who had fought 'for the new Jerusalem of a visionary republic'.[212] For many, Dominion status was 'intolerably mean and anti-climactic'[213] and, together with the experience of the Civil War, 'generated a mood of disillusionment, fatalism and cynicism which was extraordinarily strong and was intensified by the exaggerated enthusiasm and idealism of the revolutionary period'.[214] It was in this context that Catholicism came to define the young state's sense of identity and provided a focus of unity in a country which was bitterly divided – 'it remained to bind together a riven nation'.[215] In a period of postcolonial nation-building, by adopting staunch expressions of Catholic devotionalism and loyalty, the citizens of the Irish Free State sought to distinguish themselves from Protestant England.

Two events in the first decade of the Free State's existence facilitated this process and strengthened an identity expressed in religious terms. In 1929, commemorations were organised to mark the centenary of Catholic Emancipation.[216] These served to help reconcile a society recently divided by Civil War, as focus was directed on the one issue which united the majority Catholic population: its strong and deep attachment to the Catholic Church.[217] There was a public identification of the new state with a unifying and triumphant Catholicism.[218] Three years later, the Eucharistic Congress showcased Irish Catholicism to the world.[219]

The recently elected President of the Executive Council, Éamon de Valera, welcomed the papal legate Cardinal Lorenzo Lauri by attesting to the Catholic credentials of the Irish people: 'our people, ever firm in their allegiance to our ancestral faith and unwavering even unto death in their devotion to the see of St. Peter'.[220] There was a clear association being made between Irish national identity and Catholicism, an association that had its origins during the struggle for Catholic Emancipation.[221] The Catholic faith became the 'genetic code' of the nationalist movement.[222] Writing in the 1960s, Bruce Biever commented that 'Catholicism is viewed by the Irish Catholic to be simply the most effective means for the development of national pride and patriotism.'[223]

This identification of Catholicism with Irishness was easily made and reinforced in a country steeped in the Catholic faith. Paul Blanshard wrote, in 1954, that 'in practice it [Ireland] is the world's most devoutly Catholic country, not even excepting Portugal and Spain.'[224] Mass attendance was practically universal during the first five decades of independence and the daily round of life was permeated by reminders, conscious and unconscious, of the Catholic religion. Most homes displayed numerous religious objects, such as pictures and statues of the Sacred Heart, the Virgin Mary and the Infant of Prague. People wore scapulars, carried rosary beads with them and blessed themselves when they passed churches. The Angelus bell rang out from all churches at noon and six in the evening and this was an almost universal call to prayer. There was a sense of a country immersed in religion.[225] Born in 1934, writer John McGahern recalled that 'the worlds to come, hell and heaven and purgatory and limbo, were closer and far more real than America or Australia and talked about almost daily as our future reality'.[226] Thus in a country which had experienced the disappointment of unrealised revolutionary expectations, religion, more than nationalism, seemed to give meaning to life.[227]

The second factor which accounted for the religious aspect of the 1937 Constitution was the influence of the Catholic social movement in Ireland in the 1930s. Catholic activists believed that the Free State had been morally secured by the end of the 1920s. The decade had seen the enshrinement of Catholic moral values in the civil law of the country. Divorce had been banned. The Censorship of Films Act 1923 provided for the appointment of a censor empowered to refuse a licence for films deemed subversive of public morality. The Intoxicating Liquor Act 1927 reduced the number of licensed premises. The distribution and sale of books adjudged to be obscene by a committee of official censors was prohibited by the Censorship of Publications Act 1929.[228] It now remained for the Free State to be socially secured.

This was the purpose of the Catholic social movement which sought to recast Irish life – economic, social and political. Its objective was the establishment of a Christian state, defined by a leading activist, Fr Edward Cahill SJ, as 'one in which the law as well as the organised activities and general outlook of the citizens are in accordance with Christian principles'.[229] A new social system had to be reconstructed reflecting the Catholic ethos of the Irish people. The publication of the papal encyclical, *Quadragesimo Anno*, in 1931, which addressed social issues, gave Irish social activists a new sense of purpose, direction and energy. It was during the 1930s that there was 'the first serious sustained discussion of social principles in the history of Irish Catholicism'.[230]

Through a small minority of Catholics, social activists promoted their cause with enthusiasm. Organisations were formed to advance their objectives, such as Muintir na Tíre[231] and An Ríoghacht.[232] Study circles were a popular means of spreading their message. Two such groups were the St Thomas Aquinas study circle in Waterford[233] and the Columba study circle in Dublin.[234] In 1935, the social order summer school was inaugurated at Clongowes Wood College, County Kildare.[235] Public lectures and articles in journals such as *Studies* and the *Irish Ecclesiastical Record* addressed the concerns of the social movement.[236]

Catholic social activists were determined to influence public policy and opinion and the language of Catholic social theory permeated political and social discourse.[237] Before the 1933 general election, the *Irish Press* announced in its pre-election message that 'there is no social or economic change Fianna Fáil has proposed or brought about which has not its fullest justification in the encyclicals of Leo XIII or the present pontiff'.[238] In 1938, submissions were made by Catholic activists to a commission of inquiry into banking, currency and credit, which aimed to secure the publication of a report containing recommendations in accordance with Catholic social teachings.[239] Two years earlier, hardly surprisingly, efforts were made to influence the making of the state's proposed new constitution. The social order summer school of 1936 had as its subject for discussion, 'The constitutional problem from the Catholic viewpoint'. There was an attendance of 140, a fact which 'demonstrated the interest which existed within Catholic circles in the question of the Constitution'.[240]

De Valera's official biographers, Longford and O'Neill, described his awareness of, and interest in, the Catholic social movement. They provide 'a summary map of the tributaries of social thought which influenced him in the shaping of the Constitution'.[241] According to them, in the 1930s 'in Ireland a great variety of views were being propounded on the duties of the state towards its people'. De Valera 'read carefully' the writings of such Catholic professors (and Catholic social activists) as Dr Michael Browne and Dr Cornelius Lucey of Maynooth College, both of whom were to become members of the hierarchy, in *Studies, Irish Ecclesiastical Record* and other periodicals.[242] These publications were the main medium for contributors who assumed the desirability of encouraging Irish national development in accordance with Catholic theory.[243] Fr Edward Cahill presented de Valera with a copy of his 701 page book, *The Framework of a Christian State*, published in 1932, and described by Bryan Fanning as 'the most substantive post-independence elaboration of Catholic social and political thought'.[244]

Acknowledging receipt of the book, de Valera wrote to Cahill: 'Is fiú é'léigheamh agus a aith léigheamh agus is minic, d'ár liom, a raghfar chuige chun comhairle agus treorú 'fhagháil' ('It is worth reading and re-reading and it is often, I think, I will go to it for advice and direction').[245] The President's principal collaborator and adviser on the Constitution, John Hearne, was a devout Catholic and former seminarian who was, very likely, versed in Catholic social teachings. It was perhaps inevitable, given the prevailing religious climate and the activities of the Catholic social movement, that the Constitution reflected the influence of papal encyclicals.

On or about 22 October 1936, de Valera received submissions from the Jesuits on the proposed new constitution;[246] and from November 1936 onwards, Fr John Charles McQuaid, headmaster of Blackrock College, became involved in the drafting process.[247] The involvement of these parties was, in varying degrees, of importance in terms of the development of the 1937 Constitution. Whether de Valera preferred McQuaid's advice to that of the Jesuits or who wielded the greater influence is essentially irrelevant in terms of the shaping of Bunreacht na hÉireann. The contributions of both 'were grounded in the same Catholic teaching of the neo-Thomist Leo XIII and Pius XI. Both were well acquainted with the Code of Social Principles drawn up by the Catholic Action organisation, the Malines Union.'[248] They both promoted ideas with a very pronounced emphasis on the social and religious teachings of the Catholic Church.

Furthermore, the strongest philosophical themes in the shaping of the document were sovereignty and the Catholic doctrine of the natural law.[249] Interestingly, in 1934, in the course of his judgement in the matter of *The State (Ryan) v Lennon*, Chief Justice Hugh Kennedy held that Article 2A 'was void and ineffective because it was contrary to the natural law upon which he contended the 1922 Constitution was based'.[250] According to Dónal O'Donnell, 'this reasoning had an immediate impact, stimulating considerable discussion, and had an influence upon the 1937 Constitution.'[251] Certainly, Hearne would have been aware of Kennedy's arguments and, as a former clerical student, was familiar with the doctrine of natural law. 'The references to inalienable and imprescriptible rights antecedent to positive law contained in the 1937 Constitution are just one testament to the vigour this line of thought had in the aftermath of the decision.'[252]

Religion and the Constitution: the involvement of the Jesuits

The Society of Jesus became involved in the making of a new constitution as a result of correspondence between de Valera and Fr Edward Cahill. On 4 September 1936, the Jesuit wrote to the President with 'some suggestions which I hope may prove useful in drafting the new Constitution'. He advised that the government 'of which you are the head have now an opportunity which may never recur of giving the Irish state a genuinely Christian constitution'. Cahill's principal concern was that such a document give due consideration 'to the church's teachings regarding the function and duty of the state, as well as to the conclusion of traditional Catholic philosophy, and the general attitude of standard Catholic authors'. To assist de Valera, he included suggestions of 'fundamental principles' pertaining to the new basic law.[253]

De Valera replied to Cahill, inviting him to put into the form of draft articles and a preamble what he thought should be included in any new constitution.[254] On the basis of this invitation, the Jesuit order formed a committee of five priests, including Cahill, 'to advise on certain matters connected with the Constitution.'[255] The committee met on five occasions, between 24 September and 18 October 1936. A report was completed on 18 October and, in it, the Jesuits presented de Valera with the drafts of a preamble and six articles relating to religion, marriage, the family, education, private property and liberty of speech.[256] Each draft article was annotated to indicate the sources which influenced the proposed wording. These sources included the constitutions of Catholic countries, including Austria, Poland and Portugal; papal encyclicals such as *Quadragesimo Anno*; and publications by the Catholic Truth Society relating to Catholic social teachings.

The contribution of the Jesuits to the Constitution of 1937 has been overshadowed by that of John Charles McQuaid. Moreover, historians differ as to the extent of their contribution. David Fitzpatrick overstated their influence when he wrote that much of the Constitution was drafted by Jesuits and other clerical advisers.[257] Dermot Keogh has described the Jesuit involvement as 'quietly influential',[258] while Gerard Hogan has stated that their document proved to be 'enormously influential' and remained so to the end of the constitution-making process.[259]

The fact is that the Jesuit contribution was very significant. The Catholic social principles informing their submission became part of the 1937 Constitution and there is an interesting correlation between this submission and what eventually were to become Articles 41–4. The headings in the Jesuit document were replicated in the Constitution:

Jesuit submission	1937 Constitution
Article 1: Religion	Article 44: Religion
Article 3: The Family	Article 41: The Family
Article 4: Education	Article 42: Education
Article 5: Private Property	Article 43: Private Property

The Jesuits influenced the wording of some sections of the 1937 document. When de Valera was seeking a suitable phrase for the provision recognising the 'special position' of the Catholic Church, he found inspiration in their submission, a fact admitted by his biographers:[260] 'The Catholic faith, which is the faith of the vast majority of the nation, and which is inescapably bound up with the nation's history, traditions and culture, holds among religions in our country a unique and preponderant position.'[261] The preamble was also almost certainly influenced by the Jesuits.[262] The beginning of their draft reads:

In the name of the Holy Trinity and of our Lord Jesus Christ, the universal king, we, the people of Ireland, being the parent nation of the Irish race, mindful of the long centuries of persecution we have had to endure, and full of gratitude to God who has mercifully preserved us from innumerable dangers in the past;

hereby, as an independent Christian nation, establish this sovereign civil society of the Irish people.

The first four lines of the preamble of the 1937 Constitution follow this model.[263]

Crucially, articles submitted by the Jesuits concerned matters Hearne had addressed in early versions of constitutional articles drafted by him before the arrival of their document. His 'Draft Heads of a Constitution', 14 October 1936, included provisions concerned with religion, the family and private property, and which were discussed earlier. That similar subjects featured in the Jesuit submission confirmed the desirability of their inclusion in any future constitution. The Jesuits introduced a Catholic dimension to the provisions, a dimension which was to be very influential as the process of drafting progressed. Moreover, it should also be noted that McQuaid was given a copy of the report of the Jesuit committee by de Valera and had the benefit of its conclusions in the formulation of his proposals.[264]

Religion and the Constitution: the involvement of John Charles McQuaid

The mystique and mythology surrounding John Charles McQuaid extends to his involvement in the Constitution. His biographer has described him as the 'co-maker' of the document,[265] such is the perception of the influence he enjoyed. It is important to remember, however, that he was not yet the Archbishop of Dublin at the time the Constitution was drafted; he was a member of the Holy Ghost order and the headmaster of Blackrock College. His involvement in the drafting was not due to an invitation extended to him by de Valera. Rather, it arose, most likely, out of his friendship with the de Valera family and casual conversations between him and the President in the autumn of 1936.[266] Dermot Keogh has stated that McQuaid 'had a not insignificant role in the drafting process'.[267] De Valera, speaking in 1960 at a lunch to honour the centenary of Blackrock College, acknowledged that McQuaid gave him 'valuable assistance' when he was working on the Constitution, but gave no details.[268]

De Valera's official biographers gave only a limited account of his involvement: the President consulted with him on the 'social clauses' (Articles 40–5). He also sent de Valera 'paragraphs relating to private property and to free competition', in addition to two books, *Manuel Sociale* by a Belgian Jesuit, Revd A. Vermeersch , and *Code Sociale Esquisse d'une Synthese Sociale Catholique*, issued by the Union International d'Etudes Sociales in Paris in 1932.[269] Dermot Keogh and Andrew McCarthy have confirmed his influence on the formulation of Articles 41–5.[270] Moreover, de Valera's Irish language biographers recorded that McQuaid provided a satisfactory draft ('dreacht sásúil') of the preamble.[271] Undoubtedly, he was very influential but Keogh has observed that 'any definite assessment as to the nature and degree of his influence is problematic'.[272] The secrecy and absence of sources surrounding the making of the Constitution militate against such an assessment. Frequently, assessments of his involvement in the making of the 1937 Constitution have been refracted through the prism of his later career as archbishop (1940–72), when he was perceived as the 'ecclesiastical Taoiseach' and 'ruler of Catholic Ireland'.[273]

The power and influence of Archbishop McQuaid have been ahistorically attributed to Fr McQuaid. In fact, his perceived influence, while significant, has probably been overstated when considered in the context of Hearne's draft heads of 14 October 1936 and the Jesuits' submission later in the month. These heads, as has been noted already, established many of the principles which informed Articles 40–5, before any involvement by Fr McQuaid or indeed by the Jesuits. Moreover, McQuaid had the benefit of access to the Jesuit document, as noted earlier, and Hearne's drafts (see below). Whatever the extent of his influence, for the purposes of this study it is sufficient to try and determine the nature of his involvement in the actual drafting process, the attitude of Hearne to the inclusion of Catholic social principles and his reaction to McQuaid's role.

McQuaid was pleased to be involved as he, like Cahill and his confrères, hoped to ensure that a new constitution would reflect what he regarded as the essentially Christian character of the Irish nation. This would require the inclusion of articles reflecting Catholic social teachings. McQuaid outlined his ideas in a document entitled 'Directive Principles'. For him, a constitution was 'an enactment guided and deliminated by the teachings of Catholic philosophy and theology'. It enshrined 'the aim of what ought to be our Christian endeavour in social policy'. The purpose of the proposed new fundamental law should be 'to endeavour to create those circumstances of temporal life which shall realise the Christian ideal of society' and to re-establish 'throughout the whole range of society, the doctrines and practices of Christian religion'.[274]

McQuaid was in regular contact with de Valera from February to April 1937.[275] He supplied the President with notes on Catholic Church teachings on the family, marriage, private property, church–state relations and Catholic social principles. The material usually took the form of typed quotations from papal encyclicals.[276] For example, he sent de Valera over fifty pages of notes from papal documents relating to the religious article (Article 44).[277] In the matter of family and marriage, the President received references from three encyclicals of Pope Leo XIII – *Arcanum Divinae* (1880), *Sapientiae Christianae* (1890) and *Rerum Novarum* (1891) – and from three encyclicals by Pope Pius XI, *Ubi Arcano* (1922), *Divini Illius* (1929) and *Casti Connubi* (1932).[278] These notes and references facilitated the inclusion of Catholic social principles in the Constitution. Hearne's training as a seminarian was probably of great value to de Valera in interpreting and assessing McQuaid's submissions.

As the drafting process progressed, McQuaid was furnished with copies of draft articles. Among de Valera's papers is a typescript of articles, dating from the time of the Zurich draft (i.e. late December 1936/early January 1937) and, at the end of one page, there is a note: 'Part X given to Dr McQuaid'. This part referred to the section on constitutional guarantees which were to become Articles 40–5.[279] He was given a copy of the first official draft issued on 16 March 1937.[280] More significantly, McQuaid was also involved in contributing to the actual drafting of articles: for example, the ones on the family and education, which were to become Articles 41 and 42 respectively.[281]

An insight into the method adopted by de Valera to address the involvement of McQuaid in the drafting process was given by him in a letter to Seán Lemass at the height of difficult negotiations with the bishops on the Health Bill in 1953:

> I would suggest that each particular proposal of ours to which objection was made be taken up with the archbishop [McQuaid], and that he be asked to make a draft with the qualifications that would satisfy him. This draft could then be examined from our point of view and amended if necessary, until an agreed text was arrived at. This is what more or less happened in regard to the corresponding articles of the Constitution.[282]

The amendment of any of McQuaid's proposals involved Hearne, in his capacity as draftsman of the document and expert in constitutional law.

Hearne did not object to the inclusion of Catholic social principles in the Constitution. In fact, he was proud of its Christian basis. Speaking in Canada, he declared that the document laid the foundation of a 'great Christian commonwealth'.[283] Addressing an audience at the University of Notre Dame in June 1950, he told his listeners: 'We adopted a national constitution which is the most comprehensive code of Christian political principles and Christian social doctrine ever erected into a system of government by a plebiscite of our people.'[284]

It is not surprising that Hearne held such views. He was, after all, deeply committed to the Catholic faith. In fact, all those most closely associated with the making of the Constitution were not immune to the climate of Catholic religiosity which prevailed at the time. A member of the editorial committee, Maurice Moynihan, commented that 'it was unavoidable that a generation built on idealism, devoted to its church and led by a devout Catholic should reflect the predominant ethos [in the Constitution]'.[285] Most public officials were infused with the core moral and ethical values of Catholicism,[286] as the vast majority had been socialised within and educated by the Catholic Church.[287] The attitudes of the civil service elite involved in constitution-making rested on the strong devotional culture of the community at large.[288] Moreover, they were part of an Irish nationalist political culture which had, for over a century, internalised Catholicism as one of the key values of its world view.[289]

In assessing Hearne's reaction to McQuaid's actual involvement in the drafting of the Constitution, it is probable that he never had any direct dealings with the Holy Ghost priest: the President dealt with him and communicated whatever he (de Valera) decided to his legal adviser. Interestingly, Cathal Condon, in his analysis of McQuaid's contribution to the Constitution, has speculated that de Valera might not have admitted to all of McQuaid's contributions or simply down-played his role.[290] Whatever the truth of this and notwithstanding Hearne's devout Catholic views, there were tensions caused for him by the involvement of McQuaid. An insight into these tensions was provided in correspondence between Dermot Keogh and the son of one of Hearne's colleagues, Philip O'Donoghue, a member of the editorial committee. Keogh's correspondent referred to the fact that both men (Hearne and O'Donoghue) had a preference for a short concise document but were 'to witness the inclusion of other forces in the drafting process and they were, much to their deep regret, unable to control or contain that change'.[291] McQuaid's involvement was particularly extensive and intensive and Hearne did not welcome the material that began 'to cascade' on to his desk, via de Valera, from that source.[292]

Keogh's acerbic comment that 'one is tempted to speculate that he [Hearne] may have developed, as a consequence, a lifelong aversion to certain papal encyclicals' may be apposite.[293] Moreover, unlike McQuaid and indeed Cahill, Hearne did not regard the essential purpose of a new constitution as being the creation of a Catholic state. While the country's basic law could and would certainly include elements of the teachings of that church, the Constitution was also fundamentally concerned with guaranteeing and vindicating the rights of citizens. Hence, there was an important difference of emphasis which probably made Hearne's task more difficult, at the very least, as he tried to reconcile what was, at times, a conflict of vision and purpose in relation to a new constitution. In spite of McQuaid's influence, he could not divert de Valera's team of civil servants from writing a document committed to personal rights and freedoms.[294]

It was McQuaid who produced the draft article on religion that caused de Valera so much trouble, as was seen in Chapter 5. In this article, with its 'one true church' formula, the Holy Ghost priest was expressing the teachings of the Catholic Church and these accorded with the President's position as a devout Catholic and private citizen.[295] While it might have satisfied his personal beliefs, the article was not tenable in the context of his constitutional ambitions. De Valera's Irish biographers conveyed his dilemma over a conscientious issue which perturbed him: 'conas a réiteodh sé an dualgas a bhí air a chreideamh san aon eaglais fhíor a fhógairt ach gan éagóir a dhéanamh ar mhionlaigh, agus gan deacrachtaí a mheadú?' ('how to resolve his obligation to proclaim his belief in the one true church without being unjust to minorities and increasing complications'.)[296] Hearne's position was probably similar; someone who knew him personally described him as 'a strict Catholic to the letter of the law'.[297] Therefore, his private beliefs were also likely to have been consonant with those of the Catholic Church.

Such beliefs, however, had to be compromised to accommodate the exigencies of constitution-making. While he was not centrally involved in the efforts to find an acceptable formula, it is very probable that de Valera consulted him, as a trusted confidant, with an interest in and knowledge of philosophy and theology. According to Condon, the President may have been reminded by his legal advisers to consider naming the other religions that had been ignored in previous drafts.[298] As principal drafter of a constitution which sought to protect personal liberties, Hearne endorsed those other provisions of the article which guaranteed freedom of conscience and free profession of religion. Furthermore, the state guaranteed not to endow any religion and not to impose any disabilities or make any discrimination on the ground of religious profession. With the removal of the recognition of the 'special position' of the Catholic Church in 1972, the liberal character of the other provisions became more apparent. Therefore, it can be argued that Hearne would have been satisfied with the general scope and intention of the revised religious article which, after all the controversy surrounding it, represented 'an astute and not ignoble formulation of the principle of religious liberty in a predominantly Catholic country'.[299]

Hearne had another perspective on the special recognition accorded to the Catholic Church in the article on religion – that of a constitutional lawyer with a knowledge of similar provisions in the constitutions of other countries. It was a fact that there was an established religion in some European states. This was the situation in England and in the Kingdoms of Norway, Sweden and Denmark, where there were Protestant state churches and a requirement that the monarch be a member of that church. For example, the Swedish Constitution stated that 'the King shall always belong to the pure evangelical faith, as adopted and explained in the unaltered Augsburg Confession and in the resolution of the Uppsala Synod'.[300] The Norwegian Constitution, while declaring that 'the Evangelical–Lutheran religion shall remain the public religion of the state', also denied toleration to Catholic priests belonging to the Society of Jesus.[301] In England, the monarch was obliged to take an oath to maintain the supremacy of Protestantism, as King George VI did at his coronation on 12 May 1937. The Catholic Church was accorded a special position in the Polish Constitution, in an article similar to the one in Bunreacht na hÉireann.[302]

By comparison with other countries, the religious aspect as regards recognition of the Catholic Church in the 1937 Constitution was 'rather low key'[303] and made no stipulation that any officer holders had to be Roman Catholics. The article was purely descriptive in formulation. Nor were there any concerns voiced, at the time of drafting, by the leaders of the minority churches about the recognition accorded the Catholic Church. The Church of Ireland Archbishop of Dublin, Dr John Gregg, was satisfied with the section.[304] Having been shown draft copies, the President of the Methodist Church in Ireland informed de Valera that 'we find nothing either in substance or wording of the section submitted to which we could fairly take exception'.[305] Likewise, the Presbyterian Church, in its consultations with the President, expressed no reservations.[306] When the articles relating to religion and fundamental rights are considered, it is reasonable to suggest that Hearne saw them as representing a blend of liberal democracy and Catholic social teaching, while avoiding 'an affirmation of Catholic identity which would cause outright offence to the spectrum of Irish Christianity'.[307]

Hearne and the civil servants who were also associated with the Constitution were part of a more liberal Catholic culture than that represented by Cahill and McQuaid. They were wholly free of the stridency associated with certain vociferous elements in the Irish Catholic Church in the 1930s. The President was fortunate in having the expertise, wisdom and judgement of Maurice Moynihan, Arthur Matheson, Philip O'Donoghue, Michael McDunphy and, especially, John Hearne, for if he did not have the benefit of such skilled and broad-minded individuals

> it is more likely that both the content and design of the Constitution would have suffered accordingly. In the hands of others, it is likely that the Constitution would have been fatally damaged through the influence of confessional, right-wing, authoritarian thinking. While the Constitution contained some elements of this thinking (e.g., the ban on divorce, the tone and content of the preamble), the drafters also ensured ... that the Constitution contained as much of the thinking of Paine as much as it did of Catholic social teaching ... [The Constitution] ... [is] testament to the ability of the drafters to influence de Valera's thinking and to produce a document which substantially transcended the cultural values of Ireland of the 1930s.[308]

The reference to Thomas Paine is a reminder that Ireland is a liberal democratic state, an inheritance from the British constitutional tradition of which the country is a part, especially since the Act of Union. This fact can become obscured with the focus on the influence of McQuaid, the Jesuits and the Catholic Church on the Constitution. Basil Chubb has observed that the tradition of liberal democracy is 'the most persistent influence running through Bunreacht na hÉireann as a whole' and is 'most obvious' in Articles 40–4. Article 40, in particular, concerned with personal rights, provides for many of the rights associated with liberal democratic government.[309] Article 43 protects private property, while Article 44 guarantees the freedom of conscience and the free profession and practice of religion.

The focus on the inclusion of elements of Catholic social teachings can obscure a central reality of Articles 40–4: they enshrine rights and guarantees which are the essence of liberal democracy. In fact, the principles underlying the articles are a conflation of two distinct traditions: 'certain of the fundamental rights are couched in language of a secular rationalist nature, while others are clearly and strongly inspired by the Christian view of natural law'[310] and Catholic social teachings. In any assessment of Catholic influences on the 1937 Constitution, a most significant consideration is an appreciation of the many provisions reflecting the European constitutional heritage, of which Hearne was aware and upon which he drew in drafting Articles 40–4. In reality, Hugo Preuss and Thomas Paine had as much influence on the making of Bunreacht na hÉireann as the Jesuits and John Charles McQuaid.

The 1935 draft heads and the shaping of the Constitution

In terms of the practical process of drafting the 1937 Constitution, Hearne's endeavours were shaped and influenced by his draft heads prepared in 1935. They remained the basic model for the enormous task facing him.[311] Of greater significance was the fact that it was fundamentally a liberal and democratic document in the mould of the Weimar and other European constitutions, on to which the religiously inspired and other provisions were superimposed. Notwithstanding these additions, the state's new basic law, as was noted earlier, retained its roots in the tradition of liberal democracy.

The influence of the draft heads was apparent in the fact that many of the articles broadly correspond to articles in the later Constitution. In 1937, the articles were more developed and refined but they had a basis in the 1935 document, as is evident in an overview of the two:

Articles in draft heads	Provision	Articles in 1937 Constitution
Preamble	Preamble	Preamble
Article 1	Sovereignty	Article 4
Article 2	Citizenship	Article 9
Article 3	Irish language	Article 8

Articles 4–14	President	Articles 12–14
Articles 15–19	Oireachtas	Article 15
Articles 20–30	Dáil Éireann	Articles 16–17
Articles 31–3	Government	Article 28
Articles 34–5	Courts	Articles 34–7
Articles 36–7	Comptroller and auditor general	Article 33
Articles 38–42	Fundamental rights	Articles 40–4
Articles 43–5	Trial of criminal offences	Articles 38–9
Article 46	Emergency powers	Article 28
Article 47	War and defence	Article 28
Articles 48–9	Treaty-making	Article 29
Article 50	Amendment of the Constitution	Article 46

Fifty of Hearne's draft heads broadly correspond to twenty-five articles in the 1937 Constitution. These figures do not convey the full extent of the correspondence, however, as many of the articles in the 1935 document were incorporated into a smaller number in 1937. The provisions relating to the President illustrate this. In the draft heads, there were eleven articles while, in the 1937 basic law, there were two, but these incorporated most of the provisions of the draft head of 1935.

Articles in the draft heads 1935	Articles in the 1937 Constitution
Article 4	
To be elected by the people.	Article 12, 2, 1
To be at least 35 years old.	Article 12, 4, 1
To serve a term of seven years.	Article 12, 3, 1
To be eligible for re-election.	Article 13, 3, 2
May not be a member of the Oireachtas.	Article 12, 6, 1
Article 5	
An oath to be taken by the President.	Article 12, 8
Article 6	
President to be supreme commander.	Article 13, 4
All commissions to be from the President.	Article 13, 5, 2
Article 8	
Right of pardon, remit/commute sentences.	Article 13, 6

Article 9

| To appoint Prime Minister and ministers. | Article 13, 11, 2 |

Article 10

| Summon/dissolve Oireachtas. | Article 13, 2, 1 |

Article 11

| President to assent to and sign bills. | Article 13, 3, 1 |

Article 13

| Salary to be determined by law. | Article 11, 2 |

Article 14

| Powers exercisable upon the advice of the government. | Article 13, 11 |

A consideration of the draft heads serves as a reminder of one of the fundamental events in the shaping of the 1937 Constitution – the meetings between Hearne and de Valera in April–May 1935 and recorded by the latter in the 'squared paper draft'. The President's aspirations, ambitions and instructions, verbally communicated to the legal adviser, were given legal interpretation and expression by him in the 1935 draft heads. These, in turn, influenced and shaped the 1937 Constitution which represented the realisation of de Valera's vision in relation to a new basic law for the state. The six principles of an Irish Constitution, identified in the 'squared paper draft' and noted in Chapter 4, informed the development and drafting of Bunreacht na hÉireann. Significantly, the state was called 'Éire', a name redolent of a new constitutional dispensation and the destruction of the Treaty settlement.

The other principles were incorporated in the 1937 document: the sovereign independent and democratic nature of the state; territorial integrity; the sovereign power of the people; the people as the source of all authority; and only the people could change the Constitution by referendum. Included also were de Valera's other concerns, among them the creation of the office of President, the protection of fundamental rights and a preamble. Therefore, his aspirations and ambitions, as recorded in the 'squared paper draft', found expression in the Constitution, these being mediated, in a significant way, by Hearne's draft heads of 1935.

Article 29: 'International Relations'

Article 29, dealing with international relations, an innovatory feature of the Constitution introduced by Hearne, was influenced and shaped by his diplomatic experiences as legal adviser of the Department of External Affairs. This article had its origins in Article 29 of the Weimar Constitution, which accepted 'the universally recognised rules of international law', and in the Covenant of the League of Nations and the Kellogg–Briand Pact 1928. This pact rejected war as an instrument of foreign policy;[312] John Hearne represented Ireland at the talks which culminated in this agreement.[313] Its influence and that of the Covenant of the League of Nations[314] are evident in the article as composed by him.

Article 29, 1
Ireland affirms its devotion to the ideal of peace and friendly co-operation amongst nations founded on international justice and morality.

Kellogg–Briand Pact, proclamation
Persuaded that the time has come when a formal renunciation of war as an instrument of national policy shall be made ...

Article 29, 2
Ireland affirms its adherence to the principles of the pacific settlement of international disputes by international arbitration or judicial determination.

Article 13, Covenant of the League of Nations
The members of the League agree that whenever any dispute shall arise between them ... and which cannot be satisfactorily settled by diplomacy, they will submit the whole subject matter to arbitration or judicial settlement.

Article II, Kellogg–Briand Pact
The High Contracting Parties agree that the settlement or resolution of all disputes and conflicts ... shall never be sought except by pacific means.

Article 29, 3
Ireland accepts the generally recognised principles of international law as its rule of conduct in its relations with other States.

Covenant of the League of Nations
... the firm establishment of the understanding of international law as the actual rule of conduct between governments.

Seanad Éireann: shaping the articles

De Valera's attitude to the second chamber in the Oireachtas was shaped by his experiences of the Free State Seanad, the abolition of which he proposed in 1934 and achieved two years later.[315] He came to regard it as an obstruction to the realisation of his government's constitutional programme. Its rejection of the bill to abolish the oath of allegiance sealed its fate and its subsequent rejection of other government measures confirmed Fianna Fáil's resolve.[316] However, de Valera did not rule out the possibility of restoring a second chamber at a later date, recognition by him of the fact that bicameralism enjoyed considerable support in academic, commercial and ecclesiastical circles, as was noted in Chapter 4. As early as June 1933, he spoke of 'whether we should substitute another form of second chamber for it' [the Seanad].[317] Three years later, in the course of a Dáil debate in which he stated the government's intention to introduce a new constitution, he said that ministers had not yet decided on the restoration of a second chamber in the proposed new basic law.[318] He was clear, however, as to the circumstances in which it would be restored: 'whether it is possible to devise a second chamber which can be of value and not a danger'.[319]

A senate that was not a 'danger' was central to de Valera's attitude to a second House of the Oireachtas. By this he meant that it must not be a rival to the Dáil in terms of legislative authority. Speaking in June 1933, he declared that 'there can only be one master and that master, as long as we have a democratic form of government, must be the house directly elected by the people'.[320] In May 1936, he expressed the definite view that the second chamber must be ultimately subordinate to the elected house.[321] This subordination required, even demanded, that this chamber not be directly elected. On this point de Valera was adamant[322] – such an election could turn the second chamber into a rival body to the Dáil[323] thereby causing what he termed 'a clashing of authority'.[324] If he was forceful in describing the type of second house he would not countenance, he also gave an insight into the type he would consider, telling the Dáil in June 1933:

> I have not despaired of being able to devise a constitution which would give us a second house completely differentiated from this [the Dáil], with smaller numbers, which would be a consultative body, a body that would not have powers of obstruction, that would have powers of making proposals and suggestions, and whose advice would always be there for the Executive Council and for the Dáil.[325]

One such house could be organised on a vocational basis, de Valera telling the Dáil in the same debate that he could 'imagine a Seanad, for instance, in which the members would represent vocational groups'.[326] Nearly three years later, he informed deputies that he had tried 'on more than one occasion to work out the constitution of a second chamber on the basis of vocational representation'.[327] Vocationalism (or corporatism, as it was sometimes called) was a social, economic and political model proposed by Pope Pius XI in 1931 in an encyclical entitled *Quadragesimo Anno*. This appeared at a time when the world was experiencing the devastating effects of the Great Depression and, in the document, the pope commended the reconstruction of the social order so as to eliminate class warfare. The means to achieve this was the establishment of vocational groups or corporations, representative of workers and employers, to regulate the various sectors of a country's economy.[328]

The cause of vocational organisation was espoused, in particular, by supporters of the Catholic social movement in Ireland. By their advocacy, they gave papal teaching a more popular currency.[329] Such was the determination of these Catholic activists that 'vocationalism was a movement that refused to go away'.[330] The desirability of a second chamber in the Oireachtas, organised along vocational or occupational lines became an issue of particular concern for some advocates of Catholic social activism. Revd Edward Cahill wrote that a second chamber 'could very suitably be made up principally of the representatives of the [Catholic] Church, the universities and higher schools (ecclesiastical and lay), the vocational corporations and the labour unions, the agricultural interests and the great national organisations'.[331] D.A. Binchy, writing in *Studies* in March 1936, proposed that, side by side with the Dáil, there be a senate based mainly, but not exclusively, on vocational representation,[332] a view shared by Alfred O'Rahilly.[333] Revd Dr Cornelius Lucey argued for a second chamber elected on an occupational basis.[334] De Valera's biographers confirmed his familiarity with the writings of Catholic intellectuals[335] and it is very likely that he read articles relating to a vocationally organised senate which featured in Catholic journals in the 1930s.[336]

As a second parliamentary chamber had considerable support in intellectual and ecclesiastical circles, de Valera decided to establish a commission to consider its powers and method of selection, should the government decide to restore it in a new constitution. John Hearne was a member of this commission, as was discussed in Chapter 4. The President accepted a minority report which favoured a senate organised on a vocational basis.[337] He did this because he was disposed, or more correctly was not opposed, to the general idea of a second house constructed along such lines, which differentiated it from the Dáil. It was also a gesture towards the determined Catholic social movement. More importantly, this upper house had little power – it could delay legislation for only ninety days. Thus de Valera's concerns were central in shaping provisions relating to Seanad Éireann in the Constitution.

If de Valera's concerns and the minority report influenced the Constitution, so did the majority report signed by Hearne. Most of its recommendations became the basis of the articles he drafted relating to the power and functions of the restored Seanad. Interestingly, the proposed second chamber was the only aspect of the

Recommendation in majority report	Article in 1937 Constitution
Par. 6 No bill (except a money bill) may be enacted until sent to second chamber for recommendations.	20, 1.
Par. 7 A bill may be initiated in the second house.	20, 2, 1.
Par. 10 Removal of a judge and comptroller and auditor general to require resolution of Dáil and Seanad.	35, 4, 1; 33, 5, 1.
Par. 11 Seanad to have no power to reject a money bill.	20, 1.
Par. 12 Seanad may make recommendations in relation to money bills.	21, 2, 1.
Par. 15 Every minister to have the right to be heard in Seanad.	28, 8.
Par. 16 Period given to Seanad to consider bills may be abridged.	24.

Constitution on which de Valera established a formal and official body to offer opinions and recommendations, outside the closed circle of his civil service advisers. When it came to ideas regarding the means of selecting the Seanad he seemed to lack the sense of conviction and purpose which characterised most other aspects of his constitutional project. He decided to delegate this task to a commission. This did not, however, mean that he regarded it as a matter of great importance. The fact was that he never conceived the inclusion of a second chamber as a significant feature of the new Constitution, never really being convinced that a bicameral parliament was essential to representative government.[338] Should a second chamber be included, it was desirable that it be different in its composition to the Dáil and to make proposals in that respect was the principal function of the commission. The establishment of this commission was, in fact, a measure of the low priority the President ascribed to the Seanad; if it were a priority, discussions and decisions would have been confined, firmly and decisively, to his exclusive body of civil service advisers or to those invited to make recommendations, secretly and confidentially, such as the Jesuits and McQuaid.

Hearne: source of advice and inspiration

This chapter has attempted to gain an understanding of what Hearne termed 'the collective mind of lawyers and politicians' in relation to the making of the

1937 Constitution. The dominant figure was Éamon de Valera, his legal adviser giving expression to his objectives by translating them into the precise language of constitutional law. Hearne advised the President and it is evident that he valued his counsel. Clearly, Hearne had his own sense of his preferred constitution and this influenced its drafting. In particular, and most importantly, he conceived of it as a means of protecting and vindicating the rights of citizens. Thus he introduced the article on equality, advocated entrenched judicial review and even supported a dedicated constitutional court.

As was noted in Chapter 1, as early as the autumn of 1919, in his speech to the Law Students' Debating Society of the King's Inns, he expressed the view that the permanence of the legislative and executive establishments of states would depend increasingly on the advancement of their citizens' knowledge of the appreciation of their liberties and their understanding of those of others. In speeches he delivered in Canada and the United States, while serving as a diplomat, he articulated a profound sense of human dignity and the rights of the individual vis-á-vis the state and, in his drafting, he gave expression to this. He had a more developed sense of human rights and dignity than de Valera and this influenced various provisions of Bunreacht na hÉireann.

Hearne's sense of the character of the Constitution also included a profound understanding of its role in the life of the nation. He articulated his ideas in a memorandum prepared by him for de Valera and referred to earlier, 'The Constitution and National Life',[339] and in speeches delivered while on diplomatic service. He believed that there was a relationship between history and jurisprudence that was 'legitimate, inevitable and of long-standing'.[340] In effect, this meant that there was a relationship between a country's laws and constitution, and its national life.[341] With the perspective of the accomplished lawyer he had a particular interpretation of Irish history:

> During a long period of our history the whole of our national effort has been a struggle to secure for our people the right to make their own laws. That effort was inspired not merely by the determination of a great nation to throw off the yoke of alien rule. It had a deeper significance than that. It was inspired by the purpose of a people possessing an ancient civilisation, a noble heritage and the consciousness of a great future that their national laws should not only be made by themselves but should be made to foster and reflect the social and political order of a distinct Irish commonwealth.

He then enunciated a deeply held belief: 'A nation's laws are as much part of its national life as are its language, its literature, its arts and its particular outlook upon the great public questions of the age.'[342] He argued that there existed 'a close and uninterrupted relation' between the British constitutional system and the history of England and between the Constitution of the United States and the history of the American people. This same observation, according to him, was applicable to the constitutions adopted in more recent times in countries such as Russia, Portugal and Austria (before its annexation by Germany).[343]

However, in Hearne's opinion, this relationship between history and a country's constitution had not applied to Ireland for hundreds of years. Rather, the Irish nation refused to give its allegiance to laws imposed on it and which were inimical to its philosophy of life. Consequently, the Irish were characterised 'as a nation of rebels and revolutionaries, bereft of a talent for normal government and ordered political life'. They became synonymous with 'disloyalty and disorder'. Hearne asserted that 'a system of law which is divorced from the convictions, the beliefs and the spiritual character of a people is in no sense a national code'.[344]

There was, however, 'a moment in the history of every free people in which their philosophy of life passes into their national law'. In Hearne's opinion this happened in Ireland in 1937:

> Here again thought the lawyers and others who framed the national Constitution of Ireland in 1937 – the first written Constitution ever framed in Ireland by Irishmen for Irishmen – was the supreme opportunity, the first given to the Irish people for seven hundred years of enacting a fundamental law which would take account of our national thought and reflect the philosophy of life of our people.[345]

This event enabled the Irish people to express, in their new basic law, their values and beliefs, these being identified by Hearne:

> Our people stand – and have stood for more than a thousand years – for the public worship of almighty God, the freedom of the individual to profess and practise his religion according to his conscience, the institution of the family as the basis of civil society, the indissolubility of the marriage bond, the right of private property, liberty of speech and the right of association and assembly subject to public order and morality.[346]

He acknowledged that these beliefs and principles were those of a 'conservative people'.[347] Bunreacht na hÉireann was a declaration of sovereignty by a nation Hearne believed had existed for hundreds of years but which could only give expression to this fact in 1937.[348]

Clearly, for Hearne, the Constitution was much more than a recital of legal provisions; it was the encapsulation of the essence of a people by virtue of enshrining their philosophy of life. He had a philosophic, even esoteric view of the document and, consequently, this elevated and exalted the process of constitution-making. Those engaged in this task were essentially seeking, in Hearne's words, 'the restoration of an uninterrupted national tradition'.[349] In their conversations and discussions, it was likely, indeed certain, that he expressed this fundamental vision of the Constitution to de Valera. Such a view appealed to de Valera; in his speech at the inauguration of Douglas Hyde as the first President of Ireland, he used words redolent of this sentiment: 'In you we greet the successor of our rightful princes, and, in your accession to office, we hail the closing of the breach that has existed since the undoing of the nation at Kinsale.'[350]

Thus Hearne reinforced de Valera's conviction of the importance of his decision to give the state a new constitution, giving it (the decision) a greater validity and authenticity. In doing this, Hearne was effectively reprising a role he had played in 1929 and 1930, commented upon in Chapter 2. Then, by his memoranda, he had helped create an esprit de corps among the Irish delegates at the imperial gatherings of those years, giving his colleagues a greater sense of conviction and determination. In his perception of the Constitution, articulated in conversations with de Valera, he gave the President an intellectual and philosophical basis for the work and challenge of constitution-making, a basis which transcended the practical and legal concerns which attended its drafting and thereby suffused the endeavour with a nobility of purpose. For de Valera, his legal adviser became something of a Gaelic Lycurgus, a man of laws who guided and inspired the nation's leader through the legal perils of the monumental task of establishing a new fundamental law for a recently independent state at a time of severe diplomatic and legal tensions between Ireland and Britain, and against the backdrop of a European continent descending into conflict and turmoil.

Hearne's advice resonated with de Valera because both men were nationalists; the two central figures responsible for Bunreacht na hÉireann had this in common. It is important to remember and acknowledge this fact in respect of Hearne. He believed, firmly and ardently, in the sovereignty of the Irish state, regarding the Treaty as an agreement between two independent states. It was this belief which allowed him declare that 'Ireland was never a British colony.'[351] As a civil servant in the 1920s, he played a significant role in the evolution of Irish sovereignty within the British Commonwealth. He resented the refusal of the British government to accept the implications of the statement of Dominion equality heralded by the Balfour Declaration.

It was in the context of constitutional evolution that he could describe the 1922 fundamental law as possessing 'the mechanism of a crown colony of a hundred years ago ... It took little account of our nationhood'.[352] This Constitution failed to recognise 'the tone of our national thought and the trend of our national development'.[353] Hearne was a nationalist whose nationalism found expression in contributing to the evolution of the laws which defined the constitutional status of Ireland. Irish history has long recognised the contribution of political, revolutionary and cultural nationalists in the progress towards independence. In John Hearne it should recognise his contribution as a legal nationalist.

CHAPTER **7**

The Constitution of Ireland, 1937: Contemporary Reaction

The Irish public got its first glimpse of the proposed constitution when it was printed in the daily newspapers of 1 May 1937. Thus began the extensive coverage of the state's new fundamental law. The *Irish Independent* commissioned a series of articles on it by expert and public figures,[1] and reports and editorials concerned with aspects of the document featured regularly in all newspapers. On 11 May, Dáil Éireann began debating it and the deliberations continued until 14 June. The draft of the state's new basic law, the making of which had been shrouded in secrecy, was now well and truly in the glare of public attention. This chapter will consider the Dáil debate and contemporary reaction. This aspect of the 1937 Constitution's history is one in which John Hearne does not feature in a central role. Nevertheless, it is essential to consider this reaction, as it related to a document in the making of which he played, in Éamon de Valera's words, 'a fundamental part'. Though absent from the public debate – the public did not even know of his existence – in historical terms, his presence hovered over it like Banquo's ghost.

Now that the document was in the public arena, Éamon de Valera 'completely identified himself with it. He personally presented it to the people in a radio broadcast and to the Dáil ... He piloted it through the Dáil virtually single-handed, explaining and defending its provisions, where necessary sentence by sentence, word by word ...'[2] In keeping with the tradition of the anonymity of the civil service, John Hearne's contribution to the evolution and production of the new basic law went unrecorded, though there were two occasions on which he was referred to anonymously by de Valera. On 13 May, in the course of rejecting opposition criticisms of articles pertaining to the President, de Valera asserted that they had been passed by lawyers who played no part in politics. Challenged by opposition deputies to name them, he simply stated that they were 'the law advisers'. At this juncture, the Ceann Comhairle reminded members that it was not usual or proper to draw the qualifications or actions of civil servants into debates.[3] On the last day of the debate, 14 June 1937, de Valera again referred to the unnamed Hearne:

> The drafting of it [the proposed constitution], in one form or another, has taken over a year. Its principles were decided on over a year ago ... As to the actual drafting ... it is true that, as far as the literal drafting of the constitution was concerned, it has been largely left to one person, because it is better obviously, when principles are decided upon, that there should be largely a common hand running through the document. You have got a uniform style if you used that method. If you used the other you have something of a hotchpotch. But that does not mean that that draft was not criticised. It does not mean that that draft was not changed from its original form to the form in which you have it now, finally. It was changed a number of times, but the principle was to get those changes always expressed and put in their final shape ... as far as possible by the one hand.[4]

There was a particular context in which the debate on the draft constitution took place: the Civil War had crippled and poisoned the independent Irish state – 'it inaugurated a bitter ice age that froze Irish politics for a generation'.[5] In his incendiary polemic, *The Victory of Sinn Féin*, published in 1925, and dubbed at the time 'the most discussed book in Ireland',[6] P.S. O'Hegarty articulated a central tenet of supporters of the Free State: 'For the Civil War, the whole responsibility is on Mr de Valera'.[7] For followers of Cumann na nGaedheal and later Fine Gael, the Fianna Fáil leader was 'the man they could never forgive'.[8] Maryann Valiulis has observed that the events of 1922–3 became 'a perceptual prism because the Civil War became the looking glass through which both the past and future were viewed, were refracted, dictating a particular interpretation of the past and influencing actions and reactions'.[9] It was through this 'prism' of Civil War animosities that the proposed constitution was assessed and became the object for the articulation of his opponents' profound mistrust of de Valera.

The toxic character of the political climate manifested itself especially in the debate on the newly created office of President. The Dáil debate on the proposed constitution took up nearly ninety hours, of which nearly one-third (about twenty-seven hours) was devoted to the presidency. This was a disproportionate amount since the articles dealing with it account for about 13 per cent of the whole document.[10] Early in the debate, Patrick McGilligan, Hearne's former minister, asserted that the President's powers were the really 'alarming' features of the draft constitution,[11] while James Dillon proclaimed, with equal conviction, that it was possible to constitute the President 'an absolute dictator'.[12] The word 'dictator' or a derivative of it was used over two hundred times in the Dáil debate, with the vast majority of these references relating to the office of President.[13]

Fine Gael deputies had no doubt who this putative dictator would be, Desmond FitzGerald giving voice to their beliefs that, if returned to power, the Fianna Fáil government would use its parliamentary majority to give additional powers to the office, which de Valera would then assume.[14] It was precisely the section of the document providing for the granting of additional powers to the President by ordinary legislation that formed a foundational basis for Fine Gael's fears. Thus one deputy could state that this provision 'asphalts the road by which an individual could work into a dictatorship'.[15]

Another basis for opposition concern was the vesting of supreme command of the defence forces in the President, with a Fine Gael deputy cautioning: 'Every dictator wants an army behind him.'[16] The word 'dictator' had a particular power and resonance in the context of the 1930s, with the collapse of democracy throughout Europe. Deputies were very aware of developments on the continent, with Patrick McGilligan, for example, referring to the fact that, in the three Baltic states of Lithuania, Latvia and Estonia, the largely ceremonial heads of state had established dictatorships.[17] The *Irish Independent*, a journal sympathetic to Fine Gael, added its voice to opposition concerns, repeating the substance of views expressed in the course of debates. It described the document as reeking of 'Hitlerism'.[18] Concerns informed by events in European countries combined with the bitterness of Civil War divisions to make the proposed Irish presidency 'the focal point of opposition to Bunreacht na hÉireann'.[19]

Speaking in the Dáil on 13 May, de Valera observed that, in addition to the office of President, the debate on the proposed fundamental law was also being dominated by another issue – the status of women under the document.[20] He was referring to the reaction of women's groups to provisions pertaining to their gender contained in four articles. In Article 16, 1, 1 (in this chapter articles are numbered as they appear in the draft constitution as approved by Dáil Éireann in June 1937) dealing with membership of the Dáil, the omission in the proposed wording of the phrase 'without distinction of sex',[21] which appeared in the Free State Constitution,[22] caused unease and was regarded as a dilution of the legal commitment to equality of the sexes. Article 40, 1, which proclaimed the equality of all citizens before the law, was viewed with dismay because of the second sentence referring to the state having 'due regard to difference of capacity, physical and moral, and of social function'.[23]

Louie Bennett, president of the Irish Women Workers' Union, protested that this phrase tended to place women 'in a different category of citizenship from men'.[24] The words 'by her life within the home' in Article 41, 2, 1[25] was adjudged offensive. Bennett argued that it should be amended to read 'by her work for the home', thus giving recognition to the work done by women outside the domestic sphere, 'in education, in social service, in culture, in workshop and on the farm', work she described as 'indispensable to a civilised state'.[26] Finally, Article 45, 4, 2,[27] with its reference to women not being forced 'by economic necessity to enter avocations unsuited to their sex, age or strength', was regarded as a denial of the rights of women to choose their own careers in life.[28]

Women were often vehement in their denunciation of the articles: Hanna Sheehy-Skeffington wrote that women were never so united in the face of what she described as 'fascist proposals'.[29] The National University Women Graduates' Association and the Joint Committee of Women's Societies and Social Workers launched a campaign to have the offending clauses deleted[30] and their concerns received a significant degree of attention in newspapers.[31] After the Dáil passed the draft constitution on 14 June, women embarked on a campaign urging its rejection in the plebiscite. This campaign culminated in a public meeting in Dublin's Mansion House, attended by 1,500 women.[32]

Opposition politicians in the Dáil repeated the concerns voiced by the various women's groups.[33] While Cumann na nGaedheal's record on women's rights was poor,[34] de Valera's opponents were determined to harry him for political advantage. The President was equally determined in the defence of his proposals. He utterly rejected that there was any threat to the equality of women.[35] The reference to 'women in the home' was defended in an uncompromising manner, with de Valera insisting that it was a tribute to the work done by women as mothers[36] and acknowledgement of a fact that was universally recognised.[37] In the matter of Article 45, he argued that the provisions were there to protect women.[38]

What is striking about de Valera's contributions to this debate was his intransigent attitude.[39] This intransigence was due, in large measure, to his belief that he was giving expression in the new basic law to opinions that were widely held in Irish society relating to the role of women. In that regard he was correct. As Joseph Lee has commented, there seemed to have been 'more popular sympathy, including female sympathy, for de Valera's view than for that of the women graduates'.[40]

While the drafting of the article on religion had caused de Valera much anxiety, the debate on it in the Dáil was a brief and quiescent affair, with only three deputies, including de Valera himself, speaking on this provision of the proposed constitution.[41] Of course, apart from ministers, most deputies knew nothing of the difficulties surrounding the drafting of the clauses. The President made an oblique reference to these difficulties when he commented that 'it might be said that this [religious article] does not go, from the Catholic point of view, the distance that would be desired by a number, but no objection has been taken by the churches to it'. He defended the inclusion of the reference to the 'special position' of the Catholic Church by asserting that, in a democratic state, recognition must be accorded to the beliefs of the majority.[42]

A Protestant deputy, Robert Rowlette, argued that the majority position of the Catholic Church was so obvious that there was no need to give it constitutional expression. While the reference to the 'special position' of that church did not cause him any anxiety at present, such a reference might lead to unease in the future, a point upon which he did not elaborate.[43] Deputy Frank McDermott, an independent member, expressed the view that inclusion of 'the special position' of the majority church did not offend 'in any way against the principle of equal treatment of people of different religions'. It did offend, however, against the unity of Ireland and 'certain dangers will arise by putting it in, especially in connection with partition'.[44] McDermott was the only deputy who addressed the implications of this article in relation to Northern Ireland.[45]

The provisions influenced by Catholic social thinking were also approved without controversy. There was a brief discussion on the prohibition on divorce[46] and no discussion of the articles concerned with education and property.[47]

Outside the Dáil, the document won the praise of Catholic opinion. Many bishops lauded it, with the primate, Cardinal MacRory, hailing it 'as a great Christian document, full of faith in God as the supreme law-giver and ruler'.[48] The Catholic social organisation An Ríoghacht expressed satisfaction at the 'noteworthy manner' in which basic Catholic principles were recognised in the Constitution.[49] Fr Edward Cahill asserted that 'all the fundamental Christian principles ... are frankly accepted and emphasised. In the last particular, the Irish Constitution is probably unique among modern written constitutions'.[50] James Hogan, Professor of History at University College Cork,[51] writing to Alfred O'Rahilly, observed that 'it makes no bones about being the Constitution of a Catholic people' and that it was gratifying 'to see our rulers, at last, waking up to the existence of a Catholic social philosophy'.[52]

Correspondence received by de Valera, however, gives an insight into the Catholic triumphalism characteristic of Ireland in the 1930s and serves as a reminder of the challenges he faced in negotiating the article on religion. A Jesuit, Fr Thomas Hurley, suggested that an image of a Celtic cross be placed on the national flag, describing it as 'a very desirable emblem on the flag of a Catholic nation'.[53] Particular venom was directed at the provision recognising the other Christian Churches, especially at the use of the title Church of Ireland. In the opinion of Fr Edward Cahill, it was 'an authoritative approval of a piece of lying propaganda'.[54] Another Jesuit, Fr P.J. Gannon, regarded the title as the concession of 'a usurped title to a body which really is not a church at all'. He regretted the explicit mention of any Protestant 'sect' in the document.[55] A lay correspondent was even more animated in the expression of his displeasure: the real Church of Ireland was the Catholic Church and not 'the heretical alien sect' so misnamed, which was nothing but an offshoot of the lusts of Luther and King Henry VIII.[56] An Ríoghacht also lamented the recognition accorded in the document to what it termed 'the supposed marriages' between Catholics and Protestants, in spite of these being nothing more than 'legalised concubinage'.[57]

In contrast, public expressions of minority religious opinion were favourable towards the draft constitution. The *Church of Ireland Gazette* praised the recognition of the Christian faith at a time when 'state worship' was 'rampant'.[58] Speaking in Belfast in June 1937, at the general assembly of the Presbyterian Church, Revd P.W. O'Neill, out-going moderator, described the document as 'unusual in modern times' because of the recognition accorded to all religious denominations.[59] The Rabbinate Committee of the Dublin Jewish Community thanked de Valera for sending a copy of the draft to one of its representatives. The letter continued: 'They note with the greatest satisfaction and due appreciation that the "Jewish Congregations" are included in the clause giving equal recognition to the religious bodies in Éire: and they respectfully tender congratulations on the production of such a fair and just document.'[60]

The recognition accorded to Jewish congregations was a unique feature of the proposed constitution, the only constitutional provision in the world, then or since, to give such recognition. The inclusion of this clause did not, of course, signify an end to anti-Semitism in Ireland or a more generous policy towards Jewish immigration, especially during the War years.[61] Nevertheless, it was appreciated by, and of significance to, the representatives of Ireland's Jews 'at a time in history when the greatest agony of that people had already begun in Europe'[62] and which was to culminate in the Holocaust.

In Chapter 5, it was noted that the article on private property proved problematical; eventually parts of it were incorporated into Article 45, the 'Directive Principles of Social Policy'. During the Dáil debate, however, little attention was paid to this part of the document. In a speech on 11 May, de Valera described the Directive Principles as 'constant headlines', a means by which social progress would be measured. The present social system, according to him, was 'not like it ought to be anywhere in the world. One of the best ways of remedying it is to set out definite objectives you should try to reach'.[63] He insisted that these objectives could only be interpreted by parliament; hence, they were not justiciable.[64] On 4 June, there was a brief debate on them, which was dominated by their implications for the status of women. It was precisely because these principles were exempt from the jurisdiction of the courts that they were deemed meaningless by opposition critics. They were described as 'pious resolutions' by one deputy,[65] while another dismissed them as 'pious aspirations so far as social legislation and social conditions are concerned'.[66]

The Directive Principles also had their critics outside the Dáil. Alfred O'Rahilly wrote that 'we cannot afford to be socially creedless in the world'; he believed that 'their citation in law cases would be excellent publicity; it would act as an incentive towards their proper implementation'.[67] In a letter to O'Rahilly, Professor James Hogan also expressed surprise at their exclusion from the cognisance of the courts, despite 'having been stated to be fundamental'.[68] An organisation styled the League of Social Justice 'deplored' the fact that the principles were not 'mandatory' and 'not made part of the fundamental law of the state'.[69] An Ríoghacht argued that they should be omitted as they were not justiciable.[70]

One aspect of the state's proposed new fundamental law which won the approval of de Valera's opponents was his decision to restore Seanad Éireann,[71] an act described by one Fine Gael deputy as 'one of the remarkably good things in this Constitution'.[72] Addressing the Dáil, the President highlighted a number of factors which influenced the relevant articles relating to the second chamber. The vocational composition of the panels was due to 'the germ of a suggestion which we tried to work up and make practicable' and which was contained in the minority report of the Second House of the Oireachtas Commission.[73] This gave a second chamber, different in character to the Dáil.[74]

However, because the country did not have the required type of vocational organisation to make possible direct election to the upper house, de Valera explained that an indirect system of election, based on Dáil candidates at the previous general election who had received more than 500 first preference votes, was to be put in place, though this might change with the development of vocational organisation.[75] A member of the commission, Deputy Frank McDermott, expressed the view that the proposed Seanad 'should be welcome to people ... who are urging us to do more in the way of embodying the principles of various papal encyclicals into our political system here'.[76] It was welcomed by some outside the Dáil. Professor Michael Tierney, a University College Dublin academic and a staunch supporter of vocational organisation, praised de Valera's decision,[77] as did An Ríoghacht[78] and the Catholic Young Men's Society.[79]

Another member of the commission, however, Alfred O'Rahilly, objected in strenuous terms to de Valera's assertion that he was following the recommendations of the minority report which he had signed. The Cork-based academic declared: 'Personally, I would prefer no Senate at all rather than this contraption.' The proposed fundamental law contained 'pious claptrap' and the government had no intention of taking papal social teachings 'quite so literally'. The basis for O'Rahilly's deep dissatisfaction was the system of indirect election, a system which indicated that the President was 'not willing to take the first steps towards implementing the corporative ideal'.[80]

It was demonstrably apparent during the Dáil debate that de Valera was still not personally convinced of the necessity to restore the Seanad:

My attitude is that even though some of us may be largely indifferent to the question of whether or not there is a Seanad, if a large section of the people of the country think that there is something important in having a Seanad, even if we ourselves are indifferent to it, we should give way to the people who are anxious for it.

The report of the Second House of the Oireachtas Commission had convinced him that 'such a thing as an ideal Seanad' was not possible. In spite of this, he explained his decision to include one:

> The only thing that made me put a proposition for a Seanad into this measure at all is this: that there were members on the bench opposite, as I remember, who ... said: 'Very well, even a bad Seanad would be better than no Seanad at all'. It was precisely on that basis – that some Seanad, the best Seanad we can get, even though it may be adjudged a bad Seanad, is better than no Seanad at all – that this proposal is now included.[81]

This lamentable defence of his decision prompted McDermott to opine that 'the President might have been a little more encouraging and a little more inspiring than he was in his speech, or in the tone of his speech, to those who will be composing this Senate in the future'.[82]

It was the Labour Party leader, William Norton, who offered the most plausible explanation of the circumstances of the Seanad's restoration as a vocational chamber: 'It happened that the minority report produced a scheme for a second chamber and the President, wobbling on the desirability of a second chamber, immediately grasped this thing [minority report favouring a vocational senate] and so we have it in the Constitution.'[83] Norton highlighted the fact that it was different from the Seanad Fianna Fáil had abolished.[84] What the Labour deputy was saying was that this appealed to de Valera and seemed to justify his restoration of it – to restore a chamber identical to the former one was not an option.

The quality of the Dáil debate on the proposed constitution was generally poor and unsatisfactory and certainly did not reflect the gravity and importance of the subject matter, nor did it do justice to the issues involved. A number of factors contributed to this unfortunate reality. First, the poverty of discussion may be explained by the continuing bitterness engendered by the Civil War and referred to earlier. This bitterness suffused proceedings and influenced Fine Gael's negative and hostile reaction to the document. This fact was dramatically apparent in the party's attitude to the proposed office of President – an attitude which produced an animated debate. Second, the prevailing nationalist consensus meant that Articles 2 and 3 were virtually ignored, as were the implications of the draft constitution on partition and relations with Northern Ireland. Third, a similar religious consensus, Catholic in character, meant that Articles 40–5 were given only cursory attention.

The time allocated by the government for the debate may appear meagre and not conducive to in-depth deliberation: twelve days, from 11–13 May, 25 May–4 June and 10 and 14 June. Moreover, normal Dáil business was also transacted, which meant that discussion of the draft constitution descended, at times, to the level of a routine parliamentary matter. In truth, however, the allocation of time was sufficient from the perspective of the quality of the debate and the level of participation by deputies. Most did not speak; in fact, very many of them did not appear to even engage in the proceedings. This apparent lack of meaningful engagement was evident by the presence, on occasions, of fewer than twenty deputies in the chamber. This happened seven times during the twelve-day debate and twice on two days, 28 May and 4 June,[85] prompting the *Irish Independent* to comment on the absence of deputies on the former date.[86] This disengagement may be explained by a number of factors. In the case of Fianna Fáil's deputies, de Valera spoke, pontificated even, for the party and the government and there simply was no encouragement given to backbenchers to contribute to the debate. Among Fine Gael deputies there was the view that de Valera was determined to secure passage of the proposed constitution with the minimum of amendments. Thus the debate from the main opposition party's point of view was a formality, if not a charade.

There was some basis for the Fine Gael view that de Valera was seeking the passage of the state's new basic law by the Dáil with as few changes as possible. The reality was that the partisan and divisive nature of post-Civil War politics could produce no other circumstance. An indicator of the President's disposition to accommodate opposition opinion is to be found in Michael McDunphy's list of amendments to the proposed constitution tabled in the period 25 May–4 June. He recorded their fate: thirty-seven were 'defeated', thirty-three 'withdrawn' and fifteen 'accepted' and 'agreed'.[87] This evidence is indicative and by no means definitive but it suggests that the President was limited in his willingness to heed opposition concerns. Certainly on issues he deemed important or ones which had been politicised, no concessions were made. McDunphy's list recorded that seventeen Fine Gael motions relating to the office of President were defeated. Another motion that 'The Irish and English languages are recognised equally as national and official languages' suffered a similar fate.

De Valera, nevertheless, did make changes to the document in the course of the debate. None of these, however, was really fundamental. Thirteen articles in the draft were amended.[88] Some of the changes were minor or of an editorial nature. The former included: Ireland was to be the official name of the state, in addition to Éire;[89] the President was to be eligible for re-election 'once but only once';[90] and the period during which the Supreme Court was to pronounce its decision in respect of a bill referred by the President was increased from thirty to sixty days.[91] Editorial changes retained the substance of articles. Matters pertaining to the commission to discharge the functions of the President became a separate article, rather than being incorporated into the article concerned with the President. This new article was essentially composed of sections which had featured in the original article.[92] Article

40, 6, 1, ii, relating to the rights of citizens to assemble peaceably, was expressed in more concise language in the approved version.[93]

More substantial changes affected six articles. The controversy surrounding the rights of women was reflected in changes to three articles. There was an additional provision included in Article 9 which dealt with nationality and citizenship: 'No person may be excluded from Irish nationality and citizenship by reason of the sex of such person.'[94] In Article 16, 1, 1, concerned with eligibility for membership of Dáil Éireann and the right to vote, the phrase 'without distinction of sex' was included in the amended version.[95] An additional section was included in this article: 'No law shall be enacted placing any citizen under disability or incapacity for membership of Dáil Éireann on the ground of sex or disqualifying any citizen from voting at an election for members of Dáil Éireann on that ground.'[96] In a clear response to women's objections, the reference in the Directives Principles of Social Policy to the 'inadequate strength of women' not being abused by being forced into unsuitable employment was moderated. It now read: 'The State shall endeavour to ensure that the strength and health of workers, men and women ... shall not be abused ...'[97]

There were two relatively significant changes affecting the presidency. A mechanism was introduced to determine presidential incapacity – this was to be done by the Supreme Court.[98] In the matter of impeachment, the charge could be preferred by either House of the Oireachtas, rather than just by the Seanad. The other chamber was to investigate this charge and a resolution supported by two-thirds of its members was required to remove the President from office.[99] The method of election to the Seanad, based on an electorate of Dáil candidates who had received more than 500 first preference votes, was deleted.[100] The final change of significance related to the judicial determination as to the constitutional validity of laws. In the draft constitution presented to the Dáil for its approval, the power was vested in the Supreme Court;[101] this was amended by conferring this right on the High Court,[102] with the right of appeal to the Supreme Court.[103]

The proposed constitution was approved by Dáil Éireann, on 14 June 1937, by sixty-two votes to forty-eight.[104] It contained a preamble and sixty-three articles:

Preamble
Article 1: Sovereignty of the Irish nation.
Article 2: National territory whole of the island of Ireland.
Article 3: Laws to apply to the area of the state pending the re-integration of the national territory.
Article 4: Name of state – Éire.
Article 5: Éire is a sovereign, independent, democratic state.

Article 6: The sovereignty of the Irish people.

Article 7: The national flag.

Article 8: The Irish language.

Article 9: Irish citizenship and nationality.

Article 10: Natural resources of Éire belong to the state.

Article 11: All the state's revenues are to form one fund.

Article 12: The President – election, nomination and impeachment.

Article 13: Powers and functions of the President.

Article 14: Presidential commission.

Article 15: The Oireachtas.

Article 16: Dáil Éireann.

Article 17: Dáil Éireann and financial estimates.

Article 18: Seanad Éireann – composition and method of election.

Article 19: Election of senators by vocational councils.

Article 20: Legislation.

Article 21: Money bills – powers of Dáil and Seanad Éireann.

Article 22: Money bills – definition and procedure to resolve dispute between Dáil and Seanad pertaining to disputes over definition of money bills.

Article 23: Time for consideration of bills.

Article 24: Abridgement of time for consideration of bills by Seanad Éireann.

Article 25: Promulgation of bills by the President.

Article 26: Reference of bills to the Supreme Court by the President.

Article 27: Reference of bills to the people in a referendum.

Article 28: The government.

Article 29: International relations.

Article 30: The attorney general.

Article 31: The Council of State – composition and functions.

Article 32: The President obliged to consult the Council of State.

Article 33: The comptroller and auditor general.

Article 34: Powers and jurisdiction of courts.

Article 35: Independence of the judiciary, appointment and removal of judges.

Article 36: Matters pertaining to the courts to be regulated by law.

Article 37: Authority of quasi-judicial bodies.

Article 38: All persons to be tried in due course of law.

Article 39: Definition of treason.

Article 40: Personal rights.

Article 41: The family.

Article 42: Education.

Article 43: Private property.

Article 44: Religion.

Article 45: Directive Principles of Social Policy.

Article 46: Amendment of the Constitution.

Article 47: The referendum.

Article 48: Repeal of the Constitution of Saorstát Éireann.

Article 49: Government of Éire successor to government of Saorstát Éireann.

Article 50: Continuance of laws.

Articles 51–63: Transitory provisions.

Submitted to the electorate in a plebiscite held on 1 July 1937, it was accepted by 50.89 per cent (685,105 votes); 39.14 per cent (529,945 votes) rejected it. What was noteworthy was the high number of spoiled votes: 134,157 or 9.97 per cent of the valid poll.[105] The *Irish Times* protested at the poverty of the popular mandate, highlighting, in particular, the spoiled votes.[106] While it is problematical to interpret their significance, the *Irish Press*, the organ of Fianna Fáil, regarded such votes as reflecting hostility to the new basic law.[107] As he mused on the results, de Valera must have been relieved that the religious provisions never became an issue – the margin of victory would probably have evaporated had the Catholic Church been in any way openly critical of them. He was disappointed in the result,[108] which still rankled a year later when he addressed the nation on the occasion of the Constitution's first anniversary.[109] Moreover, the Constitution had created little interest throughout the country,[110] the discussion of it taking place only at elite level.[111]

Constitution Day, 29 December 1937, the day the new basic law came into operation, revealed continuing divisions over the document and no great public interest in it among a significant section of the population. The *Irish Independent* highlighted the narrow margin of approval in the plebiscite and stated that 'it is impossible for the people to have for the Constitution the respect ... required for such an instrument'.[112] The *Irish Press* adopted a contrary position, describing the occasion as 'a solemn and momentous day in the annals of Éire' because 'it marks the entry into the full status of nationhood'.[113] While this same journal declared that, on the day, 'scenes of great enthusiasm were witnessed in Dublin' and that it was marked 'with great jubilation throughout the country',[114] this does not appear to have been the case. The *Irish Times* noted that only a couple of dozen people assembled outside Government Building to witness the departure of ministers for a special mass in the Pro-Cathedral. Larger crowds had gathered when ministers were returning but 'nowhere was there to be witnessed any great display of enthusiasm'. The situation outside the capital was even more muted.[115] It was not the most propitious of beginnings for Bunreacht na hÉireann.

CHAPTER 8

Assessment of the Constitution

The Constitution of Ireland, 1937, had a difficult conception and birth. It was planned, drafted and debated by Dáil and the public at a time of deep political divisions. The hatreds and enmities of the Civil War still festered and the hostile reception accorded the document from opposition politicians and supporters represented, at times, a vicarious, if bloodless, reprise of the conflict generated by the Treaty settlement. Predictable and partisan polemics coloured assessments of the proposed new basic law and its association with the deeply divisive figure of Éamon de Valera entrenched attitudes on opposing sides. The ongoing conflict with Great Britain over annuities and the Fianna Fáil government's dismantling of the Treaty produced the additional backdrop of external tensions. Notwithstanding all these circumstances, Bunreacht na hÉireann was adopted by the Irish people, albeit by a narrow margin, in a plebiscite and it has endured for eighty years. It came to be accepted by the overwhelming majority of the state's citizens and the political and legal elite. This chapter seeks to assess aspects of it and to identify the factors which contributed to its durability.

The Constitution was primarily about sovereignty: redefining the constitutional relationship between Ireland and Britain in a manner consistent with the realisation of Irish national aspirations. With the advice and assistance of John Hearne, Éamon de Valera translated his vision of sovereignty into a political, diplomatic and legal reality, framed on the basis of the full international personality of the Irish state. As noted in Chapter 6, the document was shaped and influenced by de Valera's concept of external association as delineated in 'Document no. 2' in 1921. Thus, when the *Irish Independent* called the proposed basic law 'Document no. 3', it was recognising the origins of the constitutional species.[1] Ronan Fanning has correctly observed that 'without Éamon de Valera Ireland would never have achieved independence so quickly and certainly would not have achieved it before the Second World War';[2] and central to this achievement was his 1937 Constitution.

The new Constitution was essential to achieve de Valera's objective of the reconciliation of republican hardliners to the Irish state. Speaking in Canada, John Hearne offered a rationale for Bunreacht na hÉireann with which most republicans could identify:

> For if we inquire why it is that a written constitution usually follows a period of violence we will, I think, discover the reason to be that when a community has lost its bearings, when its foundations have been borne away, a new basis of co-operation and self-preservation has to be found and the invariable instinct has been to consciously formulate the new system in a code.[3]

Thus the new Constitution would provide the state with 'new bearings' and new 'foundations', to which most republicans could assent.[4] The *Irish Times*, in an editorial on Constitution Day, 29 December 1937, recognised that a significant purpose of the new basic law 'was to put an end to civil strife in the twenty-six counties by providing for the extreme republicans all the essentials of an independent republic'.[5] While some such republicans were not reconciled, nevertheless, in the words of Garret FitzGerald, 'it would be wrong to underestimate the seminal importance of this process of establishing within the new state a national consensus – one that soon secured the acceptance by all but a tiny handful of irreconcilables of the legitimacy and authority of the institutions of the state'.[6]

The 1937 Constitution came to provide the basis for a consensus on which the modern Irish state has been built.[7] By resolving the issue of the constitutional relationship between Ireland and Britain, which had been the prime focus of political activity for over a decade, it contributed to the diminution of the vitriolic divisiveness in Irish public life. The young state was spared 'further decades of corrosive and sterile debate on the pros and cons of the British connection'.[8] It also ended the volatility which had plagued the Constitution of the Irish Free State for over a decade: 'The 1937 Constitution represented a deliberate attempt to introduce a more rigid, entrenched constitutional order, which would remain immune from frequent change via ordinary legislation'.[9] Bunreacht na hÉireann transformed the constitutional life of the state; 'after 1937 the Constitution was more respected as a higher law' and a 'distinction between ordinary and constitutional politics was reasserted'.[10] A stable fundamental law became the foundation of Irish social, political, economic and diplomatic life.

Articles 2 and 3 were central to the reconciliation of republicans to the state. The claim to the whole of the national territory was qualified by the recognition of the actual jurisdiction of the Irish government and parliament. As noted in Chapter 6, this formula was designed, and the actual articles drafted, by Hearne. These provisions were intended to obviate the opposition of extreme republicans by a formal constitutional declaration of the sacrosanct belief in the unity of the whole island of Ireland. These articles, however, did nothing to advance the cause of actual unification, but they were never intended to really do so – they were included to maximise support for the new Constitution. The truth was that de Valera was fundamentally concerned with the interests of the actual state he ruled rather than in a putative united Ireland which seemed to preoccupy him. Sovereignty took precedence over reunification.[11]

Between sovereignty *de jure* (involving the six counties of Northern Ireland) and sovereignty *de facto* (involving the twenty-six counties of Southern Ireland), it was the latter to which he attended, the former about which he talked.[12] And he had to talk about it as he regarded himself, and was regarded by his followers, as the great national leader and the custodian of the aspiration for Irish unity. It was vital, therefore, to perpetuate the myth that a united Ireland was at the core of his nationalist vision. He had no viable policy, however, to address the intractable problem of a partitioned country.[13]

Instead, de Valera engaged in anti-partitionism, where rhetoric and propaganda substituted for constructive action.[14] Articles 2 and 3 were the high points of Fianna Fáil's anti-partition bombast, to be highlighted as proof of their trustworthy custodianship of this sacred national ideal. Furthermore, they could be employed by de Valera when playing the green card in electoral politics, to galvanise support for his party.[15] The twenty-six-county leader *par excellence*,[16] he was concerned with the state he governed; unification was relegated to a national piety, to be verbally honoured, not actively pursued.

Writing in 1987, the distinguished jurist Donal Barrington posited an interesting argument with regard to Articles 2 and 3.[17] It appeared to him to be important to relate them to Article 29, dealing with international relations, section 2 of which declares: 'Ireland affirms its adherence to the principles of the pacific settlement of international disputes by international arbitration or judicial determination.' According to Barrington, Bunreacht na hÉireann has not got one particular meaning in Article 2 and a different meaning in Article 29: 'It is one document and has only one meaning.'[18] Therefore, taking the three articles together, within the framework of the entire Constitution, he wrote that 'the most remarkable thing about it is the [Constitution's] commitment to a peaceful solution to the partition problem.'[19]

There is substance to Barrington's argument: as noted in Chapter 5, Article 29 was one of the innovations Hearne introduced into the Constitution. Section 2, in particular, was influenced by Article 12 of the Covenant of the League of Nations[20] and Article 2 of the Kellogg–Briand Pact 1925.[21] Hearne had participated in the work of the League of Nations and represented the Irish Free State at the Kellogg–Briand talks.[22] He was committed to the principle of the resolution of international disputes by peaceful means and incorporated this principle in the Constitution. His political formation as a Redmondite, his rejection of Sinn Féin extremism, his support of the Treaty settlement and the Free State and his training and practice as a lawyer clearly demonstrated a commitment to the primacy of law. For him, the matter of Irish unification would have to be resolved by non-violent means, consistent with the terms of Article 29. However, this subtle legal perspective would not always have been appreciated in the years after 1937, a fact which Barrington acknowledged.[23]

If Bunreacht na hÉireann was intended to effect the reconciliation of republicans to the state, de Valera also believed that it invested him with the authority and, more importantly, with the legitimacy to take action against hardliners who continued in their obstinate refusal to recognise this same state. As far as he was concerned, he had removed all those constitutional elements repugnant to right-minded republicans. There no longer existed any valid reason to withhold loyalty to the state. The outstanding grievance of partition would be addressed by the government legitimated by the new basic law. Within the framework of the Constitution, he would apply the rigours of the law against dissidents.[24] The laws which would be vigorously enforced against them were enacted by the representatives of the people, freely elected under the terms of a constitution adopted, and therefore enacted, by the people. Dissident republicans were no longer living in the Irish Free State; they were now living in Éire. And the forces of law and order of Éire would deal with those who subverted the authority of a state and government which claimed its legitimacy from the sovereign will of its people.[25]

The Constitution and the Irish language

For de Valera there was one thing more important than the achievement of a united Ireland, and that was the revival of Irish as a spoken language.[26] He failed in the realisation of both objectives. The Constitution gave Irish a special status, describing it as 'the national language'; and by the provisions of Article 25, 5, 4, in the case of conflict between the English and Irish texts, 'the text in the national language shall prevail'. W.T. Cosgrave thought this was nonsense, telling the Dáil that the Irish version was 'a mere translation' and according it a superior status was 'contrary to common sense'.[27] De Valera rejected the idea that the Irish text was a mere translation; according to him, the Irish drafting went on 'pari passu almost from the beginning'.[28] Certainly, on the evidence of the de Valera papers it was an aspect of the making of the document from an early stage.[29] Indeed, in a study of the Irish text prepared by Micheál Ó Cearúil, he sought to establish that the Irish version was 'in fact no mere translation',[30] but this aspect of Bunreacht na hÉireann is beyond the scope of this study.

The Constitution, however, was irrelevant in terms of the fortunes of the revival of the language. Irish nationalism privileged Irish as the quintessential expression of nationhood and the relevant articles in Bunreacht na hÉireann reflected this belief. They represented an obeisance to what was an untouchable piety – the ideals of the Gaelic League which had played such a central role in the development of the nationalist movement in the early years of the twentieth century.[31] Notwithstanding all this reverence, the Irish language continued to decline from the foundation of the state and de Valera's privileging of it in the Constitution did nothing to inspire action to arrest its descent to marginality. There were many reasons for this[32] but one was the reality that many in the political and administrative elite who spoke about the importance of the language did not or could not actually speak Irish. Even de Valera failed to bring his own party with him and he could not get his ministers to speak the language.[33] Thus there was a conspicuous lack of leadership by example. Compulsion came to characterise the policy of the state, the burden of linguistic revival being passed to school children.[34]

An address delivered by John Hearne at a St Patrick's Day banquet held in New Orleans on 18 March 1957 serves as an interesting example of the official attitude towards the Irish language and the extent to which constitutional declarations in respect of it were essentially meaningless. The speech is noteworthy for its articulation of national pieties:

> I turn now for a moment to another matter which is very dear to the hearts of all true Irishmen. I mean the restoration of the Irish language ... The revival of the language was undertaken as a sacred trust, not merely because it enshrines so much of the Irish thought and life of bygone ages, not merely as a national symbol, or because it has proved in fact to be a flexible instrument of expression of the thought of today, but because the language is inevitably bound up with the question of the summit of our civilisation.

His insistence on a popular enthusiasm for the revival of Irish was utterly misplaced. Even allowing for the occasion and the sentimentality so often engendered at such events – a St Patrick's Day banquet attended by Irish exiles – Hearne presented a version of language revival at total variance with reality:

> Never since the days of Hugh O'Neill and Hugh O'Donnell, before the Gaelic order went down to seemingly permanent disorder at Kinsale, has its place in the hearts of our people been more secure than it is today. Today, all the organs of government – executive, legislative and judicial – are bent, with due regard to prudence and justice, on the noble task of making Ireland Irish speaking once more. The Irish people have made up their minds on the vital matter which they believe to be bound up with our integrity, our coherence and our continuity as

a nation. And they are going to achieve the great national objective of Patrick Pearse of making Ireland 'not merely free, but Gaelic as well'.[35]

This speech typified the sentiments expected to be articulated by representatives of the administrative elite. Hearne was simply repeating the official platitudes shaped by the state's official aspirations and obligations towards the Irish language, these having been given expression in the Constitution he himself drafted and influenced. Even this intelligent man succumbed to the proclamation that the linguistic emperor wore new clothes, notwithstanding facts to the contrary. All the ambassador's words could not obscure the reality that 'passive, if respectful resistance' characterised the response of most of the state's population to the Irish language.[36]

Religion and the Constitution

From the perspective of the twenty-first century, Article 44, dealing with religion, is easily misunderstood. In any assessment of the religious provisions of Bunreacht na hÉireann it is essential to situate them in their contemporary context and, to do this, five considerations should be borne in mind. First, the Constitution, as noted in Chapter 6, accurately reflected the values of the vast majority of the people in the Irish state at the time and up to the 1960s, at least. It was founded on the conviction that the Irish were a religious nation; accordingly, the state was decidedly non-neutral in the matter of religion.[37] Catholicism continued to be popular, if illiberal, and sometimes intolerant.

Second, it is important to appreciate that the 'special position' conferred on the Catholic Church was a compromise, as explained in Chapter 5. The Catholic doctrine regarding the Church of Rome as the one true church was not given expression. This fact represented a rejection of a fundamental Catholic tenet by de Valera and was seriously in conflict with the teachings of that church and the opinions advanced by McQuaid, Cahill and other churchmen. It was a measure of the religious climate of the time that 'despite the assurance of a special place for the Catholic Church in the proposed Constitution, the Vatican refused to move beyond a position of strict neutrality because the draft recognised other Christian churches and because it failed to state that the Catholic Church had been founded by Jesus'.[38]

Thus, while Bunreacht na hÉireann had a distinct and undeniable Catholic flavour, it was not an ultramontane document. Far from imposing a sectarian constitution on a pluralist society, de Valera was steering a middle course between non-Catholics on the one hand and supremacist Catholics on the other.[39] Given the religious climate in the Ireland of the 1930s, with an assertive and arrogant Catholic Church, and the significant role of Catholicism in defining Irish identity, it would have been very difficult not to mention the Catholic Church in the Constitution. The challenge for de Valera was to obviate any confrontation on the religious provisions. This he did and the recognition of the Catholic Church's 'special position' was the compromise.

Third, while the constitutional recognition of the special position of the Catholic Church was a significant gesture, it should not be overstated. There certainly was a general sense at the time and subsequently that this recognition, by virtue of the fact that it was in Bunreacht na hÉireann, conferred on the Church of Rome some privileges. At the very least, it was a source of misunderstanding; as Mr Justice Barrington stated in 1998: 'there was a latent suspicion that while all citizens were equal, Roman Catholics might, in some sense, be more equal than others'.[40] However, no additional rights were conferred on the Catholic Church or its adherents,[41] Mr Justice Geoghegan observing in 1991 that 'long before Article 44, 1, 2 was abolished by referendum the provision as to the special position of the Roman Catholic Church was not considered by constitutional lawyers to have any legal implications'.[42] The Catholic Church was simply recognised as 'the guardian of the faith professed by the great majority of citizens'.

What this meant in practical terms was explained by de Valera in a memorandum prepared for Joseph Walshe when he was seeking Vatican approval of the religious clauses from the Pope, as described in Chapter 5. Obviously, the President presented the wording in as favourable and positive a light as possible from the papal perspective, in order to secure Catholic Church support:

> The premier and special position accorded to the Catholic Church as 'guardian of the faith of the great majority of citizens' will mean in practice that the Catholic Church will be the church associated with the state on all public occasions. Under our democratic Constitution the vast majority of the ministers of state are certain to be Catholic, who will profess their religion openly and will attend religious functions in a Catholic Church on all occasions in which a manifestation of religious belief is called for.[43]

There was nothing noteworthy or dramatic here – no putative exalted privileges were being blandished to elicit a favourable response. The truth was that the significance attributed to the Catholic Church in the memorandum prevailed before the 'special recognition' clause. It had been associated with the state since independence and ministers had always attended its functions. Thus de Valera was essentially assuring the Pope that the status quo ante would continue, nothing more, nothing less, notwithstanding the new special recognition accorded the Catholic Church. Even Deputy Frank McDermott, one of the few members of the Dáil to contribute to the debate on that part of the Constitution and who expressed reservations about its inclusion in relation to Northern Ireland, was of the opinion that 'It really means nothing. It does not establish the Catholic Church in a privileged position.'[44]

Certainly, the Catholic Church continued to wield great influence and authority in such areas as health and education but this was due to what Dermot Keogh has termed 'the politics of informal consensus'.[45] By this was meant that Catholic politicians and senior administrators, imbued with the values of their church, acknowledged and facilitated its role in the Irish state, as has been described in Chapter 6. Through the first fifty years or so of independence, politicians and civil servants were susceptible to the nostrums of Catholic social philosophy and moral theology by virtue of their acceptance of the moral authority of that church.[46] Primarily and fundamentally, the influence and power of the Catholic Church rested on the strong devotion and loyalty of the community at large. Catholicism provided the moral basis of social solidarity[47] and the status of the Catholic Church rested on its role within the moral community.[48] It was scarcely through the Constitution, only to a limited extent through the law and mainly through the wider cultural life and practice of the Catholic moral community that the Church of Rome enjoyed its position of unrivalled privilege and prestige in Ireland during the first five decades of independence.[49]

Fourth, all the Protestant denominations expressed official satisfaction with Article 44 in the course of de Valera's negotiations with them and this satisfaction was not dissipated after the adoption of Bunreacht na hÉireann. While some members of the minority churches stated publicly their unhappiness with the Catholic dimension of the Constitution, they were few in number.[50] Daithí Ó Corráin, in his examination of Protestant reaction to the religious article, has written that, 'if a longer view is taken it can be demonstrated that the Church of Ireland itself did not have a fixation with [Article 44] of the Constitution'.[51] In fact, in 1958, the Bishop of Limerick Charles Hodges paid tribute to the recognition accorded to non-Roman Catholic churches. Two years later, in a précis on religious liberty in Ireland prepared for the World Council of Churches, Archbishops James McCann and George Simms praised Article 44.[52] Nor did the ban on divorce upset most Protestants; divorce was as repugnant to them as their Catholic fellow citizens.[53] The presumption that they were more liberal on this issue than Catholics is inaccurate. The largest Protestant denomination, the Church of Ireland, was 'markedly reticent on the subject'.[54] Ironically, the only religious grouping to express concerted opposition to Article 44 was composed of conservative Catholics who, through an organisation styling itself Maria Duce, demanded the inclusion of the one true church formula in the Constitution.[55]

Finally, the Protestant minority community lived in a country where the influence and power of the Catholic Church seemed to permeate all aspects of public and private life.[56] Society was defined by the doctrines and values of this church, which created a moral community that was essentially homogeneous due to the numerical predominance of the majority denomination. The equation of Catholicism with Irishness reinforced this social homogeneity. Protestants, however, formed a distinctive group which did not belong to this moral community and the Catholic Church enunciated negative attitudes towards them. Such attitudes were given striking expression in the prohibition on Catholic participation in Protestant religious services and in the regulations governing mixed marriages.[57] The majority religion was flaunted without any reference to the sensibilities of the members of minority churches.[58]

At times, an observer of the Irish scene in the 1940s and 1950s – even the 1960s – might be mistaken for thinking that there was indeed an established church. Unlike in other European states, there was not. As was noted earlier, the influence of the Catholic Church rested on the loyalty of its members and the moral community to which they belonged.[59] This same loyalty secured the authority of the Catholic Church at all levels of society. The Constitution, while it reflected Catholic social teachings, was not the foundation of Ireland's entrenched Catholicism. In fact, in its strict constitutional life, the Irish state guaranteed the free expression of all religious belief, irrespective of denominational allegiance; and, in practical terms, a member of the Church of Ireland was elected first President and there has always been a Protestant presence on the superior courts. The reality was that the faith and loyalty of most of the citizens of the state ensured and secured the position of the Catholic Church in Ireland and informed attitudes towards Protestants and not articles in the Constitution.

Seanad Éireann and vocational representation

One aspect of Catholic social teaching which de Valera ignored, determinedly and decisively, was that relating to vocational organisation. Reference was made in Chapter 6 to the fact that its inclusion in the articles pertaining to the Seanad represented a gesture to the Catholic social movement. In truth, it was more a sop than a gesture,[60] as became evident when he began devising the method of election to the upper house. He had no intention of relinquishing any political power to vocational bodies. While they could nominate candidates, they had no voice in the elections. In November 1937, de Valera proposed an electorate composed of the Dáil and representatives of county and borough councils, each council to nominate seven electors.[61] This proposal formed the basis of the Seanad Electoral (Panel Members) Act 1937.[62] In making this decision, de Valera ignored suggestions made by members of a Dáil committee considering the matter of Seanad elections, which would have incorporated some elements of election by vocational bodies.[63] The effect of the procedure he preferred made Seanad elections 'the plaything of party politics at their most incestuous'.[64]

From its inception, Seanad Éireann has been a political rather than a vocational upper house. After the first election to it in March 1938, the *Irish Times* commented that 'the vocational idea was swamped by the political'.[65] A study published in 1940 by American political scientists Arthur and Mary Bromage confirmed this observation.[66] The Commission on Vocational Organisation, established in 1939,[67] reported, in 1944, that the Seanad 'falls far short of being a vocational body', a fact it attributed to the lack of direct election by professional organisations.[68] In 1954, Irish political scientist Basil Chubb wrote that 'it is one of the platitudes of Irish political life that the Senate is not, and never has been, a body representative of vocational interests and that it is, on the contrary, composed primarily of party men and dominated by party considerations'.[69] Eleven reports on Seanad reform have mainly focussed on its composition and electoral system,[70] one of them declaring that 'the arrangement for the election of members ... ensure that the Seanad is largely the creature of the government and the Dáil'.[71] Clearly, regarding a vocational Senate, 'theory is and always has been a long way from reality'.[72]

These observations, however, would not have perturbed de Valera. This was the type of Seanad he wanted. He had argued during the Dáil debate on the Constitution that the country was not sufficiently organised along vocational lines to allow for direct elections of senators. This was a true statement of fact. There were, however, some organisations and associations developed to the extent that they could serve as a starting point for such elections, an argument made by Professor James Hogan in 1937. According to him, the 'main thing was to make a start' and a list of bodies identified in the report of the Second House of the Oireachtas Commission served as a basis to achieve this.[73] De Valera was not interested. When the electoral method devised in 1938 proved unsatisfactory due to alleged corruption and abuses,[74] he simply decided to extend the vote in Seanad elections to all county and borough councillors.[75] Hogan identified the reason for this lack of interest in vocational election by de Valera and, indeed, other politicians: 'One difficulty is that every person entering the Senate from a vocational organisation in any real sense of the word thereby ousts a politician of some sort, and politicians are notoriously reluctant to give away any of their authority or to share the sweets of office with those who are not pledged politicians.'[76]

In fact, from the very first election to the newly created Senate, de Valera and Fianna Fáil were determined to ensure that they exercised as much political control over the process as possible. In November 1937, according to the minutes of the parliamentary party, the President explained the system of nomination along vocational lines.[77] In January 1938, it was agreed by the parliamentary party that no member 'would pledge his support for any candidate as the decision in reference to candidates would be a matter for the party and the organisation'. Moreover, 'it was also agreed that an effort would be made to get supporters of the government nominated by outside nominating bodies'.[78] In March 1938, just before the election, 'a preferential list of candidates' for the Seanad election was drawn up by Fianna Fáil. These candidates were arranged in the following 'classes':

List A: Fianna Fáil nominees and members of the Fianna Fáil organisation.
List B: Strong supporters.
List C: Sympathisers.[79]

These lists were intended for the guidance of TDs and councillors so as to influence the election to the party's advantage; vocational considerations were only an issue to the extent that they had to be managed in Fianna Fáil's interests.

Yet during a Dáil debate on a motion proposed by Dr Noel Browne to abolish Seanad Éireann in December 1957, de Valera expressed his supposed disappointment at how the upper house had developed since the introduction of the 1937 Constitution. He said that he had hoped that 'after a period we would be sufficiently organised vocationally in the country ... and that members ... could be elected directly by vocational bodies'.[80] The Taoiseach was being disingenuous in distancing himself from any responsibility for the failed progress of vocational organisation in Ireland. He and his government had completely ignored the report by a commission established by his government in 1939 to consider the whole matter of such organisation in Ireland.[81]

As a result of the 1957 debate, a commission was established to propose reform within the framework of the panel system as enshrined in the Constitution.[82] It reported in 1958, with a proposed scheme whereby one half of the panel members would be completely vocational.[83] Despite serious proposals towards greater vocationalisation of the Seanad, de Valera did not support the report.[84] He had no intention, and never had any intention of advancing, to any significant degree, the cause of vocationalism. His attitude to the Seanad had been fundamentally formed by his experiences of the Free State Senate, which had been 'especially anathema' to him and Fianna Fáil[85] and such considerations meant that he would not tolerate the prospect of any second chamber subverting the will of Dáil Éireann. When it came to Seanad Éireann, he was willing to consider gestures to appease Catholic activists but with due regard to the overriding concern of keeping the second chamber under the political thumb of Dáil and government.

Seanad Éireann, the only surviving example of corporate or vocational representation at national level,[86] is one of the most unsatisfactory elements of the Constitution and has attracted much criticism, with regular demands for its abolition.[87] For example, in 1987, the Progressive Democrats proposed to abolish it,[88] a proposal repeated by Fianna Fáil in its 2011 general election manifesto on the basis that 'serious questions must be asked about the continued role of an entity which is still struggling to justify its existence after three quarters of a century'.[89] A proposal for its abolition was rejected in a referendum in 2013.[90]

That the Senate has long been the subject of debate and criticism is not surprising. In many respects, it had an inauspicious constitutional birth. It was included by de Valera in Bunreacht na hÉireann without any real conviction about its need or worth; its theoretical vocational composition was intended as a sop to please the determined Catholic social movement; its actual purpose to be subservient to government and Dáil. With such a birthright, it has been regarded as an entity of no real consequence or substance, largely ignored, except for fitful interest in reforming it. Seanad Éireann has spent eighty years as the constitutional equivalent of that other Irish conundrum – the draining of the Shannon.

As has been noted earlier, there was a Dáil debate on the Seanad in December 1957. Interestingly, in May of the same year, John Hearne, who drafted the articles on Seanad Éireann and was a member of the 1936 Commission on the Second House of the Oireachtas, gave his thoughts on the subject of vocational organisation at a meeting of American lawyers in Newark. He told his audience that the Irish parliament was to be, 'in due course', vocational. 'Actually', according to him, the Senate was, 'to some extent', constituted on a vocational basis. Hearne proceeded to explain the composition of the panels. He continued by observing that Irish society was not as yet so organised vocationally 'as to lead to a fully vocational representation in both houses of parliament'.[91] What was needed to achieve the required level of such organisation was the evolution of a particular type of social structure, characterised by bodies 'private in nature but possessing legally enforceable powers in governing the various professions or economic groups'. Such a body would be the exclusive representative of all persons in that profession or sector of the economy.

Hearne cited the medieval guilds or modern bar and medical associations as examples of the social structures of which he was speaking. He was essentially describing the vocational or corporate (the terms were effectively inter-changeable) organisation of society, as advocated by Catholic social activists in the 1930s. Among the purposes of such social organisations, according to Hearne, was to construct a framework to facilitate the practice of social justice and to replace class conflict with a co-operative approach to the solution of common problems.[92]

This was an interesting, even curious, speech. The reference to parliament being vocational in due course was strange. He seemed to be suggesting that both Houses of the Oireachtas would eventually be organised in this manner. There is no evidence that de Valera envisaged such an arrangement; his meagre vocational ambitions related only to the Seanad. Hearne was misspeaking here. Moreover, he was advocating a form of social organisation in vogue in the 1930s but out of fashion, even discredited, by the 1950s. In Ireland, the Fianna Fáil government had consigned it to the margins of public discourse with its rejection of the report produced by the commission on vocational organisation in the 1940s.[93] The association of corporate organisation with fascism, especially in Italy, had done it immeasurable harm.[94] But even in the 1930s Hearne did not appear to have been a proponent of vocationalism: he did not sign the minority report of the Second House of the Oireachtas Commission proposing a vocational Senate.

His speech in America in 1957 is perhaps explained by Hearne's desire to rationalise decisions made in the 1930s with respect to the Constitution and the Seanad, with which he was associated. The most likely explanation is related to his deep commitment to his Catholic faith and to all aspects of it, including its social teachings. His address was informed by a vision of society shaped by these same teachings. This became clear in his concluding remarks:

> [Vocational] organisation would tend to form a frame of mind amongst all our citizens in which each would ask himself not only the question 'What must I do for justice's sake?' but also the question 'What can I do in the name of charity?' In such a society men would grow to a fuller stature as they fulfilled with scriptural excellence the second great commandment of the Law, which is like unto the first: 'Thou shalt love thy neighbour as thyself'. It was to a master of the Law that that revelation was first made. May it be the mission of all lawyers to weave its mighty tradition with loving and skilful fingers into the texture of systems and societies which they frame or reform, and so help to bind all men and all nations with its golden cord about the feet of God.[95]

Though not an apparent devotee of vocationalism in the 1930s, perhaps the fervent anti-communism of America in the 1950s caused Hearne to regard more favourably this scheme of social organisation. Whatever the truth, it was a strange address, iterating essentially irrelevant, jaded, even discredited concepts in the context of Ireland in the 1950s. Vocational organisation had been consigned to the margins of intellectual and social endeavour and discourse. Hearne had not identified himself with this ideal when on the Second House of the Oireachtas Commission; his espousal of it two decades later did not make much practical sense.

The presidency and the Constitution

Another institution of the Constitution – the office of President of Ireland – has enjoyed a somewhat happier history. The range of criticism it attracted while the state's new fundamental law was being debated in the Dáil suggested that the precise nature of this proposed position was unclear[96] and was an entirely abstract institution to observers in 1937.[97] Two people, however, had a very clear sense of what was envisaged for this new constitutional role – Éamon de Valera and John Hearne. John Cudahy, American Minister to Ireland, 1937–40, commented on the concept of the office held by the framers of the Constitution: 'one of permanence, a symbol of Ireland. One of dignity and representation far removed from the tumult and hurly-burly of political strife'.[98]

The reference to 'permanence' is redolent of Hearne's central idea of the Constitution as representing the restoration of an unbroken national tradition. Douglas Hyde, the first President, certainly reflected the attributes of the office as described by Cudahy. His association with the Gaelic League meant that he embodied for many the notion of an ancient Irish tradition which defined and distinguished Ireland from other nations, especially Britain. He was also a symbol of de Valera's commitment to an Irish Ireland[99] and his election was part of de Valera's determination to emphasise Irish sovereignty.[100] He was a person not associated with political strife and most definitely could not be regarded as the harbinger of the dictatorship spoken of in the Dáil debates. On his election, *Dublin Opinion* commented: 'Well, for one thing, his selection would certainly dispose of the possible menace of the uachtarán [President] becoming a dictator ... I can't quite imagine the old gentleman marching into Leinster House at the head of his troops.'[101] Thus the spectre of putative dictatorship surrounding the office was forever banished. Hyde, together with Presidents S.T. O'Kelly (1945–59) and Éamon de Valera (1959–73), helped establish the presidency on a firm footing, winning for it the support and confidence of citizens and politicians alike.[102]

Another concept of the office held by de Valera and Hearne was that its powers and functions, for the most part, were circumscribed by the requirement that these be performed on the advice of the government, a provision which 'comprehensively negates almost all presidential discretion'.[103] From the earliest stages of the making of the Constitution, the legal adviser counselled and guided his minister in the matter of the newly created office and gave legal expression to de Valera's concerns. Article 14 of the draft heads of 1935 read as follows: 'The powers and duties conferred and imposed on the President by this Constitution or by any Act of the Oireachtas shall not be exercisable and performable by him save upon the advice of the Council of Ministers.'[104] Other draft heads drawn up by Hearne in October 1936 included Article 26 which stated that the 'functions [of the President were] to be exercisable only on [the] advice of the Council of Ministers'.[105] The effect of this constitutional circumscription is that, in terms of power, Ireland has a weak President relative to many other countries and, in fact, from 1938 to the late 1980s, Presidents had the fewest constitutional powers of all countries with a directly elected head of state.[106]

American jurist Francis X. Beytagh has commented on the apparent anomaly of the only official chosen by the vote of the entire people of the state being 'relegated to such an inconsequential position in the governing of the nation'.[107] In recent decades, however, Presidents Mary Robinson and Mary McAleese transformed the character of the office through their effective and skilful utilisation of its persuasive and symbolic powers.[108] Robinson used her term of office (1990–7)[109] to create a sense of shared identity and communal endeavour;[110] while McAleese (President, 1997–2011)[111] emphasised the importance of reconciling different identities on the island of Ireland.[112] The result was that these two Presidents 'left a combined legacy of an activist presidential role, endowed with heightened public visibility and renewed sense of relevance for the people and the politics of the time'.[113] The present incumbent of the office, Michael D. Higgins, has continued to make the presidency relevant in modern Ireland.[114]

While presidential powers are limited under Bunreacht na hÉireann, presidents do have two important discretionary functions. The President's absolute right to refuse dissolution of the Dáil to a Taoiseach who has ceased to retain the support of a majority in that house has never been exercised.[115] The only substantive prerogative exercised by Presidents has been the referral, under Article 26, of bills to the Supreme Court for a determination as to their constitutionality, a provision strongly influenced by Hearne. This procedure has been used infrequently: since 1938, the Council of State has been convened to advise presidents on twenty-eight bills.[116] Fifteen bills were subsequently referred to the Supreme Court: eight were adjudged constitutional; three had sections struck down; and, in four instances, the entire bill was struck down.[117] Notwithstanding certain reservations which have been voiced regarding this constitutional provision,[118] the Constitution Review Group, reporting in 1996, described it as 'a valuable democratic safeguard'.[119] Its greatest contribution, in the words of David Gwynn Morgan, is that 'it strangles unconstitutional measures before birth'.[120]

Judicial review

At the core of Article 26 is judicial review and Bunreacht na hÉireann provides for it under the terms of Article 34. Chief Justice Susan Denham has highlighted the significance of this provision:

> Ireland led the common law world in 1937 by expressly stating in the Constitution that the jurisdiction of the superior courts shall extend to the question of the validity of any law having regard to the provisions of the Constitution. This, perhaps, more than any other aspect of the Constitution, signalled the nature of the state, its divergence from the system of government in the United Kingdom

... The power to review the constitutionality of legislation expressly given by the Constitution to the superior courts was a novel aspect of the Constitution in 1937. No such power existed expressly elsewhere in common law jurisdictions, such as the United Kingdom, Australia, or Canada.[121]

Certainly, judicial review has proven to be one of the most important aspects of the Constitution.[122] It was slow to take off, however, with only a few cases before the courts in the first twenty years of the Constitution's life.[123] The legacy of the British legal tradition, with its emphasis on parliamentary sovereignty, was still strong. As a consequence, the courts tended to interpret Bunreacht na hÉireann in a positivist or literal manner, sticking closely to the letter of the document and taking the view that there was no more to it than the words it contained.[124] In many ways, judges were searching for the role to be played by the judiciary in a young constitutional democracy.[125] The first judge to recognise the significance of the new constitutional dispensation was George Gavan Duffy, a judge of the High Court in the 1940s. He appears to have embraced a new role for the judiciary as the upholder of the Constitution but his colleagues were more cautious.[126]

John Hearne and Gavan Duffy shared a conviction regarding a new role for the judiciary. Hearne's son, Maurice, recalled conversations he had with his father in the 1940s and 1950s, while the latter was serving as a diplomat in Canada and the United States:

> My father had regularly conveyed to me when I was growing up and in school in Canada and the United States that the Constitution was constructed in such a way as it could be interpreted not simply by reference to the political, economic and social environment prevalent in the 1930s but should be regarded by the judiciary as a 'living document' relevant to political, economic and social conditions prevailing into the future. In other words, it should be viewed as a document capable of flexible interpretation by activist judges.[127]

The judicial activism favoured by Hearne became a feature of Irish life from the 1960s onwards.[128] This fact reflected the accession of a new generation of judges and changes taking place in society and political culture. It would appear, for example, that the Taoiseach, Seán Lemass, encouraged a more activist approach on the part of Supreme Court judges in their interpretation of the Constitution.[129] Newly appointed judges of the superior courts possessed a more fully developed and sophisticated understanding of the role of the judiciary in a constitutional democracy and, as occasions arose, put that understanding into effect in their decision-making.[130] The activism of the United States Supreme Court became their model as they pushed out the boundaries of judicial review in Ireland.[131] In particular, the appointment of Cearbhall Ó Dálaigh as Chief Justice and Brian Walsh to the Supreme Court in the early 1960s heralded a new era of judicial activism and the Ó Dálaigh Supreme Court began to take Bunreacht na hÉireann very seriously.[132] By the time of his resignation as Chief Justice in 1973 this document had begun to permeate all areas of Irish law[133] and, even today, the decisions from that period form the cornerstone of the country's constitutional law.[134]

John Hearne may have had an indirect but significant influence on the development of a more activist judiciary. According to his son Maurice, when his father returned to Ireland in 1960 from the United States, he was invited by the Irish-American Association to deliver a lecture on the life and times of Abraham Lincoln, the study of whose career had been one of John Hearne's most compelling hobbies while serving as Irish Ambassador in Washington. Maurice accompanied his father to the lecture in a Dublin hotel and, as they were leaving, a gentleman saluted them. Hearne inquired of Maurice who the man was and his son informed him that it was Mr Justice Ó Dálaigh of the Supreme Court. He directed Maurice to return to the hotel and introduce him to Ó Dálaigh. 'As a direct result of that meeting, the two men became good friends in a very short time and often discussed the Constitution in terms of the criteria that should be used in its interpretation. They also had lengthy discussions about the United States' Constitution on the same basis.'

In 1962, when Maurice was auditor of the Law Students' Debating Society at King's Inns, Ó Dálaigh, by then Chief Justice, insisted that John Hearne (at that time in Ghana, Africa, advising its government on constitutional matters) be invited to Maurice's inaugural meeting. Maurice later commented,'My father was delighted to return for the meeting and to resume contact with the Chief Justice and to continue their discussion on constitutional interpretation. I have no doubt that arising from these and other meetings a whole new practice of judicial activism by what became known as the Ó Dálaigh court followed.'[135]

Allowing for Maurice Hearne's filial pietas and the absence of corroborative documentation in the papers of John Hearne or of Cearbhall Ó Dálaigh,[136] his account of meetings between his father and the Chief Justice has some plausibility, not least because of his close relationship with his father and his reliability as a witness to history. Donal Barrington has recorded a remark made by Justice Ó Dálaigh, possibly in 1953, in the course of court proceedings: 'Gentlemen, we have a constitution. Yet no one seems to know what it means.'[137] This judge was determined to establish a distinctive Irish legal system reflecting the constitutional dispensation associated with Bunreacht na hÉireann.[138]

Hearne had a profound understanding of Ireland's fundamental law, allied with a deep conviction of the central part law played in the life of a state. Writing in 1937, he observed: 'A nation's laws are as much part of its national life as are its language, its literature, its arts and its particular outlook upon the great public questions of the age.'[139] His vision and sense of the Constitution would have interested the Chief Justice. It is certain that the latter valued the views of such a distinguished lawyer as Hearne, not least because of his pivotal role in the drafting of Bunreacht na hÉireann and his knowledge of American constitutional law. Maurice Hearne has correctly observed that 'it was at or about this time [the meetings between Hearne and Ó Dálaigh] that the practice of encouraging judicial review precedents in the United States began to be canvassed by lawyers in the Irish courts' and this has added 'to the richness of Irish jurisprudence'.[140] Perhaps meeting with Hearne made Justice Ó Dálaigh more receptive to the notion and importance of American jurisprudence in the development of a native Irish law.

However, in any consideration of the influence of these meetings between the two distinguished lawyers, it is an overstatement to suggest a direct cause and effect – that the meetings led to judicial activism and the greater use of American legal precedents – but they very likely served to further Ó Dálaigh's understanding of the Irish Constitution and the relevance of American judicial decision-making. They may also have reinforced his desire to make the Constitution more relevant in the application of justice. In a sense, Hearne may have been reprising a role he played in the 1920s and in the course of the making of the 1937 Constitution: his knowledge, vision and opinions were a source of inspiration to others, be they delegates at an Imperial Conference, Éamon de Valera as he undertook the Herculean task of introducing a new constitution or Cearbhall Ó Dálaigh as he sought to realise the ambition of a distinctive Irish jurisprudence.

The significance of judicial review became apparent in the 1960s when the superior courts recognised that the Constitution implicitly protected an indefinite range of citizens' rights, over and above those specifically enumerated in various articles. This concept of unenumerated or unspecified rights has become an integral part of Irish constitutional jurisprudence.[141] The foundation case was *Ryan v the Attorney General*.[142] In 1963, Mrs Gladys Ryan sought a declaration in the High Court that an act of the Oireachtas permitting the fluoridation of water was unconstitutional. She argued that it was an infringement of her right to bodily integrity. In his ruling, Mr Justice Kenny, while dismissing her claims about the danger of fluoridation, accepted that the Constitution guaranteed her right of bodily integrity. This was not specified in Article 40 but, according to Kenny, the general guarantee given in section 3, 1 of this same article 'to respect and as far as practicable ... to defend and vindicate the personal rights of the citizen' was not confined to the rights specified in section 3, 2, *viz.*, 'life, person, good name and property rights', but extended to unspecified rights. Kenny stated that 'there are many personal rights of the citizen which follow from the Christian and democratic nature of the state which are not mentioned in Article 40 ...'[143]

In effect, there were personal rights latent in the Constitution; it protected many more rights than the text, read literally, suggested.[144] It was the responsibility of judges, in the words of Justice Brian Walsh, 'to determine, when necessary, the rights which are superior or antecedent to positive law or which are imprescriptible or inalienable'.[145] In the years following the Kenny judgement, they did just that and, according to the Constitution Review Group (1996), 'the doctrine of unenumerated rights enshrined in the Constitution has become a powerful source for the identification of hitherto unrecognised rights touching upon fundamental aspects of human activity'.[146] These rights included:

the right not to be tortured or ill-treated;
the right not to have health endangered by the state;
the right to earn a livelihood;
the right to marital privacy;
the right to individual privacy;
the right to access the courts;
the right to legal representation on criminal charges;
the right to justice and fair procedure;
the right to travel within the state;
the right to travel outside the state;
the right to marry;
the right to procreate;
the right to independent domicile;
the right to maintenance;
the rights of an unmarried mother in regard to her child;
the rights of a child;
the right to communicate.[147]

It is evident that judicial review is, in the words of Francis Beytagh, 'a dynamic, not static, concept'.[148]

Dignity is the very foundation upon which respect for all human rights is based, recognising 'that each person is a unique human being and shares a common humanity with their fellow citizens of the world'.[149] As was noted in Chapter 6, it was referred to in the preamble at a time when less than 10 per cent of constitutions made any reference to it. In fact, dignity is one of the unenumerated rights protected by the Irish Constitution.[150] In 1978, Chief Justice O'Higgins, ruling in the case of *G v An Bórd Uchtála*, stated that a 'child has the right to be fed and to live, to be reared and educated, to have the opportunity of working and of realising his or her full personality and dignity as a human being'.[151] Nearly twenty years later, Justice Denham, in the course of a judgement pertaining to a ward of court who had suffered serious brain injuries, ruled: 'An unspecified right under the Constitution to all persons as human persons is dignity – to be treated with dignity. Such right is not lost by illness or accident. As long as a person is alive they have this right. Thus, the ward in this case has a right to dignity'.[152]

In Ireland an independent judiciary possessing the right of judicial review has played a vital and central role in the constitutional life of the state. In the opinion of the Constitution Review Group, 'few would dispute that the result of such judicial interpretation has been beneficial'.[153] Firstly, it has protected the rights of individual citizens. Chief Justice Cearbhall Ó Dálaigh observed that 'it was the intention of the Constitution in guaranteeing the fundamental rights of citizens that ... rights of substance were being assured to the individual and that the courts were the custodians of these rights'.[154] Judicial review has created a heightened awareness of citizens' rights among the judiciary and people of the state,[155] the latter, in particular, becoming 'conscious of the fact that they had a constitution, that it could be implemented and that, in fact, many parts of it were self-executing and did not require any supporting legislation'.[156]

Secondly, judicial review has imposed restrictions on the power of the state in its relations with its citizens by virtue of the fact that 'constitutions define and thereby limit public power';[157] in the words of Chief Justice Liam Hamilton: 'The government is the creature of the Constitution and cannot act free from the restraint of the Constitution.'[158] Judicial review has vindicated the rights of people who were not adequately protected by the democratic process, thus giving credence to the statement by Justice Brian Walsh that 'the individual has natural and human rights over which the state has no authority'.[159] Thirdly, as noted earlier, judicial review has identified unenumerated rights and this has confirmed it as a valuable constitutional safeguard. Thus judicial review is a vital element in the constitutional life of the state.

> Judicial review of constitutionality is the very essence of democracy, for democracy does not only connote the rule of the majority. Democracy also means the rule of basic values in human rights as expressed in the Constitution ... Judicial review of constitutionality enables society to be true to itself and to honour its basic conceptions. This is the basis for the substantive legitimacy of judicial review ... By means of judicial review we are loyal to the fundamental values that we took upon ourselves in the past, that reflect our essence in the present, and will direct our national development as a society in the future.[160]

Significantly, it is through judicial review and, in particular, the identification of unspecified rights that the Irish Constitution has developed. Chief Justice Susan Denham has used the analogy of 'a "living tree" which can grow within its natural limits'.[161] Crucially, its provisions are stable but not necessarily permanent.[162] In a judgement delivered in 1973, Justice Brian Walsh stated:

> According to the preamble, the people gave themselves the Constitution to promote the common good with due observance of prudence, justice and charity so that the dignity and freedom of the individual might be assured. The judges must, therefore, as best they can from their training and their experience interpret these rights in accordance with their ideas of prudence, justice and charity. It is but natural that from time to time the prevailing ideas of these virtues may be conditioned by the passage of time; no interpretation of the Constitution is intended to be final for all time.[163]

The Constitution, therefore, is reviewed by the superior courts in the light of changing circumstances – political, social and economic. It is not interpreted as having a static meaning determined eighty years ago but on the basis that 'it lays down broad governing principles that can cope with current problems'.[164] 'It is a document that speaks from 1937 but as law it speaks from to-day.'[165] The people of 1937 do not equate with the people of contemporary Ireland. Bunreacht na hÉireann must, of necessity, be construed in the present to reflect the needs of the people it serves.[166]

Did de Valera and Hearne understand and appreciate the significance of the decision to provide for judicial review? Did they realise that Articles 40, 3, 1 and 40, 3, 2 would become 'the well-spring from which the constitutional doctrine of unenumerated rights would be sourced by the judiciary?'[167] It was established in Chapter 6 that both men, definitely and deliberately, provided for judicial review, a decision taken despite the opposition of senior civil servants. Hearne, indeed, had a preference for a dedicated constitutional court which would have engaged in such judicial review. Moreover, as was noted earlier in this chapter, his son Maurice recorded that his father wanted the Constitution to be viewed as 'a document capable of flexible interpretation by activist judges'.

Two further considerations confirm his commitment to judicial review. Firstly, regard must be had to the manner in which Hearne framed the articles. According to Justice Brian Walsh, the structure and contents of the articles dealing with fundamental rights (40–4) clearly indicate that justice is not subordinate to law. In particular, the terms of Article 40, 3 expressly subordinate law to justice.[168] Thus, in the opinion of a distinguished judge, there was a demonstrable concern for justice embedded in the provisions, a concern which could only be satisfied, ultimately, by judicial review. Secondly, the section dealing with personal rights, Article 40, was drafted with deliberate vagueness: 'Had the framers of the Constitution intended to lay down particular conceptions of these principles, they could easily have done so. This omission must be deliberate; instead, the fundamental rights provisions are framed with general principles in mind, and the courts must be free to develop these principles in view of prevailing ideas and social changes.'[169]

The enumerated rights contained in Article 40, 3, 2 were not intended to be exhaustive;[170] in the words of Mr Justice Henchy of the Supreme Court: 'The infinite variety in the relationships between the citizen and his fellows, and between the citizen and the state, make an exhaustive enumeration of guaranteed rights difficult, if not impossible.'[171] The rights specified in this section are regarded as illustrative of the rights that are included in a broader category protected by the Constitution.[172] The use by Hearne of the words 'in particular' has been cited in support of this contention.[173]

Of course, Hearne and de Valera could not have fully foreseen the implications of judicial review as applied to the interpretation of Bunreacht na hÉireann, as they could not have anticipated the economic, social and political changes which formed the context for such judgements. Moreover, Séamus Ó Tuama is correct when he observed that de Valera's conception of judicial review was formed before a stronger tradition of such review emerged in the United States and he, therefore, had no means of anticipating fully its potential impact on the Irish Constitution.[174] Perhaps, some rulings would have discomforted these two conservative Catholics. Perhaps, if they could have anticipated future constitutional developments, they might have baulked at unqualified judicial review. This did not happen – they favoured the inclusion of such review without qualifications. Their decision was not an uninformed one; there were vocal opponents to the inclusion of the power of review who had made their opinions known to de Valera and Hearne.

Moreover, it is important to remember that both men understood that court judgements could be disappointing and problematic, as in the matter of the *State v Lennon* in 1934, discussed in Chapter 4, and the judicial fallout from the Offences against the State Act 1939, discussed in Chapter 6. According to his biographers, 'de Valera was always aware – some would say, too aware – of the infinite complexity of the future'.[175] With such a philosophical attitude, he may have accepted with equanimity the consequences of judicial activism, having approved of its inclusion in the Constitution.

In the exercise of the function of judicial review and the identification of unenumerated rights, the superior courts have invoked the doctrine of natural law.[176] This doctrine represented a dominant element of the background moral landscape in light of which constitutional provisions were interpreted.[177] In the course of his judgement in the McGee case in 1973, Justice Brian Walsh stated that 'the natural law as a theological concept is the law of God promulgated by reason and is the ultimate governor of all the laws of men'[178] and it came to inform much of the unenumerated rights' jurisprudence.[179] The version of natural law which inspired Irish judges was influenced by Roman Catholic theology, especially the works of St Thomas Aquinas.[180] This is not surprising: the natural law was the basis for the wording and development of many of the rights recognised and protected by the Constitution,[181] reflecting the pronounced Catholic ethos of the state at the time of the drafting of the document and in subsequent decades. References to natural law came almost instinctively to Irish judges in the 1960s and 1970s.

The right of judicial review confers enormous powers on the judiciary; judges become law-makers.[182] It was in the context of this appreciation of the power vested in judges that judicial review has been the subject of serious discussion and criticism. As early as 1967, jurist and politician, John M. Kelly, commenting on the judgement in *Ryan v the Attorney General*, wrote that the result of the ruling was to introduce uncertainty into law-making as it placed 'the Oireachtas in the position of not knowing just what personal rights it must respect and how far it can go in delimiting or abridging them'. In effect, according to Kelly, the courts have the power to act as a 'third house of the legislature'.[183] In the early 1990s, Justice McCarthy, writing extra-judicially, opined that 'in the field of unenumerated rights the judicial power can only be self-restrained'. Therefore, 'the judiciary must not err by adopting either extreme, that of the refusal to go outside the expressed terms of the Constitution at one end or of an excessive judicial law-making at the other'.[184] Professor Gerard Casey has even questioned the assumption that the task of ascertaining and declaring rights belongs to the courts[185] and that, while the United States Constitution acknowledges the existence of unenumerated rights in the ninth amendment, Bunreacht na hÉireann contains no such provision.[186]

The doctrine of unenumerated rights, one of the most influential in Irish constitutional law, has been the subject of vigorous debate,[187] with concern being voiced about the reliance by judges on natural law as the basis of their interpretation of the Constitution and the identification of new rights. The Constitution Review Group observed that the main problem associated with such reliance was 'the difficulty in determining its content: there is no single version of natural law nor is there a text of natural law to which reference can be made to ascertain its content'.[188] Writing in 1987, Gerard Hogan commented: 'If important constitutional decisions are based on what amounts to a subjective interpretation of an amorphous higher law this will ultimately lead to a lack of respect for the judicial process.' Accordingly, he cautioned that the natural law approach 'must be viewed with reserve',[189] though this was a point of view not shared by other jurists such as Richard Humphreys.[190]

By the 1990s, however, in the opinion of Hogan and Whyte, the use of explicit natural law reasoning had waned, 'probably as a result of an increasing judicial awareness that an express reliance on this approach is open to the objections that it permits reliance on standards which are often diffuse and subjective'.[191] Judges were becoming 'increasingly uncomfortable' with the implications of the doctrine of unenumerated rights[192] and the rate of judicially discovered rights slowed down significantly in the late 1980s and early 1990s.[193] Since the late 1990s, the doctrine has not been invoked in a case and no new right has been declared since then.[194] Ronan Keane, writing in 2002, agreed 'that the tide of judicial law-making had somewhat receded in recent years in Ireland as unease persists as to the underlying basis of the decision in [the] *Ryan* [case]'.[195]

Clearly, in recent decades, the standing of natural law in relation to judicial interpretation of the Constitution has gradually weakened.[196] This fact became apparent in the Supreme Court judgement in the abortion information case. In 1995, the Regulation of Information (Services outside the State for Termination of Pregnancies) Bill was referred to the court by the President to determine its constitutionality in the context of the eighth amendment (the so-called 'pro-life' amendment).[197] Counsel representing the rights of the unborn child argued that any provision either in the Constitution or in legislation which permitted the giving of information contrary to the natural law right to life of the unborn was unconstitutional. Natural law was the foundation upon which Bunreacht na hÉireann rested and ranked superior to the state's fundamental law.[198]

In its judgement, the Supreme Court rejected the contention that natural law could be invoked to invalidate constitutional amendments passed in accordance with the terms of the Constitution. The court emphasised that, under Bunreacht na hÉireann, 'it is the people who are paramount'[199] and it rejected the idea of natural law as an independent, freestanding source of constitutional authority.[200] Rather, the sovereignty of the people was identified as the foundation of the constitutional order.[201] The decline in the role of natural law mirrored the loss of status of religion, and especially of the Catholic Church, in society. The earlier Catholic ethos of the state had accorded natural law a pre-eminent position as the basis for rights, numerated and unenumerated. However, the increasingly secular ethos of this same state has marginalised its role. Just as the superior courts reflected social changes in their interpretation of the Constitution, they also reflected the impact of such changes on the philosophy which informed this interpretation.

The extent to which judges no longer emphasise Christian values when interpreting the Constitution is apparent in a consideration of references to the preamble in judicial rulings. At an earlier time, judges placed an emphasis on the invocation of the Most Holy Trinity.[202] In the 1970s, Judge Brian Walsh stated that the 'preamble acknowledged that we are a Christian people' and again referring to the preamble he associated natural human rights with natural law and the law of God.[203] In 1983, Chief Justice O'Higgins cited this part of the Constitution which 'stamped the ethical character of Christianity on the state' in his rejection of the claim that laws penalising homosexual acts between men were unconstitutional in his judgement in the *Norris* case.[204] However, in more recent times 'the interpretative leitmotif in the case law centres around the purposive focus on the principles' [declared in the preamble] of 'prudence, justice and charity' and 'the dignity and freedom of the individual'.[205] Interpretations of the law are now informed by a more secularised ideal of justice.[206]

There was one significant consequence of the doctrine of natural law as applied by the superior courts in judicial interpretation and review – the development of a distinctive Irish jurisprudence. This was an ambition of a number of senior judges in the early years of the state,[207] most notably Hugh Kennedy, first Chief Justice of the Irish Free State,[208] and George Gavan Duffy.[209] With the establishment of the Free State, Kennedy wanted the 'voice of the Gael' to be heard in the courts of the land to emphasise that a new legal order had come into being.[210] He encountered, however, the conservatism of the legal profession, not least in his efforts to change court dress,[211] and the status quo prevailed in terms of the administration of justice: 'Only the harp replacing the royal court of arms reflected the changed times.'[212]

As was noted earlier, George Gavan Duffy experienced the resistance of colleagues who did not regard the 1937 Constitution as presenting the possibility of a native constitutional jurisprudence. It was in the 1960s, with the appointment of Cearbhall Ó Dálaigh and Brian Walsh to the Supreme Court, that a beginning was really made to release the Irish system of law from near servile dependence on English judicial practice and precedence[213] – 'to move it from under the colonial shadow and go it alone'.[214] These judges realised that, if constitutional jurisprudence advanced to a sufficiently developed state, 'it would thereby be possible to effect a complete remoulding of fundamental legal principles and thus establish an entire corpus of law which would have a decidedly native foundation'.[215] The doctrine of natural law was part of the 'rebellion' against the British legal tradition and gave an Irish dimension to the ideas and principles of law.[216] It provided 'an alternative theory of rights sufficiently strong to break out of the traditional common law, Westminster model of law-making and law adjudication'.[217]

This process of establishing a distinctive Irish jurisprudence has largely been achieved by the incorporation of constitutional principles based on Bunreacht na hÉireann into standard legal concepts.[218] John Hearne, who was described as a legal nationalist in an earlier chapter, and for whom a nation's laws were such a central part of its national life and a badge of distinctive identity, would have approved.

Constitution of Ireland: a charter of personal rights

Garret FitzGerald has observed that 'the Irish Constitution offers very powerful protection for human rights vis-á-vis the executive and the legislature, probably stronger protection than in any other parliamentary democracy'.[2] As a consequence of the fundamental rights provisions included in Articles 40–4 and the identification of unenumerated rights by judicial review, Bunreacht na hÉireann has become a significant and powerful charter of the rights of people in the Irish state. This fact is highlighted when these are considered in the context of international documents concerned with human rights. In 1948, the United Nations issued the Universal Declaration of Human Rights[220] and many of the rights proclaimed in it had been enunciated in the Irish Constitution adopted eleven years before.

Right declared	Article in Irish Constitution	Article in UN Declaration
Equality before the law.	40	7
Personal liberty.	40	9
Inviolability of dwellings.	40	12
Freedom of expression.	40	19
Peaceable assembly.	40	20
Right to associate.	40	20
Right to good name.	40	12
Protection of family.	41	16
Right to elementary education.	42	26
Right to private property.	43	17

The subsequent identification of unenumerated rights increased and strengthened the personal freedoms and human rights of persons living in the Irish state. Many of the rights identified by judicial review predated their expression in the *Charter of Fundamental Rights of the European Union*, 2000.[221]

Identified unenumerated right	When identified	Article in EU Charter
Right to earn a livelihood.	*Murphy v Stewart* [1973] IR 97	15
Right to privacy.	*Kennedy v Ireland* [1987] IR 587	7

Right to marital privacy.	*McGee v Attorney General* [1974] IR 284	7
Right to marry.	*McGee v Attorney General* [1974] IR 284	7
Right to procreate.	*Murray v Ireland* [1985] IR 532	7
Right not to be ill-treated.	*The State (C) v Frawley* [1976] IR365	4
Right to bodily integrity.	*Ryan v Attorney General* [1965] IR 294	3

The referendum

While the superior courts have reflected changes in Irish society in their interpretation of the Constitution, the basic law has also been changed directly by means of referendums. Ireland is one of the few countries where every constitutional amendment requires the consent of the people.[222] Bunreacht na hÉireann provided for amendment by the Oireachtas for a period of three years after the date on which the first President entered upon office; thereafter it could only be amended by referendum, as provided for in Article 46.[223] Since the expiration of the transition period, referendums have taken place on a total of thirty-eight proposed amendments, twenty-seven of which have been accepted and eleven rejected.[224] After the stability, some might say even stagnation, of the 1940s and 1950s, Irish society began to change and the Constitution reflected this circumstance.[225] Three factors accounted for some of the most significant amendments: changing attitudes to Northern Ireland and to religion, and membership of the European Union.

From the mid-1960s, an increasing number of people in the Republic of Ireland recognised that any accommodation between it and Northern Ireland would require changes to the Constitution or its replacement.[226] In particular, Articles 2 and 3, which 'represented de Valera's most formal legacy on the partition issue,'[227] came under critical scrutiny. As early as 1967, an all-party committee on the Constitution proposed changes to these articles.[228] In its report, it stated that it would be appropriate to adopt a new provision to replace Article 3 and suggested the following wording: 'The Irish nation hereby proclaims its firm will that its territory be re-united in harmony and brotherly affection between all Irishmen.'[229] This was a much softer wording than the original and was informed by the principle of unity by consent. The outbreak of violence in Northern Ireland in 1969 and the urgent need for a solution focussed much attention on these two articles. The Good Friday Agreement

1998 included proposals for their amendment, which were adopted by referendum in the same year.[230] The amended form of Article 3 indicates the extent to which the irredentist attitudes of 1937 had been supplanted by an understanding of the need for respectful accommodation between the nationalist and unionist traditions. The article, in part, now reads:

> It is the firm will of the Irish nation, in harmony and friendship, to unite all the people who share the territory of the island of Ireland, in all the diversity of their identities and traditions, recognising that a united Ireland shall be brought about only by peaceful means with the consent of a majority of the people, democratically expressed, in both jurisdictions in the island.

The conflict in Northern Ireland also caused a more critical appraisal of Article 44, according special recognition to the Catholic Church. The *Report of the Committee on the Constitution* 1967 stated that it was 'a useful weapon in the hands of those who are anxious to emphasise the differences between North and South'.[231] There was a recommendation to delete the provision.[232] This was done in 1972[233] and 'the importance of the deletion at a symbolic level cannot be underestimated in the Irish cultural context',[234] in which the Catholic Church wielded enormous influence.

With changes in the economy and society between 1980 and 2010, the centrality and importance of religion in Irish life diminished.[235] The *Report of the Constitution Review Group* 1996 observed that 'the traditional Roman Catholic ethos has been weakened by various influences, including secularisation, urbanisation, changing attitudes to sexual behaviour, the use of contraception, social acceptance of premarital relations, cohabitation and single parenthood'.[236] Unsurprisingly, a dominant theme of those years was the dramatic changes in attitudes to the family,[237] manifesting itself in demands for contraception and divorce, in a definite repudiation of traditional Catholic teachings. The scandals which befell the Catholic Church in the 1990s did it incalculable damage and this fact, allied to ongoing economic and social changes and increasing pluralism, contributed to the greater secularisation of Irish society.

Bunreacht na hÉireann reflected these circumstances. There were two referendums on divorce: the first one, in 1986, resulted in the defeat of the proposed deletion of the constitutional prohibition,[238] while a second one, in 1995, favoured its removal by a small margin.[239] Most dramatically, in 2015, the Constitution was amended to permit same-sex marriage.[240] Thus Bunreacht na hÉireann was shorn of what had been two fundamental provisions in terms of the influence of Catholic Church teachings – marriage based on the traditional family and the prohibition on divorce – as the document was changed to accommodate the views and beliefs of an Ireland very different from the one in which it was drafted and adopted.

Ireland's accession to membership of the European Economic Community, later the European Union, has accounted for most referendums, nine in all:[241]

Year	Referendum
1972	Accession to European Economic Community
1987	Single European Act
1992	Maastricht Treaty
1998	Amsterdam Treaty
2001	Treaty of Nice (rejected)
2002	Treaty of Nice (accepted)
2008	Lisbon Treaty (rejected)
2009	Lisbon Treaty (accepted)
2012	Stability Treaty

The Constitution has been amended to accommodate the limitations on national sovereignty consequent on membership of the European Union.[242] European law has been explicit in recognising such limitations and the various referendums have been the conduit through which European law flows into Irish law and, in its sphere, the former predominates over Bunreacht na hÉireann. An institution of the European Union, the Court of Justice, has the function of ensuring that European law is observed by the member states and this stands alongside and, in certain circumstances, above the Irish courts. In 1937, it was important to declare, in its Constitution, that Ireland was a sovereign state; since 1972, the Irish people have decided, in a series of referendum decisions, to limit this same national sovereignty. The state's fundamental law has been changed to accommodate this decision.

A number of important consequences have been attendant on the referendum provisions of the Irish Constitution. They have given practical expression to the concept of the sovereignty of the people in the state's constitutional dispensation. Their effect is to confirm that, ultimately, the basic law is under the control of its citizens. Chief Justice Liam Hamilton has stated that 'the role of the people in amending the Constitution cannot be over emphasised. It is solely their prerogative to amend any provision thereof by way of variation, addition or repeal, or to refuse amendment. The decision is theirs and theirs alone'.[243]

More recently, Mr Justice Murray asserted that 'the existence of our constitutional democracy, including the constitutional framework within which it functions, owes its legitimacy exclusively to the consent of the people. That constitutional framework can only be altered with the consent of the people'.[244] Thus the citizens of Ireland are accorded a direct role in government and can engage in decisions pertaining to the basic law which defines and shapes the character of the state. It must be acknowledged that this engagement has been accepted with varying degrees of enthusiasm, as evidenced by voter turnout at referendums. The percentage poll has varied from the highest figure of 70.9 per cent in 1972 on the issue of accession to the European Community, to the lowest of 28.6 per cent in 1979 on the matters of adoption and university representation in Seanad Éireann.[245] The average turnout over the thirty-eight referendums has been 51.4 per cent,[246] with the more controversial issues recording higher percentage polls.

These issues were ones relating to social policy: divorce (first referendum, 1986), 60.8 per cent; divorce (second referendum, 1995), 62.15 per cent; and marriage equality (2015), 60.52 per cent. In 2001, the All-Party Committee on the Constitution addressed this question of voter participation in referendums and observed that it is the 'duty' of political parties and interest groups to engage in the process of debate and persuasion that can lead to as much involvement as possible in referendums by the people of the state.[247]

The referendum has been a powerful check on governments wanting to make constitutional changes that did not enjoy broad support across the political spectrum.[248] The rejection of the two proposals by Fianna Fáil to abolish proportional representation in 1959 and 1968 are evidence of this. In the words of Justice Brian Walsh: 'In the last analysis it is the people themselves who are the guardians of the Constitution'[249] and they have exercised this custodianship judiciously. The referendum also ensures that such amendments as have been approved, no matter how controversial, have a legitimacy that they would not have if the decisions had been made by the Oireachtas and politicians alone.[250] This is certainly true, for example, of the issue of marriage equality decided in 2015. Finally, the referendum provisions have allowed for amendments of the Constitution to reflect changing attitudes in society. Therefore, Bunreacht na hÉireann is capable of responding to such changes and this fact has given it greater credibility among the people of the state.

Directive Principles of Social Policy

Speaking in Villanova College, Pennsylvania, on 22 September 1950, John Hearne made an apparently dramatic declaration: 'I am endeavouring to give you a brief outline of the broad features of our plan for reconstructing society from top to bottom in the part of our national territory which we effectively control and ultimately upon the whole island.'[251] He was referring to Article 45 of the Constitution, the 'Directive

Principles of Social Policy', described by him as an article 'aimed at promoting the welfare of the whole people by securing a social order in which justice and charity shall inform all the institutions of national life':

> They [the principles] deal with the distribution of wealth; the operation of free competition in such a way as to prevent the concentration of essential commodities in the hands of a few to the common detriment. They provide for credit control, the establishment of the largest possible number of working farmers on the land in economic holdings privately owned, the promotion of private initiative in industry, the prevention of the unjust exploitation of labour, the protection of the weaker members of the community and the support of the infirm, the widow, the orphan and the aged.[252]

Seven years later, he addressed the Harvard Law School Association of New Jersey and again referred to the Directive Principles, this time in greater detail. He established the context in which they were drafted. This part of his speech represented an attack on *laissez-faire* economics, a doctrine he described as 'still around' when the Constitution was being drafted. His attack was founded on three arguments. First, such economics embodied a false notion of humanity, 'because it subordinated the human person to the imperfect policy of economic forces, instead of making man the centre of national economic life'. Second, the advocates of such economics considered the state 'a by-stander with little right to protect the common welfare and to intervene in economic affairs when the general good demanded it'. Finally, that kind of economic liberalism 'regarded economic life as a natural battleground for harsh competitive strife instead of a co-operative effort to meet man's needs, morally as well as materially, through the provident use of scarce resources'. By means of the Directive Principles of Social Policy, 'our policy-makers sought to deal with the evil of *laissez-faire* liberalist economic theory and practice, their results which still obtain in parts of Western Europe, and most of Asia, Africa and South America'.[253]

These same principles were also, according to Hearne, a rejection of 'the much graver danger of collectivism', a fact of particular relevance in a country such as Ireland which was primarily agricultural. Elaborating on this point, he told his audience: 'You will notice that every word in that declaration is sharply aimed at any attempt to apply collectivist principles to Irish agriculture by way of what had elsewhere been called in Red China, for example, "agrarian reform".'[254]

To represent the Directive Principles of Social Policy as a plan for the reconstruction of Irish society was a gross overstatement. It was a representation that needed to be heavily qualified and Hearne did this in his 1957 address:

As lawyers you will ask me at once how all these declarations are to be construed by the courts. That was a difficulty which was anticipated when they were being made. They were inserted, therefore, in the Constitution only as directives for the general guidance of the parliament. Their obligation in the making of laws was declared to be the exclusive concern of the parliament and not to be cognisable by any court established by or under the Constitution.[255]

In effect, the Directive Principles were an expression of the Constitution as a manifesto, commented upon in Chapter 6.[256] Just as the document articulated political aims, it also articulated social ones, albeit in a significantly more muted form, being non-justiciable. They were a statement of Catholic social teachings that were in vogue in the 1930s. Central to such teachings was a definitive rejection of *laissez-faire* capitalism and communism, and an appeal for a social system based on justice and charity, in accordance with the papal encyclicals *Rerum Novarum* (1891) and *Quadragesimo Anno* (1931).[257] These ideas entered Irish Catholic discourse due to their dissemination by Catholic social activists. In many respects, the Directive Principles were akin to a treatise on Catholic social teachings which was incorporated into Bunreacht na hÉireann; consequently, they had more of a philosophical than a practical import.

Hearne's enthusiasm for this article was due to his deep religious faith and his loyalty to the teachings of the Catholic Church. In that regard, he saw these principles as significant and, with them in mind, among other considerations, he told his audience in 1950 that 'it [the Constitution] has now been in operation for over twelve years and it can be said that the whole inner life of the nation has been transformed'.[258] His use of the words 'inner life' reinforces the notion that the principles possessed for him a philosophical and a religious aspect in their advocacy of the concepts of justice and charity.

It was because the Directive Principles of Social Policy were not justiciable that they were dismissed by the opposition during the Dáil debates on the proposed Constitution. In the 1930s, however, social rights were not a feature of liberal–democratic constitutions after which tradition Bunreacht na hÉireann was shaped and drafted. Such matters were political rather than constitutional, a view expressed by the Constitution Review Group in 1996: 'Whereas it is appropriate that fundamental rights are enforceable by the courts, these [social] principles, by their nature, fall to be implemented through the political process which determines, under the influence of the electorate, the progress that can be made from time to time in their application.'[259] In the words of Justice Kingsmill Moore, Article 45 'puts the state under certain duties, but these are duties of imperfect obligation since they cannot be enforced'.[260]

At most, the article was to provide an indirect obligation to strive to achieve some aims of a welfare state.[261] It also contains a vision 'of society and social policy that is comprehensive, internally consistent and founded on classical Catholic social principles, although it remains just that – a vision – for the Constitution itself does not provide means for its materialisation or for those principles being implemented by resort to the courts ...'[262]

The Directive Principles of Social Policy are, in the words of Anthony Coughlan, 'a noble enough set of guiding principles'[263] but the reality is that they have never really informed political and social discourse. While occasionally cited in the courts as an interpretative instrument,[264] they have effectively remained a dead-letter in terms of their wider social impact and application. The proximate reason is the article's non-justiciability. However, more fundamentally, the relegation of the principles to the margins of Irish life reflected the conservatism of Irish politicians, politics and society. De Valera did not envisage that he was heralding a social transformation of Ireland in his Constitution; its primary purpose was the achievement of sovereignty.

Like so many of his comrades in Fianna Fáil, he had no socio-economic philosophy of any significance.[265] In fact, the political elite which emerged from the upheavals of 1916–23 did not regard the events of those years as a prelude to dramatic social changes; Patrick Lynch has written of 'the social revolution that never was'.[266] De Valera was dismissive of the social elements of the 1916 Proclamation; it was a document about the attainment of self-government.[267] He had no revolutionary theory of society, no burning passion to redress social inequalities. His nationalist ardour was cultural and political, rather than social.[268] During his career in public life, he reflected the prevailing conservatism of Irish society, and reinforced this conservatism. In that context, it is understandable that Professor Joe Lee described the Directive Principles of Social Policy as 'mummified flatulence',[269] although it is an overly dismissive assessment.

Notwithstanding all these factors, which militated against the materialisation of the vision of the Directive Principles, their inclusion in the Constitution was an innovative feature,[270] a departure from the traditional model of the liberal–democratic constitution. They inspired similar provisions in other constitutions, such as those of India (1947) and Burma (1974). The fundamental laws of other countries have followed this path, including Pakistan (1962), Sri Lanka (1972), Bangladesh (1972), Nigeria (1979), Ghana (1992) and Namibia (1990).[271]

Moreover, while the language used is old-fashioned, Article 45 incorporated principles which have found expression nearly seventy years later in the *Charter of Fundamental Rights of the European Union*, 2000.[272] This is evident in a comparison of two important provisions in this Charter with some of the Directive Principles:

Directive Principles of Social Policy	Charter of Fundamental Rights of the European Union, 2010
Article 45, 4, 1: The State pledges itself to safeguard with especial care the economic interests of the weaker sections of the community, and, where necessary, to contribute to the support of the infirm, the widow, the orphan, and the aged.	Article 34: The Union recognises and respects the entitlement to social security benefits and social services providing protection in cases such as maternity, illness, industrial accidents, dependency or old age, and in the case of loss of employment, in accordance with the rules laid down by Union law and national laws and practices.
Article 45, 4, 2: The state shall endeavour to ensure that the strength and health of workers, men and women, and the tender age of children shall not be abused and that citizens shall not be forced by economic necessity to enter avocations unsuited to their sex, age or strength.	Article 31, 1: Every worker has the right to working conditions which respect his or her health, safety and dignity. Article 32: Young people admitted to work must have working conditions appropriate to their age and be protected against economic exploitation and any work likely to harm their safety, health or physical, mental, moral or social development ...

Thus the Directive Principles have stood the test of time and 'in many ways reflect modern concepts of justice in society',[273] though they have been effectively ignored since their adoption eighty years ago.

Women and the Constitution

Women had no involvement in the planning, shaping and drafting of the Constitution. The central figures in the process were de Valera and Hearne. The cabinet which considered the preliminary draft on 10 March 1937 was made up entirely of men. The Second House of the Oireachtas Commission, which made recommendations on Seanad Éireann, had only one woman member.[274] The editorial committee established by de Valera was composed of four male civil servants: Hearne, Maurice Moynihan, Philip O'Donoghue and Michael McDunphy. The Catholic clerics who exercised an influence on the drafting process, the Jesuits and McQuaid, were, *ipso facto*, men. Those who made observations on the various drafts and revises were, predominantly, male. The Dáil which discussed the proposed Constitution had only three women among its 152 members and these female deputies made no meaningful contribution to the debate.[275]

This is the backdrop to any assessment of the Constitution's impact on the role and condition of women in Irish society. An understanding of the history and origins of Bunreacht na hÉireann cannot blind one to 'the profound underlying patriarchy' of the state that determined the character of the 1937 document[276] and it still bears the imprint of that period. The Constitution reflected the prevailing attitudes to women – attitudes shared by most men and women – a fact noted earlier in the discussion of the Dáil debates on the provisions pertaining to women. There was a presumption of natural sex differences between women and men and an attendant commitment to the ideal of 'separate spheres'.[277] Such attitudes defined the role of women as that of wives and mothers, a fundamental belief given powerful expression in two sections of Article 41. The first, Article 41, 2, 1, 'recognises that by her life within the home, woman gives to the state a support without which the common good cannot be achieved'. Article 42, 2, 2 asserts that the state shall 'endeavour to ensure that mothers shall not be obliged by economic necessity to engage in labour to the neglect of their duties in the home'.

Thus the role of woman was conflated with that of wife and mother, a conflation which would have received near universal endorsement in the Ireland of 1937. The Constitution's emphasis on the central importance of the family as the primary unit of society underscored and reinforced this definition of the woman's role, as she was regarded as possessing a pivotal position within the family by the state, and especially by the Catholic Church, an institution whose teachings shaped societal attitudes to the family.[278]

The views of the political and civil service elite involved in constitution-making rested on the values of the community at large and the document they produced was informed by those same values. The politicians and civil servants were certainly not feminists but neither were they consciously anti-woman. Their attitudes were consonant with those of most members of Irish society – male and female – and the Constitution's formulations as they pertained to women were shaped by a social consensus about the proper role and function of women. It is in this context that Professor Mary Daly has cautioned against a 'present-centred focus' in any assessment of the provisions in Bunreacht na hÉireann relating to women, thus evaluating such provisions from the perspective of issues which did not necessarily loom large in the lives of most Irish women at that time.[279]

Yvonne Scannell has argued that there are two ways of looking at Article 41:

The first is to take de Valera at his word and to regard the first paragraph as a tribute to the work that is done by women in the home as mothers. The second paragraph, if it is to be regarded as anything other than a paternalistic declaration can be read as a constitutional guarantee that *no mother* is to be *forced* by economic necessity to work outside the home to the neglect of her duties there. The mothers covered by this guarantee would include widows, unmarried mothers, mothers whose husbands are unable or unwilling to support their families, even relatively rich mothers with heavy expenses such as those necessitated by caring for ill or handicapped children.

The alternative perspective on this provision contends that

the second way of looking at Article 41, 2 is different. To some, it is grossly offensive to the dignity and freedom of womanhood. It speaks of woman's *life* within the home (not just her work there), implying that the natural vocation of woman (the generic is used, so it means *all* women) is in the home. It is the grossest form of sexual stereotyping ... It fails to recognise that a woman's place is a woman's choice.[280]

The fact is that both perspectives are accurate. The recognition accorded to women in the home was sincerely intended by de Valera and resonated with the prevailing attitudes of the time. Though suffused with paternalism and patriarchy, it was nevertheless meant by him as a significant and honest statement when viewed in its contemporary context. While the attitudes of the 1930s accorded recognition to a woman's role in the home, they were certainly not, however, disposed to support a role outside it. The laws of the land effectively confined women to domesticity and had done so since the foundation of the state.[281] Women were denied choice of avocations in life. For almost thirty years after the Constitution's adoption the position of women in society hardly changed at all.

The 1960s heralded an era of important change in the status and role of women.[282] There were three developments which were of particular significance in that regard. First, the expansion of the economy offered women employment opportunities outside the home. Between 1971 and 1983, the number of women in the work force grew by 34 per cent and the number of married women in the work force increased by 425 per cent in the same period.[283] Second, the Irish Women's Liberation Movement was launched in 1970 and its manifesto had five demands: equal pay; equality before the law; equal education; contraception; and justice for deserted wives, unmarried mothers and widows.[284] By the 1980s, feminist issues had entered the mainstream of political life.[285] Third, Ireland's accession to the European Economic Community in 1973 imported European law into Irish law, with the consequent obligation to ensure, among other matters, equality of pay and treatment for women and men.[286]

The cumulative effect of these developments had a transformative effect on attitudes towards women and the opportunities available to them.

As a consequence of all these changes, the social values enunciated and endorsed in the Constitution began to bear 'only an approximate resemblance to those evidenced in people's daily lives' in modern Ireland.[287] Article 41, 2, with its description of a woman's life in the home, was identified as one of its more dated provisions.[288] Moreover, notwithstanding its terms, 'it has never been of any particular assistance even to women working exclusively in the home'.[289] Legally, it appears to have had little benefit. In the 1980s, the Supreme Court rejected a claim by a married woman, who was a mother and had worked exclusively within her home, that she was entitled to a 50 per cent interest in the family home.[290] In fact, it has been argued by one legal scholar that Articles 41, 2, 1 and 41, 2, 2 are probably not justiciable.[291]

As has been noted already, the Constitution conflated the roles of woman and mother. The desirable familial ideology as manifested in the 1930s, however, is now largely out of date and the 'orthodox' model of the marital family is declining, 'with a corresponding evolution of a multiplicity of alternative non-traditional units'.[292] Social change means that gender roles within the family are in a state of flux. Catriona Kennedy has noted that '[these] roles, the structure of the family and female sexuality became the sites on which many of the major battles between tradition and innovation were fought'.[293] Such developments have had significant consequences for the provisions in the Constitution as they pertain to women. Slippage has occurred in matters of gender between the Constitution and contemporary social values.[294] Supporters of an equality model of the family have attacked constitutional provisions 'as being outdated, stereotypical, biologically deterministic and even insulting to women'.[295] It has been argued that they be deleted or, at the very least, the language rendered in a gender-neutral form. The All-Party Committee on the Constitution proposed the following alternative wording in 2006:

Amend Article 41, 2, 1:
The state recognises that by reason of family life within the home, a parent gives to the State a support without which the common good cannot be achieved.

Amend Article 41, 2, 2:
The State shall, therefore, endeavour to ensure that both parents shall not be obliged by economic necessity to work outside the home to the neglect of their parental duties.[296]

While provisions of the Constitution relating to women certainly reflected attitudes prevalent in the 1930s, this same document has also vindicated their rights on occasions. In the 1970s, individual women began to challenge the constitutionality of laws which discriminated against them. In 1970, the High Court ruled that a woman had the right to earn a livelihood under the terms of Article 40 and that sex discrimination in employment recruitment was unconstitutional. The Supreme Court in 1973 upheld the right of a married woman to use contraception. Later that year, the Juries Act 1927 was declared unconstitutional in so far as it provided that women were exempt from jury service.[297]

Judicial interpretation of the Constitution has been sensitive to the matter of gender and has, to some extent, accommodated changes in the roles of the sexes in society.[298] In a 2001 ruling, Justice Susan Denham declared:

> When Article 41 was being drafted and included in the Constitution there was a negative view expressed of the role apparently consigned to women. It has been considered by some that the article was rooted in a particular Christian philosophy. It was queried as to whether it placed the woman in the home to the detriment of other areas. Whatever historical concepts and byways may be traced, the reality is that the Constitution sets out constitutional rights, duties and powers. The Constitution is a living document. It must be considered as a document of its time. Thus Article 41 is an article of the 21st century, an article of our times ... It is not to be construed as representing a norm of a society long changed utterly. Rather, it is to be construed in the Ireland of the Celtic Tiger.

Accordingly, interpreting the Constitution in this context, Justice Denham stated that Article 41, 2

> does not assign women to a domestic role. Article 41, 2 recognises the significant role played by wives and mothers in the home. This recognition and acknowledgement does not exclude women and mothers from other roles and activities. It is a recognition of the work performed by women in the home. The work is recognised because it has immense benefit for society.[299]

In a later judgement, Justice John Murray again asserted that Bunreacht na hÉireann 'is to be interpreted as a contemporary document. The duties and obligations of spouses are mutual and it seems to me that [the Constitution] implicitly recognises similarly the nature of a man's contribution in the house as a parent'.[300] The All-Party Committee on the Constitution observed, in 2004, that 'the courts are disposed to interpret 41, 2, 1 as applying to either father or mother caring in the home'.[301] Yvonne Scannell has commented that de Valera's Constitution was not consciously designed to advance the cause of women's rights but judges, through judicial review and interpretation, 'have shown that it has the capacity to do just that'.[302]

Property

In Bunreacht na hÉireann there are two provisions relating to property: Article 40, 3, 2 and Article 43. The former is included in that part of the document dealing with personal rights and may be said to protect the individual citizen's property rights, while the latter article deals with the institution of private property itself.[303] Article 43 was included in that part of the Constitution where the influence of Catholic social teachings was particularly marked and was evidence of the involvement of the Jesuits and Fr John Charles McQuaid in the drafting process. In their advocacy of the inclusion of provisions dealing with private property, they were seeking to give constitutional expression to a central tenet of Catholic social teaching, as expressed in the seminal encyclical, *Quadragesimo Anno*, issued in 1931. In the language used in the Constitution, theology certainly trumped law.

This language has been variously described as 'unhappy'[304] and 'tortured'.[305] Former Chief Justice Ronan Keane wrote that 'one cannot help wondering what the words "in virtue of his rational being" are doing in this article in the first place or what the necessary relationship is between man's rational capacity and his "right" to own property'.[306] The reality is that 'the use of confessional phrasing ... caused problems for judges required to apply Roman Catholic absolutes and ecclesiastical terminology to issues raised under a common law system which does not readily accommodate such concepts'.[307] The fact that there are two separate constitutional provisions dealing with property rights has itself given rise to confusion,[308] the courts concluding that the two inform each other.[309]

It has been frequently charged that the articles on property have impeded the adoption of socially desirable policies because of an unduly conservative interpretation of the Constitution's property provisions,[310] especially by politicians and public officials. The fate of the *Kenny Report* is often cited as evidence of this assertion. While not suggesting that this report was perfect in every respect, its fate is nevertheless of interest in the context of a consideration of the Constitution's provisions pertaining to private property. In 1971, the Minister for Local Government established a committee to report on the cost of building land, chaired by Mr Justice John Kenny. Its 1974 report recommended that development land should be compulsorily acquired by local authorities at a 25 per cent premium above its existing value.[311] The report was not acted upon, its possible unconstitutionality being cited as one reason.[312] In fact, two officials from the Department of Local Government on the committee rejected it for that reason.[313] Thus the Constitution was being presented as an obstacle to its implementation. The state's fundamental law came to be regarded by some critics of inaction on the report as a means 'to protect major differentials in the ownership of productive wealth within Irish society'.[314]

While a detailed consideration of the complexity of constitutional law as it pertains to property, and to the *Kenny Report* in particular, is beyond the scope of this study, a number of points may be made. In 1996, the Constitution Review Group commented that the courts had refrained from adopting an 'absolutist' approach to property rights.[315] There had been only about seven cases where a plaintiff established an unconstitutional interference with his or her property and 'in nearly every case the potential arbitrariness of the interference in question was fairly evident'.[316] On the basis of case-law, the All-Party Oireachtas Committee on the Constitution concluded in 2004 that 'it is very difficult to see why the recommendations contained in the *Kenny Report* would not survive constitutional scrutiny'.[317] 'We do not consider that it is correct to say that the case-law bears out the frequent criticism that the property rights provisions unduly protect the right of property or create undue difficulties for the Oireachtas where it attempts to regulate or control such property rights in the public interest'.[318]

The opinions informing the recommendations of the Constitution Review Group and the All-Party Committee apparently did not represent, however, the views of all those involved in the decision-making process. Jurist and member of Dáil Éireann John Kelly noted, in 1984, that 'the official view ... is that the statutory restrictions of the free market price [of land] in such a context would be constitutionally fragile'.[319] This was certainly the opinion of the legal adviser to the Minister for the Environment, who told a Dáil committee in the same year (1984) that the *Kenny Report* 'would have little chance of surviving a constitutional challenge in the courts based on the argument that it would amount to an unjust attack on the landowners' property right'.[320] Moreover, writing extra-juridically in 2008, Supreme Court judge Donál O'Donnell rejected the underlying principles on which the *Kenny Report* was based. He argued that a 'functioning democracy requires what I think the Irish Constitution provides: protection of all personal rights, which includes a strong guarantee of the rights to private property'.[321] In his opinion, it does not distinguish between property rights and other fundamental rights protected by the document.[322]

Certainly, the issues are complex. However, Ronan Keane has commented that 'the legislature should be capable of deciding at what point social justice or the common good requires that individuals should sacrifice the gains they have made from their shrewdness, foresight, hard work or good fortune to the greater welfare of the community'.[323] Crucially, the issues raised by the *Kenny Report* have never been tested in the courts and, therefore, there can be no legal certainties in the absence of such a test. Blaming the Constitution for a perceived lack of progress in the achievement of socially desirable objectives related to property may be reductionist. Moreover, should the Constitution be found to impede socially desirable objectives, it can be amended, should the citizens of the state decide to do so in a referendum – Bunreacht na hÉireann is not an immutable law inscribed on tablets of stone.

In recent years, the issue of corruption in relation to the planning process has been damaging to Irish politics and society.[324] There is a widespread sense that the political system facilitated some developers and speculators in their dishonest pursuit of profit and gain.[325] The attitude to the *Kenny Report* is regarded as symptomatic of this underlying corruption:

> Kenny's report, which ran to 195 pages, was frequently invoked in the decades after its publication when scandals relating to land re-zoning and attendant corrupt practices came to light, it being pointed out that such practices had their origins in the housing shortages, land prices and re-zoning practices of the 1960s and 1970s. One of Kenny's conclusions was that the demand for housing would continue to grow, and that if nothing was done to restrict them, prices would rise 'at an even more rapid rate than previously'. But as was observed twenty-five years later, 'one administration after another failed to meet the challenges of profiteering and corruption'.[326]

Ultimately, it was not Bunreacht na hÉireann which impeded the implementation of the report; this failure may be explained by politics and the attitudes in wider society to property. Blaming the Constitution obscures the real issue – the Irish relationship with property and the implications of this in terms of political objectives and social policies. Former Taoiseach, Garret FitzGerald, was of the opinion that 'the Catholic Church placed an excessive emphasis' on the right to own private property;[327] and, in an acerbic reference to the influence of the Jesuits on the Constitution, broadcaster and journalist Vincent Browne has observed: 'There was hardly any doubt where the high priests of Clongowes, Belvedere and Gonzaga stood on property rights.'[328] Such attitudes, however, only reflected those prevailing in the wider community. Preoccupation with ownership of property has been a characteristic of Irish society; it is a legacy of the experiences of the Great Famine and the Land War. Access to land remained a criterion of social success over a century or more after these historical events[329] and the values of the middle class, focusing on property ownership in its many manifestations, have come to dominate the modern Irish state.[330]

Durability of the Constitution

Bunreacht na hÉireann is one of the world's oldest constitutions. A study by Thomas Ginsburg, Zachary Elkins and James Melton of the University of Chicago Law School on the lifespan of written constitutions since 1789[331] estimated that they have lasted an average of only seventeen years. This they described as an 'unsettling' estimate 'for a document whose basic function is to express guiding national principles, establish basic rules and limit the power of government, all of which presuppose constitutional longevity'. In relation to 'durable' fundamental laws, three characteristics were identified as contributing to their more lengthy survival: inclusion, specificity and adaptability. By inclusion is meant a participatory mechanism whereby citizens are involved in the process of producing a constitution. Specificity means that the contents of a constitution cover a wide range of topics in order to survive the various pressures to which it will be subjected. This involves not only detail in particular provisions but also in the scope of the types of events the constitution covers. Adaptability relates to the capacity of the constitutional system to respond to changes in its environment. Elkins and his associates identified two primary mechanisms by which constitutional change occurs: formal amendments of the text and informal amendments that result from interpretative changes.

The model of constitutional durability presented by Elkins and his colleagues provides a useful framework in which to identify and assess the reasons for the relative longevity of the Irish Constitution. Regarding inclusion, it is important to appreciate that the modern concept of 'open government', with the consequent active encouragement of citizen participation in public and civic affairs, simply did not apply in the 1930s. Secrecy characterised the decision-making processes of governments in most countries, and certainly Ireland was no exception, with the obsessively secretive de Valera personally managing the planning, shaping and drafting of the Constitution. The fact, however, that the proposed basic law was debated by the Dáil and that, crucially, it was adopted in a plebiscite represented, at that period, a significant degree of popular participation. Ultimately, it was the electorate which decided the matter of the Constitution's approval or rejection; the plebiscite was a process of inclusion.

In terms of the constitutional model under consideration, specificity is the most difficult attribute to assess. Elkins and his colleagues concluded that durable constitutions cover a wide range of topics and that some constitutions are very, even overly specific. Seamus Ó Tuama, however, has argued that it is a matter of debate whether any constitution can be so described and that the Irish one can hardly be judged excessive in that regard.[332] Critically, Bunreacht na hÉireann does contain a number of important provisions which facilitate its capacity to cope with and survive the various pressures to which it was, is and will be subjected. These provisions include, among others, articles pertaining to the declaration of a state of emergency; the establishment of special courts; presidential referral of bills to the Supreme Court; judicial review; and the referendum. Specificity in these, and other areas, has enhanced the durability of the Constitution.

According to Elkins and his colleagues, the ability of a constitutional system to adapt to changes in its environment will determine whether it remains 'in equilibrium'.[333] Constitutions which cannot or do not change in response to political and social developments 'die young'.[334] De Valera, speaking in the Dáil in 1933, declared that constitutional adaptability was an essential prerequisite of a state's fundamental law. He described 'rigid' constitutions as 'a danger':

[T]hey have always proved a danger. If the people desire a certain change, if they feel it necessary for their well-being in changed circumstances, why should they be debarred from giving effect to their will by something that was designed in a previous period under conditions which were, probably, substantially different from the conditions that obtain now? That is how you get revolution ... I think, therefore, it is well that we should have here, not a cast-iron constitution, but a flexible constitution.[335]

A rigid fundamental law which fits its society well at the outset may be suitable if the rate of change in its environment is low but this same constitution may perform poorly if change is rapid. The Irish Constitution has witnessed a transformation of society since its inception, a fact recognised by the All-Party Oireachtas Committee on the Constitution in 2006:

The 1937 Constitution was embedded in the contemporary economic and social reality of a predominantly rural society in which agriculture provided the economic foundation ... the total population was just under 3 million. Today the population has exceeded 4 million for the first time since 1871. In 1937 the total labour force was 1.3 million; of those in employment, 614,000 or 50 per cent were in agriculture ... Seventeen per cent were engaged in industry and 33 per cent were in services. In 2003 the total labour force was 1.8 million; of those in employment only 6 per cent were in agriculture, while 28 per cent were in industry and 66 per cent were in services.[336]

The Constitution, however, has displayed a capacity for adaptability. Indeed, this fact is one of the most significant themes of this book. It has adapted by the referendum process and by judicial interpretation. The importance of judicial review cannot be overstated: 'It has given the Constitution its lasting strength and its capacity to achieve justice and to protect the dignity and freedom of the individual.'[337] If one had to identify that aspect of the constitutional system inaugurated in 1937 which, more than any other, has allowed it to survive for eight decades, it is undoubtedly the fact that it is adaptable.

Most important, however, this adaptability is balanced by a certain rigidity in the sense that the Constitution can only be changed by referendum and not simply by a Dáil majority, as was the case with the Free State Constitution. Apart from two amendments enacted by the Oireachtas, in accordance with its transitory provisions, there was no referendum until 1957 and this allowed the new fundamental law of the state to become embedded in the political and legal life of the state. This was in marked contrast to the Free State Constitution which was amended twenty-five times during the fifteen years of its existence. Bunreacht na hÉireann developed in conjunction with the social, cultural and political environment within which it came into being.[338] Its values appealed to a highly conservative and static society and, up to the 1960s, these values were, according to Bill Kissane, 'hegemonic'.[339]

The fact that the document can only be changed by referendum offers the opportunity of involvement by all the state's voters in the process of constitutional change. Thus the basic law can only be changed 'with deliberation, and not lightly and wantonly'.[340] The Irish people are afforded an opportunity of expressing their views before any change can be made. This practical expression of the doctrine of the sovereignty of the people has contributed to the sense that Bunreacht na hÉireann is regarded as the 'People's Book'[341] and 'the Charter of the Irish people'.[342]

Politically, Fine Gael and the Labour Party acquiesced in the new order established by the Bunreacht na hÉireann, not least because 'they recognised that a more powerful mass of other actors (including the Catholic Church) recognised the rules of the Constitution'.[343] The fact that, within ten years of its adoption, both parties participated in government (1948–51), in accordance with the strictures of the Constitution, facilitated their acceptance of it as the legitimate basic law of the state. Its former opponents, according to Donal O'Donnell, came to appreciate 'the care, thoughtfulness and learning which went into the drafting of the document ... and the depth, subtlety and integrity of the Constitution's provisions'.[344] A shared appreciation of Catholic social thought which inspired some of these provisions may have provided common ground between Fianna Fáil and the other parties.[345] In the case of Fine Gael, the Constitution did not really represent a radical departure from that party's version of nationalism. As a component of the first inter-party government, it was able to declare the state a republic within the constitutional framework of Bunreacht na hÉireann, thus ultimately confirming, from its perspective, Michael Collins' view that the Treaty settlement afforded Ireland the freedom to achieve greater freedom.[346]

It was not until the 1980s and later that the Constitution was amended to any great extent to reflect the changing nature of Irish society. This is significant: according to Elkins and his colleagues, constitutions do not 'crystallise until about the age fifty'.[347] By the 1980s, Ireland's basic law was approaching and later exceeded that age. It had, therefore, 'crystallised' and was established as the state's basic law. Thus Bunreacht na hÉireann refutes one conclusion of Elkins' research that 'the constitutional life cycle leads us to think of constitutions as rather fragile organisms', with only 19 per cent of them in operation by age fifty.[348] The Irish Constitution is, demonstrably, not such an organism.

Constitutional reform or replacement: a comment

While Bunreacht na hÉireann has survived eighty years, in recent times there have been calls for its radical amendment or even replacement. Senator and academic Ivana Bacik has written that it may be seen as 'a product of its time, now very much out of date';[349] in the opinion of a former minister, Liz O'Donnell, we should consider adopting a new one, 'which does not shackle us to the past';[350] while John Paul McCarthy has observed that, to modern eyes, 'this text looks on occasions like a stagnant, archaic, hidebound document steeped in the prejudices and superstitions of a time long past'.[351] In January 1988, the Progressive Democrats produced a 'Constitution for a New Republic';[352] while the 2011 Labour Party election manifesto promised a 'revised' constitution.[353] For some, the fact that the origins of the 1937 Constitution are associated with Éamon de Valera has served to confirm the need, even the urgency, of reforming or replacing the document because of the popular view that 'de Valera's Ireland was a dark, drab land, which demanded oppressive conformism, from which after a heroic contest the current generation of leaders had freed us, making today's country a vast improvement in almost every respect'.[354]

Moreover, the still prevalent popular conviction that John Charles McQuaid was a Svengali, who exercised an inordinate influence on the drafting process, serves only to further anathematise Bunreacht na hÉireann. He has come to personify the paralysing conservatism, intolerance and arrogance of the Catholic Church which wielded such influence in past decades. Anything he touched must be irredeemably tainted in the eyes of his many critics. This document, associated with de Valera and McQuaid, is often regarded as insular and introspective in character, holding up a mirror to an Ireland long gone. The articles on the Irish language and the role of women in the home, among others, are regarded as testimony to this baleful insularity. Accordingly, the Constitution must be reframed or replaced to meet the needs of a modern Ireland.[355]

Inevitably, as was noted in Chapter 6, constitution-makers reflect the social, cultural and political milieu in which a country's basic law was planned, shaped, drafted and revised. Therefore, a constitution is 'autobiographical' and 'idiosyncratic'[356] and, in that sense, will contain provisions resonant of the time of its making, hence the inclusion of Gaelic, nationalist, religious and patriarchal clauses in the 1937 document, some of which were removed in subsequent decades. However, the Irish Constitution is much more than the sum of such articles.

Bunreacht na hÉireann was not, and is not, a document insular in its conception and composition. Rather, it was a cosmopolitan production. John Hearne was a comparative constitutional lawyer of great distinction. Thus, as was commented on in Chapter 6, there was, incorporated into the text, the wisdom and experience of many countries in respect of constitution-making. A rich international heritage was mined. The provisions in the Irish Constitution were inspired, influenced or reinforced, in varying degrees, by a wide variety of constitutional texts, including the Constitutions of the Weimar Republic, Czechoslovakia, Poland, Austria, France, Spain, Portugal, the United Kingdom and the United States. Hearne's diplomatic career allowed him draw on the Covenant of the League of Nations and the Kellogg–Briand Pact. Moreover, there were significant indigenous influences woven into the text: the Proclamation of the Republic 1916; the Declaration of Independence 1919; the Democratic Programme 1919; 'Document no. 2' 1922; O'Rahilly's draft Constitution; and the Free State Constitution 1922.

Nor are some of the articles in the Irish Constitution, often instanced as expressions of its conservatism, as unique, in constitutional terms, as they are considered to be. As was argued in Chapter 6, there were comparable provisions in the constitutions of other European countries which influenced the drafting of the Irish text. More recent constitutions also include articles which resonate with clauses in the Irish Constitution. Take, for example, the Constitution of Italy which dates from 1948:

> Article 29: The Republic recognizes the rights of the family as a natural society founded on matrimony. Matrimony is based on the moral and legal equality of the spouses within the limits established by law to guarantee the unity of the family.
> Article 31: The Republic assists, through economic measures and other provisions, in the formation of the family and the fulfilment of its duties, with particular regard for large families. It protects maternity, infancy and youth, promoting the institutions necessary for such purposes.[357]

The Basic Law of the Federal Republic of Germany, adopted in 1949, affords another example:

> (1) Marriage and the family shall enjoy the special protection of the state.
> (2) The care and upbringing of children is the natural right of parents and a duty primarily incumbent upon them. The state shall watch over them in the performance of this duty.

(3) Children may be separated from their families against the will of their parents or guardians only pursuant to a law, and only if the parents or guardians fail in their duties or the children are otherwise in danger of serious neglect.

(4) Every mother shall be entitled to the protection and care of the community.[358]

The provisions on the family (the original prohibition on divorce excepted), therefore, are not Hibernian peculiarities or aberrations. In fact, much of the 1937 Constitution is not 'specifically or characteristically Irish'.[359]

What is striking in the Irish constitutional text is the language used to express many of the provisions included in the section dealing with fundamental rights, i.e. Articles 40–4. The influence of Catholic social teaching and papal encyclicals is apparent here. However, that influence has now waned. As was noted earlier, dramatic economic and social changes have impacted on religious belief and practice, with conventional Catholicism experiencing dramatic decline in the era of 'Ryanair, Father Ted and the condom-selling machine'.[360] As a consequence, Declan O'Keeffe has written of the 'degradation' in the 'legal status' of God and the natural law during the period 1973–99.[361] Many critics of the Constitution focus on the text as it was written, not as it has been interpreted. A full understanding of the document requires that it be read in the context of constitutional case-law.

It is, as has been reiterated many times in this book, a 'living' document which has evolved from its roots back in 1937. Clauses informed by Catholic Church teachings have long since broken loose of that particular inspirational source.[362] What matters in the Ireland of the twenty-first century is the inherent value of the right actually protected as distinct from its philosophical origin.[363] The rights which are protected – including personal freedom, right of assembly, right of association, freedom of conscience, freedom of religious practice, ownership of private property – are those which are fundamental to liberal democracy and liberal democratic tenets inform the Irish Constitution.

There is also an inchoate sense that Bunreacht na hÉireann failed people in the context of a country rocked by scandals associated with the abuse of children and vulnerable women in recent decades. The horrors of the industrial schools[364] and the related injustices associated with the Magdalen laundries[365] represent a negation of every decent principle, Christian, democratic and human. Well might it be asked, it has been suggested: 'Where was the Constitution when the rights of vulnerable citizens were being violated?' This is a reasonable and understandable reaction, deserving of consideration. The most immediate and direct answer is that no case was brought to the courts to vindicate the rights of these victims. The fact is that 'the sense of justice operates and, for the moment, becomes specified in particular cases';[366] and in the words of Justice Brian Walsh: 'Neither the Constitution nor the courts can be blamed for people's failure to invoke provisions of the Constitution in appropriate cases.'[367]

This failure is partly explained by the limited awareness, for the first two decades of its existence, of how important Bunreacht na hÉireann was as a basic law for a functioning democracy.[368] This began to change with an activist Supreme Court in the 1960s. Garrett Barden has commented that 'constitutions are to be discovered, that is, the constitution people have given themselves in their interaction with one another is to be discovered'.[369] It took more than two decades for the Irish people to discover their Constitution. This discovery was facilitated by a developing discernment of constitutional law as a result of disputed cases.[370]

On a wider level, the values of Irish society, for many decades, were inimical to the vindication of the rights of the most vulnerable members of the community. President Michael D. Higgins has observed that 'land and private property, a restrictive religiosity and a repressive pursuit of respectability, affecting in particular women, became the defining social and cultural ideals of the newly independent Ireland ...'[371] The unmarried mother was a cause of shame to 'respectable' families. Unregulated sexual activity threatened the stability of a social order built on the foundations of farm holdings and violated the teachings of a Catholic Church obsessed with sexual morality. In effect, there was little sympathy for the 'fallen' woman, who gave birth outside marriage, and for her child.[372] In 1927, an official report stated that 'the illegitimate child, being the proof of the mother's shame, is, in most cases, sought to be hidden at all costs'.[373] The popular view was that children in industrial schools were either criminals or born out of wedlock.[374] With such attitudes prevalent for decades, the rights of mothers and children in such circumstances were not a social priority.

On a more philosophical level, the words of John Kelly are apposite: 'The ultimate protection of human rights in a democracy lies with the people themselves. If they allow villains into government a piece of paper will not protect them from the consequences, nor must they expect a few learned men in wigs and gowns to save [them] ...'[375] For the purposes of this argument, 'government' may be interpreted as meaning any group with authority and power and, in a democratic state, the people must demand accountability from those in positions of power and be especially vigilant in relation to any organisation or institution which is evasive and obstructionist in relation to such accountability. Structures must be put in place to facilitate such vigilance and, above all else, the courts must be accessible to ensure this accountability and the vindication of human rights. 'It is inherent in the nature of Ireland's constitutional system that one of the most valued rights the citizen enjoys is the right of access to the courts.'[376] Therefore, there should be no obstacle to reasonable and necessary access, such as inordinate delays or excessive legal fees.

Notwithstanding the apologetics for Bunreacht na hÉireann, changes must be considered to the document.[377] Among the features which are most frequently criticised are its religious references and tone,[378] the so-called 'pro-life' amendment and its provisions pertaining to women.[379] Regarding the latter, American jurist Francis X. Beytagh has commented that it 'seems unproductive and futile to argue about whether the language of Article 41 is offensive to women in Ireland, for it clearly is'.[380] The failure to acknowledge economic and social rights in the enforceable provisions is regarded by some as a serious omission.[381] In order to engage citizens in the political and constitutional life of the state, there have been calls for the inclusion of a provision to permit popular initiative.[382]

Certainly, the Constitution needs to be amended so that it continues to have normative force. It is a simple fact of political, social and legal life. Society is in constant transition; its fundamental law must reflect this.

> The objective is not to strive for what one might term a 'perfect constitution' or a 'model' constitutional system. Constitutions are human instruments and thus necessarily subject to imperfections from the outset. And, with the passage of time, provisions, concepts and the like, that might have seemed desirable become outdated or prove to be unworkable. This seems both inevitable and is something to be expected.[383]

The conservative secretary of the Department of Justice in the 1930s, Stephen Roche, recognised and acknowledged this fact while serving on the Constitution Review Committee in 1934: 'The men and women of 1964 will be in a better position than we are in 1934 of saying what ought to be regarded, in 1964, as fundamental principles of government and it is impertinence on our part to try and fetter them in advance.'[384] According to Beytagh, 'each generation of persons living under a written constitution needs to reconfirm their support for that document, or else change it through the amending or rewriting process'.[385] Thus Bunreacht na hÉireann needs regular review. In fact, Taoiseach Seán Lemass said, in March 1966, that there was a case for carrying out a general review every twenty-five years or so.[386] The report produced by the Constitution Review Group in 1996, the ten progress reports by the All Party Oireachtas Committee on the Constitution between 1997 and 2006[387] and the deliberations of the Constitutional Convention, established in 2012, confirm the accuracy of this observation.[388] In reality, the recommendations of these bodies have not received the attention they deserve and should serve as the starting-point for any discussions on constitutional reform.

Aspects of the Constitution requiring change need to be identified, but such decisions should be taken in the context of an awareness and acknowledgement of the present basic law's positive features, notably its liberal–democratic character, its ability to vindicate fundamental rights of people living in the state and its adaptability to the changing circumstances of Irish society. These attributes do not receive the attention they deserve in public discourse. There is much truth in Anthony Coughlan's observation, made in 1987, that there is 'little public awareness of the Constitution'.[389] Such awareness would facilitate a more considered and fruitful public discussion. It is not judicious to discard the whole document because parts are disliked, deficient or obsolete. To quote Coughlan again: 'Constitutions are not found on supermarket shelves';[390] the making and un-making of a state's fundamental law are serious matters. Therefore, all the people of Ireland should reflect carefully and wisely on any proposals to change or replace Bunreacht na hÉireann.

CHAPTER **9**

John J. Hearne: Constitution-Maker and Civil Servant

John J. Hearne, as a civil servant, was part of an institution which played a significant role in the life of the independent Irish state. W.T. Cosgrave relied on the wisdom of civil servants after 1922 and it is striking how quickly Éamon de Valera developed a similar relationship with them after Fianna Fáil's election victory in 1932.[1] The deeply conservative de Valera 'had no interest in dismantling the state's power structures and sought only to bend them to his own purposes'.[2] Roy Foster has observed that 'if recent historiography proves one thing it is the importance of civil servants in a history whose official records are carefully obscured by the state apparatus'.[3]

However, Basil Chubb, writing about the modern service, observed that 'it is difficult to describe in general terms the part public servants play in policy making'.[4] Such a description is even more difficult when examining this role in the 1930s. De Valera's conviction in closed government and his obsession with secrecy have already been noted; he required that the civil service 'sink itself in anonymity'.[5] As a consequence, a commentator in the 1950s noted that 'most eminent public servants are featureless, dark shadows against the light of the great events in which they play their mysterious parts'.[6] Notwithstanding these difficulties, this chapter seeks to give a general assessment of Hearne's contribution to the making of Bunreacht na hÉireann in his capacity as a civil servant.

Two invaluable assessments have been made of Hearne's involvement in the process which culminated in the production of the 1937 Constitution. The first was that of Éamon de Valera, quoted in the introductory chapter. He acknowledged Hearne's role as 'architect-in-chief' and 'draftsman' of the document, describing his part in its framing as 'fundamental'.[7] A contemporary colleague and close associate of the legal adviser, Maurice Moynihan, has left an account of the working relationship between Hearne and the President:

The Constitution was de Valera's. He conceived it. Hearne did the drafting and dotted the 'i's' and crossed the 't's'. De Valera was the main architect who inspired, dictated and supervised at every stage. He was more his amanuensis than his architect. De Valera gave oral instructions to Hearne and these were put into legal language. Hearne knew Dev's line of thinking and he interpreted it into draft form. It is important not to over-estimate or under-estimate either de Valera or Hearne. They were a team in creating the Constitution.[8]

Clearly, Hearne's most obvious contribution to Bunreacht na hÉireann was as principal draftsman. When Fianna Fáil veteran C.S. Andrews recorded that he heard de Valera say 'that it was entirely the work of John Hearn [sic] ...' and that his own contribution amounted only to dotting the 'i's' and crossing the 't's' he was, almost certainly, referring to Hearne's drafting skills and their pivotal importance in the production of the document.[9] De Valera greatly valued these skills which had been called upon on many occasions, not least in producing the draft heads of a constitution in 1935. Hearne began work on the state's new basic law at the end of August 1936 and completed the first preliminary draft by 10 March 1937, a period of less than eight months. Michael Forde has commented that, 'whatever quibbles one may have with some of its clauses, it [the Constitution] is a model of superb drafting'.[10]

This achievement must be seen in the context of the difficulties, complexities and problems the drafting of even specific and isolated constitutional amendments has presented in recent decades. According to Gerard Hogan, 'it is a measure of Hearne's talent that he could – and did – draft an entire document with little enough assistance in so short a period'.[11] Addressing the Constitutional Convention in December 2012, he stated that 'it is a testament to Hearne's peerless drafting skills that the Constitution – with very few exceptions – fits together so beautifully and in an integrated whole. Seventy-five years of evolving and ever-changing constitutional case-law are living proof of this'. In a lavish encomium Hogan declared:

> Those who think we could easily start again from scratch have to ask themselves where we would be able to find another Hearne to do this work. But that is a bit like casually saying that we could easily find another Joyce or another Yeats in a new generation of writers.[12]

When de Valera wrote that Hearne was 'architect-in-chief', he was acknowledging Hearne's understanding of his ideas and vision for Bunreacht na hÉireann and the expertise with which he put a legal construct and shape on them. It was always de Valera's Constitution, a fact of which Hearne was acutely aware. Accordingly, the President was, in Moynihan's words, 'the main architect who inspired, dictated and supervised at every stage'. Hearne, however, was much more than his 'amanuensis'; hence, de Valera's description of him as 'architect-in-chief'. The legal adviser was an active participant in all key stages which anticipated the making of the state's new basic law. He was a member of the 1934 Constitution Review Committee which examined the Free State Constitution. He and de Valera discussed the issues relating to a new constitutional dispensation on 30 April and 2 May 1935, the substance of these discussions being recorded by de Valera in the 'squared paper draft'.[13] The draft heads of a constitution 1935, produced by Hearne, issued from these meetings.[14] Having been nominated by the President to draft a new constitution, Hearne drew up a 'Plan of Fundamental Constitutional Law' on 20 August 1936,[15] followed by draft heads in October of the same year.[16] This extent of involvement in the evolution of the state's new basic law facilitated the process whereby he was able to architect, in the precise language of law, de Valera's constitutional ambitions.

De Valera described Hearne's contribution to constitution-making as 'fundamental'. This is a really significant word. As defined in the *Oxford English Dictionary*, it means 'of central importance' and the employment of this word by him is of significance precisely because of 'his fastidious care with regard to words and phrases'.[17] De Valera was not casual in his use of language; rather, to quote R.V. Comerford, 'he was a paragon of circumspection in his choice of words'.[18] His biographers noted that 'he has shown an obsessional interest in dictionaries and exact meanings'.[19] This observation was confirmed by Professor T.D. Williams when he wrote that 'few politicians paid more attention to the significance of detail in the use of words'.[20] When de Valera, therefore, described Hearne's contribution to constitution-making as 'fundamental', he meant it in the full and precise sense of the word.

Crucially, Maurice Moynihan underscored the central nature of the legal adviser's role when he wrote that he and de Valera 'were a team in creating the Constitution'. The 'fundamental' part played by Hearne is apparent in his involvement in all the stages of the constitutional project, from planning to drafting. His draft heads, 1935, became the framework for Bunreacht na hÉireann. He contributed to the shaping of the entire document and, in particular, to specific and important articles. He drafted the formula used in Articles 2 and 3, pertaining to the politically and diplomatically sensitive issue of partition. He gave expression in Articles 12–14 to de Valera's desire that there be a President of Ireland. Articles 26 (referral of a bill to the Supreme Court) and 29 (international relations) reflected his ideas to a great degree. The equality provision in Article 40, 1 was originally of Hearne's devising. All of these provisions were unique features of the new Constitution, having no comparators in the Free State's basic law. Such was de Valera's appreciation of Hearne's understanding of Bunreacht na hÉireann that, when he departed for Canada as Ireland's High Commissioner in 1940, he was consulted, on the Taoiseach's instructions, regarding amendments which were under consideration, a telegram informing him: 'In view of your special knowledge of the Constitution the Taoiseach feels that final preparation of amending measures should not be undertaken before you have had time to re-examine [the] substance of the Constitution ...'[21]

The principal function of a civil servant is to advise his or her minister in the determination of policy. This entails 'collecting and appraising data, analysing problems, defining issues and evaluating possible courses of action'.[22] This is essentially what John Hearne did in the matter of the Constitution. De Valera then took his decisions, but, like any minister, he appreciated that the quality of a decision depended greatly on the nature of the official advice he received. Writing about the modern civil service, Seán Dooney observed:

> The nature of the policy making process illustrates the necessity of official advisers of ability, integrity and independence of thought. To ensure that the advice offered to his [sic] minister is the best available, a civil servant must keep up to date on the subject area of his work and know what is happening in that area in other countries ... It is desirable that their [civil servants'] outlook be fresh and receptive and that they be conversant with modern techniques and ideas.[23]

Applying these standards to Hearne, he was an adviser par excellence. He was an expert in constitutional law, familiar with current developments in the British Commonwealth and other countries. This knowledge was allied with the skills of the consummate draftsman. His independence of thought was evident, for example, in his advocacy of a constitutional court and in his advice, as recorded in the 'squared paper draft'. Commenting again on the modern civil service, Basil Chubb wrote: 'Those who prepare the memoranda, put up the papers and explain the issues to the minister might in some circumstances have an important, even decisive, influence upon the outcome.'[24] This influence will be more decisive, depending on the calibre of mind civil servants bring to their appraisal and analysis of an issue.[25] Hearne's memoranda and advice were presented by an acknowledged constitutional expert and de Valera was aware of this fact. Accordingly, the legal adviser exercised a real and significant influence on the constitution-making process initiated by his minister.

It is interesting to remember that this influential civil servant was an erstwhile Redmondite and Free State supporter, and that de Valera had not only rejected Home Rule but also the Treaty settlement and was regarded by his political opponents as the instigator of the Civil War. Tom Garvin has observed that 'the encounter between rebel-in-office and the bureaucrat has not been well documented'[26] but the professional relationship which existed between de Valera and Hearne may shed some light on such an encounter. The principal foundation of their relationship was the need of the former for the advice and assistance of legal experts in order to realise his constitutional objectives. A fortnight after the Fianna Fáil government was formed in 1932, the Attorney General wrote to Alfred O'Rahilly that matters relating to the Constitution 'have now reached a stage when they must be dealt with as matters of practical politics ... In the course of a discussion with the President we agreed that it is vital that we should have the help of men who have been considering these matters and have ... expert knowledge of them.'[27]

Pre-eminent among such men was Hearne, a key adviser to the previous Cumann na nGaedheal government on issues affecting the Free State and the British Commonwealth. Ronan Fanning has recounted what was probably a pivotal moment in the development of the relationship between minister and civil servant: 'Hearne recalled that one of de Valera's first actions as Minister for External Affairs was to ask for the files on the Commonwealth Conferences of the 1920s. Sometime later, he told Hearne he had read them with interest, adding: "I didn't know ye had done so much".'[28] De Valera recognised and acknowledged Hearne's contribution and the latter appreciated this fact. Speaking in the Seanad on 2 June 1932, the President gave public expression to his sentiments: 'Things were not quite the same in 1921 as they had been since the Imperial Conference of 1926 ... I am prepared to confess that there have been advances made that I did not believe would be made at the time. I am quite willing to confess it ...'[29] The Fianna Fáil leader came to value the freedom and flexibility made possible in confidential discussions on sensitive matters with a limited and loyal group of advisers,[30] including Hearne.

That the two men were nationalists facilitated their relationship. It is important to remember that Hearne was a nationalist whose nationalism had evolved over a period of three decades. Originally an ardent Home Ruler, he came to accept the Treaty settlement and the Free State. He worked for and contributed to the development of Dominion status and Irish sovereignty within the British Commonwealth, subsequently assisting de Valera in dismantling the Treaty. Finally, he helped to redefine Ireland's constitutional status by his involvement in the making of Bunreacht na hÉireann. It may appear, at first glance, that Hearne was a person of no principles or, at least, something of a political and legal chameleon. He was, most definitely, neither – he was, as described in Chapter 6, a legal nationalist. He was always a man of the law; he never abandoned the path of constitutional nationalism. Consequently, his nationalism was informed by and reflected evolving legal and constitutional principles and foundations as they related to Ireland's status and association with Great Britain. In his career, Hearne contributed to this evolution of laws and through them gave expression to his nationalist beliefs.

The interaction between de Valera and Hearne was helped by the fact that both men were of a conservative disposition and committed Catholics. On at least four occasions during his school and teaching career de Valera considered the priesthood,[31] while Hearne actually spent six years in clerical formation. They were both scrupulous in the discharge of their religious duties: the two men were daily communicants.[32] Moreover, they were interested in, and aware of, Catholic social teachings. While certainly not radicals, neither were they reactionaries. Thus, for example, they resisted the triumphalist intolerance of Catholic churchmen in their demands for inclusion of the 'one true church' formula and a denial of recognition of Protestant denominations as churches. They also rejected pressures from conservative civil servants to remove provisions for judicial review.

Undoubtedly, professional relations between de Valera and Hearne were enhanced by a certain temperamental compatibility. Writer Anthony Cronin noted that 'Dev was ... a hob lawyer whose ability to split hairs and evident delight in doing so was far, far greater than those of his Belvedere and Bar Library opponents.'[33] Those who worked with him on purely legal matters testified that he had the mind of a lawyer.[34] He was 'meticulous' in matters of drafting and formulae,[35] 'a sort of professor-type like [US President] Wilson, enamoured of phrases and abstractions.'[36] Former Taoiseach Jack Lynch's first ministerial appointment was as de Valera's parliamentary secretary and one of his responsibilities was liaising with the latter in drafting answers to parliamentary questions. He drove Lynch 'mad' because 'he'd keep on drafting and redrafting answers forever.'[37] Thus de Valera, something of a constitutional lawyer manqué, probably enjoyed, even revelled in, engaging with that most accomplished of legal experts, John Hearne. And according to Hearne's niece, he had great respect for de Valera.[38]

This encounter between 'rebel-in-office' and 'bureaucrat', between de Valera and Hearne, was a positive one. It was characterised by a confident and respectful trust on the part of the minister and exemplary, highly competent and dedicated professionalism on the part of the civil servant. However, the level of regard the minister had for his civil servant suggests that it was not, in fact, a typical encounter. It is important, moreover, not to overstate the extent to which de Valera was a rebel. In reality, he was a naturally cautious and conservative politician, who opted for the path of constitutionalism when he and his party entered the Dáil in 1927. The description by Seán Lemass of Fianna Fáil as a 'slightly constitutional party' was made in the heat of the moment[39] and, while certainly dramatic and eminently quotable, was essentially meaningless; as meaningless as describing a woman two months into pregnancy as 'slightly pregnant'.[40] In 1927, Fianna Fáil embarked on the road of parliamentary politics led by an erstwhile 'rebel' who later exulted in the political hegemony achieved by his embrace of constitutional politics. De Valera's espousal of such politics facilitated the development of a professional relationship with Hearne, who never deviated from constitutionalism. Though setting out from divergent political positions – Home Ruler and Sinn Féiner – there was a convergence of opinion in the 1930s as both men collaborated in the pursuit of a redefinition of Ireland's constitutional relationship with Britain.

John Hearne engaged in constitution-making at a time of great political turbulence, domestically and internationally. Irish politics were riven by the vitriolic bitterness of Civil War divisions which had been rekindled by de Valera's accession to power in 1932. The Blueshirts were a potent expression of the unresolved differences between the state's two main political parties, Fianna Fáil and Cumann na nGaedheal (later Fine Gael). Extreme republicans were actively subverting the Free State. On the international front, Ireland and Britain were at diplomatic loggerheads over annuities and de Valera's policy of dismantling the Treaty settlement. A Pandora's box of mistrust, recriminations, tensions and barely concealed hatreds distinguished the internal and external politics of the state in the 1930s.

The attitudes of the Fianna Fáil government often reflected these circumstances. The most obvious and universal contribution of politicians to policy making is through 'the formulation of general attitudes, opinions and ideologies'[41] and these are influenced by the prevailing political climate. Politicians are 'passionate, partisan, idealistic, even ideological'; civil servants, by contrast, should be 'prudent, centrist, practical, pragmatic'.[42] On the basis of this model, Hearne displayed many of the qualities of the civil servant and tempered some of de Valera's more ideological responses, such as his approach to the abolition of the oath of allegiance.

John Hearne received his earlier education from the Irish Christian Brothers and, for much of the state's independence, a considerable, even preponderant, proportion of its civil servants were pupils of the brothers' schools.[43] Unlike most of his peers, however, he had the benefit of a university education. Of all those who held the position of departmental secretary between 1923 and 1968, only one quarter were university graduates.[44] This fact of his education may partly explain why, in the discharge of his duties, the legal adviser belied aspects of the Christian-Brother-educated civil service stereotype: 'intellectually able, hardworking, but overly practical and concerned with short term objectives'.[4] Hearne was certainly intelligent and hardworking but he did think of the future implications of his advice. His whole engagement in policy making at Imperial Conferences and in relation to the Constitution was testimony to this; by definition, he was involved in projects that would impact on the longer-term development of the state and he thought in such terms. He was a practical adviser but he was much more than that. He was also a man of vision who had a philosophical sense of the state's new basic law: for him it represented, as has been quoted many times, 'the restoration of an uninterrupted national vision' and he regarded a nation's laws 'as much a part of its national life as are its language, its literature and its arts'.

Undoubtedly, John Hearne's greatest contribution to Bunreacht na hÉireann was his concern for the fundamental rights of citizens and the vindication of these same rights by a robust system of judicial review. In this concern he was motivated by his strong sense of human dignity which he regarded as a basic attribute of the human person. These beliefs were rooted in the deep religious convictions of his committed Catholicism. He was acutely aware of the reality that a new constitution was being drafted at a period of history when democracy was under threat throughout Europe. Dictatorship was replacing democratic governance and the rights of the state were overwhelming those of individual citizens. At the time of the Dáil debate on the draft Constitution, Poland, Lithuania, Yugoslavia, Austria, Estonia, Germany, Bulgaria, Latvia, Greece, Italy and Spain had all succumbed to the rule of dictators.[46]

The tyranny of dictatorial rule in Europe cast a shadow over the making of Ireland's Constitution, but those most closely involved in the process, de Valera and Hearne, rejected, decisively and definitively, the malign influences of European totalitarianism on the country's new basic law. At a time when democracy was being denied to so many of Europe's citizens, the Irish people were presented, in a plebiscite, with a constitution founded on the principles of democratic government, fundamental rights, the state's obligation to vindicate these rights and popular sovereignty. It was one of the finer moments in the history of independent Ireland.

John Hearne: the man

At this juncture it may be appropriate to give a brief account of the kind of person John Hearne was, the man behind the persona of constitution-maker and lawyer. His colleague Maurice Moynihan remembered him as 'lively, vivacious and very articulate ... highly intelligent and widely read'.[47] In his diary entry for 15 January 1935, historian Nicholas Mansergh recorded a visit to Hearne at the Department of External Affairs and described him as being in 'his best form and widely discursive'. This brief entry conveys Mansergh's pleasure at his meeting with an interesting man whose conversation was worth noting.[48] His niece remembers a humble, unassuming man with a great sense of humour. She recalls him as being very patriotic – 'one who loved every blade of grass in the country'. She visited him in Canada while he was serving there as Ireland's High Commissioner and is able to repeat his advice to her: as a young visitor she should always conduct herself with dignity, remembering that she was, in her person, a representative of Ireland abroad, 'an ambassador for her country'.[49]

Hearne possessed a remarkable toughness and resilience of character. He is remembered by one who knew him well as a man of very definite and strict views,[50] an aspect of his character apparent in his memoranda to his political superiors. These characteristics were the legacy of his involvement in Waterford's Redmondite politics. In Chapter 1, it was recorded that he played a prominent part in the March 1918 by-election, remembered by Sinn Féin participants as an especially turbulent affair. One of them noted that the contest was 'fiercely fought and marked with much rioting, intimidation and factionism'.[51] Another wrote that he later met men who had served in IRA flying columns and 'they all told me that they would prefer to repeat the service they had given in the IRA columns rather than serve in an election campaign in Waterford'.[52]

Allowing for an inevitable exaggeration, there is, nevertheless, an essential truth in the recorded impressions. This was the fractious political climate in which the young Hearne operated. He served in the Free State army during the turmoil of the Civil War; while later, as legal adviser at the Department of External Affairs, he had to contend with the arrogant obstructionism of British civil servants intent upon thwarting the Irish policy of developing the country's sovereignty. John Hearne was a reserved and scholarly man but he also experienced and successfully endured the pressures and tensions of political and diplomatic strife.

On 10 June 1933, Hearne married Monica Mary Martin (1908–79), with whom he had three sons, Maurice, David and Justin, and one daughter, Mary.

Epilogue: John Hearne's diplomatic career and later life, 1939–1969

On 20 June 1939, Hearne was called to the Inner Bar in recognition of his work on the Constitution.[53] In that same year, Ireland established diplomatic relations with Canada and he was appointed High Commissioner to Ottawa.[54] This was the beginning of a new phase in his career, that of full-time diplomat. However, his position as legal adviser at the Department of External Affairs meant that he had diplomatic experience prior to this appointment. Only a brief survey of this aspect of his career need be given here. He was involved in the work of the Free State delegation to the League of Nations, being one of the core members during the 1930s.[55] A substitute delegate in 1931 and 1932, he was a delegate for the four years from 1934 to 1938.[56] He was cool-headed and had excellent diplomatic judgement.[57] Ireland was elected to the Council of the League in 1930. This was a significant achievement for a young state seeking to assert an independent role in international affairs and not merely as a Dominion of the British Commonwealth.

The following year, Hearne made it clear how the Free State saw its role in the League of Nations: 'The Irish Free State had made it perfectly clear, both before and at the time of its election to the council, that it did not seek election on the grounds that it had associations with other states.'[58] When Fianna Fáil won the 1932 general election, Éamon de Valera found himself President of the Council of the League. On his first appearance in Geneva in September 1932, he delivered a very hard-hitting speech concerning the perception that the League of Nations was ineffectual.[59] The text may have been prepared in draft by Hearne.[60]

Hearne served as High Commissioner in Canada from 1940 to 1950. It was perhaps serendipitous that it was in Canada that the Taoiseach, John A. Costello, announced Ireland's intention to leave the Commonwealth.[61] Thus Hearne was present at the announcement of the final stage in the evolution of the country's constitutional relationship with Great Britain and the Commonwealth, the nature of which relationship had consumed so much of his professional career from 1926, when he attended his first Imperial Conference, to 1937, when he played a significant role in the making of Bunreacht na hÉireann

In 1950, he was appointed Ambassador to the United States, the first Irish diplomat to hold the post at ambassadorial level.[62] He retired on 4 November 1960 and, for the next two years, served as a parliamentary draftsman and legislative consultant to the government of Nigeria. Hearne died of cancer on 29 March 1969, at St Vincent's Private Nursing Home, Dublin. His funeral, two days later, was attended by numerous public figures, including President Éamon de Valera, Seán Lemass, Frank Aiken, Liam Cosgrave and Chief Justice Cearbhall Ó Dálaigh. John Hearne is buried in Dean's Grange Cemetery, Dublin.[63]

There were no grandiloquent words spoken over the grave of this essentially modest and self-effacing man whose contribution to the life of the modern Irish state lay hidden behind the anonymity of his civil service persona. Now, with a greater appreciation of his fundamental role in the making of Bunreacht na hÉireann, perhaps the words of Cicero may serve as an epitaph for John Joseph Hearne, constitution-maker: *Salus populi suprema lex* [The welfare of the people shall be the supreme law].

ENDNOTES

Introduction

1 The description of Constitution Day is based on accounts in the following newspapers, all published on 30 December 1937: *Irish Independent, Irish Press, Irish Times.*

2 National Library of Ireland, Ms. 25,508.

3 Basil Chubb, *The Government and Politics of Ireland* (London: Longman, second edition, 1982), p. 263.

4 Anne Chambers, *T.K.Whitaker: Portrait of a Patriot* (London: Doubleday Ireland, 2014), p. 141.

5 *Dáil Debates*, 14 December 1965, 802–3.

6 Colin Murphy, 'On the Origin of the Species', *Law Society Gazette*, October 2012, 24. This article is based on an interview with Judge Gerard Hogan, on the occasion of the publication, in 2012, of Hogan's *The Origins of the Irish Constitution 1928–1941.*

7 Terry de Valera, *A Memoir* (Dublin: Currach Press, 2004), p. 51.

8 F.S.L. Lyons, *Ireland since the Famine* (Glasgow: Fontana/Collins, 1975), p. 538.

9 Sir Andrew Gilchrist, 'Extracts from conversation with President de Valera; Mr Aiken also present, February 27, 1967'; reproduced in Diarmaid Ferriter, *Judging Dev* (Dublin: Royal Irish Academy, 2007), p. 212.

10 T. Ryle Dwyer, *De Valera: The Man and the Myths* (Dublin: Poolbeg Press, 1991), pp. 334–5.

11 Tim Pat Coogan, *De Valera: Long Fellow, Long Shadow* (London: Hutchinson, 1993), p. 703.

12 Earl of Longford and Thomas P. O'Neill, *Eamon de Valera* (London: Arrow Books, 1970), p. 290.

13 *Ibid.*, p. 291.

14 T.P. O'Neill and P. Ó Fiannachta, *De Valera*, vol. ii, p. 326. It would appear that de Valera confused the names of the two brothers and civil servants, John and Maurice Moynihan. Maurice was the person most involved with the Constitution, not John.

15 *Irish Times*, 31 March 1969.

16 *Irish Independent*, 31 March 1969.

17 Dermot Keogh, *The Vatican, the Bishops and Irish Politics 1919–1939* (Cambridge: Cambridge University Press, 1986), p. 208.

18 Dermot Keogh, 'The Irish Constitutional Revolution: An Analysis of the Making of the Constitution', in Frank Litton (ed.), *The Constitution of Ireland 1937–1987* (Dublin: Institute of Public Administration, 1988), p. 8.

19 *Irish Times*, 8 April 1987. See also Brian Kennedy, 'John Hearne and the Irish Constitution (1937)', *Eire-Ireland*, Summer 1989, pp. 121–7.

20 Dermot Keogh and Andrew McCarthy, *The Making of the Irish Constitution 1937* (Cork: Mercier Press, 2007),p. 65.

21 Seán Faughnan, 'The Jesuits and the Drafting of the Irish Constitution of 1937', *Irish Historical Studies*, xxvi, no. 101, May 1988, p. 79.

22 See Ferriter, *Judging Dev*, p. 197.

23 Bill Kissane, *New Beginnings: Constitutionalism and Democracy in Modern Ireland* (Dublin: University College Dublin Press, 2011), p. 70.

24 Gerard Hogan, 'De Valera, the Constitution and the Historians', *Irish Jurist*, 41, 2005, p. 319.

25 See O'Neill and Ó Fiannachta, *De Valera*, vol. ii, p. 328.

26 Ronan Fanning, 'Mr de Valera Drafts a Constitution', in Brian Farrell (ed.), *De Valera's Constitution and Ours* (Dublin: Gill and Macmillan, 1988), p. 36.

27 See Faughnan, 'The Jesuits and the Drafting of the Irish Constitution', p. 102.

28 Maurice Hearne, Papers relating to a proposed biography of John J. Hearne, 'Constitution April 1935–December 1937'.

29 J.J. Lee, *Ireland 1912–1985: Politics and Society* (Cambridge: Cambridge University Press, 1989), p. 202.

30 UCDA, Papers of Sean and Maurice Moynihan, P122/150(92), John Hearne to Maurice Moynihan, 7 November 1963.

31 *Eamon de Valera: A Survey by the Irish Times of the Life and Influences of a Famous Leader* (An Irish Times Publication, 1976), p. 67. The other achievement was the Anglo-Irish Agreement, 1938.

32 See Coogan, *De Valera*, p. 489.

Chapter 1

1   http://www.census.nationalarchives.ie/pages/1901/waterford/waterford urban no 4/william street/1762797/. Accessed 25 October 2014.

2   Information provided by Mrs Alice Bowen, niece of John J. Hearne. Interviewed by the author, 14 December 2013.

3   Waterford City Archives (hereafter WCA), Freedom of Waterford City Roll Book, TNC 1/5. I am grateful to Mr Richard McNamara, former executive legal officer to the Chief Justice, for this reference.

4   W.E. Vaughan and A.J. Fitzpatrick (eds), *Irish Historical Statistics: Population 1821–1971* (Dublin: Royal Irish Academy, 1978), p. 35.

5   *Ibid.*

6   Thomas Dooley, *Irishmen or English Soldiers? The Times and World of a Southern Catholic Irish Man (1876–1916) Enlisting in the British Army During the First World War* (Liverpool: Liverpool University Press, 1995), pp. 17, 20.

7   Emmet O'Connor, *A Labour History of Waterford* (Waterford: Waterford Trades Council, 1989), pp. 70–1.

8   See Dooley, *Irishmen or English Soldiers?* p. 14.

9   *Ibid.*, p. 11.

10 *Ibid.*, p. 14.

11 http://www.census.nationalarchives.ie/pages/1901/Waterford/WaterfordUrban No 4/William Street/1762797; http://www.census.nationalarchives.ie/pages/1911/Waterford/Waterford No 4 Urban part of/Johns Hill/670702. Accessed 25 October 2014.

12 R.F. Foster, *Vivid Faces: The Revolutionary Generation in Ireland 1890–1923* (London: Allen Lane, 2014), p. 52.

13 Maurice Hearne, Papers relating to a proposed biography of John J. Hearne, 'The Army and the Civil War', unpaginated.

14 This account of Richard Hearne's life is based on an obituary published in the *Waterford News*, 3 May 1929.

15 Patrick M. Egan, *History, Guide and Directory of the County and City of Waterford* (Kilkenny, 1894), p. 445. For an account of Hearne and Cahill see Michelle O'Neill, *Reminiscences of Waterford* (Waterford, 1997), pp. 53–4.

16   *Waterford News*, 24 March 1933.

17   *Ibid.*, 16 April 1948.

18   I am grateful to Mr Richard McNamara for this information.

19   See Egan, *History*, p. 230.

20   *Waterford News*, 3 May 1929.

21   *Ibid.*

22   *Ibid.*, 27 April 1900.

23   WCA, LA1/1/A/25, Minutes of Waterford Corporation, 23 February 1901.

24   *Waterford News*, 26 January 1901.

25   *Ibid.*, 1 March 1901.

26   WCA, LA1/1/A/25, Minutes of Waterford Corporation, 23 January 1902.

27   WCA, LA1/1/A/25, Minutes of Waterford Corporation, 7 January 1902.

28   WCA, LA1/1/A/25, Freedom of the City Roll, TNC 1/5.

29   *Waterford News*, 13 December 1901.

30   See Egan, *History*, p. 426.

31   *Waterford News*, 3 May 1929.

32   *Munster Express*, 10 January 1920.

33   *Ibid.*, 10 May 1929.

34   WCA, LA1/1/A/38, Minutes of Waterford Corporation, 3 May 1929.

35   Barry Coldrey, *Faith and Fatherland: The Christian Brothers and the Development of Irish Nationalism 1838–1921* (Dublin: Gill and Macmillan, 1988), p. 67.

36   Edmund Downey, *The Story of Waterford* (Waterford, 1914), p. 37.

37   See Coldrey, *Faith and Fatherland*, pp. 67–84.

38   *Ibid.*, p. 174.

39   http://www.census.nationalarchives.ie/pages/1901/Waterford   Urban   No   4/William Street/1762797/. Accessed 25 October 2014.

40   UCDA, Maurice Moynihan Papers, P122/150(92), John Hearne to Maurice Moynihan, 7 November 1963.

41   See Foster, *Vivid Faces*, p. 33.

42   John J. Hearne Papers, Address at the St Patrick's Day banquet held in New Orleans, Louisiana, 18 March 1957, p. 9.

43   I am grateful to Mr Richard McNamara for this information, which he obtained from Fr Paul Murphy, a former President of St John's College.

44   See Egan, *History*, pp. 415–16.

45   Letter from Revd Dermot Farrell, President, St Patrick's College, Maynooth, to Maurice Hearne, 23 May 1997. The departure date of students from the college was not recorded prior to 1940. This letter was part of the research undertaken by Maurice Hearne for his proposed biography of his father. My appreciation to Ms Bernadette Kilduff for furnishing me with a copy.

46   Susan Denham, 'Waterfordian John J. Hearne: A Drafter of the Irish Constitution', p. 18. This lecture was delivered in the Large Room, City Hall, Waterford, on 10 November 2014, as part of a series of talks organised by Waterford Treasures Museum to mark the 1,100 years since the foundation of Waterford City. I am grateful to Mrs Justice Denham for a copy of the lecture.

47   *Ibid.*

48   Maurice Hearne, 'Proposed Contents of Proposed Biography of John J. Hearne 1893–1969', point (e).

49   Coilin D. Owens and Joan N. Radner (eds), *Irish Drama 1900–1980* (Washington DC: Catholic University of America Press, 1990), p. 169.

50   For the full text of the play see *ibid.*, pp. 171–208.

51   *Ibid.*, p. 194.

52 Details of the clerical career of Revd Maurice Hearne, obtained from the archives of the Catholic Diocese of Waterford and Lismore. My thanks to Fr Gerry Chestnutt for accessing this information.

53 See Hearne, 'Proposed Contents', point (e).

54 Dermot Keogh and Andrew McCarthy, *The Making of the Irish Constitution 1937* (Cork: Mercier Press, 2007), p. 66.

55 Interview with Mrs Alice Bowen, 14 December 2013.

56 See Hearne, 'Proposed Contents', point (s).

57 Letter in the possession of Mrs Alice Bowen.

58 E-mail from Fr Ignatius Fennessy, OFM, to the author, 23 April 2013.

59 See Hearne, 'Proposed Contents', point (u).

60 John J. Hearne Papers, Address delivered at the Commencement Exercises, University of Notre Dame, 4 June 1950, pp. 11, 13.

61 University College Dublin, *Calendar for Session 1922–23*, p. 732.

62 I am grateful to Mr Richard McNamara for this information which he obtained from the King's Inns.

63 *Freeman's Journal*, autumn 1919, undated. I am grateful to Mr Charles Lysaght for giving me a copy of this newspaper account.

64 www.kingsinns.ie/cmsfiles/current students/Auditor1830-King's-Inns.pdf. Accessed 8 December 2014.

65 *Freeman's Journal*. See note 63.

66 Brian Walker (ed.), *Parliamentary Election Results in Ireland 1801–1922* (Dublin: Royal Irish Academy, 1978), pp. 184–5.

67 Bureau of Military History (hereafter BMH), Witness Statement no. 1,741, William V. O'Donoghue, p. 38.

68 BMH, Witness Statement no. 1,105, Nicholas Whittle, p. 9.

69 *Standard*, 16 March 1918.

70 See Whittle Statement, p. 22.

71 Dermot Meleady, *John Redmond: Parnellite* (Cork: Cork University Press, 2008), pp. 194–7.

72 Walker, *Election Results*, pp. 149, 156, 163, 169, 176, 182.

73 See Egan, *History*, p. 411.

74 For an account of this organisation see Dooley, *Irishmen or English Soldiers*, pp. 73–9.

75 *Ibid.*, p. 87. For an account of how effective Redmond's organisation was in dealing with any threats to its position from organised labour see Emmet O'Connor, 'The Influence of Redmondism on the Development of the Labour Movement in Waterford in the 1890s', *Decies*, no. 10, pp. 37–42.

76 Michael Wheatley, *Nationalism and the Irish Party: Provincial Ireland 1910–1916* (Oxford: Oxford University Press, 2005), p. 25. In his study of the Irish Party, Wheatley concentrates on five counties: Leitrim, Roscommon, Sligo, Longford and Westmeath. His observations apply equally to Waterford.

77 Patrick Maume, *The Long Gestation: Irish Nationalist Life 1891–1918* (Dublin: Gill and Macmillan, 1999), p. 204.

78 For newspaper reports of the violence and disorder see *Munster Express*, 16, 23 March 1918; *Standard*, 23 March 1918.

79 See Whittle Statement, pp. 4–8.

80 *Standard*, 27 March 1918.

81 *Ibid.*, 13 March 1918.

82 *Ibid.*, 16 March 1918.

83 *Ibid.*, 20 March 1918.

84 *Ibid.*

85 *Munster Express*, 16 March 1918.

86 See Walker, *Election Results*, p. 185.

87 William Redmond (1861–1917), younger brother of John Redmond – MP for various constituencies over a period of nearly thirty-four years. He joined the British army on the outbreak of World War One and was killed in action on 7 June 1917. For an account of his life see Terence Denham, *A Lonely Grave: The Life and Death of William Redmond* (Dublin: Irish Academic Press, 1995).

88 Darrell Figgis (1882–1925), novelist and playwright; he was involved with Erskine Childers in the Howth gun-running in 1914. He was acting chairman of the committee which framed the Constitution of the Irish Free State in 1922.

89 *Standard*, 27 March 1918.

90 *Munster Express*, 22 June 1918.

91 Dermot Meleady, *John Redmond: The National Leader* (Dublin: Merrion, 2014), p. 98.

92 See Foster, *Vivid Faces*, p. 61.

93 *Munster Express*, 2 November 1918.

94 Thomas Francis Meagher (1823–1867), born in Waterford and one of the leaders of the 1848 rebellion.

95 Thomas Sexton (1848–1932), born in County Waterford; he served as a Home Rule MP in various constituencies, 1880–96.

96 Edmund Leamy, MP, City of Waterford, 1880–85.

97 Thomas Kettle (1880–1916), MP for East Tyrone; he joined the British army in 1916. Killed in action in September 1916.

98 Senia Pašeta, *Before the Revolution: Nationalism, Social Change and Ireland's Catholic Elite 1879–1922* (Cork: Cork University Press, 1999), p. 129.

99 *Munster Express*, 2 November 1918.

100 *Freeman's Journal*, 19 November 1918.

101 *Standard*, 7 December 1918.

102 *Ibid.*, 14 December 1918.

103 *Freeman's Journal*, 13 December 1918.

104 *Ibid.*, 14 December 1918.

105 BMH, Witness Statement no. 1392, Edmund John Ryan, p. 3.

106 *Irish Independent*, 14 December 1918.

107 *Ibid.*, 16 December 1918.

108 See Meleady, *Redmond: National Leader*, p. 458.

109 John J. Hearne Papers, Text of address delivered at the annual meeting of the Harvard Law School Association of New Jersey, Newark, New Jersey, 23 May 1957, p. 1.

110 See Pašeta, *Before the Revolution*, p. 4.

111 See Wheatley, *Nationalism and the Irish Party*, p. 266.

112 See Foster, *Vivid Faces*.

113 Tom Garvin, *Nationalist Revolutionaries in Ireland 1858–1928* (Oxford: Clarendon Press, 1987).

114 See Foster, *Vivid Faces*, pp. xv–xvi.

115 *Ibid.*, p. 295.

116 *Ibid.*, p. 28.

117 Patrick Maume, 'Introduction', in Lawrence William White and James Quinn (eds), *1916: Portraits and Lives* (Dublin: Royal Irish Academy, 2015), p. 5.

118 See Foster, *Vivid Faces*, p. 260.

119 Quoted in *ibid.*, p. 21.

120 *Ibid.*, p. 1.

121 *Ibid.*, p. xxii.

122 *Ibid.*, p. 8.

123 *Ibid.*, p. 11.

124 See Garvin, *Nationalist Revolutionaries*, p. 21.
125 *Ibid.*, p. 14.
126 See Foster, *Vivid Faces*, p. 4.
127 *Ibid.*, p. 70.
128 See Pašeta, *Before the Revolution*.
129 *Ibid.*, p. 3.
130 *Ibid.*, p. 66.
131 Quoted in Senia Pašeta, 'Ireland's Last Home Rule Generation: The Decline of Constitutional Nationalism in Ireland, 1916–30', in Mike Cronin and John M. Regan (eds), *Ireland: The Politics of Independence 1922–49* (London: Macmillan Press, 2000), p. 13.
132 See Pašeta, *Before the Revolution*, p. 153.
133 *Ibid.*, p. 154.

Chapter 2

1 Interview with Mrs Alice Bowen, John Hearne's niece, 14 December 2013. Mrs Bowen knew her uncle well and he was very much in the Cumann na nGaedheal–Fine Gael political tradition.
2 Patrick Maume, *The Long Gestation: Irish Nationalist Life 1891–1918* (Dublin: Gill and Macmillan, 1999), p. 215.
3 John M. Regan, *The Irish Counter-Revolution 1921–1936: Treatyite Politics and Settlement in Independent Ireland* (Dublin: Gill and Macmillan, 1999), p. 341.
4 *Ibid.*, p. 142.
5 *Ibid.*, p. 265.
6 Michael Laffan, *Judging W.T. Cosgrave* (Dublin: Royal Irish Academy, 2014), p. 346.
7 Patrick Maume, 'Introduction', in Lawrence William White and James Quinn (eds), *1916: Portraits and Lives* (Dublin: Royal Irish Academy, 2015), p. 5.
8 See Regan, *Counter-Revolution*, pp. 83–90.
9 *Ibid.*, pp. 244–76.
10 John P. McCarthy, *Kevin O'Higgins: Builder of the Irish State* (Dublin: Irish Academic Press, 2006), pp. 1–2.
11 See Regan, *Counter-Revolution*, p. 90.
12 *Ibid.*, p. 87.
13 A phrase used by Regan of O'Higgins in *ibid.*, p. 83, but used here to encompass the entire elite.
14 John M. Regan, 'The Politics of Utopia: Party Organisation, Executive Autonomy and the New Administration', in Mike Cronin and John M. Regan (eds), *Ireland: The Politics of Independence 1922–49* (London: Macmillan Press, 2000), p. 42.
15 Quoted in Regan, *Counter-Revolution*, p. 147.
16 *Ibid.*, p. 87. The criticism was made by Michael Hayes, Ceann Comhairle (Speaker) after 1922.
17 Maurice Moynihan (ed.), *Speeches and Statements by Eamon de Valera* (Dublin: Gill and Macmillan, 1980), p. 95.
18 See Regan, *Counter-Revolution*, p. 378.
19 *Ibid.*, p. 82.
20 *Ibid.*
21 Brian Farrell, Foreword in Mary Kotsonouris, *Retreat from Revolution: The Dáil Courts 1920–24* (Dublin: Irish Academic Press, 1994), p. 3.
22 *Ibid.*, p. 23.
23 Bureau of Military History, Witness Statement 1,751, Cahir Davitt, p. 24.
24 Quoted in Tom Garvin, *1922: The Birth of Irish Democracy* (Dublin: Gill and Macmillan, 1996), p. 94.

25 *Dáil Debates*, 28 September 1922, 927–32.

26 See Davitt Statement, pp. 1–3.

27 *Ibid.*, pp. 23–4.

28 This fact was confirmed by Maurice Hearne to Mr Charles McLysaght. I thank Mr McLysaght for giving me this information.

29 See Davitt Statement, p. 24.

30 Calton Younger, *Ireland's Civil War* (London: Fontana, 1979), pp. 271–2. I am grateful to Mr John Bowen, a grand-nephew of John Hearne, for bringing this reference to my attention.

31 Irish Military Archives, Abstract of Service SDR/1235, Commandant John Joseph Hearne.

32 See Davitt Statement, p. 12.

33 *Ibid.*, p. 23.

34 *Ibid.*, p. 32.

35 Maurice Hearne, Papers relating to a proposed biography of John J. Hearne, 'The Army and the Civil War'.

36 *Ibid.*

37 See Davitt Statement, p. 25.

38 *Ibid.*, pp. 81–2.

39 Quoted in Fergal Davis, *The History and Development of the Special Criminal Court 1922–2005* (Dublin: Four Courts Press, 2006), p. 34.

40 For the text of the letter see Davitt Statement, pp. 97–8.

41 Information provided in an e-mail to the author from the Irish Military Archives, 1 May 2013.

42 Irish Military Archives, Abstract of Service SDR/1235, Commandant John Joseph Hearne.

43 John J. Hearne Papers, Address delivered at the annual meeting of the Harvard Law School Association of New Jersey, Newark, New Jersey, 23 May 1957, p. 2.

44 Basil Chubb, *The Government and Politics of Ireland* (London: Longman, second edition, 1982), p. 257.

45 *Ibid.*, p. 249.

46 Commission of Inquiry into the Civil Service, *Interim Report* (Dublin: Stationery Office, 1934), p. 61, par. 8.

47 T.J. Barrington, *The Irish Administrative System* (Dublin: Institute of Public Administration, 1980), p. 31.

48 Tom Garvin, 'The Aftermath of the Irish Civil War', in Gabriel Doherty and Dermot Keogh (eds), *De Valera's Irelands* (Cork: Mercier Press, 2003), p. 82.

49 Dermot Keogh and Andrew McCarthy, *The Making of the Irish Constitution 1937* (Cork: Mercier Press, 2007), p. 70.

50 See Maurice Hearne, 'Army and Civil War'.

51 Maurice Hearne, 'Proposed Contents of Proposed Biography of John J. Hearne (1893–1969)', point (i).

52 NAI, AGO/2000/22/142, Memorandum from Arthur Matheson to the Attorney General regarding Electricity (Supply) Bill, 1927, p. 2.

53 *Ibid.*, pp. 2–7, with time table attached as an appendix.

54 D.W. Harkness, *The Restless Dominion: The Irish Free State and the British Commonwealth of Nations 1921–31* (London: Macmillan, 1969), p. 13.

55 Michael Kennedy, 'The Foundation and Consolidation of Irish Foreign Policy: 1919–45', in Ben Torna, Michael Kennedy, John Doyle and Noel Dorr (eds), *Irish Foreign Policy*, p. 24.

56 Mahon Hayes and James Kingston, 'Ireland in International Law: the Pursuit of Sovereignty and Independence', in Ben Torna, Michael Kennedy, John Doyle and Noel Dorr (eds), *Irish Foreign Policy* (Dublin: Gill and Macmillan, 2012), p. 72.

57 *Ibid.*

58 Deirdre McMahon, 'Ireland and the Empire-Commonwealth, 1900–1948', in Judith M. Brown and Wm. Roger Louis (eds), *The Oxford History of the British Empire: The Twentieth Century*, vol. iv (Oxford: Oxford University Press, 1999), p. 156.

59 Ged Martin, 'The Irish Free State and the Evolution of the Commonwealth, 1921–49', in Ronald Hyam and Ged Martin (eds), *Reappraisals in British Imperial History* (London: Macmillan Press, 1975), p. 204.

60 Nicholas Mansergh, *The Commonwealth Experience* (London: Weidenfeld and Nicolson, 1969), p. 209.

61 See Harkness, *Restless Dominion*, p. 38.

62 NAI, DT S 4754/2, Diarmuid O'Hegarty to John Dulanty, 12 October 1926.

63 Hearne is not included by Aengus Nolan in his list of officials in his account of the 1926 Imperial Conference in *Joseph Walshe: Irish Foreign Policy 1922–1946* (Cork: Mercier Press, 2008), pp. 25–30.

64 *Ibid.*, p. 26.

65 UCDA, John A.Costello Papers, P190/101, Memorandum from John Hearne to the Attorney General, 9 August 1926. See David McCullagh, *The Reluctant Taoiseach: A Biography of John A. Costello* (Dublin: Gill and Macmillan, 2010), p. 77, for a brief discussion of Costello's memorandum on merchant shipping.

66 NAI, DT, S4754/1, 'Representatives on various committees', 25 October 1926.

67 See Mahon and Kingston, 'Ireland and International Law', p. 74.

68 See Harkness, *Restless Dominion*, p. 100.

69 For the full text of the memorandum see *ibid.*, pp. 101–4.

70 Imperial Conference, 1926, *Summary of Proceedings* (London: HM Stationery Office, 1926), p. 14.

71 *Ibid.*, p. 16.

72 *Ibid.*, p. 17.

73 *Ibid.*, pp. 16–17.

74 See Harkness, *Restless Dominion*, pp. 20–7.

75 For an account of its conclusions see Harkness, *Restless Dominion*, pp. 121–2. For the report of the nationality committee see Imperial Conference, 1926. *Appendices to the Summary of Proceedings* (London: HM Stationery Office, 1927), pp. 243–66.

76 Imperial Conference, 1926, *Summary*, pp. 37–9.

77 Imperial Conference, 1926, *Appendices*, p. 268.

78 *Ibid.*, pp. 271–7.

79 *Ibid.*, pp. 266–90.

80 Imperial Conference, 1926, *Summary*, pp. 42–5.

81 Imperial Conference, 1926, *Appendices*, p. 271.

82 *Ibid.*, p. 268.

83 Jason Knirck, *Afterimage of the Revolution: Cumann na nGaedheal and Irish Politics, 1922–1932* (Madison: University of Wisconsin Press, 2014), p. 162.

84 *Ibid.*

85 *Dáil Debates*, 15 December 1926, 712.

86 *Dáil Debates*, 15 December 1926, 726.

87 www.en.wikipedia.org/wiki/Hotel_Cecil_(London). Accessed 10 December 2014.

88 NAI, DT S4754/3, Imperial Conference 1926, 'Accommodation of Saorstát delegation and general financial arrangement'.

89 NAI, DT S4754/3, Imperial Conference 1926, 'Accommodation of Saorstát delegation and general financial arrangement', Diarmuid O'Hegarty to the Minister for Finance, 11 February 1927, 1–3.

90 NAI, DFA 2001/37/444, Personnel file of John Joseph Hearne.

91 For an account of the difficulties faced by the Department of External Affairs in its early years, see Dermot Keogh, *Ireland and Europe 1919–1948* (Dublin: Gill and Macmillan, 1988), pp. 18–26.

92 For some of the contributions from deputies during the debates, see Patrick Keatinge, *The Formulation of Irish Foreign Policy* (Dublin: Institute of Public Administration, 1973), p. 109.

93 See Keogh, *Ireland and Europe*, p. 26. The italics are those of Keogh.

94 See Harkness, *Restless Dominion*, p. 144.

95 Saorstát Éireann, *Report of the Conference on the Operation of Dominion Legislation and Merchant Shipping Legislation 1929* (Dublin: Stationery Office, 1929), pp. 8–9.

96 *Dáil Debates*, 5 June 1929, 791–3.

97 See Harkness, *Restless Dominion*, p. 147.

98 'Extracts from the general preliminary memorandum by John J. Hearne for the Irish delegation to the Conference on the Operation of Dominion Legislation, Dublin, 15 July 1929', in Ronan Fanning, Michael Kennedy, Dermot Keogh and Eunan O'Halpin (eds), *Documents in Irish Foreign Policy, 1926–1932*, III (Dublin: Royal Irish Academy, 2002), pp. 339–49. Hereafter cited as *Documents in Irish Foreign Policy*.

99 See Hearne, 'Preliminary memorandum', p. 346.

100 *Ibid.*, p. 343.

101 *Ibid.*, p. 340.

102 *Ibid.*, p. 346.

103 Hearne cited the ruling of Mr Justice Murnaghan in the case of *Alexander v Circuit Judge of Cork*, [1925] 2 IR, p. 170: see Hearne, 'Preliminary memorandum', p. 341.

104 See Hearne, 'Preliminary memorandum', p. 341.

105 *Ibid.*, p. 342.

106 *Ibid.*, p. 343.

107 *Ibid.*

108 *Ibid.*, pp. 343–4.

109 Thomas Mohr, 'The Foundations of Irish Extra-Territorial Legislation', *The Irish Jurist*, 40, 2005, pp. 107–8.

110 UCDA, Patrick McGilligan Papers, P35/136, John J. Hearne, 'Extra-territorial jurisdiction in international law'.

111 For such views see Mohr, 'Extra-Territorial Legislation', pp. 89–93.

112 See Hearne, 'Extra-territorial jurisdiction'.

113 *Ibid.*

114 *Ibid.*

115 28 & 29 Victoria, c. 63.

116 Thomas Mohr, 'The Colonial Laws Validity Act and the Irish Free State', *The Irish Jurist*, 43, 2009, p. 24.

117 See Mohr, 'Colonial Laws', pp. 31–2.

118 13 Geo. 5 Sess. 2 c.1.

119 See Hearne, 'Preliminary memorandum', pp. 345–6.

120 UCDA, Patrick McGilligan Papers, P35/137, John J. Hearne, 'The principles underlying or embodied in the Colonial Laws Validity Act, 1865'.

121 See Hearne, 'Colonial Laws Validity Act', p. 30. The emphasis is that of Hearne.

122 *Ibid.*, p. 36.

123 *Ibid.*, p. 31. The emphasis is that of Hearne.

124 Quoted in Harkness, *Restless Dominion*, p. 159.

125 See Hearne, 'Preliminary memorandum', p. 346.

126   See NAI, DT S5340/10, 'Sub-conference on Merchant Shipping Legislation: Preliminary
       Memorandum dealing with Administrative Difficulties', issued by the Dominions Office, dated 20
       September 1929, for an indication of the complexity.
127   Imperial Conference, 1926, *Summary*, pp. 18–19.
128   See Harkness, *Restless Dominion*, pp. 112-13.
129   Imperial Conference, 1926, *Summary*, p. 19.
130   NAI, DT S5340/10, John J. Hearne, 'Merchant shipping: Preliminary memorandum'.
131   *Ibid.*, p. 7.
132   *Ibid.*, p. 11.
133   *Ibid.*, p. 22.
134   See Hearne, 'Preliminary memorandum', p. 347.
135   See Hearne, 'Merchant shipping', p. 22.
136   NAI, DT S5340/10, John J. Hearne, 'Proposals for Reciprocity'.
137   *Ibid.*, B8.
138   *Ibid.*, B2.
139   UCDA, John A. Costello Papers, P190/131(5), John J. Hearne, 'Reservation of bills and
       disallowance of acts'.
140   *Ibid.*, p. 7.
141   *Ibid.*, p. 9.
142   *Ibid.*, B1.
143   *Ibid.*, B1 and B2.
144   *Ibid.*, B4.
145   *Ibid.*, B5.
146   *Ibid.*, B6.
147   *Ibid.*, C10 and C11.
148   See Harkness, *Restless Dominion*, p. 151.
149   See Hearne, 'Reservation and disallowance', C11.
150   *Ibid.*, C11 and C12.
151   *Ibid.*, C13.
152   See Knirck, *Afterimage of the Revolution*, p. 198.
153   *Ibid.*, p. 184.
154   See Harkness, *Restless Dominion*, p. 147.
155   Saorstát Éireann, *Report of the Conference on the Operation of Dominion Legislation*, p. 3.
156   NAI, DT S5340; this file contains the minutes of various meetings at the Conference.
157   NAI, DT S5340, Minutes of meeting held on 9 October, pp. 10–11.
158   UCDA, John A. Costello Papers, P190/115(22), Draft minutes of the first meeting of the Colonial
       Laws Validity Act Committee, 31 October 1929.
159   NAI, DT S5340, Minutes of meeting held on 8 October 1929, p. 41.
160   NAI, DT S 5340, Minutes of meeting held on 9 October 1929, p. 10.
161   *Report of Conference on the Operation of Dominion Legislation*, p. 17.
162   NAI, DT S5340, Minutes of meeting held on 11 October 1929.
163   NAI, DT S 5340, Minutes of meeting held on 15 October 1929.
164   UCDA, Patrick McGilligan Papers, P35/150, Minutes of meeting held on 31 October 1929, pp.
       3–4.
165   UCDA, Patrick McGilligan Papers, P35/139, Draft minutes of the first meeting of the Colonial
       Laws Validity Act Committee, 31 October 1929.
166   UCDA, John A. Costello Papers, P190/115(58), Report of Colonial Laws Validity Act
       Committee. For various drafts see UCDA, John A. Costello Papers, P190/115(24); P190/115(25)
       and P190/115(27).

167 *Report of the Conference on the Operation of Dominion Legislation*, pp. 17–26, pars 45–82.

168 *Dáil Debates*, 19 March 1930, 2064.

169 *Report of the Conference on the Operation of Dominion Legislation*, p. 19, par. 53.

170 See Harkness, *Restless Dominion*, p. 152.

171 NAI, DT S5340/13, Diarmuid O'Hegarty to Michael McDunphy, 25 November 1929.

172 NAI, DT S5340/13, 'Report from Diarmuid O'Hegarty on progress which has been made in regard to committee of experts', 12 November 1929.

173 *Report of the Conference on the Operation of Dominion Legislation*, p. 10, par. 15.

174 *Ibid.*, p. 12, par. 23.

175 *Ibid.*, p. 15, pars. 35,36.

176 *Ibid.*, pp. 16–17, pars. 40–4.

177 *Ibid.*, p. 19, par. 50.

178 *Ibid.*, pp. 26–40, pars. 83–124.

179 *Ibid.*, p. 30, par. 92.

180 Quoted in Harkness, *Restless Dominion*, p. 185.

181 See *ibid.*, p. 194, for the committee's terms of reference.

182 See *ibid.*, pp. 196–7, for the composition of all subcommittees.

183 NAI, DT S6006/6, Imperial Conference 1930, Committee on certain aspects of inter-imperial relations.

184 NAI, DT S6009/5.

185 See Imperial Conference, 1930, Summary *of Proceedings*, pp. 19–21, for the schedule containing the main provisions of the Statute of Westminster.

186 *Ibid.*, 'Annex: Draft Agreement as to British Commonwealth Merchant Shipping', pp. 32–7.

187 NAI, DT S6009/6, Imperial Conference 1930, Committee on certain aspects of inter-imperial relations, Minutes of meeting, 24 October 1930, p. 5.

188 Imperial Conference, 1930, Summary, p. 33, Article 5.

189 *Ibid.*, p. 34, Article 10.

190 *Ibid.*, p. 33, Article 2, 2.

191 NAI, DT S5340/10, Saorstát Éireann, Treaty Series 1931, No. 8, *British Commonwealth Merchant Shipping Agreement, London, 10 December 1931.*

192 See Harkness, *Restless Dominion*, p. 200.

193 *Report of the Conference on the Operation of Dominion Legislation*, p. 25, par. 75.

194 *Ibid.*, p. 25, par. 78.

195 *Ibid.*, p. 25, par. 79.

196 UCDA, Desmond FitzGerald Papers, P80/603, John Hearne to Desmond FitzGerald, 10 September 1930.

197 Quoted in Harkness, *Restless Dominion*, p. 201.

198 See Harkness, *Restless Dominion*, p. 202.

199 Quoted in Harkness, *Restless Dominion*, pp. 201–2.

200 See Harkness, *Restless Dominion*, p. 202.

201 Imperial Conference, 1930, Summary, pp. 21–2.

202 See Harkness, *Restless Dominion*, pp. 193–4.

203 *Ibid.*, p. 199.

204 *Ibid.*, p. 200.

205 *Ibid.*, p. 186.

206 Quoted in *ibid.*, p. 199.

207 *Documents in Irish Foreign Policy*, III, p. xii.

208 See Hayes and Kingston, 'Ireland in International Law', p. 76.

209 See Nolan, *Joseph Walshe*, p. 40.

210   Their dates of birth are as follows: Costello, 1891; FitzGerald, 1889; McGilligan, 1889; O'Hegarty, 1892; Walshe, 1886; and Hearne, 1893.

211   *Dáil Debates*, 16 July 1931, 2307.

212   See Harkness, *Restless Dominion*, p. 147.

213   *Ibid.*, p. 176.

214   See McCullagh, *Reluctant Taoiseach*, p. 76.

215   *Dáil Debates*, 16 July 1931, 2291.

216   Quoted in Harkness, *Restless Dominion*, p. 91.

217   See Hearne, 'Preliminary memorandum', p. 339.

218   *Ibid.*, p. 340.

219   NAI, DT S2204, Joseph P. Walshe to Éamon de Valera, Memorandum on the oath, 21 March 1932. The memorandum was written by Hearne.

220   See Knirck, *Afterimage of the Revolution*, p. 192.

221   See Martin, 'The Irish Free State and the Evolution of the Commonwealth, 1921–49', pp. 201–23. See also Donal Lowry, 'New Ireland, Old Empire and the Outside World 1922–49: The Strange Evolution of a "Dictionary Republic"', in Mike Cronin and John M. Regan (eds), *Ireland: The Politics of Independence* (London: Macmillan Press, 2000), pp. 170–1, for a brief but valuable summary of the historiography of Commonwealth evolution.

222   *Documents in Irish Foreign Policy*, III, p. xii.

223   Quoted in Paul Canning, *British Policy towards Ireland 1921–1941* (Oxford: Clarendon Press, 1985), p. 113.

224   For an examination of the history of the Privy Council and the Irish Free State, see Thomas Mohr, *Guardian of the Treaty: The Privy Council Appeal and Irish Sovereignty* (Dublin: Four Courts Press, 2016). See also Thomas Mohr, 'Law without Loyalty: the Abolition of the Irish Appeal to the Privy Council', *Irish Jurist*, 37, 2002, pp. 187–226. For a valuable contemporary account of the issues at stake see Hector Hughes, *National Sovereignty and Judicial Autonomy in the British Commonwealth of Nations* (London: P.S. King, 1931).

225   Article 2 reads as follows: 'Subject to the provisions hereinafter set out, the position of the Irish Free State in relation to the imperial parliament and government and otherwise shall be that of the Dominion of Canada, and the law, practice and constitutional usage governing the relationship of the Crown or the representative of the Crown and of the imperial parliament to the Dominion of Canada shall govern their relationship to the Irish Free State'.

226   See Harkness, *Restless Dominion*, p. 113.

227   See Hughes, *National Sovereignty*, p. 78. See Mohr, 'Law without Loyalty', pp. 191–3, for details of some of the cases.

228   See Hughes, *National Sovereignty*, p. 90.

229   Quoted in *ibid.*, p. 76.

230   In addition to these considerations the British government regarded the appeal as an important safeguard of the rights of Ireland's minority Protestant population. See Mohr, *Guardian of the Treaty*, pp. 71–89.

231   See *ibid.*, pp. 92–9, and Harkness, *Restless Dominion*, pp. 113–5.

232   'Extracts from a memorandum by John J. Hearne on the abolition of the right to appeal to the Privy Council', *Documents in Irish Foreign Policy*, III, pp. 401–8.

233   See Hearne, 'Privy Council', p. 403.

234   *Ibid.*, p. 404.

235   *Ibid.*, p. 405.

236   *Ibid.*

237   *Ibid.*, p. 406.

238   'Letter from John J. Hearne to Martin Eliasoff, 13 August 1930', *Documents in Irish Foreign Policy*, III, pp. 583–4.

239 See Harkness, *Restless Dominion*, p. 204.

240 NAI, DT S7323: 'Broadcast message of Mr McGilligan re. Privy Council, 9 November 1930'. The address was printed in *The Irish Free State Review*, vol. 41, no. 4, November 1930.

241 NAI, DT S6009, Patrick McGilligan to W.T. Cosgrave, 25 October 1930.

242 See Mohr, *Guardian of the Treaty*, p. 106.

243 See Harkness, *Restless Dominion*, pp. 206–7.

244 NAI, DT S6009, Patrick McGilligan to W.T. Cosgrave, 14 November 1930.

245 See Harkness, *Restless Dominion*, p. 207.

246 UCDA, Patrick McGilligan Papers, P35/167, 'External affairs report on discussions in London with British side, 1 May 1931'.

247 See Harkness, *Restless Dominion*, p. 207.

248 NAI, DT S2002/14/1410, Memoranda re. Bills, 27 May 1931. See also NAI DFA 3/1.

249 NAI, DFA 3/1. For an overview of all the bills see Mohr, 'Law without Loyalty', pp. 194–5.

250 See NAI, D/T S2002/14/1410, Memoranda re. Bills, p. 9.

251 See Dermot Keogh, 'De Valera, the Catholic Church and the "Red Scare", 1931–1932', in J.P. Carroll and John A. Murphy (eds), *De Valera and his Times* (Cork: Cork University Press, 1983), pp. 134–59.

252 Ciara Meehan, *The Cosgrave Party: A History of Cumann na nGaedheal 1923–33* (Dublin: Royal Irish Academy, 2010), p. 190.

253 See Laffan, *Judging W.T. Cosgrave*, p. 301.

254 Fearghal McGarry, 'Southern Ireland, 1922–32: A Free State?' in Alvin Jackson (ed.), *The Oxford Handbook of Modern Irish History* (Oxford: Oxford University Press, 2014), p. 658.

255 UCDA, W.T. Cosgrave Papers, P285/37, John J. Hearne to W.T. Cosgrave, 6 April 1932. Cosgrave's letter to Hearne is not available.

Chapter 3

1 Ronan Fanning, *The Irish Department of Finance 1922–1958* (Dublin: Institute of Public Administration, 1976), p. 216.

2 His son, Maurice Hearne, informed Mr Charles Lysaght of this fact. I am grateful to Mr Lysaght for this information.

3 Michael Laffan, *Judging W.T. Cosgrave* (Dublin: Royal Irish Academy, 2014), p. 306.

4 Richard Dunphy, *The Making of Fianna Fáil Power in Ireland 1923–1948* (Oxford: Clarendon Press, 2005), p. 147.

5 Deirdre McMahon, *Republicans & Imperialists: Anglo-Irish Relations in the 1930s* (New Haven and London: Yale University Press, 1984), p. 23.

6 Earl of Longford and Thomas O Neill, *Eamon de Valera* (London: Arrow Books, 1974), p. 275.

7 Ronan Fanning, *Eamon de Valera: A Will to Power* (London: Faber and Faber, 2015), p. 160.

8 Niall Keogh, *Con Cremin: Ireland's Wartime Diplomat* (Cork: Mercier Press, 2006), p. 9.

9 Donal Lowry, 'New Ireland, Old Empire and the Outside World, 1922–49: The Strange Evolution of a "Dictionary Republic"', in Mike Cronin and John M. Regan (eds), *Ireland: The Politics of Independence 1922–49* (London: Macmillan Press, 2000), p. 176.

10 *Ibid.*

11 Quoted in Aengus Nolan, *Joseph Walshe: Irish Foreign Policy 1922–1946* (Cork: Mercier Press, 2008), p. 59.

12 *Ibid.*, p. 85.

13 *Ibid.*, p. 72.

14 *Ibid.*, p. 63.

15 *Ibid.*, p. 82.

16 *Ibid.*, p. 63.

17 See McMahon, *Republicans and Imperialists*, p. 26.

18 See Fanning, *Eamon de Valera*, p. 160.

19 Maurice Hearne, Papers relating to a proposed biography of John J. Hearne, 'Constitution, April 1935–December 1937'.

20 UCDA, Eamon de Valera Papers, P150/2303, Memorandum by John Hearne, 'Subjects discussed with the President at regular meetings between 27 June and 18 August 1933, and 1 March and 28 May 1934'.

21 Dermot Keogh, 'Profile of Joseph Walshe, Secretary, Department of External Affairs, 1922–46', *Irish Studies in International Affairs*, vol. 3, no. 2, 1990, p. 74.

22 Joseph Lee and Gearóid Ó Tuathaigh, *The Age of de Valera* (Dublin: Ward Press, 1982), pp. 33–4. The chapter from which this quotation is taken was written by Ó Tuathaigh.

23 Diarmaid Ferriter, *Judging Dev* (Dublin: Royal Irish Academy, 2007), p. 70.

24 See McMahon, *Republicans and Imperialists*, p. 16.

25 Leo Kuhn, *The Constitution of the Irish Free State* (London: George Allen and Unwin Ltd., 1932), p. 112.

26 See Laffan, *Cosgrave*, p. 126.

27 Ciara Meehan, *The Cosgrave Party: A History of Cumann na nGaedheal 1923–33* (Dublin: Royal Irish Academy, 2010), p. 47.

28 See Lee and Ó Tuathaigh, *Age of de Valera*, p. 85.

29 See McMahon, *Republicans and Imperialists*, p. 13.

30 Quoted in Lee and Ó Tuathaigh, *Age of de Valera*, p. 63.

31 *Ibid.*

32 Nicholas Mansergh, *The Unresolved Question: The Anglo-Irish Settlement and its Undoing* (New Haven and London: Yale University Press, 1991), p. 282.

33 Joseph Lee, *Ireland 1912–1985: Politics and Society* (Cambridge: Cambridge University Press, 1989), pp. 47–55.

34 See McMahon, *Republicans and Imperialists*, p. 117.

35 *Ibid.*, p. 26.

36 NAI, DT S2264, Joseph Walshe to Eamon de Valera, 21 March 1932, including a memorandum on the oath of allegiance by John Hearne.

37 See McMahon, *Republicans and Imperialists*, pp. 26–7.

38 *Ibid.*, p. 27.

39 *Ibid.*

40 *Ibid.*, p. 47.

41 For an examination of the attitudes and responses of the British government, see *ibid.*, pp. 28–107, *passim*. See also Deirdre McMahon, '"A Transient Apparition": British policy towards the de Valera Government 1932–5', *Irish Historical Studies*, XXII, no. 88, September 1981, pp. 331–61.

42 NAI, DFA Unregistered Papers, 'Memorandum of a conversation between John J. Hearne and Sir Harry Batterbee on the general political situation between Ireland and England, London, 8 July 1932', in Catriona Crowe, Ronan Fanning, Michael Kennedy, Dermot Keogh and Eunan O'Halpin (eds), *Documents on Irish Foreign Policy*, IV, 1932–1936, p. 78. Hereafter cited as *Documents in Irish Foreign Policy*, IV.

43 UCDA, Eamon de Valera Papers, P150/2212, Memorandum to Joseph Walshe from John J. Hearne, 31 March 1932, 'Legal aspects of the oath – the question of the Irish in Great Britain'.

44 So Hearne informed Professor Alfred O'Rahilly of University College, Cork. UCDA, Alfred O'Rahilly Papers, P178/61, John Hearne to Alfred O'Rahilly, 11 May 1932.

45 Thomas Mohr, *Guardian of the Treaty: The Privy Council Appeal and Irish Sovereignty* (Dublin: Four Courts Press, 2016), pp. 130–4.

46   *Ibid.*, p. 134.
47   *Ibid.*
48   *Dáil Debates*, 27 April 1932, 570.
49   *Dáil Debates*, 27 April 1932, 573.
50   For a survey of the history of the oath of allegiance see Jim Maher, *The Oath is Dead and Gone* (Dublin: Londubh Books, 2011).
51   See 'land annuities' in S.J. Connolly (ed.), *The Oxford Companion to Irish History* (Oxford: Oxford University Press, 1998), pp. 295–6.
52   See McMahon, *Republicans and Imperialists*, p. 39.
53   UCDA, Eamon de Valera Papers, P150/2217, Memorandum, 'Treaties and parliament'.
54   UCDA, Eamon de Valera Papers, P150/2217, Memorandum, 'Authority to bind the state, Financial Agreement, 12 February 1923'.
55   See McMahon, *Republicans and Imperialists*, pp. 28–107, *passim*.
56   Imperial Conference, 1930; *Report of Proceedings* (London: HM Stationery Office, 1930), pp. 22–4.
57   See McMahon, *Republicans and Imperialists*, p. 59.
58   *Ibid.*, p. 63.
59   *Documents in Irish Foreign Policy*, IV, 'Memorandum of a conversation between Hearne and Batterbee', p. 78.
60   See McMahon, *Republicans and Imperialists*, p. 59.
61   Imperial Conference, 1930: *Report of Proceedings*, pp. 23–4.
62   See McMahon, *Republicans and Imperialists*, p. 65.
63   *Ibid.*, p. 59.
64   *Documents in Irish Foreign Policy*, IV, 'Memorandum of a conversation between Hearne and Batterbee', p. 80.
65   Deirdre McMahon, 'The Chief Justice and the Governor-General Controversy in 1932', *Irish Jurist*, 17, 1982, p. 146.
66   Brendan Sexton, *Ireland and the Crown, 1922–1936: The Governor-General of the Irish Free State* (Dublin: Irish Academic Press, 1989), p. 122.
67   See McMahon, 'Chief Justice and Governor-General', p. 146.
68   *Ibid.*, pp. 147–51; pp. 151–6.
69   *Ibid.*, pp. 151–2.
70   *Ibid.*, pp. 157–8.
71   UCDA, Eamon de Valera Papers, P150/2220, Memorandum from John J. Hearne to Seán Murphy regarding the letters patent constituting the office of Governor-General, 14 May 1932.
72   UCDA, Eamon de Valera Papers, P150/2220, Memorandum, 'The Governor-General and the Kingdom of Ireland', no date, pp. 4, 7. This memorandum is unsigned and undated, but the style is that of John Hearne.
73   NAI, DT S8532, Memorandum, Department of the President, 20 November 1932, 'Suggested appointment of Chief Justice as Governor-General', Extract from Cabinet Minutes, Cab. 6/94, 22 November 1932, Item no. 4.
74   The Appropriation Bill required signature by the Governor-General and so de Valera had to make an appointment. See 'Handwritten letter from Sean T. O'Kelly to Eamon de Valera, 19 November 1932', *Documents in Irish Foreign Policy*, IV, pp. 206–7. In this letter, O'Kelly made it clear that the Irish government's response to the controversy lacked a sense of coherent planning: 'It is unfortunate that the matter has to be settled, one way or another, so soon. If you had time to work out your line and have the British carry the baby all would be well ...'
75   For an account of Domhnall O'Buachalla's tenure see Sexton, *Ireland and the Crown*, pp. 142–70. For an account of his life and career see Adhamhnán Ó Súilleabháin, *Domhnall Ua Buachalla; Rebellious Nationalist, Reluctant Governor* (Dublin: Merrion Press, 2015).

76   See McMahon, 'Chief Justice and Governor General', p. 160.
77   NAI, DFA Unregistered Papers, 'Memorandum by John J. Hearne on the outstanding questions in British–Irish relations, 6 September 1932', *Documents in Irish Foreign Policy*, IV, p. 113.
78   *Documents in Irish Foreign Policy*, IV, 'Memorandum of a conversation between Hearne and Batterbee', pp. 78–9.
79   See McMahon, *Republicans and Imperialists*, p. 136.
80   NAI, DT 2002/14/1410, Memorandum regarding abolition of application for leave to appeal to the Privy Council, 4 June 1932.
81   For an account of de Valera's abolition of the Privy Council appeal see Mohr, *Guardian of the Treaty*, pp. 130–47.
82   Thomas Mohr, 'Law without Loyalty – the Abolition of the Irish Appeal to the Privy Council', *Irish Jurist*, 37,2002, p. 208; for the facts of the relevant case see pp. 187–9; and pp. 195–208.
83   *Ibid.*, p. 212.
84   *Ibid.*
85   NAI, DT S6757, Memorandum from John Hearne to Eamon de Valera, 'Erne Fisheries Case', pp. 3–5.
86   See Mohr, 'Law without Loyalty', p. 212.
87   For details of the appeal hearing see *ibid.* pp. 213–17.
88   *Ibid.*, p. 217.
89   See Mohr, *Guardian of the Treaty*, p. 146.
90   See Mohr, 'Law without Loyalty', p. 218.
91   See McMahon, *Republicans and Imperialists*, p. 142.
92   NAI, DJ 2005/16/1, Irish Nationality and Citizenship Act, 1935, letter from the secretary of the Department of Justice to the secretary of the Department of Industry and Commerce, 12 October 1934.
93   *Dáil Debates*, 15 November 1934, 333.
94   NAI, DJ 2005/16/1, Irish Nationality and Citizenship Act, 1935, John Hearne to Stephen Roche, 2 January 1935, p. 2.
95   *Dáil Debates*, 14 February 1935, 2049–51.
96   NAI, DT S6820, Constitution Amendment (No. 26) Bill, Memorandum from John Hearne to Maurice Moynihan, 12 November 1934.
97   *Dáil Debates*, 14 February 1935, 2024.
98   NAI, DT S6820, Aliens Bill, Memorandum from John Hearne to Maurice Moynihan, 12 November 1934, p. 1.
99   NAI, DT S6820, Memorandum from John Hearne to Maurice Moynihan, 3 December 1934.
100   *Dáil Debates*, 14 February 1935, 2149.
101   NAI, DT S6820, Aliens Bill, Memorandum from John Hearne to Maurice Moynihan, 12 November 1934, p. 2.
102   Quoted in McMahon, *Republicans and Imperialists*, p. 141.
103   For British reaction to the various bills see McMahon, *Republicans and Imperialists*, pp. 140–3.
104   F.S.L. Lyons, *Ireland since the Famine* (Glasgow: Fontana/Collins, 1973), p. 517.
105   *Dáil Debates*, 22 March 1934, 1461.
106   *Seanad Debates,* 19 May 1936, 2435.
107   *Seanad Debates*, 15 January 1936, 1780–1.
108   *Seanad Debates*, 15 January 1936, 1781.
109   *Irish Times*, 16 January 1936.
110   *Irish Press*, 16 January 1936.
111   *Irish Independent*, 16 January 1936.

112   NAI, TSCH/3/S8529, Senator W.T. Westropp Bennett to Eamon de Valera, 16 January 1936. The letter was read into the record of the house; see *Seanad Debates*, 16 January 1936, 1811–13.

113   NAI, TSCH/3/S8529, Eamon de Valera to Senator W.T. Westropp Bennett, 18 January 1936.

114   *Irish Independent*, 16 January 1936.

Chapter 4

1   For an account of Fianna Fáil's often tempestuous relationship with the Senate see Donal O'Sullivan, *The Irish Free State and its Senate* (London: Faber and Faber, 1940), pp. 301–89.

2   *Dáil Debates*, 17 May 1934, 1168. The articles Costello identified were: 6, 7, 8, 9, 18, 19, 24, 28, 43, 46, 49, 50, 61, 62, 63, 64, 65, 66, 68, 69 and 70.

3   *Dáil Debates*, 17 May 1934, 1169.

4   *Dáil Debates*, 17 May 1934, 1192–3.

5   *Dáil Debates*, 17 May 1934, 1193.

6   *Dáil Debates*, 17 May 1934, 1249.

7   NAI, DT S2979, Memorandum by Michael McDunphy, Department of the President, 24 May 1934.

8   For very informative biographical sketches of the four civil servants see Dermot Keogh and Andrew McCarthy, *The Making of the Irish Constitution 1937* (Cork: Mercier Press, 2007), pp. 65–8.

9   For the minutes of all the meetings see Gerard Hogan, *The Origins of the Irish Constitution* (Dublin: Royal Irish Academy, 2012), pp. 48–73.

10   NAI, DT S2979, Minutes of the second meeting of the Constitution Review Committee, 29 May 1934.

11   NAI, DT S2979, Memorandum by Michael McDunphy, 31 May 1934.

12   NAI, DT S2979, Minutes of the third meeting of the Constitution Review Committee, 1 June 1934.

13   NAI, DT S2979, First draft of the Constitution Review Committee Report, 9 June 1934.

14   NAI, DT S2979, Minutes of the fourth meeting of the Constitution Review Committee, 18 June 1934. The articles discussed were: 4, 6, 7, 8, 9, 10, 18, 19, 24, 28, 41, 43, 46, 49, 50, 61, 62, 63 and 64.

15   NAI, DT S2979, Minutes of the fifth meeting of the Constitution Review Committee, 19 June 1934. The articles discussed were: 65, 66, 68, 69 and 70.

16   NAI, DT S2979, Minutes of the sixth meeting of the Constitution Review Committee, 20 June 1934.

17   NAI, DT S2979, Memorandum from Michael McDunphy, 25 June 1934.

18   NAI, DT S2979, Minutes of the seventh meeting of the Constitution Review Committee, 27 June 1934.

19   See Hogan, *Irish Constitution*, pp. 68, 71, 73.

20   See *ibid.*, pp. 74–100 for the Committee's report. For an excellent overview see Gerard Hogan, 'The Constitution Review Committee of 1934', in Fionán Ó Muircheartaigh (ed.), *Ireland in the Coming Times: Essays to Celebrate T.K. Whitaker's 80 Years* (Dublin: Institute of Public Administration, 1997), pp. 342–69.

21   See Hogan, *Irish Constitution*, 'Report of the Constitution Committee, Appendix A', pp. 76–87.

22   *Ibid.*, 'Report of the Constitution Committee', par. 5, p. 74.

23   The articles were 6, 7, 8, 18, 19, 43, 51, 62, 65 and 96. See Hogan, *Irish Constitution*, 'Report of the Constitution Committee, Appendix A', pp. 76–87.

24   The relevant articles were: 9, 24, 28, 41, 46, 49, 63, 64, 66 and 68. See Hogan, *Irish Constitution*, 'Report of the Constitution Committee', pp. 76–87.

25 See Hogan, *Irish Constitution:* 'Report of the Constitution Committee, Appendix A', pp. 78–9.

26 *Ibid.*, 'Report of the Constitution Committee, Appendix E', pp. 95–7.

27 *Ibid.*, 'Report of the Constitution Committee, Appendix A', p. 84.

28 See Hogan, 'Constitution Review Committee', p. 356.

29 See Hogan, *Irish Constitution*, 'Report of the Constitution Committee, Appendix A', p. 85.

30 See Hogan, 'Constitution Review Committee', p. 357.

31 See Hogan, *Irish Constitution*, 'Report of the Constitution Committee, Appendix A', p. 82.

32 NAI, DT S2797, Memorandum by Michael McDunphy, 3 July 1934.

33 NAI, DT S2979, First Draft of Committee Report, 3 June 1934.

34 Fergal Davis, *The History and Development of the Special Criminal Court 1922–2005* (Dublin: Four Courts Press, 2006), pp. 30–42.

35 *Ibid.*, pp. 42–50.

36 *Ibid.*, pp. 50–5.

37 *Dáil Debates*, 26 April 1934, 2480.

38 NAI, DT S2979, Memorandum by Stephen Roche, 14 June 1934.

39 See Hogan, *Irish Constitution*, p. 62.

40 NAI, DT S2979, Memorandum from Stephen Roche to Michael McDunphy, 29 June 1934.

41 Article 2A was discussed in detail at the eighth and ninth meetings held on 28 and 29 June respectively. See Hogan, *Irish Constitution*, pp. 68, 71.

42 See Hogan, *Irish Constitution*, 'Report of the Constitution Committee', pars. 8 and 9, p. 75.

43 *Ibid.*, pp. 88–91.

44 *Ibid.*, 'Report of the Constitution Committee, Appendix B', pp. 88–9.

45 See Davis, *Special Criminal Court*, p. 57.

46 See Hogan, *Irish Constitution*, 'Report of the Constitution Committee, Appendix D', pp. 93–5.

47 *Ibid.*, 'Report of Constitution Committee, Appendix F', pp. 98–100.

48 *Ibid.*, 'Report of Constitution Committee, Appendices D, E, F', pp. 93–100. The Constitutions were those of Belgium, Czechoslovakia, Denmark, Estonia, Germany, Yugoslavia, Spain, Mexico, Poland, France, Sweden, Switzerland and the United States.

49 Stephen Roche was not so enthusiastic, as will be seen in Chapter 5.

50 See Hogan, *Irish Constitution*, p. 47.

51 Eugene Broderick, 'John Hearne and the Making of the 1937 Constitution', *Decies*, 69, 2013, p. 177.

52 See Hogan, 'Constitution Review Committee', p. 361.

53 See Broderick, 'John Hearne', pp. 177–8.

54 For an account of the Economic War see Cormac O' Grada, *Ireland: A New Economic History, 1780–1939* (Oxford: Clarendon Press, 1994), pp. 411–16. The struggle with the Blueshirts is recounted by Maurice Manning, *The Blueshirts* (Dublin: Gill and Macmillan, 1971) and Mike Cronin, *The Blueshirts and Irish Politics* (Dublin: Four Courts Press, 1997).

55 UCDA, Eamon de Valera Papers, P150/2370. This document is reproduced in Hogan, *Irish Constitution*, pp. 159–71.

56 Abbreviated as 'sov'.

57 Abbreviated as 'legisl'.

58 Abbreviated as 'exe'.

59 See Broderick, 'John Hearne', p. 179.

60 Abbreviated as 'I'.

61 Abbreviated as 'ackndl'.

62 Abbreviated as 'comdts'.

63 Abbreviated as 'fund'.

64 Abbreviated as 'proc'.

65 Abbreviated as 'Dec. of In'.

66 Abbreviated as 'Dem. Prog'.

67 Enacted in 1924, this act was a cornerstone of the Irish administrative system, which gave a legal basis for the establishment of the departments of state.

68 Abbreviated as 'ptd'.

69 Abbreviated as 'imperl'.

70 Abbreviated as 'shd'.

71 Abbreviated as 'amdtmt of constn'.

72 UCDA, Eamon de Valera Papers, P150/2370, John Hearne, Explanatory memorandum for preliminary draft of heads of a constitution for Saorstát Éireann, 17 May 1935.

73 See Broderick, 'John Hearne', pp. 179–80.

74 The masculine form of the pronoun was used throughout the draft and is used here for that reason.

75 The new articles in the draft heads of a constitution were: 1, 4, 5, 6, 7, 8, 9, 10, 11, 12, 13, 14, 15, 17, 25, 31, 38, 45, 46, 48, 49 and 50.

76 The following articles were transposed: 16, 19, 20, 22, 23, 28, 29, 33, 36, 39, 40, 41, 42 and 44.

77 The relevant articles were: 18, 21, 24, 26, 27 and 30.

78 Article 36.

79 The articles in the draft heads were 39, 40, 41 and 42.

80 The articles in the draft heads were: 2, 3, 18, 21, 24, 26, 27, 30, 32, 34, 35, 37, 43 and 47.

81 These articles were 34 and 35.

82 The relevant articles in the 1922 Constitution were: 64, 65, 66, 67, 68 and 69.

83 The articles included from the 1922 Constitution, identified as fundamental by the Constitution Review Committee 1934, are listed hereafter, with the corresponding article in the draft heads in brackets: 6 (41), 7 (42), 8 (39), 9 (40), 18 (22), 19 (23), 24 (16), 28 (27), 43 (19), 46 (18), 49 (47), 50 (50), 62 (36), 63 (27), 64–68 (34), 69 (35) and 70 (43).

84 *Select Constitutions of the World*, Constitution of the German Reich 1919, Article 109, p. 197.

85 *Select Constitutions of the World*, Constitution of the Polish Republic 1921, Article 96, p. 75.

86 *Select Constitutions of the World*, Constitution of the Republic of Austria 1920, Article 7, p. 88.

87 See Broderick, 'John Hearne', p. 180.

88 See Hogan, *Irish Constitution*, p. 155.

89 *Irish Times*, 15 September 2012.

90 See Hogan, *Irish Constitution*, p. 156.

91 *Irish Times*, 15 September 2012.

92 Quoted in Hogan, *Irish Constitution*, p. 187.

93 UCDA, Eamon de Valera Papers, P150/2373, Memorandum from John Hearne to Eamon de Valera, 22 October 1935.

94 UCDA, Eamon de Valera Papers, P150/2370, Memorandum from John Hearne to Seán Murphy, 10 December 1935.

95 UCDA, Maurice Moynihan Papers, P122/102(50), 'History of the Constitution of 1937'.

96 *Dáil Debates*, 3 May 1933, 543–4.

97 *Dáil Debates*, 20 June 1933, 811.

98 *Dáil Debates*, 29 May 1935, 2140.

99 Quoted in Hogan, *Irish Constitution*, p. 186.

100 UCDA, Eamon de Valera Papers, P150/2370, John Hearne to Seán Moynihan, 18 May 1935.

101 See Hogan, *Irish Constitution*, pp. 159–71. The name 'Éire' was used four times on page 1 and once on pages 2, 6 and 10. Page 4 contains the references to 'Dáil Éireann' and 'Seanad Éireann'.

102 *Dáil Debates*, 29 May 1935, 2088.

103 Quoted in Hogan, *Irish Constitution*, p. 152, footnote 1.

104   Maurice Moynihan (ed.) *Speeches and Statements by Eamon de Valera* (Dublin: Gill and Macmillan, 1980), p. 270.

105   See Keogh and McCarthy, *Irish Constitution*, p. 64.

106   UCDA, Eamon de Valera Papers, P150/2368, Memorandum from the Executive Council of the Irish Free State to King Edward VIII, 8 June 1936.

107   Earl of Longford and Thomas P. O Neill, *Eamon de Valera* (London: Arrow Books, 1970), p. 289.

108   *Dáil Debates*, 11 December 1936, 1277.

109   Bill Kissane, *New Beginnings: Constitutionalism and Democracy in Modern Ireland* (Dublin: University College Dublin Press, 2011), p. 28.

110   *Dáil Debates*, 23 June 1936, 119.

111   John J. Hearne Papers, 'The Constitution and National Life', no details, p. 3. The first page of the speech suggests that it was prepared in early December 1937 and may have been prepared for delivery by de Valera. This speech is not to be confused with one of the same title, prepared for de Valera by Hearne in June 1937. See NAI, DT S9905.

112   T.P. O Neill and Padraig O'Fiannachta, *De Valera* (Dublin: Cló Morainn, 1970), vol. ii, p. 322.

113   For details of the case and the ruling of the Supreme Court see Gerard Hogan, 'A Desert Island Case Set in the Silver Sea: *The State (Ryan) v. Lennon* (1934)', in Eoin O'Dell (ed.), *Leading Cases in the Twentieth Century* (Dublin: Round Hall Sweet & Maxwell, 2000), pp. 80–103.

114   Gerard Casey, *The Constitutional Law of Ireland* (London: Sweet & Maxwell, 1992), p. 19.

115   *Ibid.*

116   NAI, DT S9905, John J. Hearne, 'The Constitution and National Life', 12 June 1937, pp. 7–8. See note 112.

117   Donal C. Coffey, 'The Need for a New Constitution: Irish Constitutional Change 1932–1935', *Irish Jurist*, 48, 2012, p. 302. This essay gives an excellent overview of constitutional developments culminating in the Constitution of 1937.

118   See Longford and O Neill, *Eamon de Valera*, p. 290.

119   Eoin Daly and Tom Hickey, *The Political Theory of the Irish Constitution: Republicanism and the Basic Law* (Manchester: Manchester University Press, 2015), p. 24.

120   John Hearne Papers, 'The Constitution and National Life', p. 3. See note 111.

121   See Chapter 3.

122   Brian Kennedy, 'John Hearne and the Irish Constitution (1937)', *Éire-Ireland*, Summer 1989, p. 123.

123   See Moynihan, *Speeches and Statements*, p. 269.

124   Tom Garvin, *The Irish Senate* (Dublin: Institute of Public Administration, 1969), p. 14.

125   *Report of the Second House of the Oireachtas Commission* (Dublin: Stationery Office, 1936), par. 1.

126   *Report*, 'Appointment of Commission'.

127   See J. Anthony Gaughan (ed.), *The Memoirs of Senator Joseph Connolly: A Founder of Modern Ireland* (Dublin: Irish Academic Press, 1996). Connolly's description of his experiences on the commission is to be found on pp. 390–1.

128   For an account of Tierney's career see Peter Martin, 'The Political Career of Michael Tierney', *Irish Historical Studies*, xxxvii, 147, May 2011, pp. 412–26.

129   For an account of O'Rahilly's public career see J. Anthony Gaughan, *Alfred O'Rahilly: Public Figure* (Dublin: Kingdom Books, 1989); pp. 275–8 treat of his membership of the commission.

130   NAI, DT S8642/3, Second House Commission.

131   NAI, DT S8642/4/8, Second House Commission, John J. Hearne, Preliminary memorandum.

132   NAI, DT S8642/3, Second House Commission.

133   *Ibid.*

134   See Garvin, *Irish Senate*, p. 15.

135   *Report*, p. 9, par. 17.

136   *Ibid.*, p. 9, par. 18.

137   *Ibid.*, pp. 6–7, par. 6, iii.

138   *Ibid.*, p. 7, par. 8.

139   *Ibid.*, p. 8, par. 15.

140   *Ibid.*, p. 7, par. 10.

141   *Ibid.*, p. 10, par. 21.

142   *Ibid.*, p. 11, par. 25.

143   *Ibid.*, p. 11, par. 24.

144   *Ibid.*, Report by D. A. Binchy et alia (hereinafter 'Minority Report'), pp. 26–34.

145   'Minority Report', pp. 30–1, par. 14.

146   'Minority Report', p. 33, par. 19.

147   *Report*, p. 11, par. 27.

148   *Report*, 'Reservation by Mr Hearne', p. 16.

149   *Report*, p. 9, par. 18.

150   *Report*, 'Reservation to Paragraph 18', p. 13.

151   Vincent Comerford, *Ireland* (London: Hodder Arnold, 2003), p. 145.

152   *Ibid.*, p. 145.

153   *Report*, pp. 9–10, par. 20.

154   *Report*, 'Reservation by Mr Hearne', p. 16.

Chapter 5

1   Maurice Hearne, Papers relating to a proposed biography of John J. Hearne, 'Constitution April 1935–December 1937', unpaginated.

2   NAI, DT S9748A, Constitution 1937: Drafting, enactment and operation.

3   NAI, DT S9830, Seán Moynihan to the controller of the stationery office, 1 May 1937. Moynihan was secretary to the Executive Council.

4   For the text of the document see Gerard Hogan, *The Origins of the Irish Constitution 1928–1941* (Dublin: Royal Irish Academy, 2012), pp. 280–5.

5   *Ibid.*, pp. 280–1.

6   *Ibid.*

7   The abbreviation E was used in many drafts.

8   See Hogan, *Irish Constitution*, p. 282.

9   UCDA, Eamon de Valera Papers, P150/2373, 'Draft Heads of a Constitution', 14 October 1936. Two dates, in fact, are recorded on this file. The covering page reads 12 October 1936, while the file itself reads 14 October. The later date is used in this study.

10   For the text of this document see Hogan, *Irish Constitution*, pp. 298–301.

11   *Ibid.*, pp. 286–97.

12   Details of these powers were not given; rather reference was made to the relevant, though as yet unnumbered (and possibly unwritten) articles of the Constitution.

13   UCDA, Eamon de Valera Papers, P150/2373.

14   For this draft see Dermot Keogh and Andrew McCarthy, *The Making of the Irish Constitution 1937* (Cork: Mercier Press, 2007), Appendix 4, pp. 345–51.

15   UCDA, Eamon de Valera Papers, P150/2370.

16   Draft Article 13, 6.

17   UCDA, Eamon de Valera Papers, P150/2037.

18   UCDA, Eamon de Valera Papers, P150/2378.

19   See Hogan, *Irish Constitution*, p. 273.

20   UCDA, Eamon de Valera Papers, P150/2380.

21   NAI, DFA S57, 'The King Edward Crisis', 7 December 1936.

22   James McGuire and James Quinn (eds), *Dictionary of Irish Biography* (Cambridge: Cambridge University Press, 2009), pp. 171–2. The entry for John J. Hearne was authored by Dr Michael Kennedy.

23   UCDA, Eamon de Valera Papers, P150/2370, Draft Foreign Relations Bill, 6 September 1936.

24   See Hogan, *Irish Constitution*, p. 301.

25   Nicholas Mansergh, *The Unresolved Question: The Anglo-Irish Settlement and its Undoing 1912–72* (New Haven and London: Yale University Press, 1991), p. 293.

26   See Keogh and McCarthy, *Irish Constitution*, p. 90.

27   This draft is reproduced as Appendix 5 in *ibid.*, pp. 353–401.

28   UCDA, Eamon de Valera Papers, P150/2385. This copy is reproduced in Keogh and McCarthy, *Irish Constitution*, pp. 352–401.

29   See Keogh and McCarthy, *Irish Constitution*, pp. 353–4.

30   Articles 13–16.

31   Articles 17–23.

32   Articles 25–31.

33   Article 44.

34   UCDA, Eamon de Valera Papers, P150/2387.

35   Third draft, Article 7, 12.

36   Third draft, Article 12, 1.

37   Third draft, Article 13, 5.

38   In the Zurich draft, Articles 13–16 related to the Council of State and Article 20 to referral of bills to the people.

39   Zurich draft, Article 18, 2.

40   Zurich draft, Article 19, 2.

41   In the Zurich draft, the relevant articles were: private property (35) and education (38). In the third draft, they were Articles 37 and 38 respectively.

42   UCDA, Eamon de Valera Papers, P150/2390.

43   Article 7, 4.

44   Article 13, 3.

45   Article 7, 11.

46   Article 24.

47   Article 24, 1.

48   Article 24, 2.

49   UCDA, Eamon de Valera Papers, P150/2397, Memorandum from Arthur Matheson to Eamon de Valera, 4 March 1937.

50   See Hogan, *Irish Constitution*, P. 314.

51   *Ibid.*, p. 316.

52   *Ibid.*

53   UCDA, Eamon de Valera Papers, P150/2397, Memorandum from Arthur Matheson to Eamon de Valera, 1 March 1937.

54   NAI, DT S9715A.

55   See Keogh and McCarthy, *Irish Constitution*, p. 123.

56   *Ibid.*, p. 152.

57   Article 27, 4.

58   Article 32, 5, 1.

59   Article 35.

60   Articles 36 and 37.

61   Article 24, 4, 1.

62   Article 52, 5.

63   NAI, DT S9710, Cabinet Minutes, Cab. 7/599, item 3, 12 March 1937.

64   David Gwynn Morgan, *Constitutional Law of Ireland: The Law of the Executive, Legislature and Judicature* (Dublin: Round Hall, 1985), p. 27.

65   NAI, DT S9748A, Constitution 1937: Drafting, enactment and operation. Maguire was a former de Valera appointed Attorney General and Geoghegan was Minister for Justice in the first Fianna Fáil government, March 1932.

66   NAI, DT S9715A.

67   These articles were: 1, 2, 3, 4, 5, 6, 7, 8, 9, 10, 13, 15, 16, 18, 19, 20, 21, 22, 23, 24, 25, 26, 27, 28, 29, 30, 31, 32, 33, 34, 35, 36, 37, 38, 39, 40, 41, 43, 44, 45, 47, 48 and 49.

68   These articles were: 11, 12, 14, 17 and 46.

69   Article 32, 1 in the Zurich draft and Article 34, 1 in the third draft.

70   Article 39, 1, 1.

71   Article 39, 1, 2.

72   Article 39, 1, 3.

73   Article 39, 2, 2.

74   Article 40, 1.

75   NAI, DT S9715A, Maurice Moynihan to P.J. Ruttledge, 16 March 1937.

76   NAI, DT S9715B. For an excellent discussion on the observations made on the first official draft see Keogh and McCarthy, *Irish Constitution*, pp. 123–49; and Hogan, *Irish Constitution*, pp. 326–60. Hogan also reproduces the text of many of the submissions; see pp. 360–444.

77   NAI, DT S9715B, Thomas Derrig, Minister for Education, to Maurice Moynihan, 23 March 1937.

78   NAI, DT S9715B, Memorandum from the Department of Defence, 22 March 1937.

79   NAI, DT S9715B, Memorandum by William Carey, secretary to the Revenue Commissioners, to Maurice Moynihan, 7 April 1937.

80   NAI, DT S9715B, Memorandum by Michael McDunphy, 23 March 1937.

81   NAI, DT S9715B, Memorandum by J.J. McElligott, 22 March 1937.

82   Quoted in Hogan, *Irish Constitution* p. 326.

83   *Ibid.*, pp. 399–400.

84   NAI, DT S9715B, Memorandum by Michael McDunphy, 1 April 1937.

85   See Keogh and McCarthy, *Irish Constitution*, p. 124.

86   See Hogan, *Irish Constitution*, p. 375.

87   NAI, DT S9715B, Memorandum by Michael McDunphy, 1 April 1937.

88   NAI, DT S9748A, Constitution 1937: Drafting, enactment and operation.

89   NAI, DT S9830, Constitution 1937: Distribution of copies prior to publication.

90   NAI, DT S9679, Constitution 1937: Confidential printing arrangements. McDunphy recorded the fact of the meeting.

91   NAI, DT S9748A, Constitution 1937: Drafting, enactment and operation.

92   NAI, DT S9746.

93   Those articles in the first official draft were: 11, 12, 13, 15, 16, 17, 18, 19, 20, 22, 24, 25, 27, 30, 32, 43 and 44. In the first revise they were often renumbered.

94   NAI, DT S9746, Minute by Michael McDunphy, 9 April 1937.

95   NAI, DT S10159, Maurice Moynihan to all ministers and other persons, 10 April 1937.

96   See Hogan, *Irish Constitution*, p. 363. Ryan's comment related to what was Article 11 in the first official draft.

97   *Ibid.*, p. 364.

98   Article 27, 5, 2 in the first revise.

99　See Hogan, *Irish Constitution*, p. 414.

100　Article 25, 2, 1.

101　See Hogan, *Irish Constitution*, p. 416.

102　Article 30, 2.

103　NAI, DT S9715B, Memorandum from Stephen Roche to P.J. Ruttledge, 22 March 1937.

104　Article 45, 4.

105　Article 45, 6 and 7.

106　Article 45, 2.

107　See Hogan, *Irish Constitution*, p. 408, note 133.

108　Article 14, 2, 2.

109　See Hogan, *Irish Constitution*, p. 411.

110　*Ibid.*

111　NAI, DT S9746, Minute by Maurice Moynihan, 9 April 1937.

112　NAI, DT S10159.

113　Article 42, 3, 2.

114　The unchanged articles in the second revise were: 1, 2, 3, 4, 5, 6, 7, 8, 9, 10, 11, 12, 14, 15, 16, 17, 18, 19, 20, 21, 22, 23, 24, 26, 29, 30, 31, 33, 35, 36, 37, 38, 39, 46, 47, 48, 49 and 50.

115　Article 25, 2, 1.

116　See Hogan, *Irish Constitution*, p. 414.

117　*Ibid.*, p. 343.

118　NAI, DT S10299.

119　Article 25, 2, 2 in the first revise.

120　NAI, DT S10159, Memorandum by George Gavan Duffy, undated.

121　Article 25, 2, 1.

122　Article 27, 1 of the second revise. The other changes affected Article 28 by the addition of a section, 28, 1; and Article 34 by the removal of section 4, 3.

123　See Hogan, *Irish Constitution*, p. 395 for McElligott's opinion and p. 414 for McDunphy's.

124　NAI, DT S10159, Maurice Moynihan to all ministers and others, 10 April 1937.

125　NAI, DT S10159, Memorandum by James J. McElligott, 17 April 1937. See Hogan, *Irish Constitution*, pp. 486–503 for text of same.

126　See Hogan, *Irish Constitution*, p. 499.

127　Eugene Broderick, 'John Hearne and the Making of the 1937 Constitution', *Decies*, no. 69, 2013, p. 192.

128　NAI, DT S9715A, Maurice Moynihan to P.J. Ruttledge, 16 March 1937.

129　See Hogan, *Irish Constitution*, p. 418.

130　UCDA, George Gavan Duffy Papers, P152/41.

131　NAI, DFA 147/2, Charles Bewley to John Hearne, 5 April 1937.

132　Gearóid Carey, 'The Constitutional Dilemma of Article 45: An Avenue for Social Welfare and Social Rights?' *Irish Student Law Review*, vol. 5, 1995, p. 78.

133　See Broderick, 'John Hearne', p. 192.

134　NAI, DT S10160, Maurice Moynihan to ministers and officials, 23 April 1937.

135　NAI, DT S10160.

136　NAI, DT S10160, Memorandum by J.J. McElligott, 'Notes on revised draft of Articles 42–4', 24 April 1937.

137　The articles in brackets refer to the corresponding article in the second revise. The renumbering was due to the omission of articles in the third revise, which had appeared in the second. The articles which were similar in both drafts are as follows: 1, 2(3), 3(4), 4(5), 5(6), 6(7), 7(8), 8(9), 9(10), 10(11), 11(12), 14(15), 15(16), 16(17), 17(18), 18(19), 21, 22, 23, 24, 26, 28, 29, 30, 31, 32(33), 33(34), 34(35), 35(36), 36(37), 38(39), 39(40), 40(42), 41(43), 45(46), 46(47), 47(48), 48(49) and 49(50).

138 Article 19 in the third revise was composed of four sections of Article 20 in the second revise: 20, 1; 20, 2, 1; 20, 2, 2; and 20, 4. Article 20 in the third revise was composed of four sections of the same numbered article in the second revise: 20, 3, 1; 20, 3, 2; 20, 5, 1; and 20, 5, 2.

139 Article 37, 3, 1.

140 Article 37, 4, 1.

141 Article 37, 6.

142 NAI, DT S10160.

143 Earl of Longford and Thomas P. O Neill, *Eamon de Valera* (London: Arrow Books, 1974), p. 297.

144 Dermot Keogh, 'The Irish Constitutional Revolution: An Analysis of the Making of the Constitution', in Frank Litton (ed.), *The Constitution of Ireland, 1937–1987* (Dublin: Institute of Public Administration, 1988), p. 24.

145 Article 42, preliminary draft, 10 March 1937.

146 Tim Pat Coogan, *De Valera: Long Fellow, Long Shadow* (London, Hutchinson, 1993), p. 489.

147 This account is based on Keogh and McCarthy, *Irish Constitution*, pp. 150–73.

148 Article 43, 1, 2.

149 Article 43, 1, 3.

150 See Keogh, 'Irish Constitutional Revolution', p. 27.

151 UCDA, Eamon de Valera Papers, P150/2419, 'Copies of documents taken by Sean T. O'Kelly to the Nuncio, 11 April 1937'.

152 UCDA, Eamon de Valera Papers, P150/2419, Memorandum by Eamon de Valera: 'Pro Memoria': Guidelines for Joseph P. Walshe for his discussions with the Vatican, 16 April 1937.

153 See Keogh and McCarthy, *Irish Constitution*, p. 242, note 58.

154 See Hogan, *Irish Constitution*, p. 280.

155 *Ibid.*, p. 298.

156 UCDA, Eamon de Valera Papers, P150/2387.

157 See Hogan, *Irish Constitution*, p. 298.

158 NAI, DT S10159, Memorandum by J.J. McElligott: Observations on the second revise, 17 April 1937.

159 NAI, DT S10159, Memorandum by McElligott: Observations on the second revise, p. 12.

160 For an excellent account of this aspect of Irish politics see M.P. Sacks, *The Donegal Mafia: An Irish Political Machine* (London and New Haven: Yale University Press, 1976).

161 NAI, DT S9905, Constitution as approved by Dáil Éireann, 14 June 1937, Articles 51 and 52.

162 UCDA, Eamon de Valera Papers, P150/2390.

163 See Hogan, *Irish Constitution*, pp. 475–7 and pp. 500–3 for observations by Michael McDunphy and J.J. McElligott respectively.

164 The articles in the fourth revise are listed hereafter, with the corresponding number in the preliminary draft: 52(50), 54(51), 53(52), 55(53), 5 (54), 57(55), 59(56), 50(59) and 61(60).

165 NAI, DT S9830, Constitution 1937: Distribution of drafts to departments.

166 NAI, DT S9748A, Constitution 1937: Drafting, enactment and operation.

Chapter 6

1 John J. Hearne Papers, Address delivered at the annual meeting of the Harvard Law School Association of New Jersey in Newark, New Jersey, 23 March, 1957, p. 4.

2 See Chapter 3.

3 John A. Murphy, 'The 1937 Constitution – Some Historical Reflections', in Tim Murphy and Patrick Twomey (eds), *Ireland's Evolving Constitution 1937–97: Collected Essays* (Oxford: Hart Publishing, 1998), p. 12.

4   Eoin Daly and Tom Hickey, *The Political Theory of the Irish Constitution: Republicanism and the Basic Law* (Manchester: Manchester University Press, 2015), p. 22.
5   UCDA, Eamon de Valera Papers, P150/2373.
6   *Dáil Debates*, 11 May 1937, 40.
7   NAI, DT S9686, Typescript of radio address, 30 April 1937.
8   NAI, DT S9905, John J. Hearne, 'The Constitution and National Life'; Memorandum prepared for Eamon de Valera, 12 June 1937, p. 4.
9   *Ibid.*, p. 5.
10 John A. Murphy, *Ireland in the Twentieth Century* (Dublin: Gill and Macmillan, 1975), p. 89.
11 Robert Elgie, 'The President in Comparative Perspective', in John Coakley and Kevin Rafter (eds), *The Irish Presidency: Power, Ceremony and Politics* (Dublin: Irish Academic Press, 2014), Table 2.1, p. 18.
12 See Brian Murphy, *Forgotten Patriot: Douglas Hyde and the Foundation of the Irish Presidency* (Cork: Collins Press, 2016), p. 58.
13 John Coakley, 'An Ambiguous Office? The Position of Head of State in the Irish Constitution', *Irish Jurist*, 48, p. 57.
14 Garret FitzGerald, 'The Irish Constitution in its Historical Context', in Tim Murphy and Patrick Twomey (eds), *Ireland's Evolving Constitution 1937–97: Collected Essays* (Oxford: Hart Publishing, 1998), p. 32.
15 See Murphy, '1937 Constitution', p. 15.
16 www.oireachtas.ie/members/ – Directory of Members: 1919–2015, accessed 25 July 2016.
17 Donnacha Ó Beacháin, *Destiny of the Soldiers: Fianna Fáil, Irish Republicanism and the IRA 1926–1973* (Dublin: Gill and Macmillan, 2010), p. 139.
18 *Ibid.*, p. 141.
19 *Ibid.*, pp. 141–2.
20 *Ibid.*, p. 143.
21 Maurice Hearne, Papers relating to a proposed biography of John J. Hearne, 'Constitution – Postscript'.
22 UCDA, Eamon de Valera Papers, P150/2373.
23 See Maurice Hearne, 'Constitution – Postscript'.
24 *Ibid.*
25 John J. Hearne Papers, 'The National Constitution of Ireland', Address delivered at Villanova College, Pennsylvania, 22 September 1950, p. 11.
26 See Ronan Fanning, *Independent Ireland* (Dublin: Helicon, 1983), pp. 118–19; Murphy, *Ireland in the Twentieth Century*, p. 89.
27 See Coakley, 'Position of Head of State', p. 70.
28 Mervyn O'Driscoll, *Ireland, Germany and the Nazis: Politics and Diplomacy 1919–1939* (Dublin: Four Courts Press, 2004), pp. 275–6.
29 See FitzGerald, 'Irish Constitution', p. 33.
30 *Irish Times*, 29 December 1937.
31 NAI, DT S10463, Constitution of 1937, 'Attitude of British Government'.
32 John Bowman, 'Eamon de Valera: Seven Lives', in John P. Carroll and John A. Murphy (eds), *De Valera and His Times* (Cork: Cork University Press, 1983), p. 183.
33 Roy Foster, *Vivid Faces: The Revolutionary Generation in Ireland 1890–1923* (London: Allen Lane, 2014), p. 308.
34 See Bowman, 'Eamon de Valera', p. 183.
35 Frances Flanagan, *Remembering the Revolution: Dissent, Culture and Nationalism in the Irish Free State* (Oxford: Oxford University Press, 2015), pp. 38–9.
36 See Foster, *Vivid Faces*, pp. 307–8. The official biography was in 1970.

37   UCDA, Maurice Moynihan Papers, P122/105 (50–3) and P122/105(54–8). See also P122/105 (38), 'Outline of Proposed Memorandum'.

38   UCDA, Maurice Moynihan Papers, P122/105 (70), D. O'Nualláin to Maurice Moynihan, 13 December 1961.

39   UCDA, Maurice Moynihan Papers, P122/105 (82), D. O' Nualláin to Maurice Moynihan, 7 March 1963.

40   UCDA, Maurice Moynihan Papers, P122/105 (91), Maurice Moynihan to John J. Hearne, 24 October 1963.

41   UCDA, Maurice Moynihan Papers, P122/105 (131), Maurice Moynihan to John J. Hearne, 14 December 1966.

42   Gerard Hogan, *The Origins of the Irish Constitution 1928–1941* (Dublin: Royal Irish Academy, 2012), pp. 186–7.

43   *Ibid.*, pp. 280–1.

44   UCDA, Eamon de Valera Papers, P150/2373.

45   UCDA, Eamon de Valera Papers, P150/2373.

46   See Dermot Keogh and Andrew McCarthy, *The Making of the Irish Constitution* 1937 (Cork: Mercier Press, 2007), Appendix 5, p. 387, for text of Articles 32 and 34 of the Zurich draft. For the text of the articles in the third draft see UCDA, Eamon de Valera Papers, P150/2387.

47   UCDA, Eamon de Valera Papers, P150/2387.

48   UCDA, Eamon de Valera Papers, P150/2382.

49   UCDA, Eamon de Valera Papers, P150/2387.

50   Oran Doyle, *Constitutional Equality Law* (Dublin: Thomson Round Hall, 2004), pp. 52–8.

51   Gerard Hogan, 'Some Thoughts on the Origins of the Constitution': Address to UCD Constitutional Studies Group, 29 June 2012, p. 20. See also Oran Doyle, 'The Human Personality Doctrine in Constitutional Law,' *Irish Student Law Review*, 9, 2001, pp. 102–17.

52   See Doyle, *Constitutional Equality Law*, p. 52.

53   NAI, DT S9705.

54   See Gerard Hogan and Gerry Whyte, *J.M. Kelly: The Irish Constitution* (Dublin: Buttersworth, third edition, 1994), pp. 745–89.

55   Quoted in Hogan, *Irish Constitution*, p. 279.

56   UCDA, George Gavan Duffy Papers, P152/39 (1), George Gavan Duffy to Eamon de Valera, 7 April 1935.

57   UCDA, George Gavan Duffy Papers, P152/39(2), Kathleen O'Connell, personal secretary to Eamon de Valera, to George Gavan Duffy, 15 April 1935.

58   G.M. Golding, *George Gavan Duffy: A Legal Biography* (Dublin: Irish Academic Press, 1982), p. 50. The source for Golding's information was Colum Gavan Duffy, the judge's son.

59   Colum Gavan Duffy, 'George Gavan Duffy,' *Judicial Studies Institute Journal*, vol. 2, no. 2, 2002, pp. 16–17. I am grateful to Mr Justice Gerard Hogan for bringing this reference to my attention.

60   *Report of the Second House of the Oireachtas Commission* (Dublin: Stationery Office, 1936), p. 4.

61   NAI, DT S9748, Constitution 1937: Drafting, enactment and operation.

62   See Duffy, 'George Gavan Duffy', p. 29.

63   See Golding, *George Gavan Duffy*, p. 50.

64   See NAI, DT S10159, undated, for his observations on the first circulated draft and NAI DT S10159, 11 April 1937, for his observations on the second revise.

65   See Hogan, *Irish Constitution*, pp. 276–9.

66   See Hearne, 'National Constitution of Ireland', p. 17.

67   John J. Hearne Papers, Text of address given in Canada, date and place unknown, p. 3.

68   See Hearne, 'Constitution and National Life', p. 9.

69   *Ibid.*, p. 8.

70   John J. Hearne Papers, 'The Constitution and National Life', no details, p. 7. The first page of the speech suggests that it was prepared in early December 1937 and may have been prepared by Hearne for delivery by de Valera. This is not to be confused with a memorandum of the same title, also prepared by Hearne for de Valera in June 1937 and already cited in this chapter (NAI, DT S9905). See note 8.

71   John J. Hearne Papers, 'Baccalaureate Address', Commencement Exercises, University of Notre Dame, 4 June 1950, p. 11.

72   *Ibid.*

73   See Hearne, 'National Constitution of Ireland', pp. 12–13.

74   V. Bradley Lewis, 'Natural Law in Irish Constitutional Jurisprudence',www.catholicsocialscientists. org/cssr/Archival/1997/1997_171.pdf, p. 173, accessed 6 May 2016.

75   Samuel Moyn, 'The Secret History of Constitutional Dignity', http://ssrn.com/abstract=2159248, p. 1, accessed 13 April 2016.

76   UCDA, Eamon de Valera Papers, P150/2387. Various dates contained within the manuscripts suggest a date of composition in late February 1937. It is not clear if Samuel Moyn was aware of the existence of this draft which pre-dates the issuance of *Divini Redemptoris*. Its contents confirm McQuaid's familiarity with current theological ideas. However, the draft's existence does not in any sense weaken the force of Moyn's argument.

77   *Divini Redemptoris*,   www.w2.vatican.va/content/pius-xi/en/encyclicals/documents/hf_p-xi_ enc_1903193-7_divini_redemptoris.html, par. 34, accessed 13 April 2016.

78   Donal Dorr, *Option for the Poor: A Hundred Years of Vatican Social Teaching* (Dublin: Gill and Macmillan, 1983), p. 70.

79   See Moyn, 'Secret History', p. 12.

80   See *Divini Redemptoris*, par. 51.

81   Samuel Moyn, *Christian Human Rights* (Philadelphia: University of Pennsylvania, 2015), p. 75.

82   See Hearne 'National Constitution of Ireland', p. 18.

83   See Moyn, *Christian Human Rights*, p. 10.

84   See Lewis, 'Natural Law', p. 173.

85   John J. Hearne Papers, 'The Nation – the Unit of International Society', undated.

86   Article 15, 4.

87   UCDA, Eamon de Valera Papers, P150/2370, 17 May 1935, Article 50.

88   UCDA, Eamon de Valera Papers, P150/2370.

89   UCDA, Eamon de Valera Papers, P150/2373.

90   UCDA, Eamon de Valera Papers, P150/2385, Article 25.

91   For an overview of this process of deconstruction see Laura Cahillane, *Drafting the Irish Free State Constitution* (Manchester: Manchester University Press, 2016), pp. 165–7.

92   UCDA, Eamon de Valera Papers, P150/2370, p. 9.

93   *Dáil Debates*, 10 June 1937, 289.

94   *Dáil Debates*, 10 June 1937, 285.

95   John Kelly, *Fundamental Rights in Irish Law and the Constitution* (Dublin: Allen Figgis, 1967), p. 14.

96   *Ibid.*, p. 4.

97   Gerard Hogan, 'A Desert Island Case Set in the Silver Sea: *The State (Ryan) v. Lennon* (1934)', in Eoin O'Dell (ed.), *Leading Cases of the Twentieth Century* (Dublin: Round Hall Sweet & Maxwell), p. 81.

98   James Casey, 'Changing the Constitution: Amendment and Judicial Review', in Brian Farrell (ed.), *De Valera's Constitution and Ours* (Dublin: Gill and Macmillan, 1988), p. 153.

99   See Hogan, 'Desert Island Case', p. 102.

100   See Cahillane, *Free State Constitution*, p. 168.

101   UCDA, Eamon de Valera Papers, P150/2370, pp. 5, 12.

102   Gerard Hogan, 'John Hearne and the Plan for a Constitutional Court', *Dublin University Law Journal*, 2011, vol. 33, p. 76.

103   UCDA, Eamon de Valera Papers, P150/2373, Memorandum from John J. Hearne to Sean Murphy, assistant secretary, Department of External Affairs, 10 December 1936.

104   UCDA, Eamon de Valera Papers, P150/2373.

105   UCDA, Eamon de Valera Papers, P150/2373, Article XXIII.

106   UCDA, Eamon de Valera Papers, P150/2373, 'Preliminary Draft of a Constitution'.

107   See Hogan, 'John Hearne and the Plan for a Constitutional Court', pp. 79–80.

108   UCDA, Eamon de Valera Papers, P150/2373. This comment read as follows: 'Be presided over by the CJ [Chief Justice] and one other; the Pres[ident] of the H.C. [High Court] and one other; the C. Comh. [Ceann Comhairle] and Cathaoirleach [of the Seanad]; the A.G. [Attorney General]; and Presidents? 4 Judges, 1 A.G, 2 Dáil, 3 persons by PE' [President of the Executive Council].

109   UCDA, Eamon de Valera Papers, P150/2373. This annotation reads as follows: 'Chief Jus[tice] (President); Pres[ident] of HC; CC [Ceann Comhairle] and Cath [Cathaoirleach of the Seanad]; AG; 2 nom[inated] by the P [of the Executive Council]; 1 by SC [Supreme Court]; 1 by HC [High Court]'.

110   See Hogan, *Irish Constitution*, p. 274.

111   *Ibid.*, p. 341–2.

112   *Ibid.*, p. 275.

113   See Hogan, 'John Hearne and the Plan for a Constitutional Court', p. 85.

114   See Hogan and Whyte, *Irish Constitution*, p. 213.

115   *Ibid.*

116   Ronan Keane, 'Fundamental Rights in Irish Law: A Note on the Historical Background', in James O'Reilly (ed.), *Human Rights and Constitutional Law* (Dublin: Round Hall Press, 1992), p. 26.

117   See Hogan, *Irish Constitution*, p. 399.

118   NAI, DT S9715B, Stephen Roche to P.J. Ruttledge, 22 March 1937.

119   NAI, DT S10159, Stephen Roche to Michael McDunphy, 13 April 1937.

120   NAI, DT S2979. The italics are those of Stephen Roche.

121   NAI, DT S10159, Stephen Roche to Michael McDunphy, 13 April 1937.

122   Brian Walsh, Introduction, in James Casey, *Constitutional Law in Ireland* (London: Maxwell & Smart, 1992), p. x.

123   See Casey, 'Changing the Constitution', p. 156.

124   Bill Kissane, *New Beginnings: Constitutionalism and Democracy in Modern Ireland* (Dublin: University College Dublin Press, 2011), p. 70.

125   Fergal Davis, *The History and Development of the Special Criminal Court 1922–2005* (Dublin: Four Courts Press, 2006), pp. 64–70.

126   See Hogan, *Irish Constitution*, pp. 670–8; Davis, *Special Criminal Court*, p. 75. The decision in *Burke* was largely based on the view that, in accordance with the act, in 'satisfying' himself that a person was 'engaged in activities calculated to prejudice the preservation of the peace, order or security of the state' and in thereby ordering the arrest or detention of such a person, a minister was acting in a judicial manner and was, therefore, *ultra vires* the Constitution.

127   *Dáil Debates*, 3 January 1940, 1352–4.

128   *Seanad Debates*, 4 January 1940, 510.

129   *Seanad Debates*, 4 January 1940, 511–12.

130   *Seanad Debates*, 4 January 1940, 515.

131   *Seanad Debates*, 4 January 1940, 515–16.

132   [1940] IR70, *In the Matter of Article 26 of the Constitution and in the Matter of the Offences against the State (Amendment) Bill, 1940*.

133   See Hogan, *Irish Constitution*, p. 695.

134   For an account of the work of the Review Committee and the second amendment which was the result of its endeavours see *ibid.*, pp. 668–835.

135   For a description and assessment of the threat see J. Bowyer Bell, *The Secret Army: The IRA 1916–1979* (Dublin: The Academy Press, 1970), pp. 99–129; and Maurice Manning, *The Blueshirts* (Dublin: Gill and Macmillan, 1971).

136   See Davis, *Special Criminal Court*, pp. 52–5.

137   *Dáil Debates*, 29 May 1935, 2090–1.

138   See Hogan, *Irish Constitution*, pp. 88–91.

139   UCDA, Eamon de Valera Papers, P150/2370, p. 7.

140   See Hogan, *Irish Constitution*, 'Explanatory Memorandum for Preliminary Draft of Heads of a Constitution for Saorstát Éireann', p. 186.

141   Alan Greene, 'The Historical Evolution of Article 28, 3, 3 of the Irish Constitution', *Irish Jurist*, 47, 2012, p. 123.

142   John Kelly, 'The Constitution: Law and Manifesto', in Frank Litton (ed.), *The Constitution of Ireland 1937–1987* (Dublin: Institute of Public Administration, 1987), p. 209.

143   Maurice Moynihan (ed.), *Speeches and Statements by Eamon de Valera* (Dublin: Gill and Macmillan, 1980), p. 332.

144   See Hearne, 'Constitution and National Life', pp. 11–12.

145   R.V. Comerford, *Ireland* (London: Hodder Arnold, 2003), p. 145.

146   Iarfhlaith Watson, 'Irish Language, Irish Nation', in Tom Inglis (ed.), *Are the Irish Different?* (Manchester: Manchester University Press, 2014), p. 185.

147   See Moynihan, *Speeches and Statements*, p. 342.

148   Aileen Kavanagh, 'The Irish Constitution at 75 Years: Natural Law, Christian Values and the Ideal of Justice', *Irish Jurist*, 48, 2012, p. 72.

149   Ronan McCrea, 'Rhetoric, Choices and the Constitution', in Eoin Carolan (ed.), *The Constitution of Ireland: Perspectives and Prospects* (London: Bloomsbury Professional, 2012), p. 63.

150   UCDA, Eamon de Valera Papers, P150/2370, p. 8.

151   UCDA, Eamon de Valera Papers, P150/2373.

152   Dáil Éireann, *Minutes of Proceedings of the First Parliament of the Republic of Ireland* (Dublin: Stationery Office, 1994), pp. 15–16.

153   For the text of the Proclamation, see *Oidhreacht 1916–1966* (Dublin: Stationery Office, 1966), p. xii.

154   Quoted in John Bowman, *De Valera and the Ulster Question 1917–1973* (Oxford: Clarendon Press, 1982), p. 5.

155   Patrick Maume, Afterword, in Lawrence William White and James Quinn (eds), *1916: Portraits and Lives* (Dublin: Royal Irish Academy, 2015), pp. 318–19.

156   John A. Murphy, 'The Achievement of Eamon de Valera', in J.P. Carroll and John A. Murphy (ed.), *De Valera and His Times* (Cork: Cork University Press, 1983), p. 13.

157   *Ibid.*, p. 14.

158   T.P. O Neill and Padraig O Fiannachta, *De Valera*, vol. ii (Dublin: Cló Morainn, 1970), p. 323. The following constitutions were included in *Select Constitutions of the World*: Irish Free State; Kingdom of the Serbs, Croats and Slovenes; Polish Republic; Republic of Austria; Estonian Republic; Czechoslovak Republic; German Reich; Russian Socialist Federal Soviet Republic; United States of Mexico; Kingdom of Denmark; Union of South Africa; Commonwealth of Australia; French Republic; Swiss Confederation; the Dominion of Canada; Kingdom of Belgium; Kingdom of Norway; Kingdom of Sweden; and the United States of America.

159   Susan Denham, 'Waterfordian John J. Hearne: A Drafter of the Irish Constitution', p. 39. This lecture was delivered in the Large Room, Waterford City Hall, 10 November 2014, as part of the

Waterford 1,100 Talks organised by Waterford Museum of Treasures. I am grateful to Mrs Justice Denham for providing me with the text of her lecture.

160   *Ibid.*, p. 40.

161   John J. Hearne Papers, Text of address given in Canada, date and place unknown, p. 3.

162   See Denham, 'Waterfordian John J. Hearne', p. 40.

163   See Coakley, 'Position of Head of State', p. 52.

164   See pp. 169–210.

165   This was on page 5. See Hogan, *Irish Constitution*, p. 163 for a reproduction of this page.

166   See Hogan, 'Some Thoughts on the Constitution', p. 2.

167   *Ibid.*, p. 3.

168   This paragraph is based on a lecture by Mr Justice Gerard Hogan, 'The Influence of the Continental Constitutional Tradition on the Drafting of the Constitution', pp. 6–9. I am grateful to Justice Hogan for providing me with the text of the lecture.

169   *Select Constitutions of the World*, Constitution of the German Reich, pp. 186–9.

170   Gerard Hogan, 'The Influence of the Continental Constitutional Tradition on the Drafting of the Constitution', in Bláthna Ruane, Jim O'Callaghan and David Barniville (eds) *Law and Government: A Tribute to Rory Brady* (Dublin: Roundhall, 2016), pp. 160–1.

171   UCDA, Eamon de Valera Papers, P150/2373, 'Draft Heads of a Constitution', 14 October 1936, Article XXV.

172   *Select Constitutions of the World*, Constitution of the German Reich, pp. 197–8.

173   *Ibid.*, pp. 199–200.

174   *Ibid.*, p. 198.

175   *Ibid.*

176   UCDA, Eamon de Valera Papers, P150/2373, 'Draft Heads of a Constitution', 14 October 1936, Article XXVII.

177   *Select Constitutions of the World*, Constitution of the German Reich, pp. 199.

178   See *Select Constitutions of the World* for the texts of the Czechoslovak Constitution, pp. 137–67; German Constitution (Weimar), pp. 169–210; and the Polish Constitution, pp. 57–80.

179   UCDA, Eamon de Valera Papers, P150/2373, 'Draft Heads of a Constitution', 14 October 1936, Article XXVI, Section 2.

180   See UCDA, Eamon de Valera Papers, P150/2373, 'Draft Heads of a Constitution', 14 October 1936, Article XXVI, Section 3; and *Select Constitutions of the World*, Constitution of the Polish Republic, p. 78.

181   UCDA, Eamon de Valera Papers, P150/2373, 'Draft Heads of a Constitution', 14 October 1936. See *Select Constitutions of the World*, p. 76, for the relevant article in the Polish Constitution.

182   Gerard Hogan, 'Comparison between the text of the French Constitution (Second Republic) 1848 and the Constitution of Ireland 1937'. My appreciation to Mr Justice Gerard Hogan for sending me a copy of this text.

183   For a more detailed consideration of this point see Gerard Hogan, 'Address to the Constitutional Convention', Dublin Castle, December 2012, p. 6. This may be viewed athttp://www.youtube.com/watch?v=4mX3LLn316Q.

184   See Cahillane, *Free State Constitution*, pp. 154–80.

185   Tom Garvin, *1922: The Birth of Irish Democracy* (Dublin: Gill and Macmillan, 1996), p. 178.

186   See Kissane, *New Beginnings*, p. xi.

187   Garret FitzGerald, 'The Irish Constitution in its Historical Context', in Tim Murphy and Patrick Twomey (eds), *Ireland's Evolving Constitution, 1937–97: Collected Essays* (Oxford: Hart Publishing, 1998), p. 32.

188   See Cahillane, *Free State Constitution*, p. 155, note 6.

189 Brian Walsh, 'The Constitution: A View from the Bench', in Brian Farrell (ed.), *De Valera's Constitution and Ours* (Dublin: Gill and Macmillan, 1988), p. 197.

190 See Casey, 'Changing the Constitution', p. 152.

191 Gretchen M. Macmillan, *State, Society and Authority in Ireland: The Foundations of the Modern State* (Dublin: Gill and Macmillan, 1993), pp. 186–201.

192 See Cahillane, *Free State Constitution*, p. 155.

193 *Ibid.*, pp. 97–119.

194 Leo Kuhn, *The Constitution of the Irish Free State* (London: George Allen and Unwin Ltd., 1932), p. 80.

195 See Cahillane, *Free State Constitution*, p. 119.

196 See Kuhn, *Constitution of the Irish Free State,* p. 112. Kuhn's comment related to the Free State Constitution; here it is also being related to the 1937 Constitution.

197 UCDA, Eamon de Valera Papers, P150/2373, 'Draft Heads of a Constitution', 14 October 1936, Article XXVII, Section 2, 3.

198 See J. Anthony Gaughan, *Alfred O'Rahilly,* III, *Controversialist,* Part 1: *Social Reformer* (Dublin: Kingdom Books, 1992).

199 See John A. Murphy, *The College: A History of Queen's/University College Cork 1845–1995* (Cork: Cork University Press, 1995), pp. 267–97, for an account of O'Rahilly's academic career.

200 The drafting of the Free State Constitution is described by Brian Farrell, 'The Drafting of the Irish Free State Constitution', *Irish Jurist,* 5 (1970), pp. 115–40; pp. 343–56; 6 (1971), pp. 111–35; pp. 345–59. For a more recent and more comprehensive account see Cahillane, *Irish Free State Constitution.*

201 UCDA, Alfred O'Rahilly Papers, P178/63, Letter from Eamon de Valera to Alfred O'Rahilly, 27 March 1934, in which de Valera refers to returning the copy.

202 UCDA, Alfred O'Rahilly Papers, P178/61, Letter from John Hearne to Alfred O'Rahilly, 11 May 1932; P178/62(1), Letter from Alfred O'Rahilly to John Hearne, 13 May 1932.

203 For the text of O'Rahilly's Constitution see J. Anthony Gaughan, *Alfred O'Rahilly,* II, *Public Figure* (Dublin: Kingdom Books, 1989), Appendix 7, pp. 456–67.

204 Such concerns were voiced in the *Report on the Criminal Law Amendment Acts (1880–5)* 1931. The committee which produced the report was chaired by William Carrigan; the report was never published. For the text of the report see www.the-knitter.blogspot.ie/2005/06/full-carrigan-report_24.html, accessed 25 January 2017. For an account of the reaction to it see Finola Kennedy, 'The Suppression of the Carrigan Report', in Bryan Fanning (ed.), *An Irish Century: Studies 1912–2012* (Dublin: University College Dublin Press, 2012), pp. 83–92. For a comprehensive account of moral concerns during this period see Diarmaid Ferriter, *Occasions of Sin: Sex and Society in Modern Ireland* (London: Profile Books, 2009), pp. 100–214.

205 UCDA, Eamon de Valera Papers, P150/2373, 'Draft Heads of a Constitution', 14 October 1936, Article XXX.

206 Bruce Biever, *Religion, Culture and Values: A Cross-Cultural Analysis of Motivational Factors in Native Irish and American Irish Catholicism* (New York: Arno Press, 1976), p. 283.

207 Alan J. Ward, *The Irish Constitutional Tradition: Responsible Government and Modern Ireland 1782–1992* (Washington: Catholic University of America Press, 1994), p. 1.

208 Patrick Murray, *The Oracles of God: The Roman Catholic Church and Irish Politics 1922–1937* (Dublin: University College Dublin Press, 2000), p. 294.

209 Brian Walker, *A Political History of the Two Irelands: From Partition to Peace* (London: Palgrave, 2012), p. 17.

210 For an account of the Catholic social movement see J.H. Whyte, *Church and State in Modern Ireland 1923–1979* (Dublin: Gill and Macmillan, second edition, 1980), pp. 62–95. For a general overview see Eugene Broderick, *Intellectuals and the Ideological Hijacking of Fine Gael 1932–1938* (Newcastle upon Tyne: Cambridge Scholars Publishing, 2010), pp. 7–23.

211 See Flanagan, *Remembering the Revolution*.

212 See Foster, *Vivid Faces*, p. 291.

213 Tom Garvin, *Nationalist Revolutionaries in Ireland 1858–1928* (Oxford: Clarendon Press, 1987), p. 141.

214 Tom Garvin, *Preventing the Future: Why was Ireland so poor for so long?* (Dublin: Gill and Macmillan, 2004), p. 26.

215 See Fanning, *Independent Ireland*, p. 59.

216 For an account of this event see Miriam Moffitt, '"Ireland's Destiny is in the Making": The Impact of the Anniversary Celebrations of 1929 and 1932 on the Religious Character of Ireland', in Mel Farrell, Jason Knirck and Ciara Meehan (eds), *A Formative Decade: Ireland in the 1920s* (Dublin: Irish Academic Press, 2015), pp. 225–34. See also Gillian McIntosh, 'Acts of "National Communion": the Centenary Celebrations for Catholic Emancipation, the Forerunner of the Eucharistic Congress', in Joost Augusteijn (ed.), *Ireland in the 1930s* (Dublin: Four Courts Press, 1999), pp. 83–95.

217 See Moffitt, 'Ireland's Destiny is in the Making', p. 226.

218 McIntosh, 'Centenary Celebrations', p. 84.

219 For an account of the event see Moffitt, 'Ireland's Destiny is in the Making', pp. 235–41.

220 See Moynihan, *Speeches and Statements*, p. 218.

221 D. George Boyce, *Nationalism in Ireland* (London: Routledge, second edition, 1991), pp. 123–53.

222 See Flanagan, *Remembering the Revolution*, p. 4.

223 See Biever, *Religion, Culture and Values*, p. 519.

224 Paul Blanshard, *The Irish and Catholic Power* (London: Derek Verschoyle, 1954), p. 27.

225 Eugene Broderick, *The Boycott at Fethard-on-Sea 1957: A Study in Catholic–Protestant Relations in Modern Ireland* (Newcastle upon Tyne: Cambridge Scholars Publishing, 2011), p. 69. For an account of the central place of the Catholic religion in Irish life in the decades since independence see Marcus Tanner, *Ireland's Holy Wars: The Struggle for a Nation's Soul 1500–2000* (London and New Haven: Yale University Press, 2001), pp. 294–431; Eamon Duffy, *Faith of Our Fathers* (London: Continuum, 2004); and Mary Kenny, *Goodbye to Catholic Ireland* (London: Sinclair-Stevenson, 1997), pp. 1–187.

226 John McGahern, *Memoir* (London: Faber and Faber, 2005), p. 10.

227 Brian Girvin, *From Union to Union: Nationalism, Democracy and Religion in Ireland – Act of Union to EU* (Dublin: Gill and Macmillan, 2002), p. 134.

228 For an overview of these legislative enactments see Whyte, *Church and State*, pp. 24–7.

229 E.J. Cahill, *The Framework of a Christian State* (Dublin: M.H. Gill and Son, 1932), p. xv.

230 Joseph Lee, 'Aspects of Corporatist Thought in Ireland: The Commission on Vocational Organisation 1939–43', in Art Cosgrove and Donal McCartney (eds), *Studies in Irish History: Presented to R. Dudley Edwards* (Dublin: University College Dublin, 1979), p. 324.

231 Whyte, *Church and State*, pp. 68–70. Muintir na Tíre aimed at the social uplift of the Irish countryside by the application of Catholic social teachings.

232 Jesuit Archives, Cahill Papers, An Ríoghacht leaflet. The aims of this organisation were: i) To propagate among Irish Catholics a better knowledge of Catholic social principles; ii) To strive for the effective recognition of these principles in Irish public life; iii) To promote and foster Catholic Social Action.

233 Emmet O'Connor, *A Labour History of Waterford* (Waterford: Waterford Trades Council, 1989), p. 233.

234 Jesuit Archives, Coyne Papers, Letter dated 9 September 1936.

235 See Broderick, *Intellectuals*, p. 13.

236 *Ibid.*, pp. 13–14.

237 Susannah Riordan, 'The Unpopular Front: Catholic Revival and Irish Cultural Identity, 1932–48', in Mike Cronin and John M. Regan (eds), *Ireland: The Politics of Independence, 1922–49* (London: Macmillan Press, 2000), p. 100.

238 Quoted in Kieran Mullarkey, 'Ireland, the Pope and Vocationalism', in Joost Augusteijn (ed.), *Ireland in the 1930s* (Dublin: Four Courts Press, 1999), p. 99.

239 Commission of Inquiry into Banking, Currency and Credit, *Report* (Dublin: Stationery Office, 1938), Minority Report I, Appendix B, 'Catholic Social Principles', pp. 596–608; and Minority Report III, 'Some Economic Aspects of the Papal Encyclicals', pp. 676–80.

240 Sean Faughnan, 'The Jesuits and the Drafting of the Irish Constitution', *Irish Historical Studies*, xxiv, no. 101, May 1988, pp. 84–5.

241 Finola Kennedy, 'Two Priests, the Family and the Constitution', *Studies*, vol. 87, Winter 1998, p. 353.

242 Earl of Longford and Thomas P. O'Neill, *Eamon de Valera* (London: Arrow Books, 1970), p. 295.

243 See Riordan, 'Unpopular Front', p. 101.

244 Bryan Fanning, 'A Catholic Vision of Ireland', in Tom Inglis (ed.), *Are the Irish Different?* (Manchester: Manchester University Press, 2014), p. 46.

245 Jesuit Archives, Cahill Papers, Eamon de Valera to Edward Cahill, 22 March 1932.

246 'Jesuit Submission, October 1936', in Keogh and McCarthy, *Irish Constitution*, pp. 424–5.

247 See Keogh and McCarthy, *Irish Constitution*, p. 107.

248 Maurice Curtis, *A Challenge to Democracy: Militant Catholicism in Modern Ireland* (Dublin: History Press Ireland, 2010), p. 127.

249 See Daly and Hickey, *Irish Constitution*, p. 5.

250 Dónal O'Donnell, 'Review Article: Irish Legal History of the Twentieth Century', *Studies*, vol. 105, no. 147, Spring 2016, p. 104.

251 *Ibid.*

252 *Ibid.*, p. 108.

253 See Hogan, *Irish Constitution*, pp. 233–8.

254 *Ibid.*, p. 239.

255 Jesuit Constitution Committee Minutes. These have been reproduced as Appendix 7, in Keogh and McCarthy, *Irish Constitution*, pp. 413–23.

256 Jesuit Constitution Committee, 'Suggestions for a Catholic Constitution', October 1936. See *ibid.* pp. 424–43.

257 David Fitzpatrick, *The Two Irelands 1912–1939* (Oxford: Oxford University Press, 1998), p. 230.

258 Dermot Keogh, 'The Jesuits and the 1937 Constitution', in Bryan Fanning (ed.), *An Irish Century: Studies 1912–2012* (Dublin: University College Dublin Press, 2012), p. 130. This article was originally published in *Studies*, vol. 78, no. 309, 1989, pp. 82–95.

259 See Hogan, *Irish Constitution*, pp. 210, 212.

260 See Longford and O'Neill, *de Valera*, p. 297.

261 Jesuit Constitution Committee, 'Suggestions for a Catholic Constitution', in Keogh and McCarthy, *Irish Constitution*, p. 430.

262 See *ibid.*, pp. 428–9, for the text of the preamble proposed by the Jesuits.

263 See Hogan, *Irish Constitution*, p. 212.

264 See Keogh and McCarthy, *Irish Constitution*, p. 117.

265 John Cooney, *John Charles McQuaid: Ruler of Catholic Ireland* (Dublin: The O'Brien Press, 1999), p. 94.

266 See Keogh and McCarthy, *Irish Constitution*, p. 107.

267 *Ibid.*, p. 109.

268 Seán Farragher, *Dev and his Alma Mater* (Dublin: Paraclete Press, 1984), p. 174.

269 See Longford and O'Neill, *de Valera*, p. 296.

270 See Keogh and McCarthy, *Irish Constitution*, pp. 111–20.

271 See O Neill and O Fiannachta, *De Valera*, vol. ii, p. 328.

272 See Keogh and McCarthy, *Irish Constitution*, p. 109.

273 Terms used by Cooney in *John Charles McQuaid*. See the title of the biography and p. 288.

274 Clara Cullen and Margaret Ó hÓgartaigh (eds), *His Grace is Displeased: Selected Correspondence of John Charles McQuaid* (Dublin: Merrion, 2013), p. 10.

275 UCDA, Eamon de Valera Papers, P150/2390, Correspondence between John Charles McQuaid and Eamon de Valera, 16 February 1937 to 25 May 1937.

276 Dermot Keogh, 'The Irish Constitutional Revolution: An Analysis of the Making of the Constitution', in Frank Litton (ed.), *The Constitution of Ireland 1937–1987* (Dublin: Institute of Public Administration, 199), p. 20.

277 Cathal Condon, 'An Analysis of the Contribution Made by Archbishop John Charles McQuaid to the Drafting of the 1937 Constitution of Ireland' (Unpublished MA Thesis, University College Cork), p. 61.

278 *Ibid.*, pp. 101–5.

279 UCDA, Eamon de Valera Papers, P150/2371.

280 See Longford and O'Neill, *de Valera*, p. 296.

281 See Keogh and McCarthy, *Irish Constitution*, pp. 112–15.

282 Quoted in *ibid.*, pp. 109–10.

283 John J. Hearne Papers, Address delivered by John J. Hearne to the Legion of Mary, Canada, date unknown, p. 5.

284 See Hearne, 'Baccalaureate Address', p. 9.

285 Quoted in Brian P. Kennedy, 'John Hearne and the Irish Constitution (1937)', *Éire-Ireland*, Summer 1989, p. 125.

286 See Girvin, *Union to Union*, p. 124.

287 Tom Inglis, *Moral Monopoly: The Rise and Fall of the Catholic Church in Modern Ireland* (Dublin: University College Dublin Press, 1998), p. 77.

288 See Girvin, *Union to Union*, p. 125.

289 *Ibid.*, p. 124.

290 See Condon, 'Analysis', p. 221.

291 See Keogh and McCarthy, *Irish Constitution*, p. 86.

292 *Ibid.*, p. 107.

293 Dermot Keogh, 'Church, State and Society', in Brian Farrell (ed.), *De Valera's Constitution and Ours* (Dublin: Gill and Macmillan, 1988), p. 121, note 19.

294 See Kissane, *New Beginnings*, p. 67.

295 See Condon, 'Analysis', pp. 53–90.

296 See O' Neill and O'Fiannachta, *De Valera*, vol. ii, p. 335.

297 Interview with Mrs Nuala Quirke, 27 October 2016. Mrs Quirke is a member of the Cahill Family, business partners in Hearne and Cahill's. John Hearne was her mother's first cousin.

298 See Condon, 'Analysis', p. 70.

299 Joseph Lee, *Ireland 1912–1985: Politics and Society* (Cambridge: Cambridge University Press, 1989), p. 203.

300 *Select Constitutions of the World*, Constitution of the Kingdom of Sweden, Article 2, p. 552.

301 *Ibid.*, Constitution of the Kingdom of Norway, Article 2, p. 522. Article 4 required that the King profess the Evangelical–Lutheran religion. Articles 3 and 5 of the Constitution of the Kingdom of Denmark stated, respectively, that the Evangelical Lutheran Church was to be maintained by the state and that the King must be a member of that church. See *ibid.*, Constitution of the Kingdom of Denmark, p. 297.

302 Gerard Hogan, 'De Valera, the Constitution and the Historians', *Irish Jurist*, 40, 2005, p. 299.

303 Thomas Bartlett, *Ireland: A History* (Cambridge: Cambridge University Press, 2010), p. 448.

304 Dermot Keogh, *The Vatican, the Bishops and Irish Politics* (Cambridge: Cambridge University Press, 1986), p. 213.

305 UCDA, Eamon de Valera Papers, P150/2419, William Henry Massey to Eamon de Valera, 15 April 1937.

306 UCDA, Eamon de Valera Papers, P150/2419, Memorandum by Eamon de Valera, 'Negotiations with the Churches', 16 April 1937.

307 Alvin Jackson, *Ireland, 1798–1998: War, Peace and Beyond* (Chichester: Wiley-Blackwell, 2010), p. 293.

308 See Hogan, *Irish Constitution*, p. 360.

309 Basil Chubb, *The Constitution and Constitutional Change in Ireland* (Dublin: Institute of Public Administration, 1978), p. 41.

310 *Ibid.*

311 See Hogan, *Irish Constitution*, p. 156.

312 www.yale.edu/lawweb/avalon/imt/kbpact.htm, accessed 2 April 2014.

313 Colin Murphy, 'The Origin of the Species', *Law Society Gazette*, October 2012, p. 24.

314 www.avalon.law.yale.edu/20th_century/leagcov.asp, accessed 2 April 2016.

315 For a detailed account of the political struggle between Fianna Fáil and the Free State Senate see Donal O'Sullivan, *The Irish Free State and its Senate* (London: Faber and Faber, 1940), pp. 363–89 and pp. 446–72.

316 *Dáil Debates*, 18 April 1934, 1829. For a list of bills introduced by the Fianna Fáil government and delayed by the Senate see O'Sullivan, *Free State and its Senate*, Appendix F, 'Bills in respect of which the Suspensory Power was exercised by the Senate', pp. 622–5.

317 *Dáil Debates*, 20 June 1933, 783.

318 *Dáil Debates*, 28 May 1936, 1197.

319 *Dáil Debates*, 28 May 1936, 1199.

320 *Dáil Debates*, 20 June 1933, 807.

321 *Dáil Debates*, 28 May 1936, 1201.

322 *Dáil Debates*, 20 April 1934, 141.

323 *Dáil Debates*, 12 December 1935, 2660

324 *Dáil Debates*, 20 April 1934, 2141.

325 *Dáil Debates*, 20 June 1933, 810.

326 *Dáil Debates*, 20 June 1933, 784.

327 *Dáil Debates*, 28 May 1936, 1200.

328 For a discussion of *Quadragesimo Anno* see Broderick, *Intellectuals*, pp. 7–9.

329 Broderick, *Intellectuals*, pp. 9–23. See also Don O'Leary, *Vocationalism and Catholicism in Twentieth-Century Ireland: The Search for a Christian Social Order* (Dublin: Irish Academic Press, 2000), especially pp. 21–64.

330 Dermot Keogh, *Ireland and Europe 1919–1948* (Dublin: Gill and Macmillan, 1988), p. 112.

331 See Cahill, *Framework of a Christian State*, p. 481.

332 D.A. Binchy, 'Proposal for a New Senate', *Studies*, March 1936, p. 24.

333 Alfred O'Rahilly, 'The Constitution and the Senate', *Studies*, March 1936, p. 9.

334 Cornelius Lucey, 'The Principles of Constitution Making', *Irish Ecclesiastical Record*, vol. 49, 1937, p. 29.

335 See Longford and O'Neill, *de Valera*, p. 295.

336 For example, Revd Denis O'Keeffe, 'The Problem of the Senate', *Studies*, June 1936, pp. 204–14; Revd Cornelius Lucey, 'Christian Corporativism', *Irish Ecclesiastical Record*, 49, 1937, pp. 225–41; and John J. Horgan, 'The Problem of Government', *Studies*, December 1933, pp. 537–50.

337 Second House of the Oireachtas Commission, 'Minority Report', pp. 26–34.

338 *Dáil Debates*, 18 April 1934, 1830. See also *Dáil Debates*, 19 April 1934, 2109.

339 NAI, DT S9905.

340 Hearne, Speech delivered in Canada, date and place unknown, p. 3.

341 See Hearne, 'Constitution and National Life', p. 1.

342 *Ibid.*, pp. 1–2.

343 Hearne, Speech delivered in Canada, date and place unknown, p. 4.

344 See Hearne, 'Constitution and National Life', p. 4.

345 Hearne, Address delivered at Harvard Law School Association of New Jersey, p. 8.

346 See Hearne, 'Constitution and National Life', p. 8, note 70.

347 *Ibid.*, p. 4. (NAI, DT S9905).

348 For a discussion of the notion of a 'constitutional moment', see Kissane, *New Beginnings*, pp. xi–xix.

349 Hearne, Address delivered at the Harvard Law School Association of New Jersey, p. 4.

350 See Moynihan, *Speeches and Statements by Eamon de Valera*, p. 354.

351 See Hearne, 'Constitution and National Life', p. 12, note 70.

352 Hearne, Speech delivered in Canada, date and place unknown, p. 8.

353 See Hearne, 'Constitution and National Life', p. 6, note 70.

Chapter 7

1 Among the contributors were John A. Costello (6 May 1937), Diarmad O'Cuadhlaoich, a former judge of the Supreme Court set up by the first Dáil (10 May 1937) and Frank Pakenham, historian and author (13 May 1937).

2 Basil Chubb, *The Politics of the Irish Constitution* (Dublin: Institute of Public Administration, 1991), p. 21.

3 *Dáil Debates*, 13 May 1937, 431–2.

4 *Dáil Debates*, 14 June 1937, 413.

5 Michael Laffan, *Judging W.T. Cosgrave* (Dublin: Royal Irish Academy, 2014), p. 128.

6 Letter to the editor, *The Irish Statesman*, 24 June 1925; quoted in Frances Flanagan, *Remembering the Revolution: Dissent, Culture and Nationalism in the Irish Free State* (Oxford: Oxford University Press, 2015), p. 83.

7 P.S. O'Hegarty, *The Victory of Sinn Féin* (First published 1924; republished by University College Dublin Press, 1998), p. 111.

8 Maryann Valiulis, '"The Man They Could Never Forgive" – The View of the Opposition: Eamon de Valera and the Civil War', in J.P. O'Carroll and John A. Murphy (eds), *De Valera and His Times* (Cork: Cork University Press, 1983) p. 99.

9 See Valiulis, '"The Man they Could Never Forgive"', p. 93.

10 John Coakley, 'An Ambiguous Office? The Position of Head of State in the Irish Constitution', *Irish Jurist*, 48, 2012, p. 52.

11 *Dáil Debates*, 13 May 1937, 401.

12 *Dáil Debates*, 12 May 1937, 251.

13 Brian Murphy, *Forgotten Patriot: Douglas Hyde and the Foundation of the Irish Presidency* (Cork: Collins Press, 2016), p. 59.

14 *Dáil Debates*, 13 May 1937, 381–2.

15 *Dáil Debates*, 28 May 1937, 1237. See also the opinion expressed by James Fitzgerald Kenny on 13 May 1937, 343.

16 *Dáil Debates*, 13 May 1937, 344.

17 See Murphy, *Douglas Hyde*, pp. 75–6.

18 *Irish Independent*, 10 May 1937.

19 Murphy, *Douglas Hyde*, p. 59.

20 *Dáil Debates*, 13 May 1937, 421.

21   Article 15, 1, 1 of the draft constitution presented to the Dáil for its approval.

22   *Constitution of the Irish Free State*, Article 14.

23   Article 39, 1 of the draft constitution presented to the Dáil for its approval.

24   *Irish Press*, 12 May 1937; text of letter to Eamon de Valera.

25   Article 40, 2, 1 of the draft constitution presented to the Dáil for its approval.

26   *Irish Press*, 12 May 1937.

27   Article 44, 5, 2 of the draft constitution presented to the Dáil for its approval.

28   *Irish Press*, 12 May 1937.

29   Margaret Ward (ed.), *In Their Own Words: Women and Irish Nationalism* (Cork: Attic Press, 1995), p. 185.

30   Rosemary Cullen Owens, *A Social History of Women in Ireland 1870–1970* (Dublin: Gill and Macmillan, 2005) p. 272.

31   See, for example, the *Irish Independent*, 7 May, 12 May and 26 May 1937; and the *Irish Press*, 11 May, 12 May, 14 May and 17 May 1937.

32   See Owens, *Social History of Women*, p. 274.

33   See, for example, the remarks of John A. Costello, 2 June 1937, 580; and those of John Marcus O'Sullivan, 2 June 1937, 1595.

34   See Owens, *Social History of Women*, pp. 251–60.

35   *Dáil Debates*, 13 May 1937, 450.

36   *Dáil Debates*, 11 May 1937, 67.

37   *Dáil Debates*, 13 May 1937, 455.

38   *Dáil Debates*, 11 May 1937, 67.

39   See, for example, *Dáil Debates*, 11 May 1937, 64, 68.

40   J.J. Lee, *Ireland 1912–1985: Politics and Society* (Cambridge: Cambridge University Press, 1989), p. 208. See also the speech of Helena Concannon, Fianna Fáil TD, *Dáil Debates*, 12 May 1937, 244–5; and NAI, DT S9880, Letter of J. Walshe to Eamon de Valera, 15 May 1937.

41   *Dáil Debates*, 4 June 1937, 1888–95.

42   *Dáil Debates*, 4 June 1937, 1890–1.

43   *Dáil Debates*, 4 June 1937, 1891–3.

44   *Dáil Debates*, 4 June 1937, 1890, 1893.

45   For an account of reaction in Northern Ireland to the proposed constitution see Dermot Keogh and Andrew McCarthy, *The Making of the Irish Constitution 1937* (Cork: Mercier Press, 2007), pp. 199–203.

46   *Dáil Debates*, 4 June 1937, 1882–8.

47   *Dáil Debates*, 4 June 1937, 1888.

48   NAI, DT S9856, Draft Constitution, May 1937: Miscellaneous suggestions and criticisms.

49   *Irish Independent*, 3 May 1937.

50   Jesuits Archives, Cahill Papers; from the text of article published in a Spanish journal, 10 January 1938.

51   For an account of the career and views of James Hogan see Donnchadh Ó Corráin (ed.), *James Hogan: Revolutionary, Historian, Political Scientist* (Dublin: Four Courts Press, 2001).

52   UCDA, Alfred O'Rahilly Papers, P178/64(1), James Hogan to Alfred O'Rahilly, May 1937.

53   NAI, DT S9856, Fr Thomas Hurley to Eamon de Valera, 25 May 1937.

54   NAI, DT S9902, Fr Edward Cahill to Eamon de Valera, 23 May 1937.

55   NAI, DT S9902, Fr P.J. Gannon to Eamon de Valera, 7 June 1937.

56   NAI, DT S9902, Mr J. Monteith Moynihan to Eamon de Valera, 14 May 1937.

57   NAI, DT S9856, Letter from An Ríoghacht, 27 May 1937.

58   Quoted in Daithí Ó Corráin, 'Articles 41 and 44: Minority Religious Opinion 1937–1986', in Oran Doyle and Eoin Carolan (eds), *The Irish Constitution: Governance and Values* (Dublin: Thomson Round Hall, 2008), p. 56.

59 *Irish Independent*, 8 June 1937.

60 NAI, DT S9852, Rabbinate Committee of the Dublin Jewish Community to Eamon de Valera, 4 May 1937.

61 For a detailed consideration of this point see Dermot Keogh, *Jews in Twentieth-Century Ireland: Refugees, Anti-Semitism and the Holocaust* (Cork: Cork University Press, 1998), in particular pp. 88–198.

62 Brian Walsh, 'The Constitution and Constitutional Rights', in Frank Litton (ed.), *The Constitution of Ireland 1937–1987* (Dublin: Institute of Public Administration, 1988), p. 104.

63 *Dáil Debates*, 11 May 1937, 69–71.

64 *Dáil Debates*, 13 May 1937, 459.

65 *Dáil Debates*, 11 May 1937, 71.

66 *Dáil Debates*, 12 May 1937, 265.

67 Alfred O'Rahilly, *Thoughts on the Constitution* (Dublin: Browne and Nolan, 1937), p. 68.

68 UCDA, Alfred O'Rahilly Papers, P178/64(1), James Hogan to Alfred O'Rahilly, May 1937.

69 NAI, DT S9856, Letter from Michael Keating, national secretary, League of Social Justice, 2 June 1937.

70 NAI, DT S9856, Letter from An Ríoghacht, 27 May 1937.

71 See, for example, the editorial in the *Irish Independent*, 3 May 1937.

72 *Dáil Debates*, 12 May 1937, 267.

73 *Dáil Debates*, 11 May 1937, 56.

74 *Dáil Debates*, 1 June 1937, 1404.

75 *Dáil Debates*, 11 May 1937, 56.

76 *Dáil Debates*, 1 June 1937, 1410.

77 UCDA, Alfred O'Rahilly Papers, P178/65 (2), Article from the *Leader*, written by Michael Tierney. For an account and discussion of Tierney's vocational views see Eugene Broderick, *Intellectuals and the Ideological Hijacking of Fine Gael, 1932–1938* (Newcastle upon Tyne: Cambridge Scholars Publishing, 2010), pp. 41–65.

78 *Irish Independent*, 3 May 1937.

79 *Irish Independent*, 17 May 1937.

80 See O'Rahilly, *Thoughts on the Constitution*, pp. 43–4.

81 *Dáil Debates*, 11 May 1937, 56.

82 *Dáil Debates*, 11 May 1937, 78–9.

83 *Dáil Debates*, 1 June 1937, 1421–2.

84 *Dáil Debates*, 1 June 1937, 1418–23.

85 Occasions on which, according to the parliamentary record, 'notice [was] taken that twenty deputies were not present', *Dáil Debates*, 13 May 1937, 389; 26 May 1937, 1207; 28 May 1937, 1245, 1287; 1 June 1937, 1439; 4 June 1937, 1849, 1875; 10 June 1937, 287; and 14 June 1937, 380.

86 *Irish Independent*, 29 May 1937.

87 NAI DT S9904, McDunphy's copy is annotated as the 'Control copy'.

88 In addition to being amended, some of these articles were renumbered in the draft of the Constitution approved by the Dáil. The number in brackets records the new number: 4, 9, 12, 13 (14), 15 (16), 17 (18), 25 (26), 33 (34), 39 (40), 40 (41), 43 (44), 44(45) and 46 (47).

89 Article 4 in both the draft presented to the Dáil for its approval and in the approved draft.

90 Article 12, 1, 2 in both drafts.

91 Article 25, 2, 1 of the draft constitution presented to the Dáil for its approval and renumbered as Article 26, 2, 1 in the approved draft.

92 Article 14 of the draft constitution approved by the Dáil, it being essentially composed of Article 13, 11, 1 to Article 13, 11, 5 of the draft presented to the Dáil for its approval.

93   Article 39, 6, 1, ii of the draft constitution presented to the Dáil for its approval.

94   Article 9, 1, 3 of the draft constitution presented to the Dáil for its approval and of the approved draft.

95   Article 15, 1, 1 of the draft constitution presented to the Dáil for its approval.

96   Article 16, 1, 3 of the draft constitution approved by the Dáil.

97   Article 45, 4, 2 of the draft constitution approved by the Dáil.

98 · Article 12, 3, 1 of the draft constitution approved by the Dáil.

99   Article 12, 10 of the draft constitution approved by the Dáil.

100   Article 17, 3, 3 of the draft constitution presented to the Dáil for its approval.

101   Article 33, 4, 3.

102   Article 34, 3, 2.

103   Article 34, 4, 2.

104   *Dáil Debates*, 14 June 1937, 434.

105   For full details of the results see Keogh and McCarthy, *Irish Constitution*, pp. 208–11.

106   *Irish Times*, 8 July 1937.

107   See Lee, *Ireland*, p. 211, note 156.

108   *Ibid.*, p. 211.

109   Maurice Moynihan (ed.), *The Speeches and Statements by Eamon de Valera 1917–1973* (Dublin: Gill and Macmillan, 1980), p. 363.

110   See the editorial in the *Irish Times*, 15 June 1937.

111   Bill Kissane, *New Beginnings: Constitutionalism and Democracy in Modern Ireland* (Dublin: University College Dublin Press, 2011), p. xiv.

112   *Irish Independent*, 29 December 1937.

113   *Irish Press*, 29 December 1937.

114   *Irish Press*, 30 December 1937.

115   *Irish Times*, 30 December 1937.

Chapter 8

1   *Irish Independent*, 1 May 1937.

2   Ronan Fanning, *Eamon de Valera: A Will to Power* (London: Faber and Faber, 2015), p. 269.

3   John J. Hearne Papers, Speech delivered in Canada, place and date unknown.

4   It must be remembered that the Irish Free State Constitution was not regarded as a true fundamental law by such republicans.

5   *Irish Times*, 29 December 1937.

6   Garret FitzGerald, 'Eamon de Valera: the Price of his Achievement', in Gabriel Doherty and Dermot Keogh (eds), *De Valera's Irelands* (Cork: Mercier Press, 2003), p. 190.

7   *Ibid.*, p. 192.

8   See Fanning, *Eamon de Valera*, p. 269.

9   Eoin Daly and Tom Hickey, *The Political Theory of the Irish Constitution: Republicanism and the Basic Law* (Manchester: Manchester University Press, 2015), p. 118.

10   Bill Kissane, *New Beginnings: Constitutionalism and Democracy in Modern Ireland* (Dublin: University College Dublin Press, 2011), p. xiv.

11   See FitzGerald, 'Eamon de Valera', p. 196.

12   Owen Dudley Edwards, *Eamon de Valera* (Cardiff: GPC Books, 1987), p. 118.

13   For an exposition of de Valera's attitudes and policies towards partition see John Bowman, *De Valera and the Ulster Question 1917–1973* (Oxford: Clarendon Press, 1982).

14   See Stephen Kelly, *Fianna Fáil, Partition and Northern Ireland 1926–1971* (Dublin: Irish Academic Press, 2013), pp. 107–45.

15   See Bowman, *De Valera*, p. 299.

16   John A. Murphy, 'The Achievement of Eamon de Valera', in John P. Carroll and John A. Murphy (eds), *De Valera and his Times* (Cork: Cork University Press, 1983), p. 5.

17   Donal Barrington, 'The North and the Constitution', in Brian Farrell (ed.), *De Valera's Constitution and Ours* (Dublin: Gill and Macmillan, 1988), pp. 64–7.

18   *Ibid.*, p. 67.

19   *Ibid.*

20   Article 12 of the Covenant of the League of Nations stated: 'The members of the League agree that if there should arise between them any dispute ... they will submit them either to arbitration or judicial settlement ... 'See www.law.yale.edu/20th_century/leagcov.asp, accessed 3 December 2015.

21   Article 2 of the Kellogg–Briand Pact declared that 'the solution of all disputes in conflicts ... shall never be sought except by peaceful means'. See www.yale,edu/lawweb/avalon/imt/kgpact.htm, accessed 3 December 2012.

22   Colin Murphy, 'The Origins of the Species', *Law Society Gazette*, October 2014, p. 24.

23   See Barrington, 'The North and the Constitution', p. 67.

24   See Ronan Fanning, 'The Rule of Order', in J.P. O'Carroll and John A. Murphy (eds), *De Valera and His Times* (Cork: Cork University Press, 1983), pp. 160–72.

25   For an account of the relationship between de Valera and the Irish Republican Army see J. Bowyer Bell, *The Secret Army: The IRA* (Dublin: The Academy Press, 1970), pp. 99–141.

26   Diarmaid Ferriter, *Judging Dev* (Dublin: Royal Irish Academy, 2007), p. 305.

27   *Dáil Debates*, 14 June 1937, 351.

28   *Dáil Debates*, 14 June 1937, 413.

29   For example, see UCDA, Eamon de Valera Papers, P150/3279, P150/2380, P150/2384, P150/2385, P150/2388, P150/2389, P150/2390, P150/2391.

30   Micheál Ó Cearúil, *Bunreacht na hÉireann: A Study of the Irish Text* (Dublin: Stationery Office, 1999), p. 1.

31   For a consideration of the role of the Gaelic League see Kevin B. Nowlan, 'The Gaelic League and other National Movements', in Seán Ó Tuama (ed.), *The Gaelic League Idea* (Cork: Mercier Press, 1972), pp. 41–51.

32   See Reg Hindley, *The Death of the Irish Language* (London: Routledge, 1990).

33   See Ferriter, *Judging Dev*, p. 305.

34   See Adrian Kelly, *Compulsory Irish: Language and Education in Ireland 1870–1970* (Dublin: Irish Academic Press, 2002).

35   John J. Hearne Papers, Address delivered at the St Patrick's Day banquet, held in New Orleans, Louisiana, 18 March 1957, pp. 10–11.

36   Tom Garvin, *Preventing the Future: Why was Ireland so Poor for so Long?* (Dublin: Gill and Macmillan, 2004), p. 168.

37   Oran Doyle, 'Article 44: Privileging the Rights of the Religious', in Oran Doyle and Eoin Carolan (eds), *The Irish Constitution: Governance and Values* (Dublin: Thomson Round Hall, 2008), pp. 479–80.

38   Gerard F. Whyte, 'Some Reflections on the Role of Religion in the Constitutional Order', in Tim Murphy and Patrick Twomey (eds), *Ireland's Evolving Constitution 1937–97: Collected Essays* (Oxford: Hart Publishing, 1998), p. 51, note 1.

39   Michael Gallaher, 'The Changing Constitution', in John Coakley and Michael Gallaher (eds), *Politics in the Republic of Ireland* (Oxford: Routledge, 2009), p. 78.

40   Quoted in Gerard Hogan, *The Origins of the Irish Constitution 1928–1941* (Dublin: Royal Irish Academy, 2012), p. 219, note 38.

41   James O'Reilly and Mary Redmond, *Cases and Materials on the Irish Constitution* (Dublin: Incorporated Law Society of Ireland, 1980), p. 492.

42   Quoted in Hogan, *Irish Constitution*, p. 219, note 38.

43   The memorandum is reproduced in *ibid.*, p. 485.

44   *Dáil Debates*, 4 June 1937, 1890.

45   Dermot Keogh, 'The Role of the Catholic Church in the Republic of Ireland 1922–1995', in *Building Trust: Studies Commissioned for the Forum for Peace and Reconciliation* (Belfast: The Blackstaff Press, 1996), p. 112.

46   R.V. Comerford, *Ireland* (London: Hodder Arnold, 2003), p. 114.

47   Bryan Fanning, 'A Catholic Vision of Ireland', in Tom Inglis (ed.), *Are the Irish Different?* (Manchester: Manchester University Press, 2014), p. 45.

48   Brian Girvin, *From Union to Union: Nationalism, Democracy and Religion in Ireland – Act of Union to EU* (Dublin: Gill and Macmillan, 2002), pp. 134–5.

49   See Comerford, *Ireland*, p. 116.

50   See, for example, Victor Griffin, *Enough Religion to Make Us Hate: Reflections on Religion and Politics* (Dublin: The Columba Press, 2002), especially pp. 28–58. See also Robert Tobin, *The Minority Voice: Hubert Butler and Southern Irish Protestantism 1900–1991* (Oxford: Oxford University Press, 2012), *passim.*

51   Daithí Ó Corráin, 'Articles 41 and 44: Minority Religious Opinion 1937–1986', in Oran Doyle and Eoin Carolan (eds), *The Irish Constitution: Governance and Values* (Dublin: Thomson Round Hall, 2008), p. 70.

52   *Ibid.*, p. 57.

53   *Ibid.*, p. 58.

54   For an overview of the Church of Ireland attitude to divorce see *ibid.*, pp. 58–61.

55   For a discussion of Maria Duce see Keogh, 'The Role of the Catholic Church in the Republic of Ireland', pp. 135–42.

56   For an account of the experience of Protestants in the Irish state see Heather Crawford, *Outside the Glow: Protestants and Irishness in Independent Ireland* (Dublin: University College Dublin Press, 2010); Eugene Broderick, *The Boycott at Fethard-on-Sea 1957: A Study in Catholic–Protestant Relations in Modern Ireland* (Newcastle upon Tyne: Cambridge Scholars Publishing, 2011); and Kurt Bowen, *Protestants in a Catholic State: Ireland's Privileged Minority* (Dublin: McGill-Queen's University Press, 1983).

57   For a considered discussion of these points see Broderick, *Boycott*, pp. 72–5.

58   See Comerford, *Ireland*, p. 117.

59   See Broderick, *Boycott*, pp. 67–72.

60   For a consideration of de Valera's attitude to a vocational Seanad see Don O'Leary, *Vocationalism and Social Catholicism in Twentieth-Century Ireland* (Dublin: Irish Academic Press, 2000), pp. 55–74. See also Eugene Broderick, *Intellectuals and the Ideological Hijacking of Fine Gael 1932–1938* (Newcastle upon Tyne: Cambridge Scholars Publishing, 2010), pp. 119–24.

61   UCDA, Fianna Fáil Archives, Minutes of Parliamentary Party Meetings, P176/444, Minutes of meeting held on 18 November 1937.

62   For a consideration of this act see Tom Garvin, *The Irish Senate* (Dublin: Institute of Public Administration, 1969), pp. 21–3.

63   *Special Report of the Special Committee on Seanad Election (Panel Members) Bill 1937* (Dublin: Stationery Office, 1937), pp. xiii, xiv, xxii, xxiii.

64   Joseph Lee, 'Aspects of Corporatist Thought in Ireland: The Committee on Vocational Organisation', in Art Cosgrove and Donal McCartney (eds), *Studies in Irish History: Presented to R. Dudley Edwards* (Dublin: University College Dublin, 1979), p. 325.

65   *Irish Times*, 30 March 1938.

66   Arthur Bromage and Mary C. Bromage, 'The Vocational Senate in Ireland', *American Political Science Review*, vol. 24, 1940, pp. 519–38.

67 The terms of reference of the commission were 'to examine and report on: (a) the practicality of developing functional or vocational organisation in the circumstances of this country; (b) the means best calculated to promote such development; (c) the rights and powers which should be conferred and the duties which should be imposed on functional or vocational bodies ... and; (d) the legislative and administrative measures that would be required.' *Report of the Commission on Vocational Organisation* (Dublin: Stationery Office, 1943), p. 1.

68 *Report of the Commission on Vocational Organisation*, p. 436, par. 696.

69 Basil Chubb, 'Vocational Representation and the Irish Senate', *Political Studies*, vol. II, no. 2, 1954, p. 98.

70 *Report of the Working Group on Seanad Reform*, 2015, p. 17. www.merrionstreet.ie/en/ImageLibrary/20150413SeanadReformFinal1.pdf, accessed 4 October 2016.

71 All Party Oireachtas Committee on the Constitution, *Second Progress Report: Seanad Éireann* (Dublin: Stationery Office, 1997), p. 4.

72 David Gwynn Morgan, *The Constitutional Law of Ireland: The Law of the Executive, Legislature and Judicature* (Dublin: Round Hall, 1985), p. 89.

73 James Hogan, *Modern Democracy* (Cork: Cork University Press, 1938), p. 78. For the list of bodies to which Hogan referred see *Report of the Second House of the Oireachtas Commission* (Dublin: Stationery Office, 1936), pp. 31–2.

74 See Garvin, *Irish Senate*, p. 24; and J.J. Lee, *Ireland 1912–1985: Politics and Society* (Cambridge: Cambridge University Press, 1989), pp. 273–4.

75 See Garvin, *Irish Senate*, pp. 27–32.

76 See Hogan, *Modern Democracy*, pp. 77–8.

77 UCDA, Fianna Fáil Archives, Minutes of Parliamentary Party Meetings, P176/444, Minutes of meeting held on 18 November 1937.

78 UCDA, Fianna Fáil Archives, Minutes of Parliamentary Party Meetings, P176/444, Minutes of meeting held on 13 January 1938.

79 UCDA, Fianna Fáil Archives, Minutes of Parliamentary Party Meetings, P176/444, Minutes of meeting held on 1 March 1938.

80 Quoted in Jim O'Callaghan, 'Seanad Éireann – an Opportunity for Real Reform', in Eoin Carolan (ed.), *The Irish Constitution: Perspectives and Prospects* (London: Bloomsbury Professional, 2012), p. 234.

81 For a detailed consideration of de Valera's attitude to this matter see Lee, 'Aspects of Corporatist Thought', pp. 324–46.

82 See Garvin, *Irish Senate*, p. 80.

83 Seanad Electoral Law Commission, *Report*, 1959 (Dublin: Stationery Office, 1959). See Garvin, *Irish Senate*, pp. 80–5 for an excellent summary of the proposed reforms.

84 For an account of the reaction to the report see Garvin, *Irish Senate*, pp. 85–7. It should be noted that other party leaders were equally unenthusiastic about a vocational Seanad.

85 Basil Chubb, *The Government and Politics of Ireland* (London: Longmans, second edition, 1982), p. 211.

86 John Coakley and Michael Laver, 'Options for the Future of Seanad Éireann', Appendix II, All Party Oireachtas Committee on the Constitution, *Second Progress Report: Seanad Éireann*, p. 43.

87 See O'Callaghan, 'Seanad Éireann', p. 232.

88 *Ibid.*, p. 235.

89 www.michaelpidgeon.com/manifestos/docs/ff//, p. 30, accessed 14 December 2015.

90 www.rte.ie/news/2013/1005/478505-referendum-count/, accessed 15 December 2015.

91 John J. Hearne Papers, Address delivered at the annual meeting of the Harvard Law School Association of New Jersey, at Newark, New Jersey, 23 May 1957, p. 11.

92 *Ibid.*, p. 12.

93   For an account and analysis of the Fianna Fáil government reaction to this report see Lee, 'Aspects of Corporatist Thought', pp. 324–46.

94   See Broderick, *Intellectuals*, pp. 118, 129–35.

95   Hearne, Address delivered at the annual meeting of the Harvard Law School Association of New Jersey, pp. 12–13.

96   John Coakley and Kevin Rafter, 'Introduction: New Perspectives on the President of Ireland', in John Coakley and Kevin Rafter (eds), *The Irish Presidency: Power, Ceremony and Politics* (Dublin: Irish Academic Press, 2014), p. 1.

97   Michael Gallaher, 'The Political Role of the President', in John Coakley and Kevin Rafter (eds), *The Irish Presidency: Power, Ceremony and Politics* (Dublin: Irish Academic Press, 2014), p. 41.

98   Quoted in Janet Dunleavy and Gareth Dunleavy, *Douglas Hyde: A Founder of Modern Ireland* (California: University of California Press, 1991), p. 369.

99   *Ibid.*, p. 408.

100   Ciara Meehan, 'The Early Presidents 1938–1973', in John Coakley and Kevin Rafter (eds), *The Irish Presidency: Power, Ceremony and Politics* (Dublin: Irish Academic Press, 2014), p. 86.

101   Quoted in Dunleavy and Dunleavy, *Douglas Hyde*, p. 370.

102   See Meehan, 'Early Presidents', p. 100.

103   John Coakley, 'Prehistory of the Presidency', in John Coakley and Kevin Rafter (eds), *The Irish Presidency: Power, Ceremony and Politics* (Dublin: Irish Academic Press, 2014), p. 60.

104   See Hogan, *Irish Constitution*, p. 175.

105   UCDA, Eamon de Valera Papers, P150/2373, 'Draft Heads of a Constitution', October 1936.

106   Robert Elgie, 'The President in Comparative Perspective', in John Coakley and Kevin Rafter (eds), *The Irish Presidency: Power, Ceremony and Politics* (Dublin: Irish Academic Press, 2014), pp. 22–7.

107   Francis X. Beytagh, *Constitutionalism in Contemporary Ireland: An American Perspective* (Dublin: Round Hall Sweet & Maxwell, 1997), p. 136.

108   Yvonne Galligan, 'Activist Presidents and Gender Politics 1990–2011', in John Coakley and Kevin Rafter (eds), *The Irish Presidency: Power, Ceremony and Politics* (Dublin: Irish Academic Press, 2014), p. 145.

109   For an overview of President Robinson's term of office see *ibid.*, pp. 127–33.

110   *Ibid.*, p. 146.

111   For an overview of President McAleese's term of office see *ibid.*, pp. 133–43.

112   *Ibid.*, p. 146.

113   *Ibid.*

114   For discussion of aspects of President Higgins's presidency see Diarmaid Ferriter, 'Higgins's reflection on Civil War spotlights thorny issues', *Irish Times*, 27 August 2016; Fintan O'Toole, 'A head of state unlike any other', *Irish Times*, 17 September 2016; and Ronan O'Reilly, 'Out of left field – the Majesty of Michael D', *Irish Daily Mail*, 9 September 2017. At the time of writing, a book of his speeches has just been published: *When Ideas Matter: Speeches for an Ethical Republic* (London: Head of Zeus, 2017).

115   For a consideration of circumstances in which Presidents faced decisions pertaining to the exercise of this power see Dunleavy and Dunleavy, *Douglas Hyde*, pp. 428–9; Michael Gallaher, 'The President, the People and the Constitution', in Brian Farrell (ed.), *De Valera's Constitution and Ours* (Dublin: Gill and Macmillan, 1988), pp. 83–7; and Kevin Rafter, 'The Politics of a "Non-Political" Office, 1973–1990', in John Coakley and Kevin Rafter (eds), *The Irish Presidency: Power, Ceremony and Politics* (Dublin: Irish Academic Press, 2014) , pp. 121–3.

116   See Gallaher, 'Political Role of the President', p. 50, Table 3.1.

117   *Ibid.*, p. 52, Table 3.2.

118   See *Report of the Constitution Review Group* (Dublin: Stationery Office, 1996), pp. 69–73; Niamh Howlin, 'Shortcomings and Anomalies: Aspects of Article 26', *Irish Student Law Review*, vol. 13, 2005, pp. 31–48; and Beytagh, *Constitutionalism*, p. 20.

119 *Report of the Constitution Review Group*, p. 68.

120 See Morgan, *Constitutional Law of Ireland*, p. 106.

121 *A v Governor of Arbour Hill Prison* [2006] 4 IR 88, p. 146.

122 For consideration and assessment of judicial review as it applies to the Irish Constitution see Francis X. Beytagh, *Constitutionalism*, pp. 56–111; Francis X. Beytagh, 'Individual Rights, Judicial Review and Written Constitutions', in James O'Reilly (ed.), *Human Rights and Constitutional Law: Essays in Honour of Brian Walsh* (Dublin: Round Hall Press, 1992), pp. 147–62; Basil Chubb, *The Constitution and Constitutional Change in Ireland* (Dublin: Institute of Public Administration, 1978), pp. 37–51; Basil Chubb, *Politics of the Irish Constitution* (Dublin: Institute of Public Administration, 1991), pp. 60–78; Gallaher, 'Changing Constitution', pp. 84–95; K.C. Wheare, *Modern Constitutions* (Oxford: Oxford University Press, 1966), pp. 100–20; and Séamus Ó Tuama, 'Judicial Review under the Irish Constitution: More American than Commonwealth', vol. 12.2, *Electronic Journal of Comparative Law*, October 2008, pp. 1–22.

123 James Casey, *Constitutional Law in Ireland* (London: Sweet & Maxwell, 1992), p. 24; and John Kelly, 'Fundamental Rights and the Constitution', in Brian Farrell (ed.), *De Valera's Constitution and Ours* (Dublin: Gill and Macmillan, 1988), pp. 166–7.

124 See Gallaher, 'Changing Constitution', p. 86.

125 See Beytagh, *Constitutionalism*, p. 43.

126 Donal Barrington, 'The Constitution in the Courts', in Frank Litton (ed.), *The Constitution of Ireland 1937–1987* (Dublin: Institute of Public Administration, 1988), p. 111. For a brief survey of George Gavan Duffy's judicial decisions see Kelly, 'Fundamental Rights and the Constitution', pp. 166–7.

127 Maurice Hearne, Papers relating to a proposed biography of John. J. Hearne, 'Constitution – Postscript'.

128 For an overview of this judicial activism see Beytagh, *Constitutionalism*, pp. 56–111.

129 Ruadhán Mac Cormaic, *The Supreme Court* (London: Penguin, 2016), pp. 78–9.

130 See Beytagh, *Constitutionalism*, p. 57.

131 See Ó Tuama, 'Judicial Review', p. 2.

132 See Barrington, 'The Constitution in the Courts', p. 115; and Beytagh, *Constitutionalism*, p. 57; and Mac Cormaic, *Supreme Court*, pp. 72–90. For an assessment of the career of Brian Walsh see Gerard Hogan, 'The Early Judgments of Mr Justice Brian Walsh' in James O'Reilly (ed.), *Human Rights and Constitutional Law: Essays in Honour of Brian Walsh* (Dublin: Round Hall Press, 1992), pp. 37–48.

133 See Barrington, 'Constitution in the Courts', 115.

134 See Hogan, 'Early Judgments of Mr Justice Brian Walsh', p. 38.

135 See Maurice Hearne, 'Constitution – Post Script'.

136 UCDA, Cearbhall Ó Dálaigh Papers, P51.

137 See Barrington, 'Constitution in the Courts', p. 114.

138 Gerard Hogan, 'Irish Nationalism as a Legal Ideology', *Studies*, Winter 1986, p. 532.

139 NAI DT S9905, 'The Constitution and National Life', memorandum prepared by John J. Hearne, 12 June 1937, 1–2.

140 See Maurice Hearne, 'Constitution – Post Script'.

141 See Beytagh, *Constitutionalism*, p. 59.

142 R.V.F. Heuston, 'Personal Rights in the Irish Constitution', *Irish Jurist*, 11, 1976, p. 219. See *Ryan v Attorney General* [1965] IR 294.

143 *Ryan v Attorney General* [1965], 294, p. 313.

144 James Casey, 'Changing the Constitution: Amendment and Judicial Review', in Brian Farrell (ed.), *De Valera's Constitution and Ours* (Dublin: Gill and Macmillan, 1988), pp. 159–60.

145   *McGee v Attorney General* [1974] IR 284, p. 318.

146   *Report of the Constitution Review Group*, p. 222. For a survey of cases considered by the superior courts see Beytagh, *Constitutionalism*, pp. 56–111.

147   *Report of the Constitution Review Group*, p. 222.

148   See Beytagh, 'Individual Rights, Judicial Review and Written Constitutions', p. 160.

149   Susan Denham, 'Some Thoughts on the Constitution of Ireland at 75', Paper presented on 28 June 2012, at a conference on 'The Irish Constitution: Past, Present and Future', organised by the UCD Constitutional Studies Group, p. 22.

150   See Denham, 'Some Thoughts on the Constitution', p. 22.

151   *G v An Bórd Uchtála*, [1980] IR 32, p. 56.

152   *In re A Ward of Court (No. 2)* [1996] 2IR 79, p. 163.

153   *Report of the Constitution Review Group*, p. 225.

154   Quoted in Beytagh, *Constitutionalism*, pp. 57–8.

155   See Casey, *Constitutional Law in Ireland*, p. 24.

156   Justice Brian Walsh, quoted in Mac Cormaic, *Supreme Court*, p. 80.

157   Basil Chubb, *Constitution and Constitutional Change in Ireland*, p. 1.

158   *McKenna v An Taoiseach* [1995] 2 IR, p. 38.

159   *McGee v the Attorney General* [1974] IR 284, p. 310.

160   Quoted in Paul Gallaher, 'The Irish Constitution – Its Unique Nature and the Relevance of International Jurisprudence', *Irish Jurist*, 45, 2010, p. 30.

161   See Denham, 'Some Thoughts on the Constitution', p. 20.

162   Brian Walsh, Foreword, in James O'Reilly and Mary Redmond, *Cases and Materials on the Irish Constitution* (Dublin: Incorporated Law Society of Ireland, 1980), p. xii.

163   *McGee v the Attorney General* [1974] IR 284, p. 319.

164   Brian Walsh, 'The Constitution: A View from the Bench', in Brian Farrell (ed.), *De Valera's Constitution and Ours* (Dublin: Gill and Macmillan, 1998), p. 195.

165   *Ibid.*

166   See Denham, 'Some Thoughts on the Constitution', p. 19.

167   *Ibid.*, p. 17.

168   *McGee v the Attorney General* [1974] IR 284, pp. 310, 318.

169   Gerard Hogan, 'Constitutional Interpretation', in Frank Litton (ed.), *The Constitution of Ireland 1937–1987* (Dublin: Institute of Public Administration, 1998), p. 176.

170   The opinion of Mr Justice Kenny, *Ryan v the Attorney General* [1965] IR 294, p. 313.

171   *McGee v the Attorney General* [1974] IR 284, p. 325.

172   See Beytagh, *Constitutionalism*, p. 32.

173   *Ibid.*, p. 116.

174   See Ó Tuama, 'Judicial Review', p. 2.

175   Earl of Longford and Thomas P. O Neill, *Eamon de Valera* (London: Arrow Books, 1970), p. 473.

176   For a consideration of the influence of natural law on constitutional interpretation and jurisprudence see Gerard Hogan and Gerry Whyte, *J.M.Kelly: The Irish Constitution* (Dublin: Buttersworth, third edition, 1994), cxviii, pp. 677–82; Aileen Kavanagh, 'The Irish Constitution at 75 Years: Natural Law, Christian Values and the Ideal of Justice', *Irish Jurist*, 48, 2012, pp. 71–101; Declan O'Keeffe, 'God, the Natural Law and the 1937 Constitution' in Eoin Carolan (ed.), *The Constitution of Ireland: Perspective and Prospects* (London: Bloomsbury Professional, 2012), pp. 111–41; and Daly and Hickey, *Irish Constitution*, pp. 152–6.

177   See Daly and Hickey, *Irish Constitution*, p. 153.

178   *McGee v the Attorney General* [1974] IR 284, p. 317.

179   Gerard Hogan, 'Unenumerated Personal Rights: *Ryan's* Case Re-evaluated', *Irish Jurist*, 25–7, 1990–2, p. 96.

180 See O'Keeffe, 'God, the Natural Law and the 1937 Constitution', p. 114.

181 See Daly and Hickey, *Irish Constitution*, p. 5.

182 See Ronan Keane, 'Judges as Lawmakers: The Irish Experience', *Judicial Studies Institute Journal*, vol. 4, no. 2, 2004, pp. 1–18.

183 John Kelly, *Fundamental Rights in Irish Law and the Constitution* (Dublin: Allen Figgis, 1967), pp. 45–6.

184 Quoted in Hogan, '*Ryan's* Case Re-evaluated', p. 114.

185 Gerard Casey, 'Are There Unenumerated Rights in the Irish Constitution?' www.researchdepository. ucd.ie/bitstream/handle/10197/5336/Are_There_Unenumerated_Rights_in_the_Irish_ Constitution%3f.pdf?sequence=1, accessed 24 April 2016, p. 5. Casey has written: 'The subject and agent referred to in the appropriate sections of Article 40 is the State that, variously, is assigned the task of respecting, defending, vindicating and protecting various rights. But the State exercises *all* the powers of government, legislative, executive and judicial, through the appropriate organs and so it would appear to be an open question as to which of these three organs of government, alone or in combination, shoulders the designated duty of ascertaining and declaring the personal rights of the citizen.'

186 *Ibid.*, p. 3. The ninth amendment of the United States Constitution reads: 'The enumeration in the Constitution of certain rights shall not be construed to deny or disparage others retained by the people.'

187 See Mac Cormaic, *Supreme Court*, p. 334.

188 *Report of the Constitution Review Group*, p.227.

189 See Hogan, 'Constitutional Interpretation', p. 181.

190 Richard Humphreys, 'Constitutional Interpretation', *Dublin University Law Journal*, 15, 1993, pp. 59–77. This complex issue has been the subject of other scholarly contributions; see, for example Lesley A. Walter, 'Law as Literature: Illuminating the Debate over Constitutional Consistency', www.corkonlinelawreview.com/editions/2004/2004xi.pdf, accessed 6 May 2016; and Conor O'Mahony, 'Societal Change and Constitutional Interpretation', *Irish Journal of Legal Studies*, 1(2), 2010, pp. 71–115.

191 See Hogan and Whyte, *Irish Constitution*, p. cxviii.

192 See Mac Cormaic, *Supreme Court*, p. 33.

193 The observation of constitutional lawyer, Oran Doyle, cited in *ibid.*, p. 336.

194 *Ibid.*

195 See Keane, 'Judges as Lawmakers', p. 15.

196 See Daly and Hickey, *Irish Constitution*, p. 155; O'Keeffe, 'God, the Natural Law and the 1937 Constitution', p. 111.

197 For the background to this bill see Kavanagh, 'Constitution at 75 Years', pp. 86–7.

198 *Ibid.*, pp. 88–9.

199 For a summary of the judgment see *ibid.*, pp. 89–91.

200 See Daly and Hickey, *Irish Constitution*, p. 155.

201 *Ibid.*, p. 155.

202 See Kavanagh, 'Constitution at 75', p. 83.

203 See Hogan and Whyte, *Irish Constitution*, p. 6.

204 *Ibid.*, *Irish Constitution*, pp. 767–8. For a consideration of the *Norris* case see Mac Cormaic, *Supreme Court*, pp. 200–15.

205 See Kavanagh, 'Constitution at 75', p. 99.

206 *Ibid.*, p. 73.

207 For a consideration of this ambition for a distinctive Irish legal system see Bryan M.E. McMahon, 'A Sense of Identity in the Irish Legal System', in Joseph Lee (ed.), *Ireland: Towards a Sense of Place* (Cork: University College Cork, 1985), pp. 34–46.

208   For an account of Hugh Kennedy's efforts see Ronan Keane, 'The Voice of the Gael: Chief Justice Kennedy and the Emergence of the New Irish Court System 1921–1936', *Irish Jurist*, 31, 1996, pp. 205–25.

209   See G. M. Golding, *George Gavan Duffy* (Dublin: Irish Academic Press, 1982).

210   See Keane, 'Voice of the Gael', p. 221.

211   *Ibid.*, pp. 221–3.

212   *Ibid.*, p. 223.

213   See Hogan, 'Irish Nationalism as a Legal Ideology', p. 532.

214   See McMahon, 'Sense of Identity', p. 39.

215   See Hogan, 'Irish Nationalism as a Legal Ideology', p. 532.

216   See Kavanagh, 'Constitution at 75 Years', p. 99.

217   Donal O'Donnell, 'Irish Legal History in the Twentieth Century', *Studies*, vol. 105, no. 417, Spring 2016, p. 109.

218   See Hogan, 'Irish Nationalism as a Legal Ideology', p. 536.

219   Garret FitzGerald, 'The Irish Constitution in its Historical Context', in Tim Murphy and Patrick Twomey (eds), *Ireland's Evolving Constitution 1937–97: Collected Essays* (Oxford: Hart Publishing, 1998), p. 38.

220   www.un.org/en/universal-declaration-human-rights/, accessed 16 February 2016.

221   www.ec.europa.eu/justice/fundamental-rights/charter/index_en.htm, accessed 16 February 2016.

222   See Gallaher, 'Changing Constitution', p. 80.

223   *Constitution of Ireland*, Article 51. The first President entered upon office on 25 June 1938.

224   Department of the Environment, Community and Local Government, *Referendum Results 1937–2015*, p. 6.

225   For an excellent survey of these changes see Diarmaid Ferriter, *The Transformation of Ireland 1900–2000* (London: Profile Books, 2004), pp. 536–759.

226   For an examination of the relationship between the Constitution and Northern Ireland see Chubb, *The Politics of the Irish Constitution* (Dublin: Institute of Public Administration, 1991), pp. 79–95.

227   See Bowman, *De Valera*, p. 323.

228   For a brief overview of the work of the committee see Chubb, *Politics of the Irish Constitution*, pp. 83–4; and Bowman, *De Valera*, pp. 323–5.

229   *Report of the Committee on the Constitution* (Dublin: Stationery Office, 1967), par. 12.

230   Department of the Environment, *Referendum Results 1937–2015*, Referendum on the Nineteenth Amendment of the Constitution Bill 1998, pp. 60–1.

231   *Report of the Committee on the Constitution*, par. 136.

232   *Ibid.*, par. 139.

233   Department of the Environment, *Referendum Results 1937–2015*, Referendum on the Fifth Amendment of the Constitution Bill 1972, pp. 30–1.

234   Louise Fuller, *Irish Catholicism since 1950: The Undoing of a Culture* (Dublin: Gill and Macmillan, 2002), p. 194.

235   For comprehensive accounts of the changing role of religion in modern Ireland see Fuller, *Irish Catholicism*; and Tom Inglis, *Moral Monopoly: The Rise and Fall of the Catholic Church in Modern Ireland* (Dublin: University College Dublin Press, 1998).

236   See p. 296.

237   See Ferriter, *Transformation*, p. 666.

238   See Chubb, *Politics of the Irish Constitution*, pp. 57–9; Ferriter, *Transformation*, pp. 718–19.

239   Department of the Environment, *Referendum Results,* Referendum on the Fifteenth Amendment of the Constitution (No. 2) Bill 1995, pp. 52–3. The result was 818,842 votes in favour; 809, 728 against.

240 Department of the Environment, *Referendum Results*, Referendum on the Thirty-Fourth Amendment of the Constitution Bill 2015, pp. 92–3.

241 Department of the Environment, *Referendum Results*, pp. 26–7; pp. 42–5; pp. 58–9; pp. 68–9; pp. 72–3; pp.76–9; pp. 84–5.

242 This paragraph is based on Chubb, *Politics of the Irish Constitution*, pp. 96–116.

243 *McKenna v An Taoiseach (No.2)* [1995] 2IR, p. 41.

244 www.tre.ie/documents/news/nccrystal-v-theminister.pdf, par. 1, accessed 5 May 2016.

245 Department of the Environment, *Referendum Results*, pp. 26–7; pp. 32–5. The referenda on adoption and university representation in Seanad Éireann were held on the same day, 5 July 1979.

246 Calculation based on percentage turnout as recorded in Department of the Environment, *Referendum Results*. For an interesting commentary on voter turnout in referenda see Richard Sinnott, 'The Involvement of the People in the Referendum Process', Appendix 3, All-Party Oireachtas Committee on the Constitution, *Sixth Progress Report: The Referendum* (Dublin: Stationery Office, 2001), pp. 52–63.

247 See *The Referendum*, p. 23.

248 See Gallaher, 'Changing Constitution', pp. 82–3.

249 *Crotty v An Taoiseach* [1987] IR 713, p. 783.

250 See Gallaher, 'Changing Constitution', p.83.

251 John J. Hearne Papers, 'The National Constitution of Ireland', Address delivered at Villanova College, Pennsylvania, 22 September 1950, 16.

252 *Ibid.*, pp. 15–16.

253 Hearne, Address delivered at the annual meeting of the Harvard Law School Association of New Jersey, pp. 9–10.

254 *Ibid.*, p. 10.

255 *Ibid.*, pp. 10–11.

256 For a discussion of the manifesto quality of the Constitution see John Kelly, 'The Constitution: Law and Manifesto', in Frank Litton (ed.), *The Constitution of Ireland 1937–1987* (Dublin: Institute of Public Administration, 1987), pp. 208–17.

257 For an overview of Catholic social teaching in the 1930s see Broderick, *Intellectuals*, pp. 7–14. A more detailed treatment is to be found in O'Leary, *Vocationalism and Social Catholicism*, pp. 5–37.

258 See Hearne, 'National Constitution of Ireland', p. 16.

259 *Report of the Constitution Review Group*, p. 369.

260 Quoted in Hogan and Whyte, *Irish Constitution*, p. 1119.

261 Gearóid Carey, 'The Constitutional Dilemma of Article 45: An Avenue for Welfare and Social Rights?' *Irish Student Law Review*, no. 5 (1995), p. 79.

262 Anthony Coughlan, 'The Constitution and Social Policy', in Frank Litton (ed.), *The Constitution of Ireland 1937–1987* (Dublin: Institute of Public Administration, 1988), p. 145.

263 *Ibid.* p.147.

264 For a discussion of this point see Hogan and Whyte, *Irish Constitution*, pp. 1120–3.

265 See Murphy, 'Achievement of Eamon de Valera', p. 11.

266 Patrick Lynch, 'The Social Revolution That Never Was', in Desmond Williams (ed.), *The Irish Struggle 1916–1923* (London: Routledge and Kegan Paul, 1966), pp. 41–54.

267 See Fanning, *Eamon de Valera*, p. 35. This was de Valera's reply to a question by John Murray, then a university student and later Chief Justice.

268 See Murphy, 'Achievement of Eamon de Valera', p. 11.

269 See Lee, *Ireland*, p. 208.

270 See Denham, 'Some Thoughts on the Constitution', p. 18.

271 *Ibid.*, p. 19.

272 www.ec.europa/justice/fundamental-rights/charter/index_en.htm, accessed 16 February 2016.

273　See Gallaher, 'Irish Constitution', p. 28.

274　This was Mrs Helena Concannon, TD. See Second House of the Oireachtas Commission, *Report*, p. 4.

275　The opinion of Dr Yvonne Scannell in 'The Constitution and the Role of Women', in Brian Farrell (ed.), *De Valera's Constitution and Ours* (Dublin: Gill and Macmillan, 1988), p. 123.

276　Dolores Dooley, 'Gendered Citizenship in the Irish Constitution', in Tim Murphy and Patrick Twomey (eds), *Ireland's Evolving Constitution 1937–97: Collected Essays* (Oxford: Hart Publishing, 1998), p. 133.

277　Siobhán Mullally, 'On Woman in the Home', https://www.constitution.ie/AttachmentDownload.ashx?, accessed 15 February 2016.

278　For a consideration of the role of woman in the family see Inglis, *Moral Monopoly*, pp. 178–200.

279　Mary E. Daly, '"Oh, Kathleen Ní Houlihan, Your Way's a Thorny Way!": The Condition of Women in Twentieth-Century Ireland', in Anthony Bradley and Maryann Valiulis (eds), *Gender and Sexuality in Modern Ireland* (Amherst: University of Massachusetts Press, 1997), p. 102.

280　See Scannell, 'Role of Women', pp. 124–5. The emphasis is that of Dr Scannell.

281　For an overview of the condition of women in the early years of the state see Rosemary Cullen Owens, *A Social History of Women in Ireland* (Dublin: Gill and Macmillan, 2005), pp. 251–79.

282　For an insight into the issues affecting women in the 1960s see June Levine (ed.), 'The Women's Movement in the Republic of Ireland', in *The Field Day Anthology of Irish Writing*, vol. V, *Irish Writings and Traditions* (Cork: Cork University Press, 2002), pp. 177–228. This is a compilation of contemporary writings concerned with matters relating to the condition of women during this decade.

283　Catriona Kennedy, 'Women and Gender in Modern Ireland', in Richard Bourke and Ian McBride (eds), *The Princeton History of Modern Ireland* (Princeton: Princeton University Press, 2016), p. 375.

284　This manifesto, entitled *Chains or Change*, was issued in March 1971. See Scannell, 'Role of Women', p. 130. See also Maria Luddy, 'Feminism', in Richard Bourke and Ian McBride (eds), *The Princeton History of Modern Ireland* (Princeton: Princeton University Press, 2016), pp. 484–6.

285　See Luddy, 'Feminism', p. 485.

286　See Scannell, 'Role of Women', pp. 130–1.

287　Frank Martin, 'The Family in the Constitution – Principle and Practice', in Tim Murphy and Patrick Twomey (eds), *Ireland's Evolving Constitution 1937–97: Collected Essays* (Oxford: Hart Publishing, 1998), p. 83.

288　See Hogan and Whyte, *Irish Constitution*, p. 1010.

289　*Report of the Constitution Review Group*, p. 311.

290　See Hogan and Whyte, *Irish Constitution*, pp. 1010–11.

291　See Martin, 'Family in the Constitution', p. 90.

292　*Ibid.*, p. 86.

293　See Kennedy, 'Women and Gender', p. 375.

294　Alpha Connelly, 'The Constitution', in Alpha Connelly (ed.), *Gender and the Law in Ireland* (Dublin: Oak Tree Press, 1993), p. 6. For an excellent consideration of many of the issues in this regard see All-Party Oireachtas Committee on the Constitution, *Tenth Progress Report: The Family* (Dublin: Stationery Office, 2006).

295　See *The Family*, p. 106.

296　*Ibid.*, p. 127.

297　See Scannell, 'Role of Women', p. 131. See Connelly, 'The Constitution', pp. 4–27, for an overview of court decisions as they related to women up to 1992.

298　See Connelly, 'The Constitution', p. 6.

299   *Sinnott v Minister for Education* [2001] 2 IR, pp. 664–5.

300   See *The Family*, p. 108.

301   *Ibid.*, p. 120.

302   See Scannell, 'Role of Women', p. 134.

303   *Report of the Constitution Review Group,* p. 337.

304   *Ibid.*

305   Dónal O'Donnell, 'Property Rights in the Irish Constitution: Rights for Rich People, or a Pillar
       of Free Society?' in Oran Doyle and Eoin Carolan (eds), *The Irish Constitution: Governance and
       Values* (Dublin: Thomson Round Hall, 2008), p. 429.

306   Ronan Keane, 'Property in the Constitution and in the Courts', in Brian Farrell (ed.), *De Valera's
       Constitution and Ours* (Dublin: Gill and Macmillan, 1988), p. 145.

307   Louis McRedmond, *To the Greater Glory: A History of the Irish Jesuits* (Dublin: Gill and Macmillan,
       1991), p. 289.

308   See Hogan and Whyte, *Irish Constitution*, p. 1061.

309   All-Party Oireachtas Committee on the Constitution, *Ninth Progress Report: Private Property*
       (Dublin: Stationery Office, 2004), p. 21.

310   See Keane, 'Property in the Constitution', p. 146; O'Donnell, 'Property Rights in the Irish
       Constitution', p. 413.

311   For an overview of the *Kenny Report* see, *Private Property*, pp. 23–5.

312   Elaine Byrne, *Political Corruption in Ireland: A Crooked Harp?* (Manchester: Manchester
       University Press, 2012), p. 73.

313   *Ibid.*, p. 71.

314   That the Constitution's provisions on private property were being invoked for this purpose was the
       view of some members of the Constitution Review Group. See *Report of the Constitution Review
       Group*, pp. 336, 339.

315   *Ibid.*, p. 339.

316   *Ibid.*, p. 338.

317   See *Private Property*, p. 39.

318   *Ibid.*, p. 61.

319   Quoted in *ibid.*, p. 25.

320   See note 20 in *ibid.* Official advice was heavily informed by the ruling of the Supreme Court in
       Blake v Attorney General (1982) when it was held that provisions of the Rent Restriction Act 1960,
       as amended, was unconstitutional. See Hogan and Whyte, *Irish Constitution*, p. 1073.

321   See O'Donnell, 'Property Rights in the Irish Constitution', p. 414.

322   *Ibid.*, p. 427.

323   See Keane, 'Property and the Constitution', p. 148.

324   For a consideration of this issue see Byrne, *Political Corruption*, pp. 103–244.

325   Fintan O'Toole, *Ship of Fools: How Stupidity and Corruption Sank the Celtic Tiger* (London: Faber
       and Faber, 2009), pp. 105–9.

326   See Ferriter, *Ambiguous Republic: Ireland in the 1970s* (London: Profile Books, 2012), p. 596.

327   Garret FitzGerald, *All in a Life: An Autobiography* (Dublin: Gill and Macmillan, 1991), p. 65.

328   Vincent Browne, Review of Gerard Hogan's *The Origins of the Irish Constitution 1928–1941*,
       History Ireland, January/February, 2013, p. 57.

329   Maura Cronin, '"You'd be disgraced!" Middle-Class Women and Respectability in Post-Famine
       Ireland', in Fintan Lane (ed.), *Politics, Society and the Middle Class in Modern Ireland* (Basingstoke:
       Palgrave Macmillan, 2010), p. 107.

330   Diarmaid Ferriter, '"The Stupid Propaganda of the Calamity Mongers"?: The Middle Class and
       Irish Politics, 1945–97', in Fintan Lane (ed.), *Politics, Society and the Middle Class in Modern
       Ireland* (Basingstoke: Palgrave Macmillan, 2010), pp. 271–87.

331 Thomas Ginsburg, Zachary Elkins and James Melton, 'The Lifespan of Written Constitutions', www.law.uchicago.edu/alumni/magazine/lifespan, accessed 12 August 2018. This paragraph is based on this document which is unpaginated.

332 Seamus Ó Tuama, 'Revisiting the Irish Constitution and de Valera's Grand Vision', *Irish Journal of Legal Studies*, vol. 2 (2), 2011, p. 86.

333 See Elkins et alia, 'Lifespan'. See note 331.

334 *Ibid.*

335 *Dáil Debates*, 20 June 1933, 808.

336 See *The Family*, p. 19.

337 See Gallaher, 'Irish Constitution', p. 32.

338 See Kissane, *New Beginnings*, p. xvi.

339 *Ibid.*, p. xviii.

340 Phrase used by K.C. Wheare, *Modern Constitutions* (Oxford: Oxford University Press, 1966), p. 83.

341 This expression was used by the Taoiseach, Enda Kenny. See www.independent.ie/irish-news/kenny-hits-back-at-threat-to-excommunicate-tds-29244123.html, accessed 1 October 2016.

342 Phrase used by Judge Gavan Duffy during the constitutional challenge to the Offences against the State Act 1939. See Hogan, *Irish Constitution*, p. 677.

343 See Kissane, *New Beginnings*, p. xviii.

344 See O'Donnell, 'Irish Legal History', p. 113.

345 *Ibid.*

346 See *Dáil Debates*, 24 November 1948, 347–99, for the speech of the Taoiseach, John A. Costello, on the second reading of the Republic of Ireland Bill, especially 360–1.

347 See Elkins et alia, 'Lifespan'. See note 331.

348 *Ibid.*

349 Ivana Bacik, 'Future Directions for the Constitution', in Oran Doyle and Eoin Carolan (eds), *The Irish Constitution: Governance and Values* (Dublin: Thomson Round Hall, 2008), p. 135.

350 *Irish Independent*, 16 May 2015.

351 *Sunday Independent*, 25 April 2010.

352 'Constitution for a New Republic', https://irishelectionliterature.files.wordpress.com/2011/07/draft_constitution_for_a_new_republic-1998.pdf, accessed 30 April 2016.

353 'Labour Party Manifesto 2011', www.labour.ie/download/pdf/labour_election_manifesto_2011.pdf, 46, accessed 30 April 2016.

354 Declan Kiberd, 'Eamon de Valera: The Image and the Achievement', in Patrick Hannon and Jackie Gallaher (eds), *Taking the Long View: 70 Years of Fianna Fáil* (Dublin: Blackwater Press, 1996), p. 23. For an overview of de Valera's Ireland see Joseph Lee and Gearóid Ó Tuathaigh, *The Age of de Valera* (Dublin: Ward Press, 1982).

355 See, for example, the views of Dominic Hannigan TD, www.thejournal.ie/readme/column-ireland-has-moved-on-and-we-need-a-new-constitution-330806-jan2012/, accessed 17 March 2016; T.P. O Mahony, www.irishexaminer.com/viewpoints/analysis/new-constitution-needed-for-a-new-21st-century-ireland-324842.html, accessed 17 March 2016; Labour Party Manifesto, 2011, www.labour.ie/manifesto, accessed 17 March 2017; and the *Programme for Government*, 2011, 17, www.taoiseach.gov.ie/eng/Work-Of-The-Department/Programme-for-Government_2011-2016.pdf, accessed 17 March 2017.

356 S.E. Finer, Vernon Bogdanor and Bernard Rudden, *Comparing Constitutions* (Oxford: Clarendon Press, 1995), p. 7.

357 Constitution of the Italian Republic, 1948, Articles 29 and 31.

358 Basic Law of the Federal Republic of Germany, Article 6.

359 See Hogan and Whyte, *Irish Constitution*, p. xci.

360   Ian McBride, 'Religion', in Richard Bourke and Ian McBride (eds), *The Princeton History of Modern Ireland* ((Princeton: Princeton University Press, 2016), p. 314.

361   See O'Keeffe, 'God, the Natural Law and the 1937 Constitution', p. 111.

362   Gerard Hogan, Foreword, in Dermot Keogh and Andrew McCarthy, *The Making of the Irish Constitution 1937* (Cork: Mercier Press, 2007), p. 14.

363   *Ibid.*, p. 24.

364   For an account of the abuse in industrial schools see Mary Rafferty and Eoin O'Sullivan, *Suffer the Little Children: The Inside Story of Ireland's Industrial School* (Dublin: New Island, 1999); and Commission to Inquire into Child Abuse, *Report* (Dublin: Stationery Office, 2009). For a general account of the treatment of children since the 1920s see Moira J. Maguire, *Precarious Childhood in Post-Independence Ireland* (Manchester: Manchester University Press, 2009).

365   James M. Smith, *Ireland's Magdalen Laundries and the Nation's Architecture of Containment* (Notre Dame: University of Notre Dame, 2007); and the 'Report of the Inter-Departmental Committee to establish the facts of State Involvement with Magdalen Laundries', www.justice.ie/en/JELR/Pages/MagdalenRpt2013, accessed 12 August 2016.

366   Garrett Barden, 'Discovering a Constitution', in Tim Murphy and Patrick Twomey (eds), *Ireland's Evolving Constitution 1937–97: Collected Essays* (Oxford: Hart Publishing, 1998), p. 5.

367   Brian Walsh, Foreword, in Michael Forde, *Constitutional Law of Ireland* (Dublin: Mercier Press, 1987), p. xxi.

368   See Gallaher, 'Changing Constitution', p. 95.

369   See Barden, 'Discovering a Constitution', p. 6.

370   *Ibid.*, p. 9.

371   *Irish Independent*, 30 March 2016.

372   See the *Report of the Commission on the Relief of the Sick and Destitute Poor* (Dublin: Stationery Office, 1927), for an insight into attitudes which prevailed for many decades. In particular, see pars. 266–270, pp. 73–4.

373   *Ibid.*, par. 267, p. 73.

374   See Rafferty and O'Sullivan, *Suffer the Little Children,* p. 305.

375   See Kelly, *Fundamental Rights in Irish Law and the Constitution* (Dublin: Allen Figgis, 1967), p. 73.

376   Brian Walsh, 'The Constitution and Constitutional Rights', in Frank Litton (ed.), *The Constitution of Ireland 1937–1987* (Dublin: Institute of Public Administration, 1988), p. 88.

377   For a consideration of arguments in favour of radical reform see Theo Dorgan (ed.), *Foundation Stone: Notes Towards a Constitution for a 21st Century Republic* (Dublin: New Island, 2014).

378   See Bacik, 'Future Directions', p. 135. The subject of religion and the Irish Constitution is a fertile area of academic discussion; see, for example: Gerard F. Whyte, 'Some Reflections on the Role of Religion in the Constitutional Order', in Tim Murphy and Patrick Twomey (eds), *Ireland's Evolving Constitution 1937–97: Collected Essays* (Oxford: Hart Publishing, 1998), pp. 51–63; Gerard F. Whyte, 'On the Meaning of "Religion" under the Irish Constitution', in Oran Doyle and Eoin Carolan (eds), *The Irish Constitution: Governance and Values* (Dublin: Thomson Round Hall, 2008), pp. 446–62; and Oran Doyle, 'Article 44: Privileging the Rights of Religion', in Oran Doyle and Eoin Carolan (eds), *The Irish Constitution: Governance and Values* (Dublin: Thomson Round Hall, 2008), pp. 476–89.

379   Sophie Gorman, 'Why (as a woman) I detest this document', Special supplement marking the Irish Constitution at 75, *Irish Independent*, 12 December 2012, p. 15.

380   See Beytagh, *Constitutionalism*, p. 157.

381   See Bacik, 'Future Directions', p. 142. For a detailed consideration of this matter see Tim Murphy, 'Economic Inequality and the Constitution', in Tim Murphy and Patrick Twomey (eds), *Ireland's Evolving Constitution 1937–97: Collected Essays* (Oxford: Hart Publishing, 1998), pp. 163–81; and Gallaher, 'Changing Constitution', pp. 97–101.

382   See Ó Tuama, 'Revisiting the Irish Constitution', p. 83. See also Jane Suiter, 'A Constitutional Moment: Taking Advantage of a Confluence of Events', in Eoin Carolan (ed.), *The Constitution of Ireland: Perspectives and Prospects* (London: Bloomsbury Professional, 2012), pp. 474–8, for a discussion of the popular initiative.

383   See Beytagh, *Constitutionalism*, p. 130.

384   NAI, DT S2979, 14 June 1934.

385   See Beytagh, 'Individual Rights, Judicial Review and Written Constitutions', p. 160.

386   Quoted in Kelly, *Fundamental Rights*, p. 12.

387   In addition to reports already cited, the reports of the All-Party Committee on the Constitution were as follows: *First Progress Report* (Dublin: Stationery Office, 1997); *Second Progress Report: Seanad Éireann* (Dublin: Stationery Office,1997); *Third Progress Report: The President* (Dublin: Stationery Office,1998); *Fourth Progress Report: The Courts and the Judiciary* (Dublin: Stationery Office, 1999); *Fifth Progress Report: Abortion* (Dublin: Stationery Office, 2000); *Seventh Progress Report: Parliament* (Dublin: Stationery Office,2002); and *Eighth Progress Report: Government* (Dublin: Stationery Office, 2003).

388   See www.constitution.ie for a comprehensive overview of the proceedings of the Constitutional Convention. For a discussion of the convention see John O' Dowd, 'The Constitutional Convention: A Comment', in Eoin Carolan (ed.), *The Constitution of Ireland: Perspective and Prospects* (London: Bloomsbury Professional, 2012), pp. 483–94.

389   See Coughlan, 'The Constitution and Social Policy', p. 159.

390   *Ibid.*, p.160.

Chapter 9

1   Tom Garvin, 'The Aftermath of the Irish Civil War', in Gabriel Doherty and Dermot Keogh (eds), *De Valera's Irelands* (Cork: Mercier Press, 2003), p. 82.

2   Ronan Fanning, *Eamon de Valera: A Will to Power* (London: Faber and Faber, 2015), p. 159.

3   R. F. Foster, *Modern Ireland 1600–1972* (London: Allen Lane, 1988), p. 541.

4   Basil Chubb, *The Government and Politics of Ireland* (London: Longman, second edition, 1982), p. 173.

5   Owen Dudley Edwards, *Eamon de Valera* (Cardiff: GPC Books, 1987), p. 141.

6   Anonymous, 'J.J. McElligott', *Administration*, vol. 1, no. 1, Spring 1953, p. 67.

7   National Library of Ireland, Ms. 23,508.

8   Brian P. Kennedy, 'John Hearne and the Irish Constitution (1937)', *Éire-Ireland*, Summer 1989, p. 122.

9   C.S. Andrews, *Man of No Property* (Cork: Mercier Press, 1982), p. 233.

10   Michael Forde, *The Constitutional Law of Ireland* (Dublin: Mercier Press, 1987), p. 13.

11   Gerard Hogan, 'Constitution @75', Special Supplement, *Irish Independent*, 12 December 2012, p. 22–3.

12   Gerard Hogan, 'Address to Constitutional Convention', 1 December 2012, https://www.youtube.com/watch?v=4mX3LLn316Q, accessed 4 April 2016.

13   UCDA, Eamon de Valera Papers, P150/2370.

14   UCDA, Eamon de Valera Papers, P150/2370.

15   UCDA, Eamon de Valera Papers, P150/2370.

16   UCDA, Eamon de Valera Papers, P150/2373.

17   Diarmaid Ferriter, *Judging Dev* (Dublin: Royal Irish Academy, 2007), p. 66.

18   R.V. Comerford, *Ireland* (London: Hodder Arnold, 2003), p. 115.

19   Earl of Longford and Thomas P. O Neill, *Eamon de Valera* (London: Arrow Books, 1974), p. 473.

20 T.D. Williams, 'De Valera in Power', in Francis MacManus (ed.), *The Years of the Great Test 1926–1939* (Cork: Mercier Press, 1978), p. 33.

21 NAI, DFA 247/21, 4 September 1940.

22 See Chubb, *Government and Politics of Ireland*, p. 174.

23 Seán Dooney, *The Irish Civil Service* (Dublin: Institute of Public Administration, 1976), pp. 16–17.

24 See Chubb, *Government and Politics of Ireland*, p. 174.

25 See Dooney, *Irish Civil Service*, p. 16.

26 Tom Garvin, *Nationalist Revolutionaries in Ireland 1858–1928* (Oxford: Clarendon Press, 1987), p. 167.

27 Quoted in Brian Farrell, 'De Valera's Constitution and Ours', in Brian Farrell (ed.) *De Valera's Constitution and Ours* (Dublin: Gill and Macmillan, 1988), p. 200.

28 Letter from F.A. Coffey to *Irish Times*, 4 November 1996, quoted in Fanning, *Eamon de Valera*, p. 160.

29 *Seanad Debates*, 2 June 1932, 938.

30 See Farrell, 'De Valera's Constitution and Ours', p. 201.

31 Tim Pat Coogan, *De Valera: Long Fellow, Long Shadow* (London: Hutchinson, 1993), p. 36.

32 See Kennedy, 'John Hearne', p. 125.

33 Quoted in *ibid*.

34 Brian Walsh, Introduction in James Casey, *Constitutional Law in Ireland* (London: Sweet & Maxwell, 1992), p. x.

35 Deirdre McMahon, *Republicans and Imperialists: Anglo-Irish Relations in the 1930s* (New Haven and London: Yale University Press, 1984), p. 119.

36 Quoted in R. F. Foster, *Vivid Faces: The Revolutionary Generation in Ireland 1890–1923* (London: Allen Lane, 2014), p. 316. The remarks were made by Hanna Sheehy-Skeffington.

37 Quoted in Fanning, *Eamon de Valera*, p. 230.

38 Author's interview with Mrs Alice Bowen, niece of John J. Hearne, 14 December 2013.

39 John Horgan, *Seán Lemass: The Enigmatic Patriot* (Dublin: Gill and Macmillan, 1997), p. 55.

40 Declan Kiberd, 'Eamon de Valera: The Image and the Achievement', in Philip Hannon and Jackie Gallaher (eds), *Taking the Long View: 70 Years of Fianna Fáil* (Dublin: Blackwater Press, 1996), p. 25.

41 See Chubb, *Government and Politics of Ireland*, p. 173.

42 C. H. Murray, *The Civil Service Observed* (Dublin: Institute of Public Administration, 1990), p. 69.

43 See Chubb, *Government and Politics of Ireland*, p. 266.

44 *Ibid.*, p. 265.

45 M. McManus, 'Ireland', in J.E. Kingston (ed.), *The Civil Service in Liberal Democracies: An Introductory Survey* (London: Routledge, 1990), p. 101.

46 Brian Murphy, *Forgotten Patriot: Douglas Hyde and the Foundation of the Irish Presidency* (Cork: Collins Press, 1916), p. 75.

47 Quoted in Kennedy, 'John Hearne ', p. 127.

48 Dermot Keogh and Andrew McCarthy, *The Making of the Irish Constitution 1937* (Cork: Mercier Press, 2007), p. 67.

49 Author's interview with Mrs Alice Bowen, niece of John J. Hearne, 14 December 2013.

50 Author's interview with Mrs Nuala Quirke, 27 October 2016. Mrs Quirke is a member of the Cahill Family, business partners in Hearne and Cahill's. John J. Hearne was her mother's first cousin.

51 Bureau of Military History, Witness Statement no. 1,741, Michael V. O'Donoghue, p. 38.

52 Bureau of Military History, Witness Statement no. 1,104, Thomas Brennan, p. 5.

53   Supreme Court Office, Inner Bar Roll, 20 June 1939. I am grateful to Mr Richard McNamara for
      this reference.

54   NAI, DT S2555A, Cabinet Minutes, 28 July 1939.

55   Michael Kennedy, *Ireland and the League of Nations 1919–1946: International Relations,
      Diplomacy and Politics* (Dublin: Irish Academic Press, 1996), p. 223.

56   *Ibid.*, pp. 268–70.

57   Dermot Keogh, *Ireland and Europe 1919–1948* (Dublin: Gill and Macmillan, 1988), p. 26.

58   Quoted in Kennedy, *League of Nations*, p. 149.

59   For the text of the speech he delivered see Maurice Moynihan (ed.), *Speeches and Statements by
      Eamon de Valera 1917–1973* (Dublin: Gill and Macmillan, 1980), pp. 219–23.

60   See Keogh, *Ireland and Europe*, p. 40.

61   For an account of Irish diplomatic relations at this period see Ian McCabe, *A Diplomatic History
      of Ireland 1948–49* (Dublin: Irish Academic Press, 1991), especially pp. 40–9. See also John J.
      Hearne Papers, Memorandum from John A. Costello to John J. Hearne, 27 February 1968. It was
      accompanied by a one-sentence letter: 'As promised, I am sending you a copy of the memorandum
      I made on how I did not declare the republic in Canada.'

62   It would appear that Hearne was originally considered for appointment as Irish Minister to Paris.
      See NAI DT S5735B.

63   'John Joseph Hearne', in James McGuire and James Quinn (eds), *Dictionary of Irish Biography*
      (Cambridge: Cambridge University Press, 2009); *Irish Times*, 31 March 1969; and *Irish
      Independent*, 31 March 1969.

BIBLIOGRAPHY

Primary Sources

Archives

Military Archives of Ireland

Abstract of service, SDR/1235 Commandant John Joseph Hearne
Bureau of Military History, Witness Statements

National Archives of Ireland

Department of Foreign Affairs
Department of Justice
Department of the Taoiseach
Office of the Attorney General – Parliamentary Draftsman's Office

University College Dublin Archives

Papers of:
W.T. Cosgrave – P285
John A. Costello – P190
George Gavan Duffy – P152
Eamon de Valera – P150
Fianna Fáil Party – P176
Desmond and Mabel Fitzgerald – P80
Patrick McGilligan – P35
Seán and Maurice Moynihan – P122
Cearbhal Ó Dálaigh – P51
Kevin O'Higgins – P197
Alfred O'Rahilly – P178

Waterford City Archives

Corporation Minute Books, LA1/1/A/25, LA1/1/A/38
Freedom of Waterford City Roll Book, TNC 1/5

Waterford Roman Catholic Diocesan Archives

Particulars regarding Very Revd Maurice Hearne, PP

Newspapers and periodicals

Decies: Journal of the Waterford Archaeological and Historical Society
Freeman's Journal
Irish Ecclesiastical Record
Irish Historical Studies
Irish Independent
Irish Press
Irish Times
Munster Express
Studies
The Irish Jurist
Waterford Express
Waterford News
Waterford Standard

Official publications

Dáil Éireann debates
Seanad Éireann debates
Irish Law Reports
Imperial Conference, 1926. *Summary of Proceedings* (Cmd. 2768) H.C. 1926, XI, 545.
Imperial Conference, 1926. *Appendices to the Summary of Proceedings* (Cmd. 2769) H.C. 1926, XI, 607.
Saorstát Éireann, *Report of the Conference on the Operation of Dominion Legislation and Merchant Shipping Legislation* (Dublin: Stationery Office, 1929), p. 129.
Report of the Joint Committee on the Constitution of Seanad Éireann (Dublin: Stationery Office, 1929).
Imperial Conference, 1930. *Summary of Proceedings* (Cmd. 3717) H.C. 1930–1, XIV 569.
Imperial Conference, 1930. *Appendices to the Summary of Proceedings* (Cmd. 3718) H.C. 1930–1, XIV, 701.
Report of the Second House of the Oireachtas Commission (Dublin: Stationery Office, 1936).
Report of the Commission of Inquiry into Banking, Currency and Credit (Dublin: Stationery Office, 1938).
Report of the Commission on Vocational Organisation (Dublin: Stationery Office, 1944).
Commission of Inquiry into the Civil Service, *Interim Report* (Dublin: Stationery Office, 1934).
Dáil Éireann, *Special Report of the Special Committee on the Seanad Electoral (Panel Members) Bill* (Dublin: Stationery Office, 1937).
Report of the Seanad Electoral Commission (Dublin: Stationery Office, 1959).
Report of the Committee on the Constitution (Dublin: Stationery Office, 1967).
Dáil Éireann, *Minutes of Proceedings of the First Parliament of the Republic of Ireland, 1919–1921* (Dublin: Stationery Office, 1994).
Report of the Constitution Review Committee (Dublin: Stationery Office, 1996).
All-Party Oireachtas Committee on the Constitution, *Second Progress Report: Seanad Éireann* (Dublin: Stationery Office, 1997).
All-Party Oireachtas Committee on the Constitution, *Third Progress Report: The President* (Dublin: Stationery Office, 1998).

All-Party Oireachtas Committee on the Constitution, *Fourth Progress Report: The Courts and the Judiciary* (Dublin: Stationery Office, 1999).

All-Party Oireachtas Committee on the Constitution, *Fifth Progress Report: Abortion* (Dublin: Stationery Office, 2000).

All-Party Oireachtas Committee on the Constitution, *Sixth Progress Report: The Referendum* (Dublin: Stationery Office, 2001).

All-Party Oireachtas Committee on the Constitution, *Seventh Progress Report: Parliament* (Dublin: Stationery Office, 2002).

Report on Seanad Reform (Dublin: Stationery Office, 2004).

All-Party Oireachtas Committee on the Constitution, *Ninth Progress Report: Private Property* (Dublin: Stationery Office, 2004).

All-Party Oireachtas Committee on the Constitution, *Tenth Progress Report: The Family* (Dublin: Stationery Office, 2006).

Department of the Environment, Community and Local Government, *Referendum Results 1937–2015* (Dublin, 2015).

Report of the Working Group on Seanad Reform (Dublin, 2015).

Personal papers

John J. Hearne Papers, Text of speeches delivered in Canada and the United States, 1940–1960.

Maurice Hearne, Papers relating to a proposed biography of John J. Hearne.

Letter from Revd Dermot Farrell to Maurice Hearne regarding particulars of John J. Hearne's education at Maynooth College, dated 23 May 1997.

Secondary sources

Akenson, D.H. and Fallin J.F., 'The Irish Civil War and the Drafting of the Irish Free State Constitution', *Éire-Ireland*,1 (1970), pp. 10–26; 2, pp. 42–93; pp. 28–70.

Anon., *Oidhreacht 1916–1966* (Dublin: Stationery Office, 1966).

Anon., 'J.J. McElligott', *Administration*, vol. 1, no. 1, Spring 1953, pp. 67–72.

Barden, Garrett, 'Discovering a Constitution', in Tim Murphy and Patrick Twomey (eds), *Ireland's Evolving Constitution 1937–97: Collected Essays* (Oxford: Hart Publishing, 1998), pp. 1–9.

Barrington, Donal, 'The Constitution in the Courts', in Frank Litton (ed.), *The Constitution of Ireland 1937–1987* (Dublin: Institute of Public Administration, 1988), pp. 110–27.

—, 'The North and the Constitution', in Brian Farrell (ed.), *De Valera's Constitution and Ours* (Dublin: Gill and Macmillan, 1988), pp. 61–74.

Barrington, T.J., *The Irish Administrative System* (Dublin: Institute of Public Administration, 1980).

Bartlett, Thomas, *Ireland: A History* (Cambridge: Cambridge University Press, 2010).

Beytagh, Francis X., *Constitutionalism in Contemporary Ireland: An American Perspective* (Dublin: Round Hall Sweet & Maxwell, 1997).

—, 'Individual Rights, Judicial Review and Written Constitutions', in James O'Reilly (ed.), *Human Rights and Constitutional Law: Essays in Honour of Brian Walsh* (Dublin: Round Hall Press, 1992), pp. 147–62.

Biever, Bruce, *Religion, Culture and Values: A Cross-Cultural Analysis of Motivational Factors in Native Irish and American Irish Catholicism* (New York: Arno Press, 1976).

Bowman, John, *De Valera and the Ulster Question 1917–1973* (Oxford: Clarendon Press, 1982).

—, 'Eamon de Valera: Seven Lives', in J.P. Carroll and John A. Murphy (eds), *De Valera and His Times* (Cork: Cork University Press, 1983), pp. 182–94.

Broderick, Eugene, 'The Corporate Labour Policy of Fine Gael', *Irish Historical Studies*, vol. XXIX, no. 113, May 1994, pp. 88–99.

—, *Intellectuals and the Ideological Hijacking of Fine Gael, 1932–1938* (Newcastle upon Tyne: Cambridge Scholars Publishing, 2010).

—, *The Boycott at Fethard-on-Sea 1957: A Study in Catholic–Protestant Relations in Modern Ireland* (Newcastle upon Tyne: Cambridge Scholars Publishing, 2011).

—, 'John Hearne and the Making of the 1937 Constitution', *Decies: Journal of the Waterford Archaeological and Historical Society*, no. 69, 2013, pp. 171–205.

Bromage, Arthur W. and Bromage, Mary C., 'The Vocational Senate in Ireland', *American Political Science Review*, vol. 34, 1940, pp. 519–38.

Byrne, Elaine A., *Political Corruption in Ireland 1922–2012: 'A Crooked Harp?'* (Manchester: Manchester University Press, 2012).

Cahill, E., *The Framework of a Christian State: An Introduction to Social Science* (Dublin: M.H. Gill and Son, Ltd., 1932).

Cahillane, Laura, *Drafting the Irish Free State Constitution* (Manchester: Manchester University Press, 2016).

Canning, Paul, *British Policy towards Ireland 1921–1941* (Oxford: Clarendon Press, 1985).

Carey, Gearóid, 'The Constitutional Dilemma of Article 45: An Avenue for Welfare and Social Rights?' *Irish Student Law Review*, vol. 5 (1995), pp. 78–86.

Casey, James, 'Changing the Constitution: Amendment and Judicial Review', in Brian Farrell (ed.), *De Valera's Constitution and Ours* (Dublin: Gill and Macmillan, 1988), pp. 152–62.

—, *Constitutional Law in Ireland* (London: Sweet & Maxwell, 1992).

Chambers, Anne, *T.K. Whitaker: Portrait of a Patriot* (London: Doubleday Ireland, 2014).

Chubb, Basil, 'Vocational Representation in the Irish Senate', *Political Studies*, vol. ii, 1954, pp. 97–111.

—, *Cabinet Government in Ireland* (Dublin: Institute of Public Administration, 1974).

—, *The Constitution and Constitutional Change in Ireland* (Dublin: Institute of Public Administration, 1978).

—, *The Government and Politics of Ireland* (London: Longman, second edition, 1982).

—, *The Politics of the Irish Constitution* (Dublin: Institute of Public Administration, 1991).

Coakley, John, 'An Ambiguous Office? The Position of Head of State in the Irish Constitution', *Irish Jurist*, 48, 2012, pp. 43–70.

—, 'The Prehistory of the Presidency', in John Coakley and Kevin Rafter (eds), *The Irish Presidency: Power, Ceremony and Politics* (Dublin: Irish Academic Press, 2014), pp. 60–81.

— and Rafter, Kevin, 'New Perspectives on the President of Ireland', in John Coakley and Kevin Rafter (eds), *The Irish Presidency: Power, Ceremony and Politics* (Dublin: Irish Academic Press, 2014), pp. 1–16.

— and Rafter, Kevin (eds), 'The President of Ireland: Past, Present and Future', in John Coakley and Kevin Rafter (eds), *The Irish Presidency: Power, Ceremony and Politics* (Dublin: Irish Academic Press, 2014), pp. 194–209.

Coffey, Donal K., 'The Need for a New Constitution: Irish Constitutional Change 1932–1935', *Irish Jurist*, 48, 2012, pp. 275–302.

Coldrey, Barry, *Faith and Fatherland: The Christian Brothers and the Development of Irish Nationalism 1838–1921* (Dublin: Gill and Macmillan, 1988).

Comerford, R.V., *Inventing the Nation: Ireland* (London: Hodder Arnold, 2003).

Connelly, Alpha, 'The Constitution', in Alpha Connelly (ed.), *Gender and the Law in Ireland* (Dublin: Oak Tree Press, 1993), pp. 4–27.

Coogan, Tim Pat, *De Valera: Long Fellow, Long Shadow* (London: Hutchinson, 1993).

Cooney, John, *John Charles McQuaid: Ruler of Catholic Ireland* (Dublin: O'Brien Press, 1999).

Cronin, Mike, *The Blueshirts and Irish Politics* (Dublin: Four Courts Press, 1997).

Crowe, Catriona, Fanning, Ronan, Kennedy, Michael, Keogh, Dermot, O'Halpin, Eunan (eds), *Documents on Irish Foreign Policy*, vol. IV, 1932–1936, Dublin, Royal Irish Academy, 2004.

—, Fanning, Ronan, Kennedy, Michael, Keogh, Dermot, O'Halpin, Eunan (eds), *Documents on Irish Foreign Policy*, vol. V, 1937–1939, Dublin, Royal Irish Academy, 2006.

Cullen, Clara and Ó hÓgartaigh, Margaret (eds), *His Grace is Displeased: Selected Correspondence of John Charles McQuaid* (Dublin: Merrion, 2013).

Curtis, Maurice, *A Challenge to Democracy: Militant Catholicism in Modern Ireland* (Dublin: History Press Ireland, 2010).

Daly, Eoin and Hickey, Tom, *The Political Theory of the Irish Constitution: Republicanism and the Basic Law* (Manchester: Manchester University Press, 2015).

Daly, Mary E. "'Oh, Kathleen Ni Houlihan, Your Way's a Thorny Way!": The Condition of Women in Twentieth-Century Ireland', in Anthony Bradley and Maryann Valiulis (eds), *Gender and Sexuality in Modern Ireland* (Amherst: University of Massachusetts Press, 1997), pp. 102–26.

Davis, Fergal, *The History and Development of the Special Criminal Court 1922–2005* (Dublin: Four Courts Press, 2006).

Denham, Susan, 'Some Thoughts on the Constitution of Ireland at 75', Paper presented on 28 June 2012, at a Conference on 'The Irish Constitution: Past, Present and Future', organised by the UCD Constitutional Studies Group.

—, 'Waterfordian John J. Hearne: A Drafter of the Irish Constitution', Text of talk delivered in The Large Room, City Hall, Waterford, 10 November 2014, as part of the Waterford 1100 Talks, organised under the auspices of the Waterford Museum of Treasures.

Dooley, Dolores, 'Gendered Citizenship in the Irish Constitution', in Tim Murphy and Patrick Twomey (eds), *Ireland's Evolving Constitution 1937–97: Collected Essays* (Oxford: Hart Publishing, 1998), pp. 121–33.

Dooley, Thomas P., *Irishmen or English Soldiers?* (Liverpool: Liverpool University Press, 1995).

Dooney, Sean, *The Irish Civil Service* (Dublin: Institute of Public Administration, 1976).

Doyle, Oran, 'The Human Personality Doctrine in Constitutional Equality Law', *Irish Student Law Review*, vol. 9, 2001, pp. 101–21.

—, *Constitutional Equality Law* (Dublin: Thomson Round Hall, 2004).

—, 'Article 44: Privileging the Rights of the Religious', in Oran Doyle and Eoin Carolan (eds), *The Irish Constitution: Governance and Values* (Dublin: Thomson Round Hall, 2008), pp. 476–89.

Duffy, Colum Gavan, 'George Gavan Duffy', *Judicial Studies Institute Journal*, vol. 2, no. 2, 2002, pp. 1–29.

Dunleavy, Janet and Dunleavy, Gareth, *Douglas Hyde: A Maker of Modern Ireland* (University of California Press, CA, 1991).

Dunphy, Richard, *The Making of Fianna Fáil Power in Ireland 1923–1948* (Oxford: Clarendon Press, 2005).

Dwyer, T. Ryle, *De Valera: the Man and the Myths* (Dublin: Poolbeg Press, 1991).

Edwards, Owen Dudley, *Eamon de Valera* (Cardiff: GPC Books, 1987).

Elgie, Robert, 'The President in Comparative Perspective', in John Coakley and Kevin Rafter (eds), *The Irish Presidency: Power, Ceremony and Politics* (Dublin: Irish Academic Press, 2014), pp. 17–39.

Fanning, Bryan, 'A Catholic Vision of Ireland', in Tom Inglis (ed.), *Are the Irish Different?* (Manchester: Manchester University Press, 2014), pp. 44–53.

Fanning, Ronan, *The Irish Department of Finance* (Dublin: Institute of Public Administration, 1976).

Farragher, Sean P., *Dev and his Alma Mater: Eamon de Valera's Lifelong Association with Blackrock College 1898–1975* (Dublin: Paraclete Press, 1984).

Farrell, Brian, 'The Drafting of the Irish Constitution', *Irish Jurist*, 5 (1970), pp. 115–40; pp. 343–26; *Irish Jurist*, 6, 1971, pp. 111–35; pp. 345–59.

—, *Independent Ireland* (Dublin: Helicon, 1983).

—, '"The Rule of Order": Eamon de Valera and the I.R.A., 1923–40', in J.P. Carroll and John A. Murphy (eds), *De Valera and His Times* (Cork: Cork University Press, 1983), pp. 160–72.

—, 'Mr de Valera Drafts a Constitution', in Brian Farrell (ed.), *De Valera's Constitution and Ours* (Dublin: Gill and Macmillan, 1988), pp. 33–45.

—, *Éamon de Valera: A Will to Power* (London: Faber and Faber, 2015).

— and Kennedy, Michael, Keogh, Dermot, O'Halpin, Eunan (eds), *Documents on Irish Foreign Policy*, vol. III, 1926–1932, Dublin, Royal Irish Academy, 2002.

Farrell, Brian, *The Founding of Dáil Éireann: Parliament and Nation Building* (Dublin: Gill and Macmillan, 1971).

—, *Chairman or Chief? The Role of the Taoiseach in Irish Government* (Dublin: Gill and Macmillan, 1971).

—, 'The First Dáil and After', in Brian Farrell (ed.), *The Irish Parliamentary Tradition* (Dublin: Gill and Macmillan, 1973), pp. 208–22.

Farrell, Brian, 'De Valera: Unique Dictator or Charismatic Chairman', in J.P. Carroll and John A. Murphy (eds), *De Valera and His Times* (Cork: Cork University Press, 1983), pp. 35–46.

—, 'From First Dáil through Irish Free State', in Brian Farrell (ed.), *De Valera's Constitution and Ours* (Dublin: Gill and Macmillan, 1988), pp. 18–32.

Faughnan, Sean, 'The Jesuits and the Drafting of the Irish Constitution of 1937', *Irish Historical Studies*, xxvi, no. 101, May 1988, pp. 79–102.

Ferriter, Diarmaid, *The Transformation of Ireland 1900–2000* (London: Profile Books, 2004).

—, *Judging Dev* (Dublin: Royal Irish Academy, 2007).

—, *Occasions of Sin: Sex and Society in Modern Ireland* (London: Profile Books, 2009).

—, '"The Stupid Propaganda of the Calamity Mongers"?: The Middle Class and Irish Politics, 1945–97', in Fintan Lane (ed.), *Politics, Society and the Middle Class in Modern Ireland* (Basingstoke: Palgrave Macmillan, 2010), pp. 271–88.

—, *Ambiguous Republic: Ireland in the 1970s* (London: Profile Books, 2012).

—, 'De Valera's Ireland 1932–58', in Alvin Jackson (ed.), *The Oxford Handbook of Modern Irish History* (Oxford: Oxford University Press, 2014), pp. 670–91.

—, 'Twenty-First-Century Ireland', in Richard Bourke and Ian McBride (eds), *The Princeton History of Modern Ireland* (Princeton: Princeton University Press, 2016), pp. 168–92.

Finer, S.E., Bogdanor, Vernon and Rudden, Bernard , *Comparing Constitutions* (Oxford: Clarendon Press, 1995).

FitzGerald, Garret, 'The Irish Constitution in its Historical Context', in Tim Murphy and Patrick Twomey (eds), *Ireland's Evolving Constitution 1937–97: Collected Essays* (Oxford: Hart Publishing, 1998), pp. 29–40.

—, 'Eamon de Valera and the Price of his Achievement', in Gabriel Doherty and Dermot Keogh (eds), *De Valera's Irelands* (Cork: Mercier Press, 2003), pp. 185–206.

Forde, Michael, *Constitutional Law of Ireland* (Dublin: Mercier Press, 1987).

Foster, R.F., *Modern Ireland 1600–1972* (London: Allen Lane, 1988).

—, *Vivid Faces: The Revolutionary Generation in Ireland 1890–1923* (London: Allen Lane, 2014).

Gageby, Douglas, *The Last General Secretary: Sean Lester and the League of Nations* (Dublin: Town House, 1999).

Gallagher, Paul, 'The Irish Constitution – Its Unique Nature and the Relevance of International Jurisprudence', *Irish Jurist*, 45, 2010, pp. 22–50.

—, 'The Limits of Constitutionalism', in Eoin Carolan (ed.), *The Constitution of Ireland: Perspectives and Prospects* (London: Bloomsbury Professional, 2012), pp. 179–89.

Gallaher, Michael, 'The President, the People and the Constitution', in Brian Farrell (ed.), *De Valera's Constitution and Ours* (Dublin: Gill and Macmillan, 1988), pp. 75–92.

—, 'The Changing Constitution', in John Coakley and Michael Gallaher (eds), *Politics in the Republic of Ireland* (London and New York: Routledge, fifth edition, 2009), pp. 72–107.

—, 'The Political Role of the President', in John Coakley and Kevin Rafter (eds), *The Irish Presidency: Power, Ceremony and Politics* (Dublin: Irish Academic Press, 2014), pp. 40–59.

Garvin, Tom, *The Irish Senate* (Dublin: Institute of Public Administration, 1969).

Gaughan, J. Anthony, *Alfred O'Rahilly: Public Figure* (Dublin: Kingdom Books, 1989).

—, *Memoirs of Senator Joseph Connolly, A Founder of Modern Ireland* (Dublin: Irish Academic Press, 1996).

—, *Nationalist Revolutionaries in Ireland 1858–1928* (Oxford, Clarendon Press, 1987).

—, *1922: The Birth of Irish Democracy* (Dublin: Gill and Macmillan, 1996).

—, 'The Aftermath of the Irish Civil War', in Gabriel Doherty and Dermot Keogh (eds), *De Valera's Irelands* (Cork: Mercier Press, 2003, pp. 74–83) 2003.

Girvin, Brian, *From Union to Union: Nationalism, Democracy and Religion in Ireland – Act of Union to EU* (Dublin: Gill and Macmillan, 2002).

—, 'Church, State and the Moral Community', in Brian Girvin and Gary Murphy (eds), *The Lemass Era: Politics and Society in the Ireland of Sean Lemass* (Dublin: University College Dublin Press, 2005), pp. 122–45.

Golding, G.M., *George Gavan Duffy: a Legal Biography* (Dublin: Irish Academic Press, 1982).

Greene, Alan, 'The Historical Evolution of Article 28, 3, 3 of the Irish Constitution', *Irish Jurist*, 47, 2012, pp. 117–42.

Harkness, D.W., *The Restless Dominion: The Irish Free State and the British Commonwealth of Nations 1921–32* (London: MacMillan, 1969).

Hayes, Mahon and Kingston, James, 'Ireland in International Law: The Pursuit of Sovereignty and Independence', in Ben Torna, Michael Kennedy, John Doyle and Noel Dorr (eds), *Irish Foreign Policy* (Dublin: Gill and Macmillan, 2012), pp. 70–83.

Heuston, R.F.V., 'Personal Rights Under the Irish Constitution', *Irish Jurist*, 11 new series Part 2, Winter 1976, pp. 205–22.

Hindley, Reg, *The Death of the Irish Language* (London: Routledge, 1990).

Hogan, Gerard, 'Irish Nationalism as a Legal Ideology', *Studies*, vol. 75, Winter 1986, pp. 528–38.

—, 'Constitutional Interpretation', in Frank Litton (ed.), *The Constitution of Ireland 1937–1987* (Dublin: Institute of Public Administration, 1988), pp. 173–91.

—, 'Unenumerated Personal Rights: *Ryan's* Case Re-evaluated', *Irish Jurist*, 25–27, 1990–1992, pp. 95–116.

—, 'Mr Justice Brian Walsh', in James O'Reilly (ed.), *Human Rights and Constitutional Law: Essays in Honour of Brian Walsh* (Dublin: Round Hall Press, 1992), pp. 37–48.

—, 'The Constitution Committee of 1934', in Fionán Ó Muircheartaigh (ed.), *Ireland in the Coming Times: Essays to Celebrate TK Whitaker's 80th Year* (Dublin: Institute of Public Administration, 1997), pp. 342–69.

—, 'A Desert Island Case Set in the Silver Sea: *The State (Ryan) v. Lennon (1934)*', in Eoin O'Dell (ed.), *Leading Cases of the Twentieth Century* (Dublin; Round Hall Sweet & Maxwell, 2000), pp. 80–103.

—, 'Directive Principles, Socio-Economic Rights and the Constitution', *Irish Jurist*, 36, 2001, pp. 174–98.

—, 'De Valera, the Constitution and the Historians', *Irish Jurist,* 40, 2005, pp. 293–320.

—, 'John Hearne and the Plan for a Constitutional Court', *Dublin University Law Journal*, vol. 33, 2011, pp. 75–85.

—, *The Origins of the Irish Constitution 1928–1941* (Dublin: Royal Irish Academy, 2012).

—, 'Some Thoughts on the Origins of the Constitution', Paper presented on 29 June 2012, at a Conference on 'The Irish Constitution: Past, Present and Future', organised by the UCD Constitutional Studies Group.

—, 'The Influence of the Continental Tradition on the Drafting of the Constitution' in Bláthna Ruane, Jim O'Callaghan and David Barniville (eds), *Law and Government: A Tribute to Rory Brady* (Dublin: Round Hall, 2014), pp. 155–84.

—, and Whyte, Gerry, *J.M. Kelly: The Irish Constitution* (Dublin; Buttersworth, third edition, 1994).

Hogan, James, *Modern Democracy* (Cork: Cork University Press, 1938).

Howlin, Niamh, 'Shortcomings and Anomalies: Aspects of Article 26', *Irish Student Law Review*, vol. 13, 2005, pp. 26–48.

Hughes, Hector, *National Sovereignty and Judicial Autonomy in the British Commonwealth of Nations* (London: P.S. King and Son Limited, 1931).

Humphreys, Richard, 'Constitutional Interpretation', *Dublin University Law Journal*, 1993, pp. 59–77.

Inglis, Tom, *Moral Monopoly: The Rise and Fall of the Catholic Church in Modern Ireland* (Dublin: University College Dublin Press, 1998).

Jackson, Alvin, *Ireland 1798–1998: War, Peace and Beyond* (London: Wiley-Blackwell, second edition, 2010).

Kavanagh, Aileen, 'The Irish Constitution at 75 Years: Natural Law, Christian Values and the Ideal of Justice', *Irish Jurist*, 48, 2012, pp. 71–101.

Keane, Ronan, 'Property in the Constitution and in the Courts', in Brian Farrell (ed.), *De Valera's Constitution and Ours* (Dublin: Gill and Macmillan, 1988), pp. 137–51.

—, 'Fundamental Rights in Irish Law: A Note on the Historical Background', in James O'Reilly (ed.), *Human Rights and Constitutional Law: Essays in Honour of Brian Walsh* (Dublin: Round Hall Press, 1992), pp. 25–35.

—, 'The Voice of the Gael: Chief Justice Kennedy and the Emergence of the New Irish Court System 1921–1936', *Irish Jurist*, 31, 1996, pp. 205–25.

Keatinge, Patrick, *The Formulation of Irish Foreign Policy* (Dublin: Institute of Public Administration, 1973).

Kelly, John, 'The Constitution: Law and Manifesto', in Frank Litton (ed.), *The Constitution of Ireland 1937–1987* (Dublin: Institute of Public Administration, 1987), pp. 208–17.

—, 'Fundamental Rights and the Constitution', in Brian Farrell (ed.), *De Valera's Constitution and Ours* (Dublin: Gill and Macmillan, 1988), pp. 163–73.

Kelly, Stephen, *Fianna Fáil, Partition and Northern Ireland 1926–1971* (Dublin: Irish Academic Press, 2013).

Kennedy, Catriona, 'Women and Gender in Modern Ireland', in Richard Bourke and Ian McBride (eds), *The Princeton History of Modern Ireland* (Princeton: Princeton University Press), pp. 361–80.

Kennedy, Finola, 'Two Priests, the Family and the Irish Constitution', *Studies*, vol. 87, Winter 1998, pp. 353–64.

Kennedy, Michael, *Ireland and the League of Nations 1919–1946: International Relations, Diplomacy and Politics* (Dublin: Irish Academic Press, 1996).

—, 'The Foundation and Consolidation of Irish Foreign Policy: 1919–45', in Ben Torna, Michael Kennedy, John Doyle and Noel Dorr (eds), *Irish Foreign Policy* (Dublin: Gill and Macmillan, 2012), pp. 20–35.

Keogh, Dermot, 'De Valera, the Catholic Church and the "Red Scare", 1931–1932', in J.P. Carroll and John A. Murphy (eds), *De Valera and His Times* (Cork: Cork University Press, 1983), pp. 134–59.

—, *The Vatican, the Bishops and Irish Politics* (Cambridge: Cambridge University Press, 1986).

—, 'Church, State and Society', in Brian Farrell (ed.), *De Valera's Constitution and Ours* (Dublin: Gill and Macmillan, 1988), pp. 103–122.

—, *Ireland and Europe 1919–1948* (Dublin: Gill and Macmillan, 1988).

—, 'The Irish Constitutional Revolution: An Analysis of the Making of the Constitution', in Frank Litton (ed.), *The Constitution of Ireland 1937–1987* (Dublin: Institute of Public Administration, 1988), pp. 4–84.

—, 'Profile of Joseph Walshe, Secretary, Department of External Affairs, 1922–46', *Irish Studies in International Affairs*, vol. 3, no. 2, 1990, pp. 59–80.

—, *Ireland and the Vatican: The Politics and Diplomacy of Church–State Relations 1922–1960* (Cork: Cork University Press, 1995).

—, 'The Role of the Catholic Church in the Republic of Ireland, 1922–1995', in *Building Trust in Ireland: Studies Commissioned by the Forum for Peace and Reconciliation* (Belfast: Blackstaff Press, 1996), pp. 85–213.

—, *Jews in Twentieth-Century Ireland: Refugees, Anti-Semitism and the Holocaust* (Cork: Cork University Press, 1998).

—, 'The Jesuits and the 1937 Constitution', in Bryan Fanning (ed.), *An Irish Century: Studies 1912–2012*, Dublin, University College Dublin Press, 2012, pp. 119–32.

— and McCarthy, Andrew, *The Making of the Irish Constitution 1937* (Cork: Mercier Press, 2007).

Keogh, Niall, *Con Cremin: Ireland's Wartime Diplomat* (Cork: Mercier Press, 2006).

Kissane, Bill, *New Beginnings: Constitutionalism and Democracy in Modern Ireland* (Dublin: University College Dublin Press, 2011).

Knirck, Jason, *Afterimage of the Revolution: Cumann na nGaedheal and Irish Politics 1922–1932* (Madison: University of Wisconsin Press, 2014).

Kotsonouris, Mary, *Retreat from Revolution: The Dáil Courts 1920–24* (Dublin: Irish Academic Press, 1994).

Kuhn, Leo, *The Constitution of the Irish Free State* (London: George Allen and Unwin Ltd., 1932).

Laffan, Michael, *Judging W.T. Cosgrave* (Dublin: Royal Irish Academy, 2014).

Lee, Joseph, *The Modernisation of Irish Society 1848–1918* (Dublin: Gill and Macmillan, 1973).

—, 'Aspects of Corporatist Thought in Ireland: The Commission on Vocational Organisation 1939–43', in Art Cosgrove and Donal McCartney (eds), *Studies in Irish History Presented to R. Dudley Edwards* (Dublin: University College Dublin, 1979), pp. 324–46.

— and Ó Tuathaigh, Gearóid, *The Age of de Valera* (Dublin: Ward Press in association with Radio Telefís Eireann, 1982).

—, *Ireland 1912–1985: Politics and Society* (Cambridge: Cambridge University Press, 1989).

Lowry, Donal, 'New Ireland, Old Empire and the Outside World 1922–49: The Strange Evolution of a "Dictionary Republic"', in Mike Cronin and John M. Regan (eds), *Ireland: The Politics of Independence 1922–49* (Basingstoke: Macmillan Press, 2000), pp. 164–216.

Luddy, Maria, 'Feminism', in Richard Bourke and Ian McBride (eds), *The Princeton History of Modern Ireland* (Princeton: Princeton University Press, 2016), pp. 470–89.

McBride, Ian, 'Religion', in Richard Bourke and Ian McBride (eds), *The Princeton History of Modern Ireland* (Princeton: Princeton University Press, 2016), pp. 292–319.

McCabe, Ian, *A Diplomatic History of Ireland: The Republic, the Commonwealth and NATO* (Dublin: Irish Academic Press, 1991).

McCarthy, John P., *Kevin O'Higgins: Builder of the Irish State* (Dublin: Irish Academic Press, 2006).

Mac Cormaic, Ruahdán, *The Supreme Court* (London: Penguin, 2016).

McCrea, Ronan, 'Rhetoric, Choices and the Constitution', in Eoin Carolan (ed.), *The Constitution of Ireland: Perspectives and Prospects* (London: Bloomsbury Professional, 2012), pp. 59–68.

McEneaney, Eamonn (ed.), *A History of Waterford and its Mayors from the 12th to the 20th Century* (Waterford: Waterford Corporation, 1995).

McGarry, Fearghal, 'Southern Ireland 1922–32: A Free State?' in Alvin Jackson (ed.), *The Oxford Handbook of Modern Irish History* (Oxford: Oxford University Press, 2014), pp. 647–69.

—, 'Independent Ireland', in Richard Bourke and Ian McBride (eds), *The Princeton History of Modern Ireland* (Princeton: Princeton University Press, 2016), pp. 109–40.

McIntosh, Gillian, 'Acts of "National Communion": the Centenary Celebrations for Catholic Emancipation, the Forerunner of the Eucharistic Congress', in Joost Augusteijn (ed.), *Ireland in the 1930s* (Dublin: Four Courts Press, 1999), pp. 93–5.

McMahon, Bryan M.E., 'A Sense of Identity in the Irish Legal System', in Joseph Lee (ed.), *Ireland: Towards a Sense of Place* (Cork: University College Cork, 1985), pp. 34–46.

McMahon, Deirdre, 'A transient apparition: British policy towards the de Valera government 1932–5', *Irish Historical Studies*, vol. XXII, no. 8, September 1981, pp. 331–61.

—, 'The Chief Justice and the Governor General Controversy in 1932', *Irish Jurist*, 17, new series, 1982, pp. 145–67.

—, *Republicans and Imperialists: Anglo-Irish Relations in the 1930s* (New Haven and London: Yale University Press, 1984).

—, 'Ireland and the Empire-Commonwealth 1900–1948', in Judith M. Brown and Wm. Roger Louis (eds), *The Oxford History of the British Empire*, vol. IV, *The Twentieth Century* (Oxford: Oxford University Press, 1999), pp. 138–62.

—, 'Maurice Moynihan – An Appreciation', *Studies*, vol.89, no. 353, Spring 2000, pp. 71–6.

—, 'Ireland, the Empire and the Commonwealth', in Kevin Kenny (ed.), *The Oxford History of the British Empire, Companion Series: Ireland and the British Empire* (Oxford: Oxford University Press, 2004), pp. 182–219.

McManus, M., 'Ireland', in J.E. Kingdom (ed.), *The Civil Service in Liberal Democracies: An Introductory Survey* (London: Routledge, 1990), pp. 90–118.

MacMillan, Gretchen, *State, Society and Authority in Ireland: The Foundations of the Modern Irish State* (Dublin: Gill and Macmillan, 1993).

Maher, Jim, *The Oath is Dead and Gone* (Dublin: Londubh Books, 2011).

Manning, Maurice, *The Blueshirts* (Dublin: Gill and Macmillan, 1971).

Mansergh, Nicholas, 'Ireland and the British Commonwealth of Nations: the Dominion Settlement', in Desmond Williams (ed.), *The Irish Struggle: 1916–1926* (London: Routledge and Kegan Paul, 1966), pp. 129–39.

—, 'Ireland: External Relations 1926–1939', in Francis MacManus (ed.), *The Years of the Great Test 1926–39* (Cork: Mercier Press, 1967), pp. 127–37.

—, *The Commonwealth Experience* (London: Weidenfeld and Nicolson, 1969).

—, *The Unresolved Question: The Anglo-Irish Settlement and Its Undoing 1912–72* (New Haven and London: Yale University Press, 1991).

Martin, Frank, 'The Family in the Constitution – Principle and Practice', in Tim Murphy and Patrick Twomey (eds), *Ireland's Evolving Constitution 1937–97: Collected Essays* (Oxford: Hart Publishing, 1998), pp. 79–95.

Martin, Ged, 'The Irish Free State and the Evolution of the Commonwealth 1921–49', in Ronald Hyam and Ged Martin (eds), *Reappraisals in British Imperial History* (London and Basingstoke: Macmillan Press, 1975), pp. 201–23.

—, 'De Valera Imagined and Observed', in Gabriel Doherty and Dermot Keogh (eds), *De Valera's Irelands* (Cork: Mercier Press, 2003), pp. 84–103.

Maume, Patrick, *The Long Gestation: Irish Nationalist Life 1891–1918* (Dublin: Gill and Macmillan, 1999).

Meehan, Ciara, *The Cosgrave Party: A History of Cumann na nGaedheal 1923–33* (Dublin: Royal Irish Academy, 2010).

—, 'The Early Presidents 1938–1973', in John Coakley and Kevin Rafter (eds), *The Irish Presidency: Power, Ceremony and Politics* (Dublin: Irish Academic Press, 2014, pp. 82–101).

Moffitt, Miriam, '"Ireland's destiny is in the making": The Impact of the Anniversary Celebrations of 1929 and 1932 on the Religious Character of Ireland', in Mel Farrell, Jason Knirck and Ciara Meehan (eds), *A Formative Decade: Ireland in the 1920s* (Dublin: Irish Academic Press, 2015), pp. 225–46.

Mohr, Thomas, 'Law without Loyalty – The Abolition of the Irish Appeal to the Privy Council', *Irish Jurist*, 37, 2002, pp. 187–226.

—, 'The Foundations of Irish Extra-Territorial Legislation', *Irish Jurist*, 40, 2005, pp. 86–110.

—, 'The Colonial Laws Validity Act and the Irish Free State', *Irish Jurist*, 43, 2008, pp 21–44.

—, *Guardian of the Treaty: The Privy Council Appeal and Irish Sovereignty* (Dublin: Four Courts Press in association with the Irish Legal History Society, 2016).

Morgan, David Gwynn, 'Judicial Activism – Too Much of a Good Thing', in Tim Murphy and Patrick Twomey (eds), *Ireland's Evolving Constitution 1937–97: Collected Essays* (Oxford: Hart Publishing, 1998), pp. 107–19.

Moyn, Samuel, *Christian Human Rights* (Philadelphia: University of Pennsylvania Press, 2015).

Moynihan, Maurice, *Speeches and Statements by Eamon de Valera 1917–1973* (Dublin: Gill and Macmillan, 1980).

Mullarkey, Kieran, 'Ireland, the Pope and Vocationalism: the Impact of the Encyclical *Quadragesimo Anno*', in Joost Augusteijn (ed.), *Ireland in the 1930s* (Dublin: Four Courts Press, 1999).

Murphy, Brian, *Forgotten Patriot: Douglas Hyde and the Foundation of the Irish Presidency* (Cork: Collins Press, 2016).

Murphy, John A., *Ireland in the Twentieth Century* (Dublin: Gill and Macmillan, 1975).

—, 'The Achievement of Eamon de Valera', in J.P. Carroll and John A. Murphy (eds), *De Valera and His Times* (Cork: Cork University Press, 1983), pp. 1–16.

—, *The College: A History of Queen's/University College Cork 1845–1995* (Cork: Cork University Press, 1995).

—, 'The 1937 Constitution – Some Historical Reflections', in Tim Murphy and Patrick Twomey (eds), *Ireland's Evolving Constitution 1937–97: Collected Essays* (Oxford: Hart Publishing, 1998), pp. 11–27.

Murphy, Tim, 'Economic Inequality and the Constitution', in Tim Murphy and Patrick Twomey (eds), *Ireland's Evolving Constitution 1937–97: Collected Essays* (Oxford: Hart Publishing, 1998), pp. 163–81.

Murray, C.H., *The Civil Service Observed* (Dublin: Institute of Public Administration, 1990).

Murray, Patrick, *Oracles of God: The Roman Catholic Church and Irish Politics 1922–37* (Dublin: University College Dublin Press, 2000).

—, 'Obsessive Historian: Eamon de Valera and the Policing of his Reputation', *Proceedings of the Royal Irish Academy*, vol. 101C, no. 2, 2001, pp. 37–65.

Nolan, Aengus, *Joseph Walshe: Irish Foreign Policy 1922–1946* (Cork: Mercier Press, 2008).

Nowlan, Kevin B., 'The Gaelic League and other National Movements', in Seán Ó Tuama (ed.), *The Gaelic League Idea* (Cork: Mercier Press, 1972), pp. 41–51.

Ó Beacháin, Donnacha, *Destiny of the Soldiers: Fianna Fail, Irish Republicanism and the IRA, 1926–1973* (Dublin: Gill and Macmillan, 2010).

O'Callaghan, Jim, 'Seanad Éireann – An Opportunity for Real Reform', in Eoin Carolan (ed.), *The Constitution of Ireland: Perspectives and Prospects* (London: Bloomsbury Professional, 2012), pp. 217–37.

O'Connor, Emmet, 'The Influence of Redmondism on the Development of the Labour Movement in Waterford in the 1890s', *Decies*, 10, pp 37–42.

—, *A Labour History of Waterford* (Waterford: Waterford Trades Council, 1989).

Ó Corráin, Daithí, 'Articles 41 and 44: Minority Religious Opinion 1937–1986', in Oran Doyle and Eoin Carolan (eds), *The Irish Constitution. Governance and Values* (Dublin: Thomson Round Hall, 2008), pp. 53–70.

O'Donnell, Dónal, 'Property Rights in the Irish Constitution: Rights for Rich People, or a Pillar of Free Society?' in Oran Doyle and Eoin Carolan (eds), *The Irish Constitution: Governance and Values* (Dublin: Thomson Round Hall, 2008), pp. 412–30.

—, 'Irish Legal History of the Twentieth Century', *Studies*, vol. 105, no. 417, Spring 2016, pp. 98–120.

O'Hegarty, P.S., *The Victory of Sinn Féin* (first published 1924, re-issued Dublin: University College Dublin Press, 1998).

O'Keeffe, Declan, 'God, the Natural Law and the 1937 Constitution', in Eoin Carolan (ed.), *The Constitution of Ireland: Perspectives and Prospects* (London: Bloomsbury Professional, 2012), pp. 111–41.

O'Leary, Don, *Vocationalism and Social Catholicism in Twentieth-Century Ireland: The Search for a Christian Social Order* (Dublin: Irish Academic Press, 2000).

O'Mahony, Conor, 'Societal Change and Constitutional Interpretation', *Irish Journal of Legal Studies*, 2010, 1(2), pp. 71–115.

O'Neill, T.P. and Lord Longford, *Eamon de Valera* (London: Arrow Books, 1970).

O'Neill, Tomas agus O'Fiannachta, Padraig, *De Valera*, vol. ii (Dublin: Cló Morainn, 1970).

O'Rahilly, Alfred, *Thoughts on the Constitution* (Dublin: Browne and Nolan Limited, 1937).

O'Reilly, James and Redmond, Mary, *Cases and Materials on the Irish Constitution* (Dublin: Incorporated Law Society of Ireland, 1980).

O'Sullivan, Donal, *The Irish Free State and its Senate* (London: Faber and Faber, 1940).

Ó Tuama, Séamus, 'Revisiting the Irish Constitution and de Valera's Grand Vision', *Irish Journal of Legal Studies*, vol. 2(2), 2011, pp. 54–87.

—, 'Prospects for Constitutional Democracy in Ireland', in Eoin Carolan (ed.), *The Constitution of Ireland: Perspectives and Prospects* (London: Bloomsbury Professional, 2012), pp. 453–68.

Owens, Coilin and Radner, Joan (eds), *Irish Drama 1900–1980* (Washington, D.C: Catholic University of America Press, 1990).

Owens, Rosemary Cullen, *A Social History of Women in Ireland, 1870–1970* (Dublin: Gill and Macmillan, 2005).

Pašeta, Senia, *Before the Revolution: Nationalism, Social Change and Ireland's Catholic Elite 1879–1922* (Cork: Cork University Press, 1999).

—, 'Ireland's Last Home Rule Generation: The Decline of Constitutional Nationalism in Ireland 1916–30', in Mike Cronin and John M. Regan (eds), *Ireland: The Politics of Independence, 1922–49* (London: Macmillan Press, 2000), pp. 13–31.

Regan, John M., *The Irish Counter-Revolution: Treatyite Politics and Settlement in Independent Ireland* (Dublin: Gill and Macmillan, 1999).

Riordan, Susannah, 'The Unpopular Front: Catholic Revival and Irish Catholic Identity 1932–48', in Mike Cronin and John M. Regan (eds), *Ireland: The Politics of Independence 1922–49* (Basingstoke: Macmillan Press, 2000), pp. 98–120.

Scannell, Yvonne, 'The Constitution and the Role of Women', in Brian Farrell (ed.), *De Valera's Constitution and Ours* (Dublin: Gill and Macmillan, 1988), pp. 123–36.

Sexton, Brendan, *Ireland and the Crown 1922–1936: The Governor-Generalship of the Irish Free State* (Dublin: Irish Academic Press, 1989).

Tushnet, Mark, 'National Identity as a Constitutional Issue: the Case of the Preamble to the Irish Constitution of 1937', in Eoin Carolan (ed.), *The Constitution of Ireland: Perspectives and Prospects* (London: Bloomsbury Professional, 2012), pp. 49–57.

Valiulis, Maryann, 'The Man They Could Never Forgive, The View of the Opposition: Eamon de Valera and the Civil War', in J.P. Carroll and John A. Murphy (eds), *De Valera and His Times* (Cork: Cork University Press, 1983), pp. 92–100.

Vaughan, W.E., and Fitzpatrick, A. (eds), *Irish Historical Statistics: Population 1821–1871* (Dublin: Royal Irish Academy, 1978).

Walker, Brian, *A Political History of the Two Irelands: From Partition to Peace* (London: Palgrave, 2012).

Walsh, Brian, 'The Constitution: a View from the Bench', in Brian Farrell (ed.), *De Valera's Constitution and Ours* (Dublin: Gill and Macmillan, 1988), pp. 188–97.

—, 'The Constitution and Constitutional Rights', in Frank Litton (ed.), *The Constitution of Ireland 1937–1987* (Dublin: Institute of Public Administration, 1988), pp. 86–109.

Ward, Alan J., *The Irish Constitutional Tradition: Responsible Government and Modern Ireland 1782–1992* (Washington: Catholic University of America Press, 1994).

Ward, Margaret (ed.), *In Their Own Voice: Women and Irish Nationalism* (Cork: Attic Press, 1995).

Wheare, K.C., *The Statute of Westminster 1931* (Oxford: Clarendon Press, 1931).

—, *Modern Constitutions* (Oxford: Oxford University Press, 1966).

Wheatley, Michael, *Nationalism and the Irish Party: Provincial Ireland 1910–16* (Oxford: Oxford University Press, 2005).

Whyte, Gerard F., 'Some Reflections on the Role of Religion in the Constitutional Order', in Tim Murphy and Patrick Twomey (eds), *Ireland's Evolving Constitution 1937–97: Collected Essays* (Oxford: Hart Publishing, 1998), pp. 51–63.

—, 'On the Meaning of "Religion" under the Irish Constitution', in Oran Doyle and Eoin Carolan (eds), *The Irish Constitution: Governance and Values* (Dublin: Thomson Round Hall, 2008), pp. 446–62.

Unpublished theses

Broderick, Eugene, 'Irish corporatism 1931–1939', Unpublished MA Thesis, University College Cork, 1991.

Condon, Cathal, 'An analysis of the contribution made by Archbishop John Charles McQuaid to the drafting of the 1937 Constitution of Ireland', Unpublished MA Thesis, University College Cork, 1995.

Online publications

Ginsburg, Thomas, Elkins, Zachary, Melton, James, 'The Lifespan of Written Constitutions', www.law.uchicago.edu/alumni/magazine/lifespan, accessed 29 January 2017.

Moyn, Samuel, 'The Secret History of Constitutional Dignity', http://ssrn.com/abstract=2159248, accessed 29 January 2017.

Ó Tuama, Séamus, 'Judicial Review under the Irish Constitution: More American than Commonwealth', *Electronic Journal of Comparative Law*, October, 2008, http://www.ejcl.org/122/art122-2.pdf, accessed 29 January 2017.

Walter, Lesley A., 'Law as Literature: Illuminating the Debate Over Constitutional Consistency', www.corkonlinelawreview.com/edition/2004/2004xi.pdf.

INDEX